The Drama of Complaint

The Drama of Complaint

Ethical Provocations in Shakespeare's Tragedy

EMILY SHORTSLEF

Great Clarendon Street, Oxford, OX2 6DP,
United Kingdom

Oxford University Press is a department of the University of Oxford.
It furthers the University's objective of excellence in research, scholarship,
and education by publishing worldwide. Oxford is a registered trade mark of
Oxford University Press in the UK and in certain other countries

© Emily Shortslef 2023

The moral rights of the author have been asserted

All rights reserved. No part of this publication may be reproduced, stored in
a retrieval system, or transmitted, in any form or by any means, without the
prior permission in writing of Oxford University Press, or as expressly permitted
by law, by licence or under terms agreed with the appropriate reprographics
rights organization. Enquiries concerning reproduction outside the scope of the
above should be sent to the Rights Department, Oxford University Press, at the
address above

You must not circulate this work in any other form
and you must impose this same condition on any acquirer

Published in the United States of America by Oxford University Press
198 Madison Avenue, New York, NY 10016, United States of America

British Library Cataloguing in Publication Data

Data available

Library of Congress Control Number: 2023930786

ISBN 978–0–19–286848–0

DOI: 10.1093/oso/9780192868480.001.0001

Printed and bound in the UK by
Clays Ltd, Elcograf S.p.A.

Links to third party websites are provided by Oxford in good faith and
for information only. Oxford disclaims any responsibility for the materials
contained in any third party website referenced in this work.

Acknowledgments

It's a joy to acknowledge the many debts I have incurred in the ten years I have spent thinking about the ideas that slowly and circuitously became this book. First and foremost I want to thank Jean Howard, to whom I owe so much, and for whose extraordinary mentorship, intellectual guidance, generosity, and friendship I am so very grateful. I am also thankful to Crystal Bartolovich, Dympna Callaghan, Julie Crawford, Molly Murray, and Alan Stewart for their invaluable support and engagement with my work during my time as a graduate student at Columbia and at Syracuse, and to Beverly Matiko and L. Monique Pittman, whose undergraduate literature classes at Andrews University were so formative for me.

At the University of Kentucky, which provided vital institutional support, I wish to thank my colleagues in the Department of English; my fellow early modernists Joyce Green MacDonald and Jeff Peters; and the friends who make Lexington a happy place to live as well as work: Brandy Anderson, Molly T. Blasing, Jordan Brower, Jeff Clymer, Gerónimo Sarmiento Cruz, Michael Genovese, Regina Hamilton-Townsend, Martin Aagaard Jensen, Jap-Nanak Makkar, Andrew Milward, Robin Rahija, Michelle Sizemore, Michael Trask, and especially Hannah Pittard. For helping me navigate the tenure process, I am also grateful to Jonathan Allison, Jill Rappoport, and Kristen Pickett. At Oxford University Press, I am grateful to Ellie Collins for supporting this project and to Karen Raith for shepherding it through the review process. For their helpful suggestions at the revision stage, I am thankful to the two anonymous readers of the manuscript. An early version of Chapter 2 appeared in *Exemplaria* 29.2 (2017); I thank the journal for permission to reprint it here.

This book has benefitted from conversations with audiences at meetings of the Shakespeare Association of America, the Renaissance Society of America, the Modern Language Association, and the Ohio Valley Shakespeare Conference; from seminars and workshops at the 2016 Mellon School of Theater and Performance Research at Harvard University; and from research made possible by an RSA-Huntington Fellowship. For invitations to present and publish work, incisive feedback, and helpful professional advice, I am thankful to Cristina León Alfar, Claire Bourne, Brooke Conti, Lynn Festa, Penelope Geng, Marissa Greenberg, Jessie Hock, Wendy Beth Hyman, Kent Lehnhof, Julia Lupton, Dianne Mitchell, Ryan Netzley, Sarah C. E. Ross, Carolyn Sale, Matthew J. Smith, Rosalind Smith, and Andrew Sofer. My thinking and writing have been enriched by the conversations I've had over the years—in hotel ballrooms, bars, restaurants, or living rooms,

vi ACKNOWLEDGMENTS

around seminar or dinner tables—with Jude Webre, Bryan Lowrance, Ashley Brinkman, Liza Blake, Kathryn Vomero Santos, Musa Gurnis, Christine Varnado, Alexander Paulsson Lash, Seth Williams, Matthew Harrison, Bethany Packard, Matt Hunter, Rinku Chatterjee, Megan Herrold, and Lucía Martínez Valdivia. I am especially glad for the friendship and good company of Heidi Craig; Erin Kelly; John Kuhn; Emily Vasiliauskas; and my fellow AU Shakespeareans, Vanessa Corredera, Kristin Denslow, and L. Monique Pittman.

Several friends helped me finish this book, and I want to express my special gratitude to them here. Thank you to Jordan Brower, who read the manuscript and offered so much moral support in the final stretches; to Vanessa Corredera, whose steady encouragement always arrived at exactly the right time; and to Mary Kate Hurley, Nicholas Osborne, Ashley Lee, and Buffy Turner, both for cheering me on and for giving me time away.

For their love and support I am thankful to Per Olof and Marie-Louise Bengtsson, and to Stephanie Bengtsson, sister-in-law and friend. I am more grateful than I can say to my sister Caitlin Shortslef and to my parents, Dennis and Cecelia Shortslef, whose faith has been unwavering, and from whom I learned both to love words and to be a reader. Finally, my deepest gratitude and greatest debt are to Frederick Bengtsson, who has lived with this book as I have, and whose intellect has shaped it for the better. His patience, good humor, and love made it possible for me to write—and to stop writing—it.

Table of Contents

Introduction: Scenes of Complaint — 1

1. Signs of Life: Existential Complaint and the Creaturely Ethics of Complaining — 26

2. Ethical Demands: Judicial Complaint and the Call of Conscience — 63

3. "Me and My Cause": Spectral Complaints and Sublime Motives — 94

4. Lamentable Objects: Good Audiences and the Art of Female Complaint — 135

5. "Nobody, I Myself": Deathbed Complaint and the Authority of Happiness Scripts — 171

Bibliography — 199
Index — 217

Introduction

Scenes of Complaint

A woman is complaining. A man, older and worldly, approaches. "Comely distant sits he by her side," and from this remove he invites her to reveal the "grounds and motives of her woe" so that he may, if he can, "her suffering ecstasy assuage."[1] The woman needs no further prompting. Hers is a familiar lament: a story of seduction and betrayal, of having fallen for the flattering lies of a beautiful young man who so skillfully pressed his suit to her that she could not help but yield. Now, her youth, beauty, and name ruined—"his passion, but an art of craft"—she repeats the amorous plaints that captivated her (line 295). She is heard not only by the "reverend man" but by an unseen person who has been present from the beginning, before the man has arrived or the woman herself has come into view, someone whose attention was caught by the echoing sound of her plaintive cries ("My spirits t'attend this double voice accorded, / And down I laid to list the sad-tuned tale" [lines 3–4]). It is from the voyeuristic perspective of this witness that Shakespeare's *A Lover's Complaint* is narrated.

This narrative frame—atypical of its genre, and evocative of theatrical spectatorship in its representation of a dialogic exchange unfolding before a distanced third figure—is abandoned once the woman begins to speak. The poem never returns to the narrator's voice, nor does it reveal the older man's response to her words. *A Lover's Complaint* simply ends with the woman arriving at a startling conclusion to her own story. Having recounted the events that led to her fall, and having rehearsed at length the complaints that seduced her, she imagines herself as she is now, wiser and penitent, transported to a counterfactual past or conjectural future in which her erstwhile lover complains to her as he did before:

> Who, young and simple, would not be so lovered?
> Ay me, I fell, and yet do question make
> What I should do again for such a sake.
> Oh, that infected moisture of his eye!

---

[1] Shakespeare, *A Lover's Complaint*, lines 65, 63, 69. Hereafter cited parenthetically. Unless otherwise noted, citations of Shakespeare's work are from *The Norton Shakespeare*. The authorship of this poem, first printed in *Shake-speare's Sonnets* (1609), has been a matter of some debate. On the case for Shakespeare's authorship, see Jackson, *Determining the Shakespeare Canon*.

The Drama of Complaint: Ethical Provocations in Shakespeare's Tragedy. Emily Shortslef, Oxford University Press.
© Emily Shortslef 2023. DOI: 10.1093/oso/9780192868480.003.0001

2 THE DRAMA OF COMPLAINT

> Oh, that false fire which in his cheek so glowed!
> Oh, that forced thunder from his heart did fly!
> Oh, that sad breath his spongy lungs bestowed!
> Oh, all that borrowed motion, seeming owed,
> Would yet again betray the fore-betrayed,
> And new pervert a reconcilèd maid.
>
> (lines 320–9)

In a marked departure from other early modern poems of female complaint that close by affirming the value of chastity and warning readers about men's artful deceptions, Shakespeare's complainer finds no moral in her story.[2] She just sees herself falling once more, "perverted"—turned aside, led astray—by the convincingly performed complaint she hears. The poem can thus be said to underscore the seductive rhetorical power of those erotic complaints that invite their addressees to be "lovered." But in showing how the woman gets increasingly enthralled by the story she is telling—the remembered story of the young man's addresses and her own response to those plaints—what *A Lover's Complaint* brings to light, more unusually, is the compelling force of a *scene* of complaint. That is, the poem captures the way in which the plaintive situation itself, the interaction between speaker and addressee, seen as if from the outside, becomes an eroticized object—an object that excites the interest and curiosity of the "reconcilèd maid," compelling her to "question make" of herself.[3] The conclusion suggests that the recounted scene entangles her in its dynamics, its drama of desire, precisely because it offers her the pleasure of changing direction all over again, the pleasure of becoming newly unresolved, of forgetting what she knows. Understood in this way, the nested scene of complaint on which the poem closes—the remembered exchange between the woman and her lover that she narrates from her temporal distance—also bears, obliquely, on the primary scene of complaint to which the poem never explicitly returns, the exchange between the woman and the reverend man that the narrator hears from his spatially removed vantage point. Through the doubling of these scenes, the poem posits the scene of complaint as a

---

[2] Compare George Whetstone's "Cressid's Complaint" (1576), a warning to "you ramping gyrles, which rage with wanton lust" to "Disdaine my life, but listen to my mone, / Without good heede, the hap may be your owne." Whetstone, *The Rocke of Regard*, 18. For an overview of early modern experiments in female complaint relevant to Shakespeare's poem, see Kerrigan, *Motives of Woe*. Although voyeurism and ventriloquism are conventional features of the female complaint poem, what makes *A Lover's Complaint* unusual, as Kerrigan notes, are "Shakespeare's almost unparalleled refusal to close the frame" and "the text's failure to draw a moral" (50).

[3] On the religious connotations of "reconcilèd" and the resonances between the woman's exchange with the "reverend man" and the Catholic sacrament of confession, see Kerrigan, *Motives of Woe*, 49–51.

catalyst that sets desire and thought in motion, and it highlights the unstable, vertiginous position of the audience that witnesses an artful scene of complaint.

The conclusion of Shakespeare's single complaint poem articulates the complex dynamics and compelling force that *The Drama of Complaint* identifies in Shakespearean theatrical scenes of complaint. These scenes are among the most electrifying and iconic of Shakespeare's tragedy: Lear howling at the heavens with Cordelia's body in his arms; the spirits of Richard III's victims tormenting him with their accusations and curses; *Hamlet's* Ghost, issuing its "dread command" for revenge and remembrance; Richard II, mirror in hand, lamenting as his kingly identity dissolves; Desdemona, crying out from behind the curtains on her death-bed. This book argues that these scenes play pivotal roles in their plays' staging of provocative thought experiments about ethical subjectivity. It thus contributes to a growing body of scholarship on the way that Shakespearean drama practices and enables ethical thinking. At the same time, it is a book about the kind of thinking performed and elicited by poetic forms of complaint. My aim here is complementary to but different from the body of literary criticism that under-stands complaint as a powerful rhetorical mode for expressing sorrow, eliciting pity, and diagnosing sociopolitical ills. Tracing the entanglement of poetic forms of complaint with forms of ethical thought, this book builds a case for the philo-sophical affordances of complaint, its capacities for giving shape to ways of desir-ing, acting, and living consonant with early modern conceptions of the good.

The following chapters pursue this double argument by elaborating the ethical thinking performed in, around, and through scenes of complaint in five of Shakespeare's tragedies, and in five corresponding poetic forms of complaint pro-lific in sixteenth- and seventeenth-century literary texts and genres. Each chapter maps a particular formation of normative early modern ethical thought whose importance to the play comes into relief when the play is read alongside the poetic form of complaint staged in its scene of complaint. Existential complaint in *King Lear* engages ethical scripts informed by theological conceptions of creatureliness that detail the moral perversity of finite human creatures "complaining" about their suffering. *Richard III's* scenes of external and theatricalized judicial com-plaint intersect with popular understandings of conscience as an internal scene of plaintive accusation and response. *Hamlet's* scene of spectral complaint converges with moral psychological inquiries into the enigma of motivation. Performances of female complaint in *Richard II* emphasize new ethical paradigms of virtuous literary reception developing in concert with the period's emergent aesthetic the-ory, while *Othello's* scene of deathbed complaint plays on and complicates con-ventional narratives about domestic happiness. Together, these chapters show how Shakespeare reworks the conventional ethical schemas of contemporary poetic forms of complaint, reconfiguring important ethical concepts and provok-ing audiences to reconsider what they know about the good life.

4 THE DRAMA OF COMPLAINT

1. Forms of Desire

At its most basic, a complaint is an utterance animated by discontent, fueled by the sense that something is not as it should be. Or, put differently, every complaint is animated by desire, a longing for something to be otherwise. When early modern writers philosophize about what they see as the human condition, they describe an unevenly distributed but universal unhappiness for which complaint is the common language. "As there is no sea without tempest, warre without danger, or journey without travell: so there is no life without griefe…neither did I ever see nor know that man who hath no cause to be grieved, or to complaine," the French Protestant moralist Pierre de La Primaudaye notes in the prefatory epistle to *The French Academie* (1586).[4] Joseph Hall—satirist, Neostoic essayist, and Bishop of Exeter—makes the same observation in his *Meditations and Vowes* (1605): "Every man hath his turne of sorrow; whereby, some more, some lesse, all men are in their times miserable, I never yet could meet with the man that complayned not of somewhat."[5] The soliloquy that would become the period's best-known theatrical speech, itself a complaint, is a litany of the things about which a person might complain (and as such, a catalog of the stock topoi of complaint literature): the "slings and arrows of outrageous fortune," the aches of the heart and pains of the flesh, the stings of time, "th'oppressor's wrong" and "the law's delay," unrequited love, undervalued virtue and undeserved position, the loathsomeness of life and the fear of death—all the indignities and injuries and vicissitudes that, for Hamlet as for La Primaudaye, being means bearing.[6] Gesturing at once to all the meanings of the word—everyday grumbling, legal bills, poetic expressions of grief and grievance—the curate Henry Peacham prefaces his advice for constructing complaints in his rhetorical manual *The Garden of Eloquence* (1577) with the quip, "What is more common than complaint."[7]

Poetic forms of complaint suffused the texts that Shakespeare and his contemporaries studied, heard, read, performed, and wrote.[8] These complaints comprise a corpus that is vast and—because the term was, as John Kerrigan notes, "applied to many sorts of articulate dissatisfaction"—notoriously incohesive, crossing

---

[4] La Primaudaye, *The French Academie*, Aiiir. The second volume of this compendium of moral philosophy, also translated into English by Thomas Bowes, appeared in print in 1594.

[5] Hall, *Meditations and Vowes*, 115. This text would go through six editions by 1621.

[6] *Hamlet*, 3.1.57, 70, 71.

[7] Peacham, *The Garden of Eloquence*, 66. "Complaint," which derives from the Latin *plangere* (to beat the breast, lament) was used from the end of the thirteenth century to refer to everyday utterances of dissatisfaction; laments and other poetic expressions of grief; accusations made against another person; and grievances brought before a juridical authority for redress. *OED*, s.v. "complaint." *The Princeton Encyclopedia of Poetry and Poetics* notes that complaint was "an established rhetorical term by the time of Aristotle's *Rhetoric* (1395a)." See p. 287.

[8] Throughout this book I use the descriptor "poetic" to signal a contextual and functional distinction from legal bills of complaint: by "poetic" or "literary" complaints I mean those that appear within fictional texts, and/or are spoken by fictionalized personae, and/or are addressed to an audience other than (or in addition to) an actual judicial or legislative authority.

INTRODUCTION 5

genres and spanning erotic, philosophical, sociopolitical, historical, elegiac, and religious themes.[9] Love lyrics scattered through poetic miscellanies and prose romances were called complaints, as were poems of religious sorrow and longing modeled on the Penitential Psalms, as were broadside ballads like *A Complaynt agaynst the wicked enemies of Christ* (1564), whose speaker mourns the martyrdom of Protestants under Queen Mary's rule and fantasizes about inflicting revenge on Catholics ("to tosse and to turne them, / To hewe them in peces to Broyle and to burne them"). Some complaints, such as the mid-sixteenth-century anti-enclosure poem "A Ruful Complaynt of the Publyke Weale to Englande," give voice to highly particularized grievances, while others telegraph more perennial discontents (a case in point is Richard Barnfield's *The Complaint of Poetry, for the death of Liberality* [1605], in which Poetry complains that no one values her enough to financially support poets). Exemplary complainers included Job, cursing; Mary Magdalen, lamenting; Boethius, engaged in his querulous exchange with Lady Philosophy; and Piers Plowman, exhorting. Typical targets of complaint included cruel ladies, perfidious men, uncharitable aristocrats, and blind, fickle Fortune. Complaint specifies no particular content, no particular formal features, only an attitude: a lack of contentment on the part of its speaker. The nine poems compiled in Edmund Spenser's *Complaints* (1591) include sonnets and dream visions translated from Petrarch and Du Bellay on the transitory nature of worldly pleasures and achievements; a pointed "complaint against the times" that doubles as an elegy for Sir Philip Sidney and Robert Dudley, Earl of Leicester; a poem of lamentation in which the Muses bemoan their neglect; a satirical animal fable critical of William Cecil, Lord Burghley; and a mock-heroic epyllion on the mutability topos.[10] Some of the most significant sixteenth-century experiments in historical prosopopoeia took shape as complaints, from the complaint opus *A Mirror for Magistrates* (1559), a popular and frequently expanded collection of narrative verse monologues spoken by the ghosts of historical personages who lament their tragic falls and counsel readers to live virtuously, to Michael Drayton's *Englands Heroicall Epistles* (1597), a set of passionate verse epistles—imagined as the correspondence between legendary couples from English history—modeled on the amorous epistolary complaints of Ovid's

---

[9] Kerrigan, *Motives of Woe*, 7. Smith, O'Callaghan, and Ross ("Complaint") describe early modern forms of complaint as developing from medieval traditions, some modeled on precedents in the literature of antiquity, which include (1) the amorous complaints of Chaucer and Lydgate, shaped by French love poetry as well as Ovid's *Heroides*; (2) religious complaints inspired by the Psalms, Books of the Prophets, and other biblical narratives; and (3) popular complaints of sociopolitical protest and critique ("complaint against the times" and "clamour") influenced by emerging forms of legal complaint and petition. Kerrigan (*Motives of Woe*) also mentions the important influence of the lamentations of Greek tragedy, as well as philosophical complaints about the vicissitudes of earthly life and the sufferings of the body, such as Alain de Lille's twelfth-century *De planctu naturae*.

[10] These complaints are, respectively, *The Ruines of Rome*, *The Visions of Bellay*, and *The Visions of Petrarch*; *The Ruines of Time*; *The Teares of the Muses*; *Prosopopoia, or Mother Hubberds Tale*; and *Muiopotmos*.

6 THE DRAMA OF COMPLAINT

Heroides. (As Lynn Enterline has suggested, the *Heroides'* clear influence on the proliferation of female-voiced complaint in the 1590s reflects its place in the curriculum of the Tudor grammar school, where schoolboys were required to compose and perform passionate complaints in the voices of iconic female complainers.)[11] The textual archive includes complaints of consolation (Richard Mulcaster's *A Comforting Complaint* [1603], an elegy on Elizabeth's death); supplication (*The Lamentable Complaint of the Commonaltie, By Way of Supplication to the High Court of Parliament, For a Learned Ministerie* [1588]); warning (John Lane's *Tom Tel-Troth's Message, and His Pens Complaint* [1600], whose speaker "blaz[es] Englands iniquities," rebuking the "world bad, men worse, men in world, worldly men, / [who] Doe give occasion to my plaintife pen;") and devotion (Katherine Parr's *The Lamentacion of a Sinner* [1547], a prose text that juxtaposes expressions of personal penitence, a discussion of Reformed soteriology, and prayers for the conversion of sinners.)[12] Even this brief overview indicates the multiple genealogies of complaint, the array of genres with which it fuses, the plural rhetorical modalities of complaining—lamenting, grumbling, or accusing, or pleading, or confessing, or demanding—and the volume and diversity of the utterances and texts classifiable as complaint.[13] Indeed, for William Scott, author of *The Model of Poesy*, a poetic treatise composed in the late sixteenth century, "plaintive" poetry is simply that which "consists in complaining the absence and want of something which possessed we persuade ourselves would be of pleasure and use to us."[14]

Critical accounts of complaint invariably acknowledge that such elasticity presents "definitional woes"—complaint, Jake Arthur and Rosalind Smith rightly observe, "can often feel like a case of *you know it when you see it*."[15] This "motile, slippery" quality, Wendy Scase suggests, has made complaint "a problematic category in modern critical vocabulary."[16] In a recent essay, Smith, Michelle O'Callaghan, and Sarah C.E. Ross note that "complaint's distinctive blurring of boundaries—material, textual, rhetorical, and emotional—has meant that it has not, until recently, gained great critical purchase as an analytic term," despite its unmistakable "centrality as a mode to early modern poetic practice."[17] To demonstrate and develop the analytical value of complaint these and other scholars have

---

[11] Enterline, *Shakespeare's Schoolroom*.   [12] Lane, *Tom Tel-Troth's Message*, B1r, F3v, B1r.

[13] On the combination of complaint with various modes of narrative in early modern literature, see Kietzman, *"Means to Mourn Some Newer Way": The Role of the Complaint in Early-Modern Narrative*.

[14] Scott, *The Model of Poesy*, 28.

[15] Arthur and Smith, "Women's Complaint," 293, authors' emphasis.

[16] Scase, *Literature and Complaint*, 1.

[17] Smith, O'Callaghan, and Ross, "Complaint," 339. Among literary scholars there is no firm consensus on what defines complaint as a literary form, nor is there consensus on whether it is best understood as a form, a mode, or a genre. For instance, the entry for "complaint" in the *Oxford Companion to English Literature* defines it as "A poetic form derived from the Latin *planctus*, bewailing the vicissitudes of life...or addressed to a more particular end" (s.v. "complaint"), while David Mikics' *A New Handbook of Literary Terms* defines "complaint" as "a literary genre based on seemingly interminable lamenting" (67).

INTRODUCTION 7

created working definitions and imposed winnowing categories on the sprawling field of complaint, typically grouping complaints together on the basis of common theme (religion, love, politics), the gender of the speaker or author (female-voiced complaint, complaint written by women), or shared poetic features (narrative verse complaint, epistolary complaint). This work has shown complaint to have been a versatile and emotionally powerful language for mourning loss, for protesting injustice, for eliciting various kinds of sympathetic identifications, and for convoking communities of like feeling or common cause, not least because of what Arthur and Smith identify as the "primary poetic effect" of complaint tout court: its "amplification of the speaker's distress."[18] It is the intrinsically dramatic, situational quality of such performed distress that motivates my own framing of the field of complaint as an expansive repertoire of various expressions of unhappy desire, all highly conventional, but each unhappy in its own way.

Though unmoored from any one literary genre, complaint has a special affinity with tragedy, whose traditional subject matter—suffering, injustice, trauma, catastrophe, loss, bad luck, love gone wrong—provides ample cause and occasion for complaining. "My part it is and my professed skill / The Stage with Tragick buskin to adorne, / And fill the Scene with plaint and outcries shrill / Of wretched persons, to misfortune borne," declares Melpomene, Muse of Tragedy, in Spenser's *The Teares of the Muses* (1591).[19] Early modern writers considered speeches of complaint formally integral to tragedy: "tragicall verse," according to one sixteenth-century poetic treatise, consists of "dolefull complaynts, lamentable chaunces, and what soeuer is poetically expressed in sorrow and heauiness."[20] This is a perfect description of de casibus tragedy, its tales told by ghosts who "bewaile...theyr greevous chaunces, heavy destenies, and woefull misfortunes," as William Baldwin, editor of the first edition of *A Mirror for Magistrates* (a continuation of John Lydgate's fifteenth-century *Fall of Princes*) puts it.[21] Complaint was also prominent in the Euripidean and Senecan traditions that shaped early

[18] Arthur and Smith, "Women's Complaint," 293–4. See, for example, Felch, "Anne Lock and the Instructive Complaint;" O'Callaghan, "A Mirror for Magistrates"; Shortslef, "Second Life"; Ross, "Hester Pulter's Devotional Complaints."

[19] Spenser, *The Teares of the Muses*, lines 151–4, first printed in *Complaints* (1591). All citations of Spenser are from *The Shorter Poems*.

[20] Webbe, *A Discourse of English Poetrie*, D2v. *The Mirour for Magistrates*, 109r. All citations of the *Mirror* are from this 1587 omnibus edition, edited by John Higgins. For an overview of early modern tragic practice and theory, see Reiss, "Renaissance theatre and the theory of tragedy;" Hoxby, *What Was Tragedy?*; Bushnell, "The Fall of Princes"; and Cadman et al., *The Genres of Renaissance Tragedy*.

[21] The tragic de casibus complaint was so ubiquitous and so conventional that it was an easy target for mockery. In one of several satirical verses on contemporary poetic trends printed in *Virgidemiarum* (1602), Joseph Hall pokes fun at the predictable formulae of these "rufull plaint[s]":

> Then brings he [the poet] up some branded whining Ghost,
> To tell how old misfortunes had him tost.
> Then must he ban the guiltlesse fates above,
> Or fortune fraile, or unrewarded love.
> And when he hath parbrak'd his grieved minde,
> He sends him downe where earst he did him find.

(p. 12)

8   THE DRAMA OF COMPLAINT

modern tragic drama.[22] "Weepyng verse of sobbes and sighes" is how Jasper Heywood describes *Troas*, his 1559 translation of Seneca's *Troades*, the story of the sufferings of the Trojan women in the aftermath of their city's destruction, which opens with the lamenting Hecuba—"A mirrour...to teache you what you are"—complaining of "the fates which from above / the wavering Gods downe flinges."[23] As in these models, so in early modern tragic drama, including stage plays, university dramas, and closet dramas, complaints regularly punctuate the falls from "heigh degree / Into myserie" that constitute the plots of tragedy.[24] The final speeches of dying characters are often complaints, last gasps of an attachment to life that persists in the leaving of it, as when Christopher Marlowe's Bajazeth, the conquered emperor of the Turks, complains before braining himself against the cage in which Tamburlaine has confined him:

> O life more loathsome to my vexèd thoughts
> Than noisome parbreak of the Stygian snakes
> Which fills the nooks of hell with standing air,
> Infecting all the ghosts with cureless griefs!
> O dreary engines of my loathèd sight
> That sees my crown, my honor, and my name
> Thrust under yoke and thralldom of a thief!
> Why feed ye still on day's accursèd beams
> And sink not quite into my tortured soul?[25]

Yet complaining does not exclusively mark falls: as often, a complaint is just the beginning of tragedy. Complaints frequently open tragic plays, forecasting the dramatic action by declaring or explicating the cause of a character's discontent, as Shakespeare's Troilus complains that he is "mad / In Cressid's love" and that "she is stubborn, chaste against all suit," or Queen Videna, lamenting that "nowe the Daie renewes my griefull plainte," expresses her displeasure at her husband's plan to divide his kingdom in the first lines of Thomas Sackville and Thomas Norton's *Gorboduc* (1565), or Elizabeth Cary's Mariam laments her ambivalence at Herod's reported death ("One object yields both grief and joy"), her knowledge

---

[22] On the influence of Euripides, see Pollard, *Greek Tragic Women on Shakespearean Stages*. On Senecan drama, see Braden, *Renaissance Tragedy and the Senecan Tradition* and Perry, *Shakespeare and Senecan Tragedy*.

[23] Seneca, *Troas*, preface; B3v, A3r. The description of Hecuba as a "mirror" is from a Chorus written by Heywood himself.

[24] Chaucer, "The Monk's Tale," in *The Canterbury Tales*, VII. 1976–7. Quoted from *The Riverside Chaucer*. On complaint as a conventional speech in early modern tragic drama, see Clemen, *English Tragedy Before Shakespeare*.

[25] Marlowe, *Tamburlaine the Great, Part 1* (1590), 5.1.255–63. Quoted from *English Renaissance Drama*.

of his tyranny insufficient to "repulse some falling tear / That will, against my will, some grief unfold."[26]

Neither the specific passion nor the more general wretchedness at issue in these tragic speeches is exclusively that of their fictional speakers. Rhetorical handbooks described plaintive speeches of sorrow, anguish, or outrage as passionate performances capable of stirring passion in audiences, making such speeches especially attractive to sixteenth- and seventeenth-century dramatists, who, as Blair Hoxby has argued, "located the essence of tragedy in the passions that it imitated and aroused."[27] (A claim affirmed by the allegorical figure of Tragedie in the anonymous play *A Warning for Fair Women* [1599], who says that she "must have passions that must move the soule /..../ Extorting teares out of the strictest eyes.")[28] A mediator of such passion, Spenser's Melpomene is figured as nothing less than a complaining corpus, with a voice that cries to the heavens as she observes and stages the sad scenes of human existence ("a Tragedy, / Full of sad sights and sore Catastrophees"), bearing witness to human misery.[29] Many tragic complaints articulate this view of existence, their speakers depicting themselves as representatives of a woeful human condition for which one can do nothing but lament, as Estrild complains at Locrine's death in the anonymous *Lamentable Tragedie of Locrine* (1595):

> O fickle Fortune! O unstable world!
> What else are all things that this globe contains,
> But a confusèd chaos of mishaps?
> Wherein, as in a glass, we plainly see,
> That all our life is but as a tragedy.[30]

This tragic conception of human subjectivity is reflected not only in the formulaic things that tragedy's complainers say about the misery of humankind, but in the proverbially "bootless" act of complaining itself, an action consisting of nothing more than words that the speaker fears are futile, and without meaning.[31] This is the logic that underlies Macbeth's reaction on being told of Lady Macbeth's

---

[26] *Troilus and Cressida*, 1.1.48–49, 92; Norton and Sackville, *Gorboduc*, Aiiir; Cary, *The Tragedy of Mariam* (1613), 1.1.10, 53–54, quoted from *English Renaissance Drama*.

[27] Hoxby, "Passions," 564. While Milton suggests in the preface to *Samson Agonistes* (1671) that tragedy arouses the passions of pity and fear to purge its audiences of these and other excessive passions, sixteenth-century English writers, though clear about the centrality of pathos to tragedy, have less to say about the ends it serves. On the pertinence of Aristotelian catharsis and the *Poetics* more generally to early modern tragedy, see Smith, "Tragedy 'Before' Pity and Fear."

[28] *A Warning for Fair Women*, lines 44–6.   [29] *The Teares of the Muses*, lines 157–8.

[30] *The Lamentable Tragedy of Locrine*, 5.6.50–54.

[31] Lee Patterson has suggested that the ubiquity of complaint in late medieval writing reflects a longstanding poetic concern with the efficacy of language as "a form of action that mediates between the subject and the world." Patterson, *Acts of Recognition*, 182.

10 THE DRAMA OF COMPLAINT

untimely death, when he describes life as an ephemeral tragedy composed of such histrionic complaints:

> Out, out, brief candle.
> Life's but a walking shadow, a poor player
> That struts and frets his hour upon the stage
> And then is heard no more. It is a tale
> Told by an idiot, full of sound and fury,
> Signifying nothing.[32]

Just as the discontent that drives complaining accounts for its intimacy with tragedy, so does that dissatisfaction underpin a more surprising connection between complaint and ethics, which was understood in early modern England as the study of how one might "attaine that chiefe goodness of the children of men," the supreme good identified by Aristotle as eudaimonia, the happiness that is the very height of human flourishing.[33] Complaints are energized by the same striving for happiness that Aristotle attributes to human nature. Complaining can even be understood as a form of ethical thinking itself, insofar as it involves a judgment that one's well-being depends on the acquisition of a particular object of positive desire that might bring one closer to happiness ("something which possessed we persuade ourselves would be of pleasure and use to us," to return to William Scott's phrase) or on the removal of an object of negative desire that causes displeasure.[34] Poetic forms of complaint are structured around the riveting and galvanizing force of these objects, which seem to promise or deny a satisfaction which the complainer experiences as lacking (as one melancholy shepherd in Philip Sidney's *The Countess of Pembrokes Arcadia*, complaining to another shepherd of the woman he desires, laments that "She holds the balance of my contentation").[35] Such objects of desire are, of course, virtually infinite. We complain for want of God's presence, or for unrequited love, Scott observes, but "we have other plaintiffs as we have other calamities and losses, whether of goods,

---

[32] *Macbeth*, 5.5.23–28.

[33] Hall, *Salomons Divine Arts, of Ethickes, Politics, Oeconomicks*, 1–2. As Jill Kraye notes, "from antiquity to the Renaissance, the enquiry into man's supreme good or *summum bonum*, that is, the attempt to determine the ultimate purpose for which he was born, was generally accepted as the defining characteristic of ethics." The Aristotelian identification of eudaimonia as the *summum bonum* is generally echoed by early modern English writers, for whom the *Ethics* was one of the most important works of moral philosophy, with scholastic and neo-Platonic modifications whereby human flourishing or happiness is defined as the knowledge of God and life in accordance with his will. See Kraye, "Moral Philosophy," 316, 349.

[34] Scott, *The Model of Poesy*, 27.

[35] This line exists only in a song contained in the Second Eclogues of the so-called Old Arcadia, which was written between the late 1570s and early 1580s and circulated in manuscript. I am quoting from *Sir Philip Sidney: The Countess of Pembroke's Arcadia (The Old Arcadia)*, ed. Duncan-Jones, 124.

honour, friends, health, or whatsoever worldly fading joy we hold dear."[36] Indeed, the "complaint against nature" that the preacher Godfrey Goodman makes in a sermon called *The Fall of Man* (1616) figures humans as gluttonous "meere-cormorants" whose "infinite desire" is enflamed by a world that forever fails to satisfy it: because "wee receive no contentment at all," he argues, we are perpetual "importunate suitors," always seeking satisfaction, and thus always complaining.[37] The complainer essays an answer to—or, in the case of the complainer who does not exactly know why she is so unhappy, initiates an inquiry into—the fundamental ethical question of what the good life is, the question of what is required for happiness and what gets in its way.

To be clear, while I am proposing that complaints always have an ethical charge, insofar as the complaint scenario foregrounds questions of happiness, I am not suggesting that either the object that a complainer desires or the ultimate aim of their desire is necessarily *good*—at least not by any normative measure. The distance between the satisfaction the complainer pursues and the good posited by normative morality is the very subject of the wry lament of Sidney's Astrophil, who lusts after the virtuous Stella: "So while thy beauty draws the heart to love, / As fast thy virtue bends that love to good," he tells her, "But ah, desire still cries: 'Give me some food.'"[38] Astrophil is hardly alone. The pulse of the amorous complaint in particular is fundamentally pleasure-seeking—a point made openly by the speaker of the lyric titled "An absent dame thus complaineth" in George Gascoigne's *Works* (1587), who, comparing herself to a greyhound stayed from chasing the "game" it spots, "plain[s] for lacke of time & place" to enjoy her lover and "taste / The dulcet fruites of my delight."[39] The pursuit of something decidedly at odds with the complainer's well-being is on display in those amorous complaints whose speakers find enjoyment in their hunger, their very lack of contentment, as when the *Arcadia*'s lovesick Gynecia, claiming that "Bitter grief tastes me best, pain is my ease," describes herself as "Sick to the death, still loving my disease."[40] As Catherine Bates has argued, in complaints like these, we find a "depiction of human desire" as "irrational, insane, obsessive, driven, self-destructive, addictive, masochistic in a compulsively repetitive way, wholly immune from considerations of worth or desert or from the pursuit of happiness or satisfaction, but no less irresistible for that."[41] Her point of reference is Freud, but this conception of desire would not have been at all unfamiliar to early moderns. Arguing against the Aristotelian axiom that human flourishing is the natural telos of

---

[36] Scott, *The Model of Poesy*, 28.   [37] Goodman, *The Fall of Man*, 49.

[38] Sidney, *Astrophil and Stella* (1591), Sonnet 71, lines 12–14. Quoted from *The Major Works*.

[39] Gascoigne, *Herbes*, printed in *The Whole Woorkes*, pp. 139, 138, 139.

[40] Book Three, 634. Quoted from the expanded and revised printed edition of 1593, in *Sir Philip Sidney: The Countess of Pembroke's Arcadia*, ed. Evans.

[41] Bates, "The Enigma of *A Lover's Complaint*," 434, 435. On plaintive lyric, masochism, and the way in which early modern representations of desire anticipate those of psychoanalytic theory, see also Sanchez, *Erotic Subjects*.

12 THE DRAMA OF COMPLAINT

desire, Calvin suggests that the world of created things is so corrupted by Original Sin that desire's orientation is fundamentally perverse: "What is that ende of our creation?" he asks, "Even the same from which we are altogether turned away."[42] Unpinned from any innate sense of the good, having no natural orientation to the "right" objects, desire in the Calvinist paradigm might well be said to take its direction from "an erotics that is above morality" (a Lacanian phrase particularly apt in this context, since Lacan notes that such desire, evident in the clinical scenes of complaint that ground Freudian psychoanalysis, comes to the fore in the theological discourse of the sixteenth century).[43] In brief, complaints reveal a desire whose ethical measure—whose logic of the good—is not necessarily or always commensurable with the metrics of traditional moral philosophy and religious belief. Far from it. Yet in the early modern literature of complaint, those metrics are never far from the scene either, as we will see.[44]

The dramas of intense and often ambivalent desire staged by the complainer are central to the taxonomy that this book constructs. Indeed, this way of thinking about complaint opens a way of reading for pattern across the different texts, genres, and discourses in which the protean, "singularly amorphous" complaint appears.[45] I approach the field of complaint as a field of formulaic scenarios of desire: signature situations, each with its own familiar objects, speakers, and addressees, its own characteristic relational dynamics. Complaining about the fundamental conditions of their life, and trying to understand the meaning of their unhappiness, the speaker of what I call existential complaint desires an end to their suffering, a conclusion and a telos. The speaker of judicial complaint demands justice from someone obligated to respond by virtue of their place in an institutional or social structure. The ghosts who utter spectral complaints command their addressees to do whatever they ask, to be the instruments of their desire. The speakers of female complaint want a sympathetic reception, a mirroring of their passion, from their audiences. Confessing to and repenting a transgression,

---

[42] Calvin, *Institution of Christian Religion*, 71v (2.1.3).

[43] Lacan, *Seminar VII*, 103. Lacan speaks of "the filiation or cultural paternity that exists between Freud and a new direction of thought…that is apparent at the break which occurred toward the beginning of the sixteenth century, but whose repercussions are felt up to the end of the seventeenth century" (120).

[44] Although it is beyond this book's focus, I want to note the moral questions that arise (for fictional complainers and their interlocutors, as well as for critics) whenever a speaker persists in complaining, despite knowing that the object they desire cannot be had. These questions often center on the good that complaining itself does: is complaining therapeutic or counterproductive? Does it alleviate or enflame bad feelings? Does it help the complainer move on or keep them stuck? Does the complainer have an unhealthy attachment to their complaints? See, for instance, Paul Salzman's recent discussion of the difference between complaints that demonstrate what popular psychotherapy calls "clean pain"—mourning through which the complainer turns back to sociality—and complaints that are "tied up in dirty pain: that is, an obsessive focus on self-criticism, diminishing worth and self-torment," a distinction that recalls Freud's famous discussion of the difference between mourning and melancholia. Salzman, "The Politics of Complaint," 142.

[45] Dubrow, "A Mirror for Complaints," 400.

the speaker of deathbed complaint longs for the community they have disrupted to be reformed, and for themselves to be reintegrated into it. Each of these situations comprises a *form* of complaint—a more or less consistent and recognizable configuration—repeated across early modern texts as an intrinsically dramatic, and not infrequently histrionic, *scene*. (I typically use "form" when I am describing the generalizable structure and pattern that accrues meaning through its repetition—form being, in my understanding, a "recurring pattern that makes something the thing it is"—and "scene" when I am discussing particular instantiations of the form).[46] With the exception of existential complaint, in name and/or general characteristics these forms overlap to varying extents with categories recognized and discussed by other critics, but for each of these constellations I offer a novel definition that reflects the conceptual work the form does.

The argument that this book advances likewise follows from seeing forms of complaint as dramas of desire. Thematizing the pursuits of particular objects of desire by complainers, and the pressures felt or resisted by addressees, these forms of complaint occasion self-conscious reflections—from fictional speakers and from writers alike—on happiness and the good. As this book will show, the writers of these texts used these forms not only to construct ethical arguments, but to try to make these arguments matter to audiences, to make them aware of what they, too, should want.

2. Forms of Ethical Thought

The analyses of existential, judicial, spectral, female, and deathbed complaint in the following chapters attend to the pressures mediated by these forms. Such pressures pertain both to the fictionalized speech situations represented in scenes of complaint and to the encounters that readers and audiences have with these forms. Among the former are the internal and external forces that spark a complainer's desire and motivate complaint in the first place. Complainers frequently describe themselves as subject to psychophysiological pressures that demand expression in speech: invoking both the humoral-materialist understanding of

---

[46] This is one of many possible definitions of "form," as Sandra Macpherson notes ("A Little Formalism," 388). The understanding of form as a particular arrangement or ordering of material, iterated with frequency and consistency, has been central to the revival of formalism(s) seen in literary studies over the past twenty-some years, a critical movement heralded in a special issue of *Modern Language Quarterly* (61: 1, 2000) on "Reading for Form," edited by Susan Wolfson. It's necessary to note, however, that the methodologically and ideologically diverse work done under this aegis rejects a single, unified definition or shared consensus about what "form" is, a fact already noted in Marjorie Levinson's "What is New Formalism?" (*PMLA*, 122: 2, 2007) and more recently defended as a virtue by Jonathan Kramnick and Anahid Nersessian in "Form and Explanation" (*Critical Inquiry*, 43, 2017). For an especially influential reading of form as a patterned arrangement that crosses genres and discourses, see Levine, *Forms* (2015).

14 THE DRAMA OF COMPLAINT

passion as bodily turbulence and the conventional wisdom expressed in such adages as "The heart, and stomach, eazed are, through playntes, & teeres, from pensyve eye," they describe their complaints as the therapeutic discharge of something within that threatens their well-being, even their very life.[47] Other pressures have obvious external causes. "Oft have I heard your Majesty complain / Of Tamburlaine, that sturdy Scythian thief, / That robs your merchants of Persepolis," the councilor Meander says to Mycetes, King of Persia, launching into a complaint about Tamburlaine's encroachment, in response to the king's request that he "Declare the cause of my conceivèd grief, / Which is, God knows, about that Tamburlaine."[48] This exchange gestures to a different kind of external pressure as well, for it follows from the hapless Mycetes' confession, in the opening line of *Tamburlaine*, that he is unable to perform the complaint with which a tragedy conventionally begins: "I find myself aggrieved, / Yet insufficient to express the same, / For it requires a great and thund'ring speech."[49] Scenes of complaint are miniaturized psychosocial dramas. Yet they do less to construct interiority, I would suggest, than to emblematize outwardness, emphasizing what Timothy Reiss has described as the *possibility* of the self—its capacity to be acted on by external forces, and to suffer, as a consequence of its embeddedness in natural and social worlds.[50]

Often the susceptibility that matters most in a scene of complaint is that of the addressee. A type of passionate utterance—a speech act that "work[s] on the feelings, thoughts, and actions of others coevally with its design in revealing our desires to others and ourselves"—a complaint not only expresses the pressures that a complainer feels but also attempts to exert pressure on someone else.[51] Fictional encounters between a complainer and another person frequently foreground issues of obligation and ethical judgment, emphasizing the responsibility of the addressee or witness to hear and respond to the complainer. Some are legal situations; in others, patently distressed complainers who supplicate more

---

[47] Quoted from the commonplace book of Thomas Butts (c. 1581). On the significance of humoral theory for tragedy in particular, see Paster, "The tragic subject and its passions." As Paster's work has shown, early moderns understood these passions to result from the body's permeability to, and its complex interactions with, the external environment. See, for instance, Paster, *Humoring the Body*.

[48] Marlowe, *Tamburlaine*, 1.1.35–37, 29–30.   [49] *Tamburlaine*, 1.1.1–3, 29–30.

[50] On possibility, see Reiss, *Mirages of the Selfe*, 2. This term, he suggests, "names experiences of being whose common denominator was a sense of being *embedded in and acted upon by*...circles" that included "the material world and immediate biological, familial and social ambiences, as well as the soul's...cosmic, spiritual or divine life." As he notes, "these circles *preceded* the person, which acted as *subjected to* forces working in complicated ways from 'outside.' But because of the embedding, that 'outside' was manifest in all aspects and elements of 'inside'—of *being* a person" (2, author's emphases).

[51] Cavell, *Philosophy the Day After Tomorrow*, 186. On passionate utterances, see especially 7–27, 155–91. Cavell's category of the passionate utterance is only one instance of the critical expansion of J. L. Austin's category of performatives—utterances that do, rather than simply describe, something—from exclusively illocutionary speech acts (where "the issuing of the utterance is the performing of an action") to include perlocutionary speech acts, whose performative force manifests in the effects that follow from the utterance. On these distinctions see Austin, *How to Do Things with Words*, 6.

INTRODUCTION   15

powerful addressees to grant their requests may figuratively invoke legal scenarios by presenting themselves as plaintiffs, speaking in the language of forensic oratory, and insisting on the righteousness of their causes.[52] Thus Lucrece pleads with Tarquin to recall the aristocratic codes of honor and friendship ("holy human law and common troth"), her tears making "motion" before his power:

> Be moved with my tears, my sighs, my groans.
> All which together, like a troubled ocean,
> Beat at thy rocky and wreck-threat'ning heart
> To soften it with their continual motion.[53]

Faced with a plea that catalyzes his moral reason and judgment, that offers him an opportunity to reflect on his intended action and change course, Tarquin refuses to hear (his "heart granteth / No penetrable entrance to her plaining"), a fact that the narrator suggests only adds to the moral weight of his crime.[54] In a similarly decisive scene in Samuel Daniel's verse history *The Civil Wars* (1595), the Genius of England appears as a weeping woman in a dream to Bolingbroke on the eve of his rebellion, pleading with him in a lengthy speech of complaint to "stay here thy foote, thy yet unguilty foote."[55] These scenes of complaint, whose function is to show that these men could have chosen otherwise, represent ethical crossroads for their addressees. Scenes of this sort may contain an implicit address to another audience as well. Think of Shylock's complaint, pointing beyond Shakespeare's Venice to Shakespeare's England:

> Hath not a Jew eyes? Hath not a Jew hands, organs, dimensions, senses, affec-
> tions, passions—fed with the same food, hurt with the same weapons, subject to
> the same diseases, healed by the same means, warmed and cooled by the same
> winter and summer as a Christian is? If you prick us do we not bleed? If you
> tickle us do we not laugh? If you poison us do we not die, and if you wrong us
> shall we not revenge?[56]

When complainers speak from disadvantaged positions or from the margins of a social world, complaining appears as a form of action at its most minimal, in conditions of extremity—the thing that one does when one can do nothing else.

Several forms of complaint popular in the period, leveraging what Alison Thorne calls complaint's "persuasive, ethical, and diagnostic qualities," stage these

---

[52] On the formative impact of judicial structures and procedures on poetic practices of complaint in late medieval England, see Scase, *Literature and Complaint*. On complaints in forensic orations, see Skinner, *Forensic Shakespeare*.
[53] Shakespeare, *The Rape of Lucrece*, lines 571, 588–91.   [54] *The Rape of Lucrece*, lines 558–9.
[55] 1.90.1, from Daniel, *The First Fowre Bookes of the civile wars*, 16.
[56] *The Merchant of Venice*, 3.1.49–55.

16   THE DRAMA OF COMPLAINT

kinds of scenes, directly addressing and exerting moral pressure on readers.[57] In one form, a complainer (sometimes adopting the suffering voice of a corporate persona or an abstraction) demands remedy, redress, and relief from the privileged and the powerful, whom the complainer reminds of the responsibilities attached to their place in the social hierarchy.[58] By granting the demand, the complainer suggests, the addressees pursue their own good too. A prime example is Arthur Standish's prose pamphlet *The Commons Complaint* (1611), which complains of deforestation and food shortages and offers horticultural advice to landowners for preventing food shortages and the riots that ensue. Standish tells the landowners that by "reliev[ing] the wants" of the complaining commons, they fulfill, in part, "the cause of [their] creation," bringing them closer to the eternal blessedness that is the promised end of the Christian ethical paradigm.[59] Another form of complaint, more sharp and satirical than deferential or flattering to its readers, aims "to wound and worke upon the conscience," as William Holbrooke says in his preface to *Loves Complaint, For Want of Entertainement* (1609), a homily preached at St. Paul's intended "to shewe unto you your want of Love, by your manifest injustice, and want of Rejoycing in true and honest dealing and religion."[60] The speakers of these complaints position themselves as moral physicians, diagnosing addressees' sins and urging them to heal themselves.[61] In this vein, Thomas Kingsmill's *A Complaint against Securitie in these perillous times* (1602) warns "that because of these perilous times Catholike warres, forreine & civill daungers, late seditions, and uprores…it is not a time to injoy vines or olives, to rest in chaires or footstools," but instead to exercise the spiritual virtues of righteousness, mercy, and charity.[62] In *Christs Teares Over Jerusalem*—a polemic whose speaker impersonates Christ's lament over Jerusalem, then excoriates contemporary Londoners for their sins—Thomas Nashe, writing in the plague year of 1593, suggests that his vice-ridden readers might take remedy from his "coursespun webbe of discontent: a quintessence of holy complaint."[63] Whether a

---

[57] Thorne, "'O, lawful let it be,'" 115.

[58] On topical complaints, see Manley, *Literature and Culture in Early Modern England*, 63–122. On the continuities and differences between complaint and the more explicitly politically-charged modes of "railing" and "ranting," see Prendergast, *Railing, Reviling, and Invective in English Literary Culture*.

[59] "Whereupon good Reader, it insueth, that by the observing of these small directions, thou mayest performe some part of the cause of thy creation, by giving glorie to thy Creator, honour, pleasure, and profit to thy King, Countrey, and to thy selfe also, by feeling and relieving thy Christian brothers wants, and by a charitable industrie, thou mayest raise meanes to disburthen them of all their grievances present and to come, and in the end, by the mercie of our good God, thou mayest bee partaker of his loving promises in the Gospell, Come you blessed of my Father." Standish, *The Commons Complaint*, B1r–v.

[60] Holbrooke, *Loves Complaint*, B1v.

[61] On the differences between the closely related modes of complaint and satire see Peter, *Complaint and Satire in Early English Literature* and Combe, "The New Voice of Political Dissent." Both critics describe complaint as more mournful, more abstract and vague in its critiques and suggestions for reform, and more socially and politically conservative than satire.

[62] Kingsmill, *A Complaint against Securitie*, B3r–v.

[63] Nashe, *Christs Teares Over Jerusalem*, unpaginated prefatory material.

consummate instance or a parody of the form (it is hard to say with Nashe), *Christs Teares* vividly makes the point that Susan M. Felch attributes to all these "prophetic" and "instructive" complaints, whose speakers imagine themselves as mediators of a divine warning: "the one who refuses to listen will die."[64] A final didactic form of complaint is the "mirror" genre, with its prophylactic moral lessons "Verye profitable for all sorte of estates to reade and looke upon."[65] Spoken in the person of a legendary or historical figure presented as a negative exemplar, these prosopopoetic complaints include those of King Herod, King David, and Judas from Anthony Munday's *Mirrour of Mutabilitie* (1574), the complaints of such "wicked and ungodlye worldelinges" as Tarquin, Tantalus, and Helen in Richard Robinson's *The Rewarde of Wickednesse* (1574), and the complaints of *A Mirror for Magistrates* and its offshoots, which combine moral didacticism with political counsel. This form of complaint supports the cultivation of Aristotelian ethos—moral character—by urging readers to habitually practice those actions and pursue those objects that will lead them toward happiness and away from the unfortunate "haps" that befell the complainers.

Other forms of complaint invite a reader to identify with the desire of the complainer, to desire the good that they desire. Elegiac complaints ask the addressees to mourn with the complainer for the loss of a common object, as in one 1603 elegy for Elizabeth, in which Melpomene asks all "good Subjects" to "conjoyne in one" and "Let griefe be Nector to rejoyce their hearts."[66] (Such restoration is the very purpose of "the forme of poeticall lamentations," according to the sixteenth-century poetic theorist George Puttenham, who suggests of such works that "It is a piece of joy to be able to lament with ease and freely to pour forth a man's inward sorrows and the griefs wherewith his mind is surcharged...by making the very grief itself (in part) cure of the disease.")[67] Invoking a community whose desire it redirects to a new object—in this case, the new King—elegiac complaint aims to convert loss into gain, grief into pleasure. Other forms of mournful complaint, by contrast, might encourage their addressees to follow the complainer in detaching their desire from all temporal objects. For instance, the final sonnet of *The Visions of Petrarch*, Spenser's translation of a French translation of a sequence from the *Rime Sparse*, concludes with the speaker's expression of contempt for the world ("I wish I might this wearie life forgoe, / And shortly turne vnto my happie rest") and his counsel for readers to feel the same as he does: "When ye these rythmes doo read, and vew the rest, / Loath this base world, and thinke of heauens blis."[68]

---

[64] Felch, "Anne Lock and the Instructive Complaint," 32.
[65] This line is from the title page of Richard Robinson's complaint collection *The Rewarde of Wickednesse*.
[66] T. W., *The Lamentation of Melpomene*, B1v–B2r.
[67] Puttenham, *The Art of English Poesy*, 135.
[68] Spenser, *The Visions of Petrarch*, lines 89–96.

18 THE DRAMA OF COMPLAINT

What I am trying to suggest, and what the rest of this book will develop in more detail, is the extent to which the wide-ranging literature of complaint was deeply informed by—and in turn gave a certain shape to—normative early modern ethical thought, which shared with complaint a prevailing interest in questions of the individual's well-being and happiness. Aaron Garrett's observation that "self-help was a (or even *the*) central issue" of early modern English moral philosophy indexes the latter's privileging of ethics, which (in early modern thought as in the Aristotelian tradition) was described as the branch of moral philosophy specifically concerned with the good governance of the individual.[69] Neema Parvini has recently explicated the profoundly eclectic nature of early modern ethical thought, informed as it was by heterogeneous traditions that included Aristotelian virtue ethics, Stoic and Neostoic moral philosophy, Platonic and Neoplatonic metaphysics, and Ciceronian skepticism.[70] Early modern ethical thought was also deeply religious: as John D. Cox notes, at every point on the confessional spectrum "questions about ethics were inseparable from religion...because God was perfect goodness."[71] The result is a synthetic discourse in which variegated strands of classical moral philosophy are interwoven with the Christian narrative of humanity's creation, Fall, and redemption through grace (the work of patching together these different and sometimes contradictory ideas often occurs in the prefaces and other paratextual material of writers, editors, and translators). The ethical thought explored in the following chapters is normative in the sense that it is prescriptive; it both reflects and reproduces culturally dominant norms. It is also culturally commonplace, ordinary, and ubiquitous. It circulates in a broad array of nonfictional discourses, including theological treatises; sermons; devotional manuals; popular moral essays and collections of maxims and scriptural verses; didactic literature; treatises on human nature, the soul, or the workings of the body; antitheatrical discourse and defenses of poetry; and compendia of moral philosophy. It informs aphoristic speech and representations of moral reasoning and counsel in fictional texts. One would not have needed to be especially conversant with the canonical texts, or the finer points, of classical moral philosophy or Reformed theology to know this everyday ethical thought. It was, as Parvini puts it, "swirling around," distilled into "the cultural ether" as the commonsense knowledge that subtended early modern social life and its practices.[72] Such embodied knowledge concerns "howe to live well, and

---

[69] Garrett, "Seventeenth-Century Moral Philosophy," 230. Author's emphasis.

[70] Parvini, *Shakespeare's Moral Compass*.

[71] Cox, *Seeming Knowledge*, 161. Debora Shuger argues that "In the Renaissance religious discourse enfolds more than such specifically theological concerns...Religion during this period supplies the primary language of analysis. It is the cultural matrix for explorations of virtually every topic: kingship, selfhood, rationality, language, marriage, ethics, and so forth." See Shuger, *Habits of Thought*, 6. Hall suggests that "the end of all...the whole of Man, the whole dutie, the whole scope, the whole happinesse" lies in the knowledge of God and the keeping of his commandments. Hall, *Salomons Divine Arts*, 12–13.

[72] Parvini, *Shakespeare's Moral Compass*, 71, 73. Parvini notes the relative stability of this thought in the period.

how to shew our selves helpefull and officious to the world"—the purview of moral philosophy, as Joseph Hall suggests in one of his own self-help manuals, *Two Guides to a Good Life* (1604).[73]

In contrast to critical work on complaint that evaluates the efficacy of complaining and limns the agency exercised by complainers, this book aims to understand the more abstract, conceptual, ideological projects that writers advanced through particular forms of complaint, projects that are not identical with the particular desires and demands of complainers.[74] It looks at how particular scenes of plaintive desire are consistently linked to the articulation of particular "happiness scripts," or conventional blueprints for how to desire and act so as to achieve a certain measure of happiness.[75] (The "final end" of ethical knowledge being, in Sidney's words, to "lead and draw us to as high a perfection as our degenerate souls, made worse by their clayey lodgings, can be capable of.")[76] These scenes encourage identifications with ways of desiring, and attachments to objects of desire, deemed good in normative ethical thought. By putting the right objects of desire in complainers' mouths, or depicting complainers as tragic exemplars of self-destructive impulses, the victims of their own bad choices, forms of complaint were enlisted not only to construct, but to render desirable, ethical paradigms that point audiences in the right direction. With their tableaux of familiar unhappy scenarios, these forms suggest how to "use rightly what wee have" to "redresse, morall, and adorne [our] life"—how to make it right, good, and beautiful—by wanting and pursuing the right things. This literary history is important for understanding why forms of complaint were such a rich poetic and ethical resource for Shakespeare, whose dramatic career took shape in the 1590s, the decade that saw a "sudden intensification" of complaint.[77]

3. Shakespeare's Ethical Poetics

Early modern audiences, having been repeatedly told that fiction was either good or bad for them, were primed to attend to the ethical benefit they might receive from reading or from theatrical spectatorship. One of these actual primers— Plutarch's widely-read essay on reading poetry, titled "How a Young Man Ought

---

[73] Joseph Hall, *Two Guides to a Good Life* (London, 1604), B5r.

[74] This book's methodology aligns with what has been called "historical formalism," which sees literary forms as "social products shaped by specific historical circumstances to perform specific ideological tasks." Cohen, "Between Form and Culture," 32. On historical formalism in early modern literary studies, see Dubrow, "Guess Who's Coming to Dinner"; Rasmussen, *Renaissance Literature and Its Formal Engagements*; Burton and Scott-Baumann, *The Work of Form*.

[75] I borrow the concept of the happiness script from Sara Ahmed, who suggests that such scripts "redescribe social norms as social goods." See Ahmed, *The Promise of Happiness*, 2. I will return to the topic of happiness scripts at more length in Chapter 5.

[76] *The Defence of Poesy*, in *Sir Philip Sidney: The Major Works*, 219.

[77] Smith et al., "Complaint," 343.

20 THE DRAMA OF COMPLAINT

to Heare Poets, and How He May Take Profit By Reading Poemes" in Philemon Holland's 1603 translation—suggests that poetry is a gateway drug to philosophy. Poetic fictions, Plutarch proposes, "make an overture and way into the minde of a young ladde, that it may encline the rather to Philosophicall reasons and discourses," through poetic speeches that "move affections & passions in the readers...work[ing] strange events in them, even contrarie to their opinion and expectation," and representations of impassioned persons that "stir up the affection, & holdeth in suspense and admiration [their] mindes."[78] What this suggests is that early modern audiences may have approached poetic texts and theatrical performances with anticipation: prepared for novelty, prepared to be moved and, paradoxically, prepared to be surprised by their own reactions.

Since the late eighteenth century, Shakespeare has been heralded as a creator of fictional characters and situations that reward moral philosophical inquiry, offering insight into matters of practical reasoning, moral deliberation, volition, freedom, responsibility, choice.[79] The last fifteen years, however—roughly concurrent with the discipline's broader "ethical turn"—have seen increased critical attention to Shakespeare as an ethical thinker. One strand of this criticism, historicist in its objectives, seeks to do with regard to early modern ethical thought what the new historicist criticism of the 1990s and early 2000s did with regard to early modern theology and political theory: it reveals how Shakespeare's plays refract the ethical texts, ideas, and debates that comprised his contemporary intellectual surround and remain alive in the moral philosophy and critical theory of later periods.[80] Another strand, while also cognizant of the interlocutors that shaped Shakespeare's thinking, puts Shakespeare's plays in dialogue with a cast of thinkers from antiquity to modernity to illuminate their mutual concerns and productive tensions, "with some sense...of their significance for the way we live now."[81] While the former explicates what Shakespeare thought and the latter practices "thinking with" Shakespeare, these approaches converge in recognizing the plays as forms of ethical thinking, texts that explore and pose questions of living well in relation to

---

[78] Plutarch, *Morals*, 33.

[79] Recent contributions to this tradition include Nuttall, *Shakespeare the Thinker*; Zamir, *Double Vision*; and the essays in Bristol, *Shakespeare and Moral Agency*.

[80] In their introduction to *Shakespeare and Renaissance Ethics* (2014), Patrick Gray and John D. Cox note the relative paucity of scholarship by literary scholars and Cambridge School historians on Shakespeare's engagement with contemporary ethical thought, compared to the attention given to his participation in early modern discussions of political theory and theology. See Gray and Cox, "Introduction," 2–3. In addition to the essays collected in that volume, recent examples of this work include Gray, *Shakespeare and the Fall of the Roman Republic*; Parvini, *Shakespeare's Moral Compass*; Lewis, *Hamlet and the Vision of Darkness*; Engle et al, *Shakespeare and Montaigne* (2021).

[81] The phrase is Julia Reinhard Lupton's, from *Thinking with Shakespeare* (8), one of the foremost examples of this strain of criticism. See also Kuzner, *Shakespeare as a Way of Life*, which suggests that Shakespeare "imagin[es] skeptical practices for everyday existence" (4); Witmore, *Shakespearean Metaphysics*; Kottman, *A Politics of the Scene* and *Tragic Conditions in Shakespeare*; Curran, *Shakespeare's Legal Ecologies*; and Gold et al., *Of Levinas and Shakespeare*.

others—questions that are not finally separate from matters of politics or religion, or from history, but that cross these domains, arching over them.

Central to this work is the conviction that subjectivity is fundamentally relational. Building on Reiss's account of possibility, critics like Patrick Gray and James Kuzner have argued that Shakespeare's plays model a way of "think[ing] about ethics outside the frame of the self-determining subject."[82] Gray, for instance, argues that Shakespeare's Roman plays align the denial of possibility with tragic outcomes and make a case for "an ideal that instead embraces the most basic, inescapable facts of our human condition: embodiment, vulnerability, sympathy, dependence."[83] Suggesting that Shakespeare "advocates an intersubjective openness," Kuzner argues that such openness entails the risks and pleasures of self-loss at the same time that it is the condition of community: such is the "virtue of vulnerability."[84] Against an older critical tradition that aligned Shakespeare with autonomous selfhood and Kantian moral philosophy, these and other scholars suggest that his work belongs to a very different intellectual genealogy of the subject, and hence of ethics: a lineage that Gray grounds in Christian theology; Kuzner locates in strands of Roman republicanism as well as the work of theorists like Judith Butler and Jean-Luc Nancy; and Julia Reinhard Lupton finds in Hannah Arendt's existentialist phenomenology ("a philosophy oriented around human being in the trembling vulnerability of our multiple dependencies on each other and our permanent exposure to the scars, mutations, and new births delivered by the slings and arrows of our own signifying practices").[85] Theatrical drama emerges in this criticism as the privileged medium for presenting the subject in its relationality, and for showing how such relationality conditions agency, action, and responsibility.

Chapters 1 and 2 of this book show how Shakespeare and other early modern writers turned to tragic scenes of complaint to theorize relationality. Chapter 1 focuses on the complainer as a figure of the creaturely subject, continually shaped by an authoritative divine power whose afflictions the subject must respond to correctly. Chapter 2 focuses on the addressee as a figure for the ethical demands of conscience. The ethical thought these chapters take up is deeply informed by Calvinist theology, which Adrian Streete suggests provided early modern thinkers with "a dominant set of conceptual tools" for understanding the world and their place in it, regardless of their precise location on the doctrinal spectrum.[86] Calvinist theology is also central to Chapter 3, but there I also introduce a subject that becomes increasingly important in Chapters 4 and 5, which shift from

---

[82] Kuzner, *Open Subjects*, 29.   [83] Gray, *Shakespeare and the Fall of the Roman Republic*, 29.
[84] Kuzner, *Open Subjects*, 6, 23.   [85] Lupton, *Thinking with Shakespeare*, 14.
[86] Streete, *Protestantism and Drama in Early Modern England*, 83. The extent to which Calvinist theology was hegemonic in early modern England is a matter of longstanding debate among historians, but Streete's salutary point is that that theology was so culturally pervasive that one could not wholly escape its categories.

22   THE DRAMA OF COMPLAINT

exploring how theology informs ethical thought to exploring how early modern writers imagine literature as a site of ethical instruction, experimentation, and judgment. These final three chapters, then, focus on particular subgenres of tragedy whose signature forms of complaint enable that thinking.

Chapter 1 situates *King Lear*'s closing command to "Speak what we feel" in the context of early modern ethical discourse—namely, Calvinist and Neostoic counsel on virtuous responses to suffering—and tragic-existential meditations on human finitude. In these discourses, the figure of the complainer, positioned in scenes of existential complaint, emblematizes human wretchedness and exemplifies unvirtuous conduct in the face of suffering. First I show how this figure is grounded in theological conceptions of creatureliness that link affliction to transcendent, divine providence and define ungrudging acceptance of that suffering as the measure of ethical subjectivity. Then, turning to *Lear*, a play that transposes the drama of creatureliness to an immanent world while taking up the same ethical questions about responding to suffering, I argue that its scenes of existential complaint reverse the valences of complaining, directing the audience's attention to earthly sites of sovereign authority and suggesting the ethical necessity of complaining in response to what the play calls "the weight of this sad time."

Having begun with a tragedy that reflects on ethical comportment through the figure of the complainer, Chapter 2 pivots to a tragedy that explores ethical responsibility by emphasizing the ethical demand that arrives in the form of a complaint, compelling a response. In early modern texts, the poetic form that focalizes this responsibility is judicial complaint, whose vision of justice is premised on a divinely-authored moral law that grounds and mediates human relations. After first exploring the conventional co-articulation of judicial complaint and conscience (figured in theological and popular writing as an internal voice of accusatory complaint that speaks as the voice of God within), this chapter examines Shakespeare's theorizing of conscience in *Richard III*, in which the ghosts of Richard's victims surround him as he sleeps, complain of his crimes, and demand justice, until he awakes with what he describes as a conscience that afflicts him. While the ghost scene is often read as a theatricalized depiction of the internal drama of conscience, I contend that Shakespeare, in a departure from the account of this event offered in his historiographical sources, represents the ghosts as real presences that cause Richard's experience of conscience, rather than metaphorical figures that symbolize his inner torment. I argue that in underlining the ontological difference between Richard and the complaining ghosts, and in formally linking their complaints to a chorus of judicial complaints that demand to be heard and answered throughout the play, Shakespeare refigures conscience as an experience that responds to the complaints of a human other. By rearranging the relation between judicial complaint and conscience, the play situates social complaints as the paradigmatic ethical demand, which it grounds in a fundamental *human* relationality.

INTRODUCTION 23

Diverging from well-known critical readings of *Hamlet*'s Ghost as a symptom of post-Reformation anxieties about the dead and Hamlet's "dull revenge" as a problem for which a rational cause can be found, Chapter 3 argues that *Hamlet*'s scene of spectral complaint initiates the play's persistent exposure of a propulsive force that does not aim at the good, and its relentless representation of the psychological and philosophical insufficiency of reason. The first part of the chapter, which focuses on the link between tragic falls and irrationality in the de casibus monologues of spectral complaint in *A Mirror for Magistrates*, shows how the spectral complaint form captures a tension in early modern moral psychology between classical moral philosophy's belief in the will's natural inclination to obey reason, and Reformed theology's account of an evil concupiscence that compels beyond rational intention and volition. The spectral complaint's formal history of representing the enigmas of the desiring mind is the context in which I then situate *Hamlet*'s scene of spectral complaint and the questions of motive and cause it catalyzes. From the Player's tears for Hecuba to Gertrude's coupling with Claudius, I show how *Hamlet* repeatedly highlights the phenomenon of being driven to act by a sublime motive—a motive that exceeds rational intention and strains the understanding—that Shakespeare consistently links to an enigmatic, "ghostly" command that sets its addressee into motion. Arguing that the play's oscillation between scenes of senseless action and inaction (the latter most evident in Hamlet's inability to act despite having "cause and will and strength and means" to do so) challenges the classical psychic hierarchy of motives in which reason is sovereign, I suggest that in its insistent entertaining of this morally unsettling idea, *Hamlet* confronts its audience with a culturally disavowed (though rhetorically affirmed) truth about desire, and gestures to an irrational basis for ethical subjectivity.

While early modern literary theory frequently examines the question of the good or evil ends furthered by poetry, in Chapter 4 I explore literary moments that address the question of what it means to be a good audience. The chapter argues that in their conventional representation of spectators who give an impassioned complainer the sympathetic reception she asks for, poetic forms of female complaint uniquely register a shift in ethical paradigms of virtuous literary reception that corresponds with (and, in female complaint, is mutually articulated with) the historical emergence of early modern aesthetic theory. Focusing on several key texts of female complaint—Shakespeare's *The Rape of Lucrece*, Samuel Daniel's *The Complaint of Rosamond*, Michael Drayton's *Matilda*—I show how these imagine the ethical duty of the viewer to consist not in the self-application of moral lessons, but in the sympathetic affirmation of the artfully constructed sadness of an aesthetic object. The female complaint form imagines and delineates an aesthetic space governed by its own internal ethical logic. This is the fantasy that I argue grounds *Richard II*'s famously metapoetic, plaintive king's attempt, in concert with the female complaints of his queen, to turn himself into a lamentable

24   THE DRAMA OF COMPLAINT

object to be judged for his sadness as a tragic aesthetic object, rather than his failings as a historical subject. By simultaneously inviting and problematizing such sympathetic reception, the play offers what I suggest is an immanent critique of this new ethical paradigm, neither recuperating art's ethical utility nor valorizing sympathy, but making sympathetic reception itself the object of ethical judgment for the "good audience."

The final chapter of *The Drama of Complaint* links what critics have described as *Othello's* complicated and ambiguous relationship to the didactic moral warning against interracial marriage foregrounded in its source text to the play's formal experimentation with deathbed complaint. In the early modern domestic tragedies whose tropes and conventional plotlines inform *Othello*, the deathbed complaint—spoken by a character who professes their unhappiness and repents the actions that have brought them to this unhappy state—is the privileged rhetorical form for validating the ideological happiness script that shapes the play. The deathbed complaint that Shakespeare gives to Desdemona, however, is markedly different, not only in its content but in its form. Tracing the formal fragmentation and distribution of the parts of the deathbed complaint throughout the last act of the play, I suggest that *Othello* relinquishes its own ethical authority with regard to its informing happiness script and puts the burden, and the responsibility, of ethical judgment on the interpretive labor of audiences, who must assemble the pieces for themselves.

It is something of a critical commonplace that "tragedy has proved acutely sensitive to epistemic conflicts whose effects are also felt and suffered at the level of everyday life."[87] The religious, political, and scientific paradigm shifts now associated with the sixteenth and seventeenth centuries entailed precisely the unsettling of shared knowledge ("the common ground itself was in crisis," as Steven Mullaney puts it) and, as Mitchell Greenberg suggests, "ushered in new ways of configuring the place of the human subject in a radically changing symbolic system."[88] Echoing Mullaney's claim that Shakespearean tragedy "can operate brilliantly as a vehicle for political, social, and historical thinking," *The Drama of Complaint* explores how the period's intellectual discontent registers in the ethical topologies of Shakespeare's work that pass through scenes of complaint.[89] What its chapters trace is neither a systematic, cohesive articulation of a new moral philosophy, nor a sustained critique of an older model, but rather a set of fragmentary thought experiments about ethical subjectivity that respond creatively to ideological fractures by mapping new notions of the good through experimentation with forms of complaint.[90] In his study of Shakespeare's

---

[87]   Mullaney, "'Do You See This?'" 154.

[88]   Mullaney, "'Do You See This?'" 152; Greenberg, "The Concept of 'Early Modern,'" 76.

[89]   Mullaney, "'Do You See This?'" 158.

[90]   My approach to Shakespeare as an ethical thinker is analogous to how David Loewenstein and Michael Witmore approach Shakespeare's religious thinking: they suggest that Shakespeare should be

engagement with early modern skepticism, Kuzner suggests that in some plays "there comes a moment when characters, readers, or both become aware that a frame by which they understand selfhood, ethics, or freedom is not the only or the natural one."[91] What happens in these moments, he argues, is a shift to another frame, a choice not even necessarily recognized as such by the character or the reader. It is such perspectival shifts that this book identifies in scenes of complaint—both in their cultural familiarity and their dramatic reframing—in *King Lear, Richard III, Hamlet, Richard II*, and *Othello*. These shifts direct desire to new objects and ends, rerouting energies trapped in old scripts and plots.

seen "as a writer whose plays engage creatively and dramatically with various—and sometimes contradictory and dissonant—facets of religious culture in early modern England and Europe without, in the end, his being a deeply or consistently religious writer who makes clear-cut confessional choices" ("Introduction," 5).

[91] Kuzner, *Shakespeare As a Way of Life*, 6.

1

Signs of Life

Existential Complaint and the Creaturely Ethics of Complaining

Who do you think you are to complain? Lady Philosophy's reproving question—a rebuke to Boethius's laments about his unjust imprisonment—echoes across the texts of early modernity, as commonplace as the complaints to which it is a persistent counterpoint.[1] It is the question that Gertrude poses to the melancholy Hamlet ("all that lives must die.../ Why seems it so particular with thee?"), the question with which Milton's Adam interrupts his complaints about divine justice ("Wilt thou enjoy the good, / Then cavil the conditions?"), and the question that marks the turning point of Donne's Holy Sonnet 5 ("But who am I, that dare dispute with thee / O God?").[2] Each of these questions is a riff on the one posed to Job, complainer par excellence, in the whirlwind: who is this that speaks without knowledge?[3] Such questions are tropes of a transdiscursive, historically resilient rhetoric in which a range of unbecoming ways of responding to suffering are bound together in the figure of the complainer, who has neither sufficient right nor reason to complain, and should be ashamed of doing so. In this rhetoric, "complaining" and its proximate terms (whining, murmuring, grudging, griping, quarreling) operate as shorthand for speech acts unbefitting their speaker's place in the order of things.

This chapter argues that the ethical paradigm reflected in sixteenth- and seventeenth-century criticisms of complaining correlates with an understanding of subjectivity grounded in the theological, and specifically Calvinist, conception of creatureliness. That is, for early modern writers, complaining bears on ethical subjectivity because humans are mere creatures, a word that in Julia Reinhard Lupton's gloss "indicates a made or fashioned thing, given its existential urgency by the sense of continued or potential process, action, or emergence in relation to

---

[1] "What right has thou to plaine...thou that arte put in the commune realm of al." Lady Philosophy is here ventriloquizing Fortune's rejoinder to Boethius's complaint about her ill treatment of him. I am quoting from *Boece*, Chaucer's translation of *De consolatione philosophiae*, in *The Riverside Chaucer*, Book II, Prosa 2.

[2] *Hamlet*, 1.2.72–75. Except where otherwise noted, all citations of Shakespeare's work are from *The Norton Shakespeare*, eds. Greenblatt et al. Milton, *Paradise Lost*, 10.758–59. Donne, *John Donne: The Major Works*, 175, lines 9–10.

[3] Job 38:1–2. *The Geneva Bible*.

The Drama of Complaint: Ethical Provocations in Shakespeare's Tragedy. Emily Shortslef, Oxford University Press.
© Emily Shortslef 2023. DOI: 10.1093/oso/9780192868480.003.0002

a sublime maker."[4] Calvinist thought turns frequently to the vast disparity between the sublimity of the divine creator and the abjectness of humans, finite in knowledge and being, and—uniquely spoiled by sin—the most unhappy of created things.[5] In the lurid stock phrases of one devotional text,

> Man is made of the earth, conceived in sinne, and borne to paine...By birth uncleane, a child of wrath, a worker of iniquitie, an open sepulcher, a worme, the meate of wormes, dounge and wormes, deprived of Gods glorie, a winde, ignorant of the time when he came into the world, and when he shall depart, a beast by his owne knowledge, from whom nothing can proceede but that which is corrupt, a rotten carkasse, in whom there is no help, in whom dwelleth no good thing...nothing, yea lesse than nothing.[6]

In his sermons on the Book of Job, Calvin, having sounded these same mortifying depths, marvels at the tendency of such "wretched carrions" to presumptuously complain ("grudge") against God when they suffer, rather than acknowledging his authority to do with them as he will:

> And although we be but wretched carions: yet notwithstanding there is such a malapertnes in us, as we would controll God in all his works, & can noe finde in our hearts to submit our selves unto him, & to say, Well, Lorde, holde thou the soveraigntie over all thy creatures, and let none grudge against thee[.][7]

As Calvin's assessment of the instructive value of Job's notorious complaints underlines ("Here ye see to what purpose the holy Ghost setteth downe the complaintes that Job made: namely, that we should not followe that which is to be condemned in him"), complaining represents, in negative, the ethical ideal most fundamental to this conception of creatureliness: ungrudging consent to the inscrutable will of the sovereign creator, whose word makes and sustains human life.[8] This ideal follows from the doctrine of a "singular providence" that, as Calvin explains in the *Institutes*, "peculiarly direct[s] the doing of every creature," including the seeming misfortunes that it suffers.[9] The ongoing work of providence—a force "no lesse belonging to [God's] handes than to his eyes," a matter not only of omniscience but of continual shaping action—is, for Calvin, "what this meaneth

---

[4] Lupton, *Thinking with Shakespeare*, 14.
[5] On the very different conception of creatureliness articulated in the discourse of natural history, which challenges human exceptionalism as well as the notion of a firm divide between the human and the animal, see Shannon, *The Accommodated Animal*.
[6] Powel, *The Resolved Christian*, 4.
[7] Calvin, *Job*, 264. Hereafter cited parenthetically. On the popularity of Calvin's sermons on Job, and the influence and availability of his work more generally, see Lemon, *Addiction and Devotion*, 28–35. Golding's translation sold well enough to appear in six folio editions between 1574 and 1584.
[8] Calvin, *Job*, 247.   [9] Calvin, *Institution of Christian Religion*, 56r (1.16.1); 58r (1.16.4).

28   THE DRAMA OF COMPLAINT

that God is the creator."[10] By the same logic, the quality of incompletion, of being ever worked upon, defines creatureliness, as Lupton points out: in her words, the creature is "a thing always in the process of undergoing creation...actively passive or, better, *passionate*, perpetually becoming created, subject to transformation at the behest of the arbitrary commands of an Other."[11] In what follows, I explore early modern discussions of human suffering that are underpinned by this theological framework, focusing on their shared consensus that such suffering reflects—in some unfathomable, profound way—the "perpetuall govern[ing]" of providence in the life of a creature.[12]

Enter the complainer: a figure, crafted from the materials of theology, that I suggest is both a figure of *feeling* through whose suffering early modern writers imagined the operative power and terrible effects of this enigmatic force, and a figure of passionate *speaking* who laments, protests, or otherwise responds, in language, to its afflictions.[13] This figure thus has two complementary, sometimes superimposed, faces. Returning to a trope mentioned in this book's introduction, the first section of this chapter explores the complainer's emblematic function as a mirror of the human creature in all its inherent wretchedness, a walking seismograph of Original Sin. Here I look at representative instances of tragic-existential discourse, particularly scenes of what I call existential complaint, whose speakers shuttle between expressions of sorrow or rage in response to particular injuries and truisms about the painful vicissitudes of what they call "man's life" in a harsh world—a life that is at once too short and too long, and subject to all sorts of indignities. Take the complaint of Plangus in Philip Sidney's *The Countess of Pembrokes Arcadia* (1593), who, grieving the imprisonment of his beloved Erona, laments the state of "wretched human kind.../ Balls to the stars, and thralls to Fortune's reign."[14] Likening humans to "players placed to fill a filthy stage" (p. 296), Plangus suggests that the baby's cry contains the seed of a later and fuller knowledge of misery:

---

[10] Calvin, *Institution of Christian Religion*, 57v (1.16.4), 56r (1.16.1). On the cultural pervasiveness of the belief in God's providential intervention in the world, see Walsham, *Providence* and Rosendale, *Theology and Agency*.

[11] Lupton, "Creature Caliban," 1, author's emphasis. The structural opposite and conceptual counterpart of the creature is the sovereign, the figure of sublime authority with the power to create and destroy life, institute and suspend law at will. A great deal of critical work at the intersections of political theology and early modern literary studies has explored the significance of early modernity to the conceptual and representational history of sovereignty via the work of Carl Schmitt, Ernst Kantorowicz, and Walter Benjamin, as well as Giorgio Agamben. See Hammill and Lupton, eds., *Political Theology and Early Modernity* and Lorenz, *The Tears of Sovereignty*.

[12] Calvin, *Institution of Christian Religion*, 56r (1.16.1).

[13] Throughout this chapter I use the capacious term "feeling" (the early modern meanings of which include "the general impression or effect produced on a person by an object"; "a physical sensation or perception"; and "the condition of being emotionally affected") to describe the experience of suffering (*OED*, s.v. "feeling").

[14] Book Two, p. 296. All quotations of the *Arcadia* are from Sidney, *The Countess of Pembroke's Arcadia*, ed. Evans. Hereafter cited parenthetically.

All [is] but jests, save only sorrow's rage.
The child feels that; the man that feeling knows,
With cries first born, the presage of his life,
Where wit but serves to have true taste of woes.

(p. 296)

This lifelong acquaintance with complaint bespoken by Plangus's very name (from the Latin *plangere*, to strike, beat; to bewail, lament) animates his anguished question: "Alas, how long this pilgrimage doth last! / What greater ills have now the heavens in store[?]" (p. 296). A stock tragic assertion, his claim to suffer at the will of "the heavens" also reflects the widely held theological belief (here formulated in *The Vineyard of Vertue* [1579]) that "the godly ones are not here afflicted by chance, but by the will and knowledge of God."[15] A passionate relation to this enigma structures existential complaint, the poetic form that I argue stages a particular drama of creatureliness: the complainer's attempt to make sense of their suffering, to not only have it *come to* an end, but to *know* its end, its purpose.[16] These complaints are often what one might call metaplaintive—that is, they are complaints that thematize the act of complaining. Additionally, their writers tend to take a (critical, ironic, pitying, or even skeptical) distance from their complaining subjects. My focus will be on scenes of existential complaint whose writers, I suggest, urge their audiences to see complaining as a response to suffering that traffics in fantasy. Plangus's complaint about the "cruel cunning" (p. 296) of the heavens ("if heaven there be" [p. 297]), for instance, is made to an interlocutor, Basilius, who tells him he is "deceive[d]" by his passion, "wrapped in foggy mist" (p. 298). It's this nebulous thinking, and its attendant "blasphemous words," that Basilius attempts to correct:

[15] Robinson, *The Vineyarde of Vertue*, 12v.
[16] See, for instance, George Herbert's "Complaining" (1633). The complainer—who refers to himself as a creature, "Thy clay that weeps, thy dust that calls" (line 5)—begs God to either withdraw his afflictions or end the complainer's life:

> …Am I all throat or eye,
> To weep or crie?
> Have I no parts but those of grief?
> Let not thy wrathfull power
> Afflict my houre,
> My inch of life: or let thy gracious power
> Contract my houre,
> That I may climbe and finde relief.

(lines 13–20)

Quoted from Herbert, *The English Poems of George Herbert*, pp. 500–1. "Complaining"—whose title, as Helen Wilcox observes, eschews the sense of a finished poem (a "complaint") in favor of suggesting a "ceaseless activity" (501)—perfectly encapsulates the tragic-existential notion of complaining as coextensive with creaturely life.

30   THE DRAMA OF COMPLAINT

> We think they hurt, when most they do assist.
> To harm us worms should that high Justice leave
> His nature? Nay, himself? For so it is.
> What glory from our loss can he receive?
> But still our dazzled eyes their way do miss,
> While that we do at his sweet scourge repine,
> The kindly way to beat us to our bliss.

(p. 300)

Basilius urges Plangus to "tame these childish superfluities," to not "yield to female lamentations," but rather "some grammar learn of more congruities" (p. 300). In short, he urges him to speak more appropriately, more reasonably, in a manner more befitting the man that he is. Notice Basilius's use of the first-person plural pronoun ("We think they hurt"). These scenes of existential complaint frame complaining—the irrational activity of a particular mind, in extremity—as a fantasmatic interpretation of suffering that epitomizes the weakness characteristic of the human mind more generally.

Turning to discussions of suffering in ethical discourse, the chapter's second section explores how the interpretive pressure that may give rise to irrational complaint in everyday life is managed by the theologically-informed scripts of philosophical consolation that early modern writers proffer as virtuous responses to suffering (often, as in this passage from the *Arcadia*, in or around scenes of existential complaint). As we've already seen, these texts valorize uncomplaining submission to what a higher, perfectly rational power has determined, a point where the ethical teachings of Calvinist theology harmonize especially well with the Stoic dictum that the *summum bonum* of virtue depends on aligning one's will with the immanent logos of Nature.[17] Here, through what I describe as the rhetoric of complaint-shaming, the figure of the complainer is deployed as the embodiment of a way of thinking and speaking that is not only irrational and erroneous, but also rebellious and sinful. For Arthur Golding, the translator of Calvin's sermons on Job, the silencing of complaint is the conclusion that must follow from a recognition of God's absolute sovereignty. Noting in his preface that readers may find it easy to play the plaintiff ("All men canne skil to complaine with Job, that this short life of ours is fraught with many miseries, afflictions, and adversities, and verie experience sheweth it to bee so"), Golding attempts to foreclose such

---

[17] On the convergence of Stoic moral philosophy and Reformed ethics, see Cochran, *Protestant Virtue and Stoic Ethics* and Schoenfeldt, *Bodies and Selves*. On the perceived compatibility of the two systems of thought see Kraye, "Moral Philosophy," 367–70. Despite a general recognition of the affinities between Stoic and Christian thought early modern writers often call attention to the difference between what they describe as Stoic philosophy's notion of a fully deterministic fate, and divine providence, which Calvin insists is not to be blamed for sin, as Adam was given the freedom to fall of his own volition.

language by reminding these would-be complainers of the lowly place from which they speak.[18] "We consider not that God beeing our maker and governour, hath by good right a soveraigne dominion over us and all other his creatures, to order and dispose at his good wyll and pleasure," he writes, "and that the same his doing is wrought by incomprehensible power, wisedome, and rightfulnesse, so as there cannot justly any fault or blame bee founde in any of his proceedinges."[19] Such counsel was widely propounded in ethical discourse and underlines, repeatedly, the limits of human power and understanding. While "want of wisdom causeth us complaine, / Of every hap, wherby we seme opprest /.../ Yet for our good, God worketh every thing," intones one of the de casibus tragedies of *A Mirror for Magistrates* (1559).[20] "When crosses afflict him, he sees a divine hand invisibly striking with these sensible scourges: against which hee dares not rebell, nor murmure," reads the sketch of "The Patient Man" in Joseph Hall's *Characters of Vertues and Vices* (1608).[21] Interwoven with claims about the incomprehensible cause and telos of human suffering, the theological framework that casts humans as creatures works to produce ethical subjects who maintain the right relation to the authoritative power that manifests in suffering by remembering what they lack, and silencing their complaints. In their very inability to comprehend their suffering, they are to be reminded at once of their own creaturely finitude and the sublime authority of the creator.

Together, these sections show how figurations of the complainer and scenes of existential complaint in tragic-existential and ethical discourses delineate interpretive responses to the suffering constitutive of human existence, and they show how the theological conception of creatureliness underwrites the early modern framing of these responses as alternately virtuous or transgressive, rational or irrational, masculine or feminine. The final section focuses on *King Lear*, a play whose representations of intense suffering are surrounded by fragments of these tragic-existential and ethical discourses, but which is set in a fictional world in which the theological framework that informs them has no particular authority. Shakespeare's transposition of the creaturely drama of existential complaint to an immanent world, I argue, allows for a repurposing of the figure of the complainer and a reversal of the ethical valences of complaining, a reversal encapsulated in the play's closing command to "Speak what we feel, not what we ought to say."[22]

---

[18] Calvin, *Job*, A2r.   [19] Calvin, *Job*, A2r.
[20] "The Tragedy of George Plantagenet, Duke of Clarence." Quoted from *The Mirour for Magistrates*, 181v.
[21] Hall, *Characters*, 43.
[22] 5.3.323. All citations of the play are from *King Lear*, ed. R. A. Foakes (London: Bloomsbury Arden, 1997). Hereafter cited parenthetically.

32 THE DRAMA OF COMPLAINT

1. Creaturely Pressures and Existential Complaint

No one would deny that the same creaturely abjection that should silence complaint would also seem to ceaselessly provoke it. "Having but the bare name of life," human existence, the moralist Pierre de La Primaudaye observes, "is in effect and truth a continuall paine."[23] From the beginning, its soundtrack is one of complaint. As George Gascoigne's translation of Innocent III's *De contemptu mundi* observes,

> men generally are borne, without knowledge, without speach, without virtue, without power, weeping, wayling, weake, feeble, and but little differing from brute beasts...we are all borne crying, that we may thereby expresse our misery...eche of these soundes is the voyce of a sorrowful creature, expressing the greatnesse of his grefe.[24]

Here as in Plangus's complaint, the human creature is figured as a born complainer, its reflexive first cry an impassioned response to its own impotence through which the infant exercises the single power it possesses, the capacity to express its feeling.

If in early modern thought the infant's first cry—sign of life and signifier of sorrow—is the archetype of existential complaint, its primal scene is the Fall, the "falling away" from God by which Adam, in Calvin's words, "destroyed all his owne posteritie [and] perverted the whole order of nature."[25] Among the manifold early modern retellings of this "dolefull tragedie" is Francis Sabie's *Adam's Complaint* (1596), a poem of existential complaint in which the "first causer of all maladies and errors" laments the terrible new world sparked by his sin, a second creation unfolded from the divine fiat that bars humankind from "happie bliss."[26] Exiled from Eden, Sabie's Adam chastizes himself as a sinful creature, the "bringer in of woe" for all his offspring:

> O haplesse Adam (quoth he) unkind father,
> Unnaturall Parent, childrens fatall foe:
> From whence all mankind doe such curses gather:
> Authour of death, first bringer in of woe.
> No sooner fram'd of thine al-making God,
> Then purchasing his sin-correcting rod.

---

[23] La Primaudaye, *The French Academie*, Aiiir.

[24] "The View of Worldly Vanities," from Gascoigne, *The Droomme of Doomes Day*, A3r. On this Latinate medieval tradition of philosophical rumination on the decay of the creation, see Peter, *Complaint and Satire*.

[25] Calvin, *Institution of Christian Religion*, 72v (2.1.5).

[26] Sabie, *Adam's Complaint*, C4v, C1v, B1r.

························

Of lumpish-earth Jehovah me created,
To th'end I should not glorie in my feature:
And I againe to earth must be translated
By Gods just doome, the end of every creature.[27]

Calvinist theology stresses that life exists under the sign of this deferred death sentence: fatally infected with the inherited disease of Original Sin, the infant, in Calvin's evocative phrase, "draw[s] forth a life as it were entangled with death."[28] Marked from the beginning by "Gods just doome," the life of the human creature was thus imagined to be painfully alive to feeling, subject to impressions, sensations, perceptions, and passions that constantly agitate the body and mind.

This intensity of feeling is one of the dominant themes of tragic-existential discourse, a decidedly mournful mode of representation that inventories, across a range of genres and texts, what Hamlet in his signature existential complaint calls "The heartache and the thousand natural shocks / That flesh is heir to."[29] Here "flesh" is a metonym not for the corporeal body as opposed to the soul, but rather (in keeping with Luther and Calvin's retooling of this Pauline concept to signify the corruption of the body and soul alike) a metonym for "the human as creature in distinction from the Creator," in Lisa Freinkel's phrase.[30] The picture that emerges in tragic-existential discourse is of a life fundamentally deformed by death, deprived of the fullness of being and overcharged with painful sensations, the perturbations of passion, the punctual stings of guilty conscience, and a keen sense of existential lack. "O wretched state of man," a lament in a sixteenth-century volume of pseudo-Augustinian meditations intones: "He hath lost blessednesse, to which he was made, and founde miseries, to whiche he was not made. The thyng is gone without which nothyng is luckie, and the thyng remayneth whiche of it selfe is all together unluckie."[31] In similar language, Calvin's commentary on the second chapter of Genesis describes the death incurred by Adam's sin as a gradual "depriving of life," and life as a state of overanimated deprivation, stripped of all but a "soule [that] feeleth Gods curse."[32]

Arguing for the exceptionality of human suffering, the theological narrative that underpins tragic-existential discourse links that exceptionality to the workings of the mind. When he laments the "many punishments [that] are proper and peculiar to man" in his sermon-treatise *The Fall of Man* (1616), Godfrey Goodman suggests that humans are "more susceptible of wrongs" than other animals, not only because the human body is less fit for survival, but because the

---

[27] Sabie, *Adam's Complaint*, B1r–C3v.
[28] Calvin, *Institution of Christian Religion*, 65r (1.7.10).   [29] *Hamlet*, 3.1.61–62.
[30] Freinkel, *Reading Shakespeare's Will*, 121.   [31] *Certaine select Prayers*, S1r.
[32] Calvin, *Genesis*, 71.

34 THE DRAMA OF COMPLAINT

human mind, uniquely endowed with reason, is aggrieved and "perplexed" by its suffering.[33] "Having a feeling, and a stronger apprehension of his owne wrongs," the wounded human, Goodman argues, suffers pain in excess of the injury itself:

> when the smart is once past in the skinne, or in the flesh, yet still the thorne seemes to take deepe hold in the braine. And thus man disquiets himselfe with his owne thoughts, that he should be thus dealt withal, perplexed and tormented like a slave; that it should not bee in his power to prevent the like mischief, but he must lie open and naked to all dangers; he must stand upon his guard, yet like a disarmed and weaponlesse man, must wholly commit himselfe to their mercie: these very thoughts, as they come neerest the heart, so are they a farre greater corrosive, then the wounds in the flesh.[34]

For Goodman, the "thorn" that "seemes to take deepe hold in the braine" is the shock of indignation, upon experiencing an injury, at finding oneself "open and naked to all dangers." (Recall Hamlet's specification that it is "in the mind" that a person "suffer[s] / The slings and arrows of outrageous fortune.")[35] This thorn is the first link in a chain of unhappy thoughts, the point of orientation for a "disquieting" way of thinking that concerns one's place in the created order as both its earthly sovereign and a "slave," subject to another's command. In brief, then, the theological conception of creaturely subjectivity highlights the mind's suffering under the impress of a divine word that creates and curses, that deals life and death at the same time.[36] In tragic-existential discourse, the complainer—a figure who has nothing if not "a feeling of his own wrongs," all-too-conscious of the fact of his suffering—embodies, from birth, this anguish.

Of course, to be conscious of the fact of suffering is not necessarily to understand it correctly. What early modern writers depict as the disorderly, irrational thinking of the distressed mind is on display in the following theatrical scenes of existential complaint, which feature complainers whose interpretations of their suffering read as fantasies.[37] Centered around complaints frequently punctuated by nonverbal signifiers (cries, wails, groans, sighs); repetitive, minimally symbolic sounds of suffering ("O, o, o"); and the bodily language of distress (prostration,

---

[33] Goodman, *The Fall of Man*, 70, 69.   [34] Goodman, *The Fall of Man*, 69–70.
[35] *Hamlet*, 3.1.56–57.
[36] This formulation gestures to an affinity between the theological conception of the creature and psychoanalytic understandings of subjectivity. Indeed, it is precisely the theological resonances of the term that the critical theorist Eric Santner evokes by referring to the dimensions of subjectivity explored by psychoanalysis as "creaturely," insofar as the unconscious and its formations are "a by-product of exposure to what we might call the *excitations of power*...enigmatic bits of address and interpellation." Santner, *On Creaturely Life*, 24, author's emphasis.
[37] I'm drawing loosely here on both the early modern and psychoanalytic senses of the term; indeed, Adrian Streete suggests that early modern "construction[s] of the fantasy as a faculty that offers various 'fictions' to the self" may "contribute in some way to a pre-history of the unconscious." Streete, *Protestantism and Drama*, 113.

the tearing of garments or hair, the beating of the breast), these scenes involve complainers who describe themselves as persecuted by a cruel power that wishes them ill, an opaque cause of suffering in excess of its phenomenal cause in illness, loss, or pain afflicted by other humans. (As, for instance, Marlowe's dying King of Arabia, horrified by Tamburlaine's army, wonders—in a question that recalls Tamburlaine's boast that he is "termed the scourge and wrath of God"—"What cursèd power guides the murdering hands / Of this infamous tyrant's soldiers?")[38] Often named as "the gods," Fate, or Fortune—a fact that underscores the fantasmatic dimension of these complaints, insofar as such names were commonly described as illusory fictions or misrecognitions of divine providence—this force appears as a hypercathected object in these scenes. In Robert Greene's *Selimus* (1594), for instance, the Turkish emperor Bajazet, aggrieved by his treacherous sons and suffering what he calls "swelling seas of never-ceasing care, / Whose waves my weatherbeaten ship do toss" imagines these passions to have been stirred up by, and under the control of, Fortune, whose "crossness" toward him he bemoans to one of his officers.[39] He complains:

> Come, Aga, let us sit and mourn a while,
> For Fortune never shewed herself so cross
> To any prince as to poor Bajazet.
> ....
> Ah, where shall I begin to make my moan?
> Or what shall I first reckon in my plaint?
> From my youth up I have been drowned in woe,
> And to my latest hour I shall be so.
> ....
> But out, alas, the god that vails the seas,
> And can alone this raging tempest stent,
> Will never blow a gentle gale of ease
> But suffer my poor vessel to be rent.
>
> (18.1–34)

Imagining himself to be—and to always have been—suffering at the will of Fortune, Bajazet suggests that he can anticipate Fortune's moves: "alas," he says, the interjection suggesting pleasure at his own resignation, she will continue to withhold "ease." He addresses this "blind procurer of mischance" directly in the complaint's closing lines, begging her to become even crosser still, and thus put

---

[38] Marlowe, *Tamburlaine the Great, Part 1*, 3.3.44, 5.1.403–4. Quoted from *English Renaissance Drama*.

[39] Greene, *Selimus*, scene 18, lines 15–16, 2. Quoted from *Three Turk Plays*, ed. Vitkus. Hereafter cited parenthetically.

him out of his misery: "Thy cruel hand, even when thou wilt, enhance / And pierce my poor heart with thy thrilliant steel" (18.35, 37–38). The unusual adjective figures the stroke of death as the final blow of Fortune, at once the cruelest and the kindest of the shocks that have shaped his entire life.

For Bajazet, "mak[ing] my moan" has a defensive function: it gives order to suffering, allowing him to make sense of it by narrativizing it, by making himself the afflicted protagonist of a lifelong tragedy. (Hence the officer's eagerness to join in: "Cease, Bajazet—now it is Aga's turn. / Rest thou awhile and gather up more tears, / The while poor Aga tells his tragedy" [18.39–41]). In Thomas Kyd's *The Spanish Tragedy* (1592), the Viceroy of Portugal, mistakenly believing his son Balthazar to be dead, interprets his "distress" as the affliction of Fortune, whose attention he seeks:

> But wherefore sit I in a regal throne?
> This better fits a wretch's endless moan.
> *Falls to the ground.*
> ....
> Yes, Fortune may bereave me of my crown.
> Here, take it now! Let Fortune do her worst.
>   [*He takes off his crown.*]
> She will not rob me of this sable weed;
> Oh, no, she envies none but pleasant things.
> ....
> Fortune is blind and sees not my deserts;
> So she is deaf and hears not my laments;
> And could she hear, yet is she willful mad,
> And therefore will not pity my distress.
> Suppose that she could pity me, what then?
> What help can be expected at her hands [?]
> ....
> Why wail I, then, where's hope of no redress?
> Oh, yes, complaining makes my grief seem less.[40]

The stock claim that complaining lessens grief usually relies on the language of humoral theory, describing the relief of expelling excessive passion from the overcharged body in the outbursts of words, sighs, and tears. Yet it would seem that the grieving Viceroy—falling to the ground, taking off his crown—finds not only comfort but pleasure in his histrionic performance itself, by which he imagines himself as the victim of an alternately envious, indifferent, and "willful mad" Fortune who has both afflicted him and ignored his distress. Another play

---

[40] Kyd, *The Spanish Tragedy*, 1.3.8–32. Quoted from *English Renaissance Drama*.

attributed to Kyd, *The Tragedy of Soliman and Perseda* (1592), materializes, as part of the play-world's objective reality, the complainer's fantasy of an all-powerful force who directs and watches the complainer's suffering from a remove: in the play's main narrative, characters complain that someone is enjoying their suffering ("Ah, fickle and blind guidresse of the world, / What pleasure hast thou in my miserie?"), and at the end of each act a gleefully sadistic Chorus of Death, Fortune, and Love convenes to squabble about which of them "Hath in the Actors showne the greatest power."[41] A way in which the play itself attempts to give form to the powerful forces that shape human life, this metatheatrical framing device accentuates the finitude that the characters lament by revealing to the audience the forces that are beyond these complainers' full comprehension, and whose governing power they can only feel.

If scenes of existential complaint in tragic-existential discourse are generally meant to mirror the perplexed mind trying to make sense of its condition, these particular scenes, by distancing the audience from the pitiful, self-dramatizing complainer caught up in fantasy, call attention to a certain foolishness that their writers suggest is as intrinsic to human existence as suffering. Calvin suggests that it is precisely "the dulnesse of our understanding," which is illuminated by the enormity of suffering, that opens the space of fantasy: because the purposive divine will is beyond our comprehension, he writes in the *Institutes*, the thought may "creepeth into our mindes, that mens matters are turned and whirled about with the blinde saw of Fortune," or "the flesh [may] stirreth us to murmure, as if God did to make himselfe pastime tosse them like tennise balles."[42] Against such temptations to fantasize and to complain, we are to remember that "God hath an assured good reason of his purpose," and "assuredly holde" that "howsoever the causes be secret and unknowen to us…they are layde up in hidden store with him."[43] I want to shift now to consider how ethical discourse offers an alternative way of managing and responding to the interpretive pressures that inform scenes of existential complaint—pressures that surface in the everyday lived experience of suffering. In these didactic texts and passages, those who suffer are told, rather than left to wonder, what God wants of them, and they are told how to respond to the message that radiates in suffering: not with the tearful, querulous, and fantasmatic complaints sketched in these scenes, but with words of humble submission.

2. Philosophy against Complaining

The early modern ethical discourse of suffering responds to several historically specific pressures, including the intimacy of early modern life with death and a

---

[41] *The Tragedye of Solyman and Perseda*, D3v, C3r.
[42] Calvin, *Institution of Christian Religion*, 60r (1.16.9); 61r (1.17.1).
[43] Calvin, *Institution of Christian Religion*, 61r (1.17.1).

38 THE DRAMA OF COMPLAINT

social world whose hierarchies were naturalized and understood as divinely instituted.[44] Another historical pressure, I want to suggest, is the significance attached to passion by the theological narrative of creatureliness that teaches that God "sheweth the perfectnesse of his mightie power in these frayle earthen vessels of our weake and mortall bodies."[45] To the extent that it persistently described human suffering as an especially intimate and peculiar way in which divine providence shapes the lives of fallen human creatures, this culturally authoritative narrative can be said to have made enigmatic signifiers of grief, pain, and adversity of all kinds—to have, by situating such feeling as a form of divine communication, created a pressure to translate these irreducibly opaque addresses into a determinate demand that the sufferer could fulfill by responding in the right way.[46] These ethical scripts guide, and reproduce, that interpretive process.

The reader of early modern ethical discourse who wants to know how *not* to act in the face of suffering need look no further than the complainer. While Calvinist theology primarily casts the complainer as a figure of insubordination—a petulant creature "fling[ing] himself out of his bounds against God"—Stoic moral philosophy accentuates the unvirtuous irrationality of complaining, depicting the complainer as an ignorant fool who quarrels, futilely, with an incontrovertible law.[47] "Good men...ought not to complaine of Fate," Seneca declares in *De Providentia*, but "Whatsoever befalleth them, let them take it in good part, and turne it to their good," reconciling themselves to "the commandement of an eternall law" by willing for themselves what this higher power has decreed.[48] Having bent their will to their fate, those who are virtuous can happily say:

> I am not compelled, I suffer nothing unwillingly; neither doe I serve God but assent unto him, and so much the rather, because I know that all things happen by an eternall and unchangeable ordinance of God.[49]

This fatalistic way of thinking, which dovetails with the Calvinist understanding of divinely ordained affliction, is central to discussions of suffering in early modern ethical discourse, though the latter departs from Stoic thought in aligning virtue with decidedly self-abasing submission to the will of God. The operative

---

[44] On the question of whether Neostoic moral philosophy lent itself to political quietism or political resistance in early modern England see Cadman, *Sovereigns and Subjects*.

[45] The phrase is Golding's, from his preface to Calvin, *Job*, A2r.

[46] On enigmatic signifiers as authoritative and incomprehensible addresses (words and phrases as well as images, gestures, sounds, and other non-linguistic signs) that excite the interpretive activity through which humans become enmeshed in a relational, sociosymbolic world, see Laplanche, *New Foundations for Psychoanalysis*. For another account of how early modern subjectivity and the experience of suffering were shaped by Calvinist theology see Hirschfeld, "Hamlet's 'first corse,'" which argues that the Fall narrative "constitute[s] a shared early modern narrative for structuring individual traumatic experience" (430).

[47] Calvin, *Job*, 262.   [48] Seneca, *The Workes*, 499, 498.   [49] Seneca, *The Workes*, 506.

SIGNS OF LIFE   39

simile in the following aphorism from the *Meditations and Vowes, Divine and Morall* (1605) of Joseph Hall (termed "our spiritual Seneca" by Sir Henry Wotton), for example, stresses the gulf that separates the cosmic lawgiver from the creatures in thrall to that law: "A Man under Gods affliction, is like a bird in a net, the more hee striveth, the more hee is entangled. Gods decree cannot bee eluded with impatience. What I cannot avoyde, I will learne to beare."[50]

Teaching readers how to bear this decree is the aim of much of the period's ethical discourse on suffering, a discourse dominated by humanist traditions of consolation that promote reason as the cure for the disruptions of immoderate passion and employ the figure of the complainer to epitomize irrational and immoral responses to suffering. "We are not here to give a law, but to receive it, and to follow that which we find established," the French Catholic Neostoic moral philosopher Pierre Charron reminds readers in his discussion of sadness in his treatise *Of Wisdome* (1608).[51] Across different genealogical strands of moral philosophy, writers—drawing on a rhetoric of complaint-shaming that frequently mobilizes gender, race, and social status—make "complaining" the mark of bad character and align virtue with uncomplaining submission to providence or fate.[52] Plutarch's widely known letter of consolation to Apollonius on the death of his son, for instance, suggests that only "the woorse sort of people" (namely, women and non-Greek "barbarians") complain about their losses.[53] Advising the "wise man and wel brought up" to "mainteine that which is decent & beseeming his own person," he urges his grieving friend to recall that in "all our worldly affaires, we are to be content with our portion allotted unto us, and without grudging and complaint, gently to yield our selves obedient."[54] These are exactly the terms in which Stoic and Calvinist thinkers define their mutually valorized virtue of patience: "a voluntarie sufferance without grudging of all things, whatsoever can

---

[50] Wotton, *Life and Letters*, 370. Hall, *Meditations and Vowes*, 127.

[51] *Of Wisdome*, 96–7. In a passage resonant with Claudius's rebuking of Hamlet for his "unmanly grief / [that] shows a will most incorrect to heaven / A heart unfortified or mind impatient, / An understanding simple and unschooled" (1.2.94–97), Charron suggests that even the passion of grief alone, if worn with too much "heaviness," effectively constitutes "a rash and outragious complaint against the Lord and common law of the whole world, which hath made all things under the Moone changeable and corruptible."

[52] On the gendering of displays of passion, see Vaught, *Masculinity and Emotion*. On the relation between discourses of self-improvement and racialized identity, see Akhimie, *Shakespeare and the Cultivation of Difference*. Though it is beyond the purview of this chapter, I want to note the historical permutations of the figural logic of the complainer, including its enduring imbrication with racist and sexist logics, the continued prevalence of shame in its affective economy, and the way in which "complaining" still operates as a signifier for allegedly unreasonable, ungrateful, or inappropriate expressions of dissatisfaction, grief, or anger made by certain kinds of people (who are dismissed as "complainers," while others' grievances are legitimized). Ethical conduct, as Akhimie notes, remains "a social and discursive arena in which in which power relations are negotiated, defined, and redefined" (1), and the castigation of complaining and complainers often reflects and reinforces the exclusions and injustices that cause complaint in the first place. For a reflection on complaint and power relations grounded in an account of formal complaints about sexual harassment and racism at academic institutions, see Ahmed, *Complaint!*

[53] Plutarch, *Morals*, 523.   [54] Plutarch, *Morals*, 510.

40 THE DRAMA OF COMPLAINT

happen to, or in, a man."[55] If we habitually practice patience, Hall promises, "whatsoever happeneth," we are "prepared to digest and turne it to the best."[56] It is for this reason that Seneca suggests that the "great man" should welcome afflictions: these "pressure[s] of the mind" present opportunities to fortify oneself for one's eventual encounter with death.[57] It is unsurprising, then, that these commonplaces are routinely cited in death scenes on the early modern stage, sometimes as admonitions made to someone dying badly (as the councilor Assaracus in *The Lamentable Tragedy of Locrine* [1595] advises the dying Brutus to "Cease your laments," since "whatsoe'er the Fates determined have, / It lieth not in us to disannul"), sometimes as the resolutions of those reconciled to their fate, as Mortimer, condemned to execution in the final scene of Marlowe's *Edward II* (1592), says, "Why should I grieve at my declining fall?"[58] Indeed, the refusal to complain as death approaches is dramatic shorthand for masculine rationality and strength, if not, in every instance, moral virtue.[59]

Not complaining is not easy. For the reader who would learn patience, ethical discourse teaches habits of rational thought that comprise a virtuous way of "digesting" the excessive passion that threatens to erupt in complaint. The Stoic "philosophicall remedy," as Charron notes, involves correcting the erroneous judgments that have authorized passion in the first place.[60] Such is the counsel offered by Hall's *Two Guides to a Good Life* (1604), which suggests that at the first stirrings of passion we must "bridle them by the authoritie of virtue and reason," "perswad[ing] our selves" that what we have incorrectly identified as an evil is in fact something that has no bearing on us, an "indifferent," in Stoic terminology.[61] In this scenario the impassioned complainer, typically guided by an interlocutor who personifies reason, comes to understand that they have been thinking and speaking incorrectly. The oft-translated sixth-century *De consolatione philosophiae* tracks the gradual quieting of Boethius's complaints as Lady Philosophy reasons with him, while in Justus Lipsius's Neostoic dialogue *De Constantia*, published in Latin in 1583 and translated into English in 1595, Lipsius's complaints about the war-ravaged Low Countries are countered by his friend Langius ("What wilt thou querulous complaint doe?... There is no other refuge from necessity, but to wish that, that she willeth") until at last, in the text's final lines, Lipsius proclaims himself cured: "I have escaped the evill, and found the good."[62] The other method for cutting off complaint is to "divert our thoughts, and turne them another way."[63]

---

[55] [Lipsius], *Two Bookes of Constancie*, C1r.   [56] Hall, *Two Guides to a Good Life*, I3r.

[57] Seneca, *De Providentia*, in *The Workes*, 503. On Stoic virtue as wholly independent of external circumstances and contingencies, including one's health, social standing, and prosperity, see Nussbaum, *The Therapy of Desire*, especially Chapter 10.

[58] *Locrine*, 1.2.42, 33–4. Quoted from *The Lamentable Tragedy of Locrine*, ed. Gooch. Marlowe, *Edward II*, 5.6.63. Quoted from *English Renaissance Drama*.

[59] On dying as performance in and outside the theater, see Vinter, *Last Acts*.

[60] Charron, *Of Wisdome*, 523.   [61] Hall, *Two Guides to a Good Life*, D1r.

[62] Lipsius, *Two Bookes of Constancie*, 54–5, 127.   [63] Charron, *Of Wisdome*, 523.

This is the practice recommended by Reformed theologians, who, acknowledging the legitimacy of passion, suggest that its excesses may be managed by redirecting thought from the pain of suffering to the will of God.[64] Discussing how to "tame and subdue to his [God's] ordinaunce all contrary affection," Calvin suggests that the plaints of those who grieve must give way to another phrase:

> this alway shalbe the conclusion, But the Lord willed so. Therfore let us follow his wil. Yea even in the middest of the prickings of sorrow, in the middest of mourning and teares, this thought must needes come betweene, to encline our heart to take cheerefully the very same thinges, by reason whereof it is so moved.[65]

In a similar key, the English Calvinist theologian William Perkins instructs that Christ himself—subject in his human form both to the pangs of suffering and to the will of God—is to be

> our example in this case, who in his agonie praied, *Father, let this cup passe from me*, yet with a submission, *not my will but thy wil be done*: teaching us in the very panges of death to resigne our selves to the good pleasure of God...without all manner of grudging or repining[.][66]

Whether in the midst of complaining or on its verge, those who suffer are to recall that their afflictions refract, however obliquely and opaquely, God's "good pleasure." It is on that sublime cause, rather than its painful effects, that they are to fix their minds. In an echo of *De Providentia*'s account of afflictions as a form of tough love, intended to make the sufferer more virtuous, one of the aphorisms about suffering from the *Meditations and Vowes* tells readers what to tell themselves when they are in pain: "When I sustaine more, it shall more comfort me, that God findes mee strong; than it shall grieve mee, to be pressed with an heavy affliction."[67] All of these texts, we might say, counsel readers as to what they should think about what they feel, and what they should *say* in response to those thoughts and feelings: they lay out the response that the divine creator wants to hear from his creatures.

Such instruction is inscribed into those scenes of existential complaint that double as sites of ethical thought. Scenes of this sort are vital to Thomas Becon's dialogue *The Sicke Man's Salve* (1561), a devotional text in the *ars moriendi*

---

[64] On Reformed theology's defenses of passion and rejection of Stoic apatheia, see Strier, *The Unrepentant Renaissance*.

[65] Calvin, *Institution of Christian Religion*, Hh4v (3.8.9), Hh5r (3.8.10).

[66] Perkins, *A salve for a sicke man*, 169–70, author's emphasis.

[67] Hall, *Meditations and Vowes*, 47. "God hath a fatherly mind towards good men, and he loveth them strongly. And let them, saith he, have labors, losses, and pains, to the end they may recover a true strength." Seneca, *The Workes*, 500.

42 THE DRAMA OF COMPLAINT

tradition that went through twenty-nine editions before the seventeenth century, "wherein," as its title page promises, "the faithfull Christians may learne...how to behave them selves paciently and thankfully in the tyme of sickenes." Here the dying, complaining Epaphroditus is visited by several friends who press philosophical consolation on him in the form of "the comfortable sentences" of scripture, mostly from the Book of Job.[68] Their conversation consists of a pattern, repeated several times: Epaphroditus complains, his friends comfort at length, and then he briefly reiterates—now as his own beliefs—their words. Epaphroditus's sickness, his friends suggest, is "God's loving visitation," which is "for your commodity and salvation" (13). "This sicknes, which I now suffer, is the loving visitation of God, and a token of Gods good wil toward me," he realizes (26). His assimilation of this Neostoic commonplace allows him to renounce complaint and submit to God:

> The Lords will be done in me. He knoweth what is most meete for me a wretched sinner: let him therfore worke hys good pleasure in me...Onely o heavenly father, I besech thee for Christes sake to geve me a patient and thankfull hart, that I never grudge against thy blessed will, but be obedient unto it in all things.
>
> (43–44)

The Sicke Man's Salve (which essentially replaces Job's well-meaning but erroneous friends with the philosophizing interlocutors of Neostoic dialogues) offers proof of the comfort offered by the alternative mental pathway for passion that philosophy teaches, where grief is digested and calmed by practicing patience, rather than aggravated by complaining. More importantly, the manual helps to train readers in these habits. It is only by habitually practicing resignation to the will of God, Calvin explains, that one becomes "so framed in minde" as to "have that quietnesse & sufferance" that "godly mindes ought to have," a disposition capable of "extend[ing] to all chances whereunto our present life is subject."[69] Such texts do not simply teach readers to memorize consolatory maxims: rather, they help them to internalize the way of thinking—the mental framework— instantiated by those aphorisms and commonplaces, to install in the mind the habitual forms of thought, the arguments of reason, that will consistently intercept the perturbations of passion before they are discharged in complaint. Leading the reader to embody the ethical ideal of submission to a higher will, such philosophical consolation is more than a remedy for the losses of the past and afflictions of the present: it is a constructive practice meant to be formative of future interpretations of suffering.

It is precisely the power of such habits of mind that we see in one of the most compelling scenes of not complaining on the early modern stage: the Duchess's

---

[68] Becon, *The Sicke Mans Salve*, 46. Hereafter cited parenthetically.
[69] Calvin, *Institution of Christian Religion*, Hh1v (3.7.10).

death scene in John Webster's *The Duchess of Malfi*, first performed around 1613. Forced to part from each other, Antonio presses Neostoic consolation on the Duchess, who at first resists the thought of "slavishly" resigning herself to her suffering:

> ANTONIO   Oh, be of comfort!
> Make patience a noble fortitude.
> ....
> DUCHESS   Must I, like to a slave-born Russian,
> Account it praise to suffer tyranny?
> And yet, O heaven, thy heavy hand is in't.
> I have seen my little boy oft scourge his top,
> And compared myself to't. Naught made me e'er
> Go right but heaven's scourge stick.
> ANTONIO   Do not weep.
> Heaven fashioned us of nothing, and we strive
> To bring ourselves to nothing.[70]

Here Neostoic ethical subjectivity converges with tragic heroism in the two-part rhetorical performance of renouncing complaint and embracing fate, speech acts coupled in the Duchess's "And yet," the hinge where her protest disappears into a recognition of God's "heavy hand" in her suffering. Her complaint stops in its tracks, her rhetorical question swallowed up in the apostrophe to heaven, as she remembers a lesson she has "oft" learned before: her likeness to a child's top beaten by "heaven's scourge stick" (the same trope invoked by Sidney's Plangus, who likens man to "a top which nought but whipping moves" [p. 297]). The speech thus enacts the process by which an internalized way of thinking redirects a complaint. Her death scene shows the payoff of such a practice. As her tormentors try to strike fear into her, the Duchess pointedly refuses to complain ("be tedious"), and wills her death instead:

> BOSOLA   Yet methinks
> The manner of your death should much afflict you,
> This cord should terrify you?
> DUCHESS   Not a whit.
> ....
> I would fain put off my last woman's fault:
> I'd not be tedious to you.
>
>   (4.2.210–24)

---

[70] Webster, *The Duchess of Malfi* (1623), 3.5.73–84. Quoted from *English Renaissance Drama*. Hereafter cited parenthetically.

44   THE DRAMA OF COMPLAINT

The Duchess meets her death with masculine equanimity, her "I would fain put off my last woman's fault" a simultaneous assertion of her soul's willingness to part from her mortal body—to "not be tedious" by clinging to it—and her choice to forgo the "tedious" and "womanish" complaint Bosola expects from her. And just as *De Providentia* promises, her Christianized *amor fati*, her uncomplaining submission to her fate of returning to the "nothing" out of which she was created, allows her to retain a modicum of autonomy, as evinced in her defiant declaration to Bosola: "I am Duchess of Malfi still" (4.2.138). Compare with the complainer, who speaks from a place of irrationality, impotence, and self-loss.[71]

And yet, given the limitations of what Bosola (repeating the standard tragic-existential view) calls "womanish and fearful mankind" (5.5.120), even the strictest moralists concede that under the right wrong circumstances, anyone might slip into complaint. The intensity of suffering can cause a temporary breach in one's rational defenses. "We are not ourselves / When nature, being oppressed, commands the mind / To suffer with the body," Lear says, voicing a conventional defense of complaining frequently invoked by Shakespearean characters (2.2.296–98). This argument stresses the complainer's impotence in relation to a pressure too great to be bound by reason, a feeling so intense that it cries out of its own volition. It is on these grounds that Montaigne proposes, in an essay on his kidney stones, that moral philosophy should reclassify complaining as a mere reflex of the voice, rather than an ethical index: "Let her grant to pain this cowardice in the voice . . . and let her assign these voluntary complaints to the category of the sighs, sobs, palpitations, and pallors that nature has put out of our control."[72] (The phrase "voluntary complaints" is Montaigne's witty inversion of the Stoic virtue of reconciling one's will to fate: he wills for himself what is determined by the involuntary motions of the body.) Calvin himself concedes that extreme suffering suspends reason: Job, he argues, fell short of outright blasphemy, for he was "so overpressed with his miserie" that "he spake not as one that consented to such meaning."[73] He was just venting, a modern commentator would say. Shakespeare's Titus Andronicus, using the language of early modern humoral theory, describes his plaints as the unpreventable discharge of his body's excessive bitterness. Kneeling and weeping with Lavinia, he declares himself unable to "bind" or digest his passion:

---

[71] In Senecan tragedy, as Curtis Perry notes, "the signature flights of rhetorical excess" that are "used to express passionate extremity" demonstrate exactly the dangerous irrationality and loss of self-control criticized in Stoic moral philosophy. Perry, *Shakespeare and Senecan Tragedy*, 111. These Senecan complaints were an important rhetorical model for early modern theatrical tragedy, as Wolfgang Clemen has shown, including for those passionate tragic speeches that I am calling existential complaints. See Clemen, *English Tragedy Before Shakespeare*.

[72] Montaigne, "Of the Resemblance of Children to Fathers." Quoted from *The Complete Essays of Montaigne*, 576.

[73] Calvin, *Job*, 53, 52.

MARCUS   But yet let reason govern thy lament.
TITUS   If there were reasons for these miseries,
Then into limits I could bind my woes.

....

Then give me leave, for losers will have leave
To ease their stomachs with their bitter tongues.[74]

This conventional plea for "leave" to complain—a plea for temporary license to cross the line of propriety and let passion speak, unbound by reason—hinges on the status of the complainer as a "loser," weakened by the force of suffering, a person whose complaints can do no real harm anyway. It is fitting that these rejoinders to moral philosophy are so often articulated in dialogic argument with ethical injunctions against complaining rendered in the rhetoric of complaint-shaming. To be sure, such debates reflect competing early modern ideas about the claims of passion and the range of expressions compatible with virtue.[75] But they are similarly rooted in a theological conception of creatureliness in relation to which the figure of the complainer—whether excoriated for futile complaints or defended for being unable to patiently bear the weight of suffering, whether framed as a negative exemplar or an object of pity—is an emblem of tragic human finitude.

In scenes of existential complaint that stage the complainer's conversion from fantasmatic complaining to philosophical consolation, the recognition of those limits is at once the catalyst to conversion and its surest proof. Several stanzas of Michael Drayton's *Matilda* (1594), a verse tragedy narrated by Matilda's complaining ghost, chart this passage. Matilda's ghost, recounting the aftermath of her murder, describes her father complaining, demanding to know the intention of "Yee powers Divine": "What ment you, first to give her vitall breath / ... / And of her presence to deprive the earth?" he demands.[76] But then he recognizes in this address to the heavens his own impertinence, and repents the transgression, blaming it on his "extremitie." He admits that the heavens "know what's good, and what is ill," and that he, a mere creature, does not:

O pardon Heavens these sacriligious words,
This irreligious open blasphemie:
My wretched soule no better now affords,
Such is the passion of mine agonie,
My desperate case in this extremitie.

....

---

[74] *Titus Andronicus*, 3.1.219–34.
[75] On increasing skepticism about humanist consolation in late-sixteenth-century England, see Pigman, *Grief and English Renaissance Elegy*.
[76] Drayton, *Matilda*, G4r.

46 THE DRAMA OF COMPLAINT

> O heavens, perforce we must attend your time,
> Our succours must awaite upon you still,
> In your just waights you ballance everie crime,
> For us you know what's good, and what is ill;
> Who understands your deepe and secret skill?
> In you alone our destinies consist,
> Then who is hee which can your power resist?[77]

The scene recapitulates the conclusion of the Book of Job, minus the latter's *deus ex turbine*. His complaints silenced by the rhetorical questions posed to him in the whirlwind, Job obtains his proverbial patience in just such a moment of "abashed" anagnorisis that, for Calvin, constitutes the moral of the story:

> too whome or agaynst whome shall wee make our complaynt? Then let us learne, that when wee have considered all well, wee must not blame God, nor commence action against him: but onely find fault with our selves. For the final point whereunto wee must come, is to know the shortnesse of our life, and too be abashed at it when we thinke thereof.[78]

Drayton's conversion scene demonstrates the same "effectual remedie against wrath and impatience" proposed by Calvin: "Thinke upon the Providence of God," he urges in the *Institutes*, in order to "call backe [the] minde to this point. It is the Lordes will, therefore it must bee suffered, not onely because it is not lawfull to strive against it, but also because hee willeth nothing but that which is both just and expedient."[79] It is only from our limited perspectives, Calvin argues, that our afflictions seem nonsensical and arbitrary. From the transcendent perspective of providence, they are perfectly just. Titus says he could restrain his grief "If there were reasons for these miseries." Ultimately what Neostoic and Calvinist ethical discourses teach, in the rational counsel of their philosophizing figures and through their scenes of complaint, is *that* those reasons exist, while *what* they are is beyond creaturely comprehension or question ("The order, meane, ende, and necessity of those thinges that happen, doth for the most part lie secret in the purpose of God").[80] In depicting the conversion of complainers, who come to recognize their fantasies as such and repent, these scenes aim to convert everyday experiences of suffering from occasions of complaint to occasions of self-remembrance. They work to facilitate this perspectival shift in no small part by pointing to the structural place that scenes of existential complaint fixate on: the "beyond" of human life. The "beyond" is the site of an answer, and the end that

---

[77] Drayton, *Matilda*, G4v–H1r. [78] Calvin, *Job*, 248.
[79] Calvin, *Institution of Christian Religion*, 64v (1.17.8).
[80] Calvin, *Institution of Christian Religion*, 60r (1.16.9).

the complainer, or potential complainer, wants. This is exactly the point to which Adam, the paradigmatic human, looks in the final stanza of *Adam's Complaint*: heartened by the promise of "Man reconciled to his God by grace / ... / Free from all cares, and worldly wretchedness" in a heavenly afterlife, he breaks off his complaint and determines to "Fight manfully" for the remainder of his earthly existence.[81]

In the mythic, pre-Christian setting of *King Lear*, the very existence of this beyond, this point of transcendence, is a matter of pronounced uncertainty that comes to the fore nowhere so forcefully as in scenes of suffering.[82] Characters repeatedly invoke the gods, Nature, or "the stars" to make sense of otherwise inexplicable affliction: Edgar construes Gloucester's vicious blinding as proof that "The gods are just and of our pleasant vices / Make instruments to plague us" (5.3.168–69); Gloucester himself suggests that "as flies to wanton boys are we to the gods, / They kill us for their sport" (4.1.38–39); Kent, trying to account for the difference between Cordelia and her cruel sisters, concludes that "It is the stars, / The stars above us govern our conditions, / Else one self mate and make could not beget / Such different issues" (4.2.33–36). Similarly, Albany welcomes the news of Cornwall's death at the hand of Gloucester's servant as proof of the gods' existence and their retributive justice ("This shows you are above, / You justicers, that these our nether crimes / So speedily can venge" [4.2.79–81]). These moments— all of which center on markedly strained acts of interpretation—show characters simultaneously trying to understand the meaning of shocking events by recourse to the heavens and trying to find, in those seemingly senseless events, confirmation that some such fundamental moral order does indeed govern the world. Yet when they call upon the gods, nothing happens. Gloucester's cry to the gods ("O cruel! O you gods!" [3.7.69]) does not prevent Cornwall from putting out his eyes, and despite his prayer ("the gods defend her") Albany's order to halt Cordelia's hanging arrives too late (5.3.254). The anguished question Kent poses as he looks on the dying king and dead daughter ("Is this the promised end?"), paired with his subsequent declaration that "All's cheerless, dark and deadly," encapsulates the despair that has come, by the end of the play, to permeate its fictional world (5.3.261, 288). The cumulative effect is the sense of a play-world that lacks—and whose characters feel the lack of—a transcendent frame that would give meaning to human existence. *Lear* is thus commonly read as a tragedy especially attuned to the birth-pangs of secular modernity, an epistemic rupture that Walter Benjamin, who famously tracks its pulsations in the aesthetics of the seventeenth-century German baroque *Trauerspiel*, or "mourning play," uses the

---

[81] Sabie, *Adam's Complaint*, D1v.
[82] On the absence of the gods, see Elton, *King Lear and the Gods*; Loewenstein, "Agnostic Shakespeare?"

48   THE DRAMA OF COMPLAINT

language of creatureliness to describe.[83] (For Benjamin, the *Trauerspiel* limns "the misery of mankind in its creaturely estate," registering humanity's melancholy immersion in a world no longer enlivened by the promise of redemption, severed from a transcendent source of legitimation and meaning).[84] The absence of this transcendent point of orientation from *Lear*'s play-world—which necessitates a reconceptualizing of creatureliness and its dramas—allows Shakespeare to imagine different answers to the same ethical questions about suffering that the play, like these other early modern texts, explores through scenes of existential complaint and the figure of the creaturely complainer. Complaining may not make sense of suffering, but the world *Lear* imagines is a world in which it makes no sense not to complain.

3. Speaking Feeling in *King Lear*

King Lear ends on a note both sententious and imperious, with a speech addressed to its onstage and theatrical audiences alike:

> The weight of this sad time we must obey,
> Speak what we feel, not what we ought to say.
> The oldest hath borne most; we that are young
> Shall never see so much, nor live so long.
>
> (5.3.322–25)

In suggesting that those who feel "the weight of this sad time" must say what they feel—rather than saying something else—these lines announce their distinction from the call to collective mourning conventionally located at the close of a theatrical tragedy: here, the speaker acknowledges, lamentation violates a norm of some sort, here words of mourning are not—as they would ordinarily be—simply

---

[83] Hugh Grady reads *Lear* as a *Trauerspiel* that registers the evacuation of divine meaning from the world, and the gradual waning of belief in providence. See Grady, "Presentism." Jonathan Dollimore makes the more polemical argument that the play (like other Jacobean tragedies, in his reading) critiques providentialist ideology. See Dollimore, *Radical Tragedy*, 18–19, 194–203. For Stephen Greenblatt, the play attests to a widespread nostalgia for the communal experience of pre-Reformation ritual, a loss recuperated by and as theatrical ritual. See Greenblatt, *Shakespearean Negotiations*, 94–128. Curtis Perry has recently offered a fascinating contribution to this discussion by attributing the play's "presumptive modernity" to Shakespeare's return to "the antisocial energies" of Senecan tragedy, in which the self comes unhinged from its relations to a social world. See Perry, *Shakespeare and Senecan Tragedy*, 113.

[84] Benjamin, *The Origin of German Tragic Drama*, 146. In Benjamin's telling, the *Trauerspiel* reflects a hollowed-out version of the creatureliness focalized in medieval religious drama ("Whereas the middle ages present the futility of world events and the transience of the creature as stations on the road to salvation, the German *Trauerspiel* is taken up entirely with the hopelessness of the earthly condition. Such redemption as it knows resides in the depths of this destiny itself rather than in the fulfillment of a divine plan of salvation" [81].)

"what we ought to say." My claim is that the speech is subtended by, and takes on its fullest meaning in relation to, the matrix of ethical thought that this chapter has been exploring, a web of ideas, images, and tropes in which sorrow is figured as a pressure that elicits a reaction and speaking feeling is understood as an ethically significant choice, a matter of what one ought or ought not to do.

Feeling is especially important to the play, which repeatedly turns to sensations, passions, and thoughts that approach, and often arrive at, the point of being too much to bear.[85] Among its most commonly noted motifs are descriptions of bodies that feel so much they break, burst, or crack under the strain.[86] Edgar attributes Gloucester's death to his inability to withstand the tension of opposing passions:

> his flawed heart,
> Alack, too weak the conflict to support,
> 'Twixt extremes of passion, joy and grief,
> Burst smilingly.
>
> (5.3.195–98)

Edgar's eyewitness account of the event to Albany is permeated with the language of this life-threatening excess of feeling, from his expressed wish for a similar extinction ("O, that my heart would burst!"), to his retelling of Kent throwing himself on Gloucester's corpse in grief until his own "strings of life / Began to crack," to Albany's woeful admission that he himself is "almost ready to dissolve / Hearing of this" (5.3.181, 215–16, 202–3). Together these images articulate "the limits of the human," a threshold explicitly acknowledged in Kent's description of the cataclysmic storm: "Man's nature cannot carry / Th'affliction, nor the fear" (3.2.48–49).[87]

Such limits—limits that are sounded and attested to by feeling—are indeed at the very core of the understanding of "man's nature" developed in *Lear*.[88] The play, which critics have often interpreted as "emblematic of subjectivity in its most acute, most essential aspect," is clearly in dialogue with tragic-existential discourse, as evinced in its frequently aphoristic language, its echoes of the morality play, its resonances with the Book of Job and citations of Stoic moral philosophy, its universalizing assertions, and its characters' shared tendency to speak about

---

[85] Many of the play's usages of "feel" focalize consciousness. Gloucester, for instance, laments "hav[ing] ingenious feeling / Of my huge sorrows" and wishes that he, like Lear, were mad ("Better I were distract; / So should my thoughts be severed from my griefs, / And woes by wrong imaginations lose / The knowledge of themselves" [4.6.274–75, 276–9]).

[86] On this pattern, see Spurgeon, *Shakespeare's Imagery*, 339.

[87] Mousley, "Care, Scepticism, and Speaking in the Plural," 111.

[88] Turner, *The English Renaissance Stage*, 183. On the critical history of reading *Lear* as an existential play, either of nihilistic despair (as exemplified in Jan Kott's 1964 *Shakespeare Our Contemporary*) or redemptive hope, see Grady, "Presentism."

50   THE DRAMA OF COMPLAINT

themselves and others in quasi-allegorical abstractions.[89] (Think of the way Lear describes Poor Tom as if he were an object lesson: "Is man no more than this? Consider him well…thou art the thing itself. Unaccommodated man is no more but such a poor, bare, forked animal as thou art" [3.4.101–6]). This thematic also manifests in the play's insistence on the wretchedness and fragility of human life—not to mention its interest in the extent of human foolishness and cruelty—and in its manifold images of decay and corruption. Such pessimism informs the apocalyptic desires and fears that converge around the event of the storm, when Lear's earlier calls for the infertility of Goneril and Regan blend into his demand for the destruction of all nature's reproductive capacities, misogynistic sentiments resonant with the same tragic-existential meditations on Original Sin alluded to in the Gentleman's comment to Lear that he "has one daughter / Who redeems nature from the general curse / Which twain have brought her to" (4.6.201–3). And, as is typical of tragic-existential discourse, the play stresses human creatureliness, foregrounding this concept through copious references to nonhuman animals: tigers, lions, wolves, bears, boars, dogs, owls, snakes, rats, worms, and leviathans.[90] When the play's characters talk about "man's nature," or "natural" human behavior, they do so not in relation to the law of a transcendent divine creator but by comparing themselves to these animals. Thus social disorder is figured as the inversion of proper creaturely hierarchies, strange metamorphoses in which humans have become like, and are therefore now more beastly than, these beasts. "Tigers, not daughters, what have you performed?" Albany says to Regan and Goneril, "A father, and a gracious aged man / Whose reverence even the head-lugged bear would lick, / Most barbarous, most degenerate, have you madded" (4.2.41–44). The news of Gloucester's blinding—in his own household, by his guests, with the implicit consent of his son—motivates Albany's prediction of a universal and even more monstrous bloodbath to come, if the gods do not reinstate order by punishing these transgressions: "If that the heavens do not their visible spirits / Send quickly down to tame these vile offences, / It will come," he insists, "Humanity must perforce prey on itself, / Like monsters of the deep" (4.2.47–51). The conspicuous lack of any such divine intervention—here or elsewhere in the plot—serves to emphasize the immanence of this play-world, closing it off from an outside, unbeknownst to the characters who inhabit it.

While the framework of theology has no authority or explanatory purchase within the fictional world of the play, *Lear's* two scenes of existential complaint reveal with particular clarity how the theological conception of creatureliness

---

[89] On *Lear's* intimacy with the Book of Job, see Hamlin, "The Patience of Lear."

[90] This aspect of the play's language has been most comprehensively explored by Laurie Shannon, who argues that in showing humans to be "cosmically unaccommodated" relative to nonhuman animals, *Lear* represents human exceptionalism in negative terms, deconstructing human claims to privilege and sovereignty. See Shannon, *The Unaccommodated Animal*, 141.

nevertheless animates Shakespeare's text. These scenes have become especially iconic Shakespearean images of suffering, and more specifically of suffering that explodes into language as characters try to understand the shadowy forces that they believe afflict them from above.[91] The first shows Lear, cast out by his daughters and exposed to "the tyranny of the open night...too rough / For nature to endure," ranting at the storm that comprises Act 3 (3.4.2–3). The second is the final scene of the play, beginning from the moment in Act 5 when Lear enters with Cordelia's body, expressing his desire to "howl" with such force "That heaven's vault should crack" (5.3.257). Each frames the former king as a creaturely complainer, and his complaints—one addressed to the elements, the other aiming at the dome of the sky that in ancient cosmology formed the boundary between earth and the gods—as flights of fantasy, both delusional and futile. But each scene, I want to suggest, also stages or creates the possibility for a secular equivalent of the conversion moments that so often occur in scenes of existential complaint in ethical discourse. At these moments, the play directs the audience's attention to an *earthly* site of sovereign authority that it suggests amplifies suffering, an authority it consistently figures through the theological analogies characteristic of early modern notions of political sovereignty. This is the context in which "Speak what we feel" comes to be meaningful as a command.

To "speak what we feel" is not, of course, in every context synonymous with complaining (even in the play, the most obvious instance of speaking feeling is the sycophantic profession of love that Lear tyrannically demands from his daughters in the opening scene). Yet I would suggest that *Lear* does align the particular form of speaking commanded by "the weight of this sad time"—and prohibited by an ethical norm—with complaining. Indeed, throughout the play, complaining has been framed as precisely the opposite of what one "ought to say" in the face of suffering, just as it is in early modern ethical discourse. Both Lear and Gloucester fight the urge to burst into this shameful speech, which they describe as unmanly and unvirtuous, antithetical to the will of the gods. Turned out by his daughters, Lear struggles against a feminized rising passion ("*Hysterica passio*, down, thou climbing sorrow") that threatens his resolve to "let not women's weapons, water-drops, / Stain my man's cheeks" (2.2.247, 466–67).[92] He begs the gods for assistance—"You heavens, give me that patience, patience I need!"— and determines that he will die before he complains: "I have full cause of weeping,

---

[91] Insofar as I am interested in the play's exploration of vertical human relations my reading differs from those that emphasize horizontal and cross-species relations. Leah Marcus, for instance, puts forward a reading informed by early modern and modern vitalism that suggests the play's interest in "the articulation of a new set of vibrant connections among beings and even things: what modern vitalists would call an 'assemblage'—a network of 'affective bodies' in which agency is horizontally distributed rather than hierarchical and in which interaction does not necessarily take place in its most customary and easily measurable forms." See Marcus, "*King Lear* and the Death of the World," 428.

[92] On the return of Lear's repressed femaleness, see Adelman, *Suffocating Mothers*.

52 THE DRAMA OF COMPLAINT

but this heart / Shall break into a hundred thousand flaws / Or e'er I'll weep" (2.2.460, 473–75). Similarly addressing the gods, Gloucester describes his decision to "Shake patiently my great affliction off" as the alternative to "fall[ing] / To quarrel with your great opposeless wills" (4.6.36, 37–38). After the existential reset of his suicidal fall, and Edgar's reframing of his life ("Thy life's a miracle") he again resolves to "bear / Affliction till it do cry out itself / 'Enough, enough' and die"—to carry on stoically until his afflicted body gives out on its own, an event he imagines as an involuntary burst into a dying complaint (4.6.55, 75–77). The ethical tension between the dictum of patience and the intensity of feeling comes to a head in Act 4 when Lear (mad and "smell[ing] of mortality") meets Gloucester (blind and reborn, as it were) at Dover and proposes to "preach" to him (4.6.129, 176). Here Shakespeare weaves threads of ethical thought and tragic-existential discourse together. Gloucester perceives in Lear's madness an emblem of the world's slow death, its "wear[ing] out to naught," while Lear—before he acknowledges Gloucester's identity—greets him as a generic human who can "feelingly" know the world through an array of senses, and who therefore knows exactly how badly "this world goes":

> GLOUCESTER   O, let me kiss that hand!
> LEAR   Let me wipe it first, it smells of mortality.
> GLOUCESTER   O ruined piece of nature, this great world
> Shall so wear out to naught. Dost thou know me?
> ....
> LEAR   You see how this world goes.
> GLOUCESTER   I see it feelingly.
> LEAR   What, art mad? A man may see how this world goes
>   with no eyes. Look with thine ears.... Thou hast seen a
>   farmer's dog bark at a beggar?
> GLOUCESTER   Ay, sir.
> LEAR   And the creature run from the cur—there thou mightst
>   behold the great image of authority: a dog's obeyed in office.
> ....
> If thou wilt weep my fortunes, take my eyes.
> I know thee well enough, thy name is Gloucester.
> Thou must be patient. We came crying hither:
> Thou knowest the first time that we smell the air
> We wawl and cry. I will preach to thee: mark me.
> GLOUCESTER   Alack, alack the day!
> LEAR   When we are born we cry that we are come
> To this great stage of fools.

(4.6.128–79)

Perceptible here in the trope of the crying infant is the figure of the complainer as the emblem of creaturely wretchedness.[93] At the same time, that figure's other face—the antithesis of virtuous patience—flickers into view in Lear's aphoristic insistence that "Thou must be patient," a fragment of ethical discourse lodged in his memory, a maxim he can recall, if not practice, even in his distracted state of mind.[94] In the storm scene, too, he briefly interrupts his own complaining with this same remembered script, in a line that to an early modern audience would have immediately called to mind Job, that sometime complainer become unlikely model of patience: "No, I will be the pattern of all patience, / I will say nothing" (3.2.37–38).

I would suggest that the opposition at stake here is not simply that between patience (saying nothing) and complaining (speaking feeling), but also between, on the one hand, the philosophical knowledge represented by the maxim that one must be patient, and, on the other, a "feeling" knowledge of the world—"this great stage of fools"—that would lead one to complain. To say that *Lear* is about the unravelling of a social world is to state a critical commonplace. Lear's observation to Gloucester that "a dog's obeyed in office" recalls Gloucester's own description of "strange, strange!" mutations at the very beginning of the play: "Love cools, friendship falls off, brothers divide: in cities, mutinies; in countries, discords; in palaces, treason, and the bond cracked 'twixt son and father...The King falls from bias of nature—there's father against child" (1.2.117, 106–12). This cracking of bonds and "unnatural" dissolution of relationships, read alongside the play's images of breaking bodies and its apocalyptic visions of events in nature, suggest a world whose whole fabric is coming undone—a point that comes increasingly to the forefront of the narrative as this crisis reaches its apex in the civil war dramatized in Acts 4 and 5. If, as Lupton suggests, "*Lear* remains truer to the essence of Jobean complaint, at once courting and resisting all consolation, than any other work by Shakespeare," it is precisely because it keeps this disintegrating world—the world of the complainer—in view.[95]

The character who embodies the figure of the complainer is Lear himself. Indeed, Shakespeare repeatedly frames the erstwhile king in his abject misery as an allegorical exemplar of human unhappiness, a creaturely "wretch." "I am even / The natural fool of fortune," Lear tells Gloucester, while the Gentleman who has come to apprehend him describes his madness as "A sight most pitiful in the meanest wretch, / Past speaking of in a king" (4.6.186–87, 4.6.200–1). The storm

[93] Though this is a commonplace, these lines are often taken to be an allusion to Plangus's complaint in Sidney's *Arcadia*, the text that is the source of the Gloucester subplot. See McKeithan, "*King Lear* and Sidney's *Arcadia*," 45–9.

[94] Shakespeare has Ophelia, in her madness, say the same phrase as she sings and passes out flowers.

[95] Lupton, "The Wizards of Uz," 177.

54   THE DRAMA OF COMPLAINT

scene, which shows Lear "contend[ing] with the fretful elements," demanding "that things might change, or cease," is framed through a conversation between Kent and a Knight who describes Lear's behavior in terms that signal his irrationality (3.1.4, 7). In stark contrast to the creatures that know to shelter themselves from the storm, Lear, the Knight reports,

> Bids the wind blow the earth into the sea,
> Or swell the curled waters 'bove the main,
> That things might change, or cease; tears his white hair,
> Which the impetuous blasts with eyeless rage
> Catch in their fury and make nothing of,
> Strives in his little world of man to outscorn
> The to and fro conflicting wind and rain;
> This night wherein in the cub-drawn bear would couch,
> The lion and the belly-pinched wolf
> Keep their fur dry, unbonneted he runs,
> And bids what will take all.
>
> (3.1.5–15)

The Knight's account clearly aligns Lear, "striv[ing] in his little world of man," with the tropes of human finitude common to existential complaint. Tragic scenes of existential complaint frequently show complainers trying to make sense of turbulent "storms" of passion (as Greene's Bajazet bewails the winds and waves of grief that assault him, for instance, and attributes these to Fortune's cruelty). Pitted against an actual storm, Lear experiences it as an enigmatic phenomenon, an event whose purpose he tries to discern.[96]

Lear's complaint reflects the fantasy that he constructs in response to the storm's enigma. Speaking both as an afflicted wretch who desires the end of his suffering and as a sovereign who would enact destruction with a word, Lear commands the storm to both strike him ("Singe my white head!") and to cut off the very source of generation ("Crack nature's moulds"), foreclosing further creation:

> Blow winds and crack your cheeks! Rage, blow!
> You cataracts and hurricanoes, spout
> Till you have drenched our steeples, drowned the cocks!
> You sulphurous and thought-executing fires,
> Vaunt-couriers of oak-cleaving thunderbolts,

---

[96] There is a long critical tradition of debating the relation between the storm and Lear's passion. Recently Gail Kern Paster has argued that in line with the early modern belief in the analogical correspondences and shared traits between natural phenomena and the passions, Shakespeare uses the storm as a heuristic for exploring whether, as Lear asks, the cause of "unkindness" is in nature. See Paster, " 'Minded Like the Weather.' "

Singe my white head! And thou, all-shaking thunder,
Strike flat the thick rotundity o'the world,
Crack nature's moulds, all germens spill at once
That make ingrateful man!

(3.2.1–9)

Here he fantasizes that the storm is his prosthesis, executing his will with the authority he no longer possesses. Notice that its personified face is that of a complainer whose passion is a form of power: the storm's cheeks crack with rage rather than age, its angry tears unleash devastation ("cataracts and hurricanoes"), its sighs are forceful winds, and it is able to immediately translate fiery thoughts into sovereign action in the form of Jove-like "oak-cleaving thunderbolts." In short, all that is impotent in him is recuperated in the storm. Even when he admits that the elements are not his to command ("You owe me no subscription") he still imagines that it wants something with him, identifying himself as its "slave" and inviting it to visit its "horrible pleasure" on him. This phrase, with its allusion to a capricious sovereign will, seems to remind him of the "two pernicious daughters" whom he thinks *do* owe him obedience, prompting his indignation:

Rumble thy bellyful! Spit fire, spout rain!
Nor rain, wind, thunder, fire are my daughters;
I tax not you, you elements, with unkindness.
I never gave you kingdom, called you children;
You owe me no subscription. Why then, let fall
Your horrible pleasure. Here I stand your slave,
A poor, infirm, weak and despised old man.
But yet I will call you servile ministers
That will with two pernicious daughters join
Your high-engendered battles 'gainst a head
So old and white as this. O ho! 'tis foul.

(3.2.14–24)

Lear's complaint ends with a final shift: having accused the elements of being the "servile ministers" of his daughters, he closes by describing these same elements as "dreadful summoners" sent to haul the guilty before a divine tribunal:

Let the great gods
That keep this dreadful pudder o'er our heads
Find out their enemies now. Tremble, thou wretch,
That hast within thee undivulged crimes[.]
....

56   THE DRAMA OF COMPLAINT

> Close pent-up guilts
> Rive your concealing continents and cry
> These dreadful summoners grace. I am a man
> More sinned against than sinning.
>
> (3.2.49–60)

He closes with a protestation of his innocence, tinged with self-righteous self-pity. He imagines his daughters punished, and himself vindicated, by the higher power that he assumes to be controlling the storm. The existence of such a power is, indeed, the one point of consistency in his complaint: though the identity of this figure shifts, *someone* is always making the storm the instrument of its will.

Here it is worth taking a step back and recalling the reason that Lear is exposed to the storm in the first place. In defiance of "the offices of nature, bond of childhood, / Effects of courtesy, dues of gratitude," Goneril and Regan have turned him and his retinue away from their households (2.2.367–68). Daniel Juan Gil reads this act as an instance of what Agamben theorizes as "'raw' sovereign power," the effect of which is to strip Lear of what makes him human—the "more than nature needs" that Lear argues distinguishes "Man's life" from a beast's—and exclude him from the play's social world (2.2.399, 400).[97] There, as Lear puts it, he feels "Necessity's sharp pinch!" and becomes "a comrade with the wolf and owl" (2.2.456, 455)—the latter an echo of Job's description of himself as having become "a brother to the dragons, and a companion to the ostriches."[98] We might see their expulsion of him as a repetition of how Lear "disclaimed all [his] paternal care" of Cordelia, when—invoking the "the orbs / From whom we do exist and cease to be"—he consigns her to the status of a "barbarous Scythian" or a cannibal, casting her out to the very margins of the category of the human (1.1.114, 112–13, 117).[99] Here he has de-created by sovereign fiat the daughter who has described her

---

[97] Gil, *Shakespeare's Anti-Politics*, 108. Gil argues for the play's interest in new forms of life that become possible when the subject has been excluded from a sociopolitical community and comes unhinged from the creative-destructive sovereign power on which its social identity has depended.

[98] Job 30:29. *The Geneva Bible.*

[99] Lear's speech, in full, reads:

> Well, let it be so. Thy truth then be thy dower,
> For by the sacred radiance of the sun,
> The mysteries of Hecate and the night,
> By all the operation of the orbs
> From whom we do exist and cease to be,
> Here I disclaim all my paternal care,
> Propinquity and property of blood,
> And as a stranger to my heart and me
> Hold thee from this for ever. The barbarous Scythian,
> Or he that makes his generation messes
> To gorge his appetite, shall to my bosom
> Be as well neighboured, pitied and relieved,
> As thou my sometime daughter.
>
> (1.1.109–21)

"bond" to him as that of a creature to its maker ("Good my lord, / You have begot me, bred me, loved me" [93, 95–96]). It is clear from Lear's complaint that the sheer indignity of his ejection from Goneril and Regan's households is the "bemadding" event (3.1.34). Notice how his address to the elements is interrupted by a complaint against his daughters ("In such a night / To shut me out? Pour on, I will endure. / In such a night as this? O Regan, Goneril" [3.4.17–19]). What torments Lear is a feeling in excess of the storm: the "tempest in my mind / [That] doth from my senses take all feeling else, / Save what beats there, filial ingratitude" (3.4.12–14). The unfailingly loyal Kent suggests that Lear has just cause to be aggrieved: indeed, he urges the Knight to go to Dover and "mak[e] just report / Of how unnatural and bemadding sorrow / The King hath cause to plain," to raise a group of supporters (3.1.33–35). We might say, then, that the storm scene shows Lear complaining in exactly the wrong way, in the wrong place, about the wrong thing, and to the wrong audience, the fantasmatic quality of his complaint all the clearer for the justness of his cause to complain.

Yet this scene also stages a conversion that—like the religious conversion moments in other scenes of existential complaint—involves a shift in perspective. And, as is often the case, this conversion involves the intervention of another person, a friend. Lear's complaint is interrupted by the disguised Kent, who comes to lead Lear and the Fool into Poor Tom's hovel. What Kent offers is not philosophy but physical shelter, itself figured as a type of friendship ("Some friendship will it lend you 'gainst the tempest," he says [3.2.62]). Before entering the hovel, Lear says "I'll pray, and then I'll sleep" (3.4.27). This is already an odd gesture—an incongruously Christian moment of devotion—and it is also strange that no divinities are addressed in the "prayer" that follows. Instead Lear addresses the "poor naked wretches" who are unsheltered from the storm, and then, having recalled his own neglect of their unhoused state, he instructs those in power ("pomp") to "take physic" by "exposing" themselves "to feel what wretches feel":

> [*Kneels.*] Poor naked wretches, wheresoe'er you are,
> That bide the pelting of this pitiless storm,
> How shall your houseless heads and unfed sides,
> Your looped and windowed raggedness, defend you
> From seasons such as these? O, I have ta'en
> Too little care of this. Take physic, pomp,
> Expose thyself to feel what wretches feel,
> That thou mayst shake the superflux to them
> And show the heavens more just.
>
> (3.4.28–36)

This speech has occasioned many rich critical discussions about Shakespeare's conceptualization of the sociopolitical possibilities and limitations of empathy,

58 THE DRAMA OF COMPLAINT

pity, compassion, and charity, in part because of the link it suggests between "feeling" and a just distribution of resources.[100] So too, critics have discussed this moment as an ethical turning point for Lear himself, in which "feeling" opens the door to fellow-feeling.[101] My own interest lies less in this speech's articulation of a particular social vision, or its significance for Lear individually, than in its widening of the frame of the existential complaint scene for the play's audience. Here the audience is invited to "see" all these other, hitherto-unseen complainers: the unsheltered, uncared-for "wretches" whom the figure of the unhoused king represents, and whose unheard complaints (how shall we be defended from this?) he ventriloquizes. As importantly, the speech redefines "the heavens": the power that "shake[s] the superflux," Lear suggests, comes from human agencies and figures of authority whose forms of justice have the potential to be "more just" than the heavens (or, as the worldly mode in which heavenly justice appears, are capable of proving that the gods they represent are indeed just). Rather than the conventional conversion of the complainer, then—a conversion that involves a shift in the complainer's personal perspective on his suffering as he contemplates the divine—Lear's "prayer" enacts a shift in the *audience's perspective* on creaturely suffering and its causes.

In sum, then, this scene of existential complaint enables the audience to see a fuller cast of complainers and to trace "feeling" to human forms of sovereign power that amplify the effects of suffering, here represented by the storm: exceptional sovereign violence in Goneril and Regan's expulsion of Lear, ordinary sovereign dereliction in Lear's inattention to the "poor naked wretches" of his kingdom. The words Albany speaks to Regan, Goneril, and Edmund as they prepare to face Cordelia's army in Act 5 similarly bring into view a multitude of "wretches" complaining about and to sovereign authority: "the King is come to his daughter, / With others whom the rigour of our state / Forced to cry out," Albany says, referring to a mass of aggrieved people who, he admits, "most just and heavy causes make oppose" (5.1.21–23, 27). Here, as in Lear's prayer, human sovereign authority emerges as both an amplifier of feeling and—less certainly—a potential, though far from sure, provider of "shelter" from its weight.[102] Thus I want to suggest that the scene enables us to make a triangulation between the *personal* ethics that some critics have seen articulated by the play (a code of conduct that acknowledges the insufficiency of Stoic consolatory scripts and allows for passion), the *social* ethics that other critics have identified (instantiated in various acts of

---

[100] For a recent discussion of these issues, see Johnson, " 'To Feel What Wretches Feel.' "

[101] On the storm as an ethical turning point for Lear, see Kearney, " 'This is above all strangeness.' "

[102] In an essay on the play's exploration of the fundamentally "political nature" of human life (an Aristotelian idea misunderstood in early modernity as referring to general social relationality), Jeffrey Griswold argues that the play's representations of frail and "unaccommodated" bodies communicates the necessity of political forms and structures of belonging and care. See Griswold, "Human Insufficiency and the Politics of Accommodation in *King Lear*," 75.

compassion and fellow-feeling), and a *political* ethics that has to do with recognizing the "just and heavy causes" that compel speaking out in opposition.[103]

The play's closing scene, a metaplaintive scene of existential complaint, imagines that collective spoken feeling might be a weapon that draws the attention of the sovereign ear. As Albany, Edgar, and Kent wait to learn whether the reprieve Edmund has sent will reach the castle in time to spare Cordelia and her father from death, Lear enters, carrying Cordelia and crying:

> Howl, howl, howl, howl! O, you are men of stones!
> Had I your tongues and eyes, I'd use them so
> That heaven's vault should crack: she's gone for ever.
> I know when one is dead and when one lives;
> She's dead as earth.
>
> (5.3.255–59)

As in the storm, Lear is an emblem of human misery here, a point made by Kent, who says, "If Fortune brag of two she loved and hated, / One of them we behold" (5.3.278). The specifically creaturely coordinates of that misery are underscored by the howl, an approximation of animal sound that nevertheless—precisely because it appears as a repeated, spoken *word*—emphasizes a uniquely human unhappiness. Moreover, this "howl" is not just an expression of outrage but is also a grammatical imperative ("Howl, howl, howl, howl!") that summons its addressees to speak feeling, to symbolize suffering. A certain moral righteousness infuses this imperative: a common caricature of Stoic impassivity, Lear's phrase "men of stones" shames his onlookers for their silence. To cease being "men of stones"—to be human—is in this formulation contingent on turning words and tears into something *like* stones, projectiles to aim at heaven's vault.[104] And yet the action Lear calls for, the action he casts as an ethical good, would seem no more than a collective exercise in tragic futility: the gods are absent and Cordelia is "gone for ever." Why bother to howl? This sense of despair resounds in the negations that punctuate Lear's last words, all those "nos" and "nevers" that insist on Cordelia's lifelessness:

> No, no, no life!
> Why should a dog, a horse, a rat have life
> And thou no breath at all? O thou'lt come no more,
> Never, never, never, never, never.

....

---

[103] For a recent version of this argument about the play's anti-Stoicism see Lehtonen, "The Intelligence of Negative Passion." Edgar is the figure most closely associated with Stoic moral philosophy. For the various acts of compassion in the play, see Geng, *Communal Justice in Shakespeare's England*.

[104] Shakespeare references this same Senecan trope in Act 4 of *Titus Andronicus*—also as an image of futility—when Titus writes complaints addressed to the gods, then attaches them to arrows he shoots into Saturninus's court ("sith there's no justice in earth nor hell, / We will solicit heaven and move the gods / To send down Justice for to wreak our wrongs" [4.3.50–52]).

60   THE DRAMA OF COMPLAINT

> Do you see this? Look on her: look, her lips,
> Look there, look there!   *He dies.*[105]

$$(5.3.304-7)$$

Framed by an exhausted "Howl" and an image of creaturely death (an image doubly marked by the verbal and visual emphasizing of "no breath"), this scene of existential complaint defies the didactic gestures typical of such scenes. The scene contains no moral commentary, only Kent's suggestion that Lear is fortunate to be free of the torture that is life in the world: "O, let him pass. He hates him / That would upon the rack of this tough world / Stretch him out longer" (5.3.312–14). The scene would seem to similarly defeat the critical impulse to redeem or recuperate. In a critique of earlier humanist readings that saw in the play an affirmation of the human spirit, some critics have suggested that this final scene confronts the theatrical audience with a traumatic dimension of human life, something senseless and unassimilable. John Joughin, for instance, argues that the meaninglessness of Cordelia's death constitutes an "ethical demand" that the audience bear witness to the senselessness of the horror they have seen: rather than turning to illusory consolations, they must register the "irruptive excess" that the play transfers to them—a surplus of affect without meaning.[106]

And yet the ethical command to which Shakespeare gives the last word is the imperative to speak, to symbolize, to make meaning:

> The weight of this sad time we must obey,
> Speak what we feel, not what we ought to say.
> The oldest hath borne most; we that are young
> Shall never see so much, nor live so long.

$$(5.3.322-25)$$

Again, the speaker of these lines articulates—precisely as an ethical imperative, and with an admission of contradicting a conventional "ought"—exactly the response to feeling that the early modern ethical discourse this chapter has explored cautions against. Its countering of that discourse is rhetorically signaled by the fact that the speech is spoken by a figure of authority (the 1608 Quarto assigns it to Albany, the surviving sovereign, while the 1623 Folio gives it to Edgar, the play's Chorus-like tragic commentator), and in a manner that mimics the didacticism of the philosopher figures of ethical discourse, who remind complainers of the higher power whose law they "must obey." Here, in contrast,

---

[105] Lear's final words are ambiguous—he may die believing that she is breathing, or he may be emphasizing the fact that she has "no breath at all," as he has said. See Foakes, n. 309–10, p. 390.

[106] Joughin, "*Lear*'s Afterlife," 69, 70. For similar arguments see Raman, "Protesting Bodies" and Clody, "The Mirror and the Feather."

SIGNS OF LIFE   61

it is "the weight of this sad time" that must be obeyed, and obeyed by *speaking feeling*—specifically, by complaining, the speaking that is the opposite of Stoic and Christian "patience."

There would seem to be something almost perverse about this command, given its proximity in placement, tone, and sentiment to Lear's futile order to "howl": why should feeling be spoken if no good can come of speaking feeling? Nevertheless, I want to suggest that these words are the potential prelude to this scene's conversion moment—a moment that, like its equivalents in other scenes of existential complaint, involves the opening of a new horizon and a corresponding shift in perspective for both the complainer and the audience, who are here aligned. The storm scene has indicated what that shift entails: it is a shift away from the sky and the heavens, and toward the earth and its sites of authority, a shift from the "beyond" of eternity to the here and now of "this sad time"—where, as tragic-existential discourse reminds us, things are always in flux, never settled, always ending and beginning.

Because this is where the play ends, this conversion moment is of necessity a *virtual* one, held out as a possibility to two distinct audiences. One is comprised of the fictional characters, who at this moment in the narrative are just beginning to undertake the reconstruction of their sociopolitical world by arranging—in an echo of the play's opening—the distribution of sovereign authority.[107] For these survivors, the lines bear upon the future of the living, asking them to consider what role the speaking of feeling might play in forming that future: put differently, the lines suggest that speaking feeling does indeed have some such role there. Amanda Bailey, picking up on just this possibility and noting its resonance with Brian Massumi's discussion of the politics of affect, suggests that "Here feeling is recognized as the 'reservoir of political potential' of the collective."[108] In this context, the grammatically negative future-tense statement that concludes the speech ("The oldest hath borne most; we that are young / Shall never see so much, nor live so long") may be heard as a hopeful intention, a decision to build a life quantitatively less full of sorrow and thus qualitatively less "long," less unbearable.

For Stanley Cavell, whose famous essay on *Lear* becomes a meditation on witnessing suffering within and outside the theater, the conclusions of Shakespeare's tragedies are thresholds between two "arena[s] of action," one in which we are helpless to act as an effect of the position in which we are placed, and one in which we habitually position ourselves such as to render action impossible.[109] The point is not that in every instance we can act—indeed, there are limits on our

---

[107] When Albany asks Edgar and Kent to "Rule in this realm and the gored state sustain," it is unclear whether he is suggesting that they each rule over a portion of a divided kingdom; inviting them to rule alongside himself in a united kingdom; or using "rule" in a much more limited sense and simply restoring them to their former positions (5.3.319). On these different possibilities see Foakes' editorial notes in the Arden edition, 392.

[108] Bailey, "Speak What We Feel," 38.   [109] Cavell, "The Avoidance of Love," 113.

62 THE DRAMA OF COMPLAINT

power inherent to our finitude—but rather that we are not in every instance unable to act, or relieved of the ethical responsibility to do so. He suggests that tragedy distances us from our customary, often unconscious defenses against action so that we might recognize them, as well as their potentially tragic consequences, as our own choices, rather than expressions of fate. It "make[s] us practical, capable of acting," Cavell argues, precisely because "it gives us a chance to stop," to change direction.[110]

By virtue of its placement, *Lear*'s concluding summons to a "we" who must speak what we feel also addresses the theatrical audience, an audience whose members, as Penelope Geng puts it, "have a genetic and political future" themselves.[111] As the speech calls the play's characters to a world they are tasked with renovating, so it ushers its audience out to their own world, their own "sad time." Articulated in the conventional narrative location for recapitulating the moral insight a play has yielded, the command to "Speak what we feel" is positioned so as to become impressed on listeners. Hence the formulation of these lines as a proverb, a rhetorical form that Craig Dionne suggests was designed to "magically, endlessly, produce further rumination" for audiences trained in humanist educational practices.[112] I would not go so far as to say that Shakespeare orders audiences to become complainers. I would, however, suggest that the command to "Speak what we feel, not what we ought to say" calls into question the absolute validity of the ethical injunctions against complaining that early modern audiences knew so well, urging them—and future audiences, too—to weigh those injunctions against "the weight of this sad time," whatever *this* sad time is. *Lear* does not in any straightforward manner tell—let alone show—its audiences exactly why they should complain, or provide evidence confirming that it is good (or that it will end well) for them to do so. In this sense the logic of the closing command resembles the theological ethical discourse whose norms it counters: in proposing that there is something we "must" do in response to suffering, the speaker issues an imperative that assumes, on the part of its addressee, something like faith. But despite—and precisely because of—the bleakness of its world, the play does not give up on complaining, and it suggests that its audiences shouldn't either.

[110] Cavell, "The Avoidance of Love," 118, 104.
[111] Geng, *Communal Justice in Shakespeare's England*, 121.   [112] Dionne, *Posthuman Lear*, 21.

2
Ethical Demands
Judicial Complaint and the Call of Conscience

This chapter turns from the poetic form of existential complaint to that of judicial complaint: a demand for justice, vaguely evocative of those enacted in legal contexts, addressed to someone obligated to respond. It also turns from the figure of the complainer to the figure of the addressee, a figure that I will argue functions in ethical discourse to theorize ethical responsibility. In the early modern texts I will be exploring, this figure helps to flesh out the internal drama of the "complaining" conscience that pleads with or accuses the self from within the mind, on behalf of the moral law. I want to begin, however, by noting that a scene of plaintive address and obligatory response has also been important to more recent and very different conceptualizations of ethical responsibility—namely, to an influential strand of ethical and phenomenological thought in contemporary critical theory, rooted in Hegel's account of recognition, that invokes the trope of a primal "scene of address" that marks the subject's difference from the world and itself. Readers familiar with the latter strand of thought will recognize the oddity of my reference to the scene of address—used by theorists to articulate an antinormative, extrajudicial, non-repressive ethics of relationality—in the context of a discussion about judicial complaint, conscience, and the moral law. But what makes this critical trope illustrative for our purposes is that it explicitly foregrounds a human relationality felt in moments of encounter and address that I will suggest comes alive in this chapter's exemplary scene of judicial complaint: the climactic ghost scene in *Richard III* in which Shakespeare's villainous king, prompted by the complaining ghosts of his victims, has a fleeting but intense experience of something he calls conscience.

Allow me, then, to briefly summarize the critical trope of the scene of address. For critics who ground ethics in heteronomy rather than Kantian autonomy, an idealized, dyadic scene of plaintive address is the key figure for the inaugural scene of ethical subjectivity and responsibility, signifying a traumatic experience of an external ethical demand that charges the subject with an impossible mandate.[1] A touchstone is Levinas's face-to-face encounter, the trope for a preontological confrontation with absolute alterity that "tear[s] consciousness up from its

---

[1] On the traumatic-impossible nature of the ethical demand as it is conceptualized in heteronomous ethics, see Critchley, *Infinitely Demanding*, 39.

The Drama of Complaint: Ethical Provocations in Shakespeare's Tragedy. Emily Shortslef, Oxford University Press.
© Emily Shortslef 2023. DOI: 10.1093/oso/9780192868480.003.0003

64   THE DRAMA OF COMPLAINT

center," imposing an ethical demand that brings into being a subject ineluctably responsible for the other.[2] Replacing the metaphysical and theological underpinnings of this Levinasian scene with poststructuralist and psychoanalytic supports, Judith Butler has influentially theorized an ethical responsibility assumed in interlocutory acts of address and response, as the subject responds to the address of the injured other. Taking aim against a moral philosophical tradition centered on autonomy and accountability (and against the charge that critical theory and ethical thought are antithetical), Butler's work locates ethical responsibility in "a primary relation to alterity by which we are animated," deriving an ethics that acknowledges vulnerability and the limits of self-knowledge from the fact that the subject first emerges through an unwilled exposure and responsiveness to the disorienting proximity and enigmatic addresses of the other.[3] ("Scene[s] of address" that they suggest "can and should provide a sustaining condition for ethical deliberation, judgment, and conduct.")[4] In its specifically sonic dimensions, this scene of address also appears in Adriana Cavarero's construction of a relational ontology that grounds ethics and politics, insofar as she casts a convocational "duet between mother and infant" as the originary scene of a "sonorous bond" that underwrites and resonates in social speech, in which "uniqueness and relation" are communicated extra-semantically, through the acoustics of voices speaking together.[5] In each of these models, the scene of address tropes a constitutive relation to otherness that prevents autonomy and renders the subject simultaneously vulnerable to and responsible for the other, a fundamental relationality that anchors an ethics irreducible to prescriptive moral norms and prohibitive legal codes.[6] Ethical responsibility is imagined as a matter of responding to an ethical demand that calls out, as it were, from the singularity of the other and addresses the subject in their own singularity. This abstract ethical demand materializes in the form of an expression of injury and a demand for recognition: a complaint.

Shakespeare also constructs a scene of plaintive address to theorize an abstraction of ethical thought: the experience of conscience, for early moderns the paradigmatic ethical demand. Like these later accounts, *Richard III*'s representation of conscience captures a fundamental relationality posited as the ground of ethical subjectivity and responsibility. Early modern writers and their audiences, however, understood this relationality to be between the human and the divine, and saw its preventing of autonomy as an axiomatic truth rather than a provocative

---

[2] Levinas, *Totality and Infinity*, 207.   [3] Butler, *Giving an Account of Oneself*, 100.

[4] Butler, *Giving an Account of Oneself*, 49.

[5] Cavarero, *For More than One Voice*, 180, 169, 180.

[6] For Levinas, this more fundamental law is the commandment of what he terms the infinite, the voice of God that breaks through human finitude in the "destitute" face of the other. For Butler, in a very different idiom, the law that underwrites the scene of address is the alterity of the signifying field in which subjects are produced as non-identical with themselves. Of vital importance for both Levinas and Butler is the nonequivalence of this law to any juridical code or to the norms of any specific sociopolitical order. See Levinas, *Ethics and Infinity*, 89–90. See Butler, *Giving an Account*, 13–17.

critical stance. Indeed, in distinction to the role that conscience would assume in post-Kantian moral philosophy as the internal judge of the moral law which man gives to himself, early modern accounts of conscience, including Shakespeare's, unequivocally stress the heteronomous nature of its demand.[7] Conscience was routinely described by theologians and represented in popular literature as a traumatic imprint of divine alterity in the soul that binds the subject to the moral law. In the words of the Calvinist theologian William Perkins, the period's most prolific expositor of conscience,

> Morall law concernes duties of love partly to God & partly towards our neigh-
> bours it is contained in the decalogue or 10 commandements & it is the very law
> of nature written in all mens hearts...in the creation of man: & therfore it binds
> the consciences of all men at all times, even of blind and ignorant persons that
> neither knowe the most of it nor care to know it.[8]

For the bishop John Woolton, conscience is "a certaine natural intelligence of the law...planted in the internall man by God."[9] Justus Lipsius suggests that it is the way in which God "by this image of his commeth unto us, yea (which more is) even into us."[10] Perkins calls conscience "a thing placed by God in the middest betweene him and man."[11] William Ames, a Puritan cleric tutored by Perkins at Christ's College, asserts that it "stands in the place of God himselfe."[12] Generally thought to reside in the faculty of reason as something "distinct from the Understanding, from the Memorie, Will, and Heart of Man...an other thing created of God, besides all these," conscience is an excessive thing that was also thought to represent a negative space, a fissure in the self where the divine dwells.[13] It names a certain *openness* where an unbreakable bond—an attachment and an obligation—between the human and the divine has formed.

Language issues from this openness, including the language of complaint. Commonly figured as an internal voice, conscience was said to facilitate communication between the self and God, speaking to each as the representative of the other. A fifteenth-century verse dialogue attributed to William Lichfield and printed several times in the sixteenth century as *The Remors of Conscyence*, for

---

[7] On the intellectual history of conscience, I have consulted Ojakangas, *The Voice of Conscience* and Strohm, *Conscience: A Very Short Introduction*.

[8] Perkins, *A Discourse of Conscience*, 14. Rebecca Lemon describes Perkins as "one of England's most popular religious writers, with seventy-six editions of his work appearing before his death in 1602." Lemon, *Addiction and Devotion*, 34.

[9] Woolton, *Of the Conscience*, B4v. Conscience conjoins abstract knowledge of the law (*synteresis* or *synderesis*) with the ability to judge its applicability to specific situations (*syneidesis* or *conscientia*). On these distinctions, see Braun and Vallence, *Contexts of Conscience*, x–xviii.

[10] Lipsius, *Two Bookes of Constancie*, 11.   [11] Perkins, *A Discourse of Conscience*, 5.

[12] Ames, *Conscience, with the Power and Cases Thereof*, 7.

[13] Bernard, *Christian See to Thy Conscience*, 4.

66 THE DRAMA OF COMPLAINT

instance, depicts an exchange between God and Man in which God, pleading with Man to "Open thyn eeres vnto my call and cry," calls Man to repentance by reminding him of the primary demand of the moral law—"love thy soverayne as it is skyll"—and Man repents, having "receyued in conscyence this complanynge."[14] These internal dialogues were often imagined as recurring dyadic scenes of judgment in which conscience—a divine surrogate who knows all that the person has felt, thought, and done, and can say how they stand in relation to the moral law—speaks alternately as a witness, a judge, and a plaintiff, pleading with or accusing the person in whom it dwells, as "an other person within."[15]

As Abraham Stoll has argued in a recent study of poetic representations of conscience, the post-Reformation turn to private conscience as the privileged seat of moral authority, in tandem with Reformed theology's "fundamental move toward inwardness," gave special urgency to late sixteenth-century theorizations of conscience, theorizations that are richly figurative.[16] Among these is *Richard III*'s ghost scene. Awaking from a dream during which the ghosts of his victims have appeared before him to name his crimes and demand his death, the terrified Richard cries that his conscience has accused him of "Murder, stern murder, in the direst degree!" with "a thousand several tongues," as if it were a plaintiff—or a body of plaintiffs—bringing grievances before a court of law:

> My conscience hath a thousand several tongues,
> And every tongue brings in a several tale,
> And every tale condemns me for a villain.[17]

Richard's interpretation of the ghosts' accusations as complaints made by his conscience echoes the assessment of the sixteenth-century historical chroniclers, Shakespeare's sources, who suggest of the "straunge vision" the king was reported to have experienced on the eve of his death that "this was no dreame, but a puncion and pricke of hys synfull conscience... [which] at the last daie of extreme life is wonte to shew and represent to us our faultes and offences."[18] The theatrical

---

[14] Anon., *The Remors of Conscyence*. A2r, A2v.   [15] Perkins, *A Discourse of Conscience*, 7.

[16] Stoll, *Conscience in Early Modern English Literature*, 11–12. Notwithstanding the profound philosophical shift associated with the Reformation—whereby, in Paul Strohm's words, conscience "came to be seen less as a body of ecclesiastical precepts imported from the 'outside in,' and more as a set of deeply lodged convictions speaking from the 'inside out'"—the positions attributed to conscience in Protestant religious discourse are normative ones, in both senses of the term: they reiterate existing norms and claim normative status for their own prescriptions. See Strohm, *Conscience: A Very Short Introduction*, 17. On early modern conscience as uniting private conviction with communal norms, see DiGangi, "Entangled Agency," 385–99. Victoria Kahn discusses conflicts of obligation between conscience and sovereign authority as taken up by Perkins and other Calvinist theologians in *Wayward Contracts*, 64–73.

[17] All citations of the play are from *Richard III*, ed. Siemon. 5.3.197, 193–5. Hereafter cited parenthetically.

[18] Hall, *Union*, 53. This interpretation of Richard's dream originates in Polydore Vergil's *Anglica Historia* (1534–55).

scene also reflects conventional understandings of conscience formalized in early modern treatises such as Woolton's *Of the Conscience* (1576) and Perkins' *A Discourse of Conscience* (1596). Like Richard, who imagines that the "thousand several tongues" of his conscience "Throng to the bar, crying all, 'Guilty, guilty!'" (5.3.199), Woolton and Perkins describe conscience as a witness that "accuses" and a judge that "condemns."[19] Woolton, in fact, even cites the historian Polydore Vergil's report of Richard III's unsettling vision as proof that no person, however hardened, can indefinitely evade the accusing testimony that his conscience lays before him.[20]

Critics too have typically described the complaining ghosts as players in Richard's internal drama, and with good reason: the actions Woolton ascribes to the versatile guilty conscience—"An evill Conscience is a witnesse of our debtes, a Judge, a tormenter, she accuseth us, she judgeth us, she punisheth us, and she condemneth us"—correspond perfectly to those performed by the ghosts, who not only accuse Richard but also sentence him to death.[21] "Despair and die," each ghost orders the king; "I shall despair," he announces; despairing, he will die the following morning in battle, defeated by Henry Tudor, Earl of Richmond (5.3.126, 200). The Shakespearean scene clearly hews very closely to the conventional narratives of conscience familiar to early modern audiences from theological literature, sermons, and morality plays, in which a person's own conscience speaks, as the Elizabethan proverb had it, "in steede of a thousand witnesses."[22]

And yet it is worth lingering on the ways in which the theatrical appearance of the king's conscience exceeds, even as it patently evokes, these accounts. Consider that the same ghosts that accuse Richard also bless the sleeping Richmond, a dramaturgical decision that strongly implies the ghosts' ontological distinction from Richard.[23] For the theatrical audience, the felt sense of such a distinction would only be amplified by the fact that the ghosts of *Richard III* appear as embodied presences on stage who complain in their own voices (in contrast to the anonymous contemporary play *The True Tragedy of Richard the Third* (1594), whose Richard merely describes a "wounded conscience" that has caused him to dream of ghosts that "complain and crieth for revenge").[24] *Richard III* even makes

---

[19] Woolton, *Of the Conscience*, A1v.   [20] Woolton, *Of the Conscience*, F1v.

[21] Woolton, *Of the Conscience*, A2r. See, for instance, Holderness, *Shakespeare: The Histories*; Wilks, *The Idea of Conscience*; Wheeler, "History, Character and Conscience in *Richard III*"; Hughes, "The 'Worm of Conscience' in *Richard III* and *Macbeth*"; Long, "Toward an Early Modern Theory of Trauma."

[22] Woolton, *Of the Conscience*, A1v.

[23] Among the critics who have made this case are Walsh, *Shakespeare*, 155, and Wells, "Staging Shakespeare's Ghosts."

[24] *The True Tragedie*, H1v. The earliest performance date of this play (part of the repertory of The Queen's Men) is unknown, as is its relationship to Shakespeare's play. See Walsh, *Shakespeare*, 74–107. *The True Tragedie* emphasizes Richard's internal drama, and links the complaints of his conscience to the pressures of kingship:

> The hell of life that hangs upon the Crowne,
> The daily cares, the nightly dreames,
> . . . .

68 THE DRAMA OF COMPLAINT

Richard's own senses testify against his claim that the complaining voices he has heard have come from within, for on waking he observes that "The lights burn blue" (5.3.180), a phenomenon traditionally thought to signal the presence of ghosts (an effect created in the early modern theater by low-burning candles on the stage). His description of a physical environment that still registers the traces of the ghosts—a moment in which the play's presentational and representational levels converge—tacitly affirms to the theatrical audience the reality of the complaining ghosts they have witnessed. Shakespeare orchestrates the scene in such a manner, then, as to undermine Richard's retrospective identification of the plaintiffs in his tent as the projections of his guilty conscience, and to flag the ghosts as real opponents rather than figures of an internal conflict given shape in his dream. Put more forcefully, the scene's staging underscores the insufficiency of the notion of an irruptive internal drama to account for what we have seen. Turning the familiar figure of the externalized complaining voice of conscience into actual external plaintiffs who speak not as the several-tongued voice of Richard's conscience but for and as themselves, Shakespeare positions Richard's experience of conscience as the *effect* of his exposure to the ghosts' complaints, rather than their point of origin, their *cause*.

By reconfiguring conscience's archetypal inward scene of plaintive, accusatory address as an external scene of judicial complaint, *Richard III* reconceptualizes conscience as the paradigmatic experience of an ethical demand. As this chapter shows, in depicting conscience as a response to the complaint of another person, the play articulates a notion of conscience that is neither incompatible nor identical with the early modern formulations outlined above, but supplements them in focalizing an ethical pressure that indexes a constitutive and specifically *human* relationality. The scene of judicial complaint, I want to suggest, is one of Shakespeare's privileged theatrical forms for representing the responsibility that this relationality entails.

1. Hearing Judicial Complaint

In the climactic last scene of *Measure for Measure*, Isabella, seeking to "wring redress" for Angelo's transgressions, falls to her knees and appeals to the Duke, demanding that he hear her complaint:

> Strikes such a terror to my wounded conscience,
> That sleepe I, wake I, or whatsoever I do,
> Meethinkes their ghoasts comes gaping for revenge,
> Whom I have slaine in reaching for a Crowne.
> Clarence complaines, and crieth for revenge.
> My Nephues bloods, Revenge, revenge, doth crie.
> The headlesse Peeres comes preasing for revenge,
> And every one cries, let the tyrant die.

ETHICAL DEMANDS   69

> ISABELLA   Justice, O royal Duke! vail your regard
> Upon a wronged—I would fain have said a maid.
> O worthy prince, dishonor not your eye
> By throwing it on any other object
> Till you have heard me in my true complaint
> And given me justice, justice, justice, justice.
> DUKE Relate your wrongs: in what, by whom? Be brief.[25]

This exchange catalyzes a scene of judgment. Isabella's accusation of Angelo sparks the investigation that reveals the truth, passing through the questioning of witnesses and Mariana's testimony to Angelo's confession and the Duke's ruling. It is because the Duke cannot in this public setting ignore her demand for a hearing that, having hatched a plan with Isabella and Mariana to expose Angelo, he has called for a "dispatch of complaints" immediately upon his supposed return to Vienna (4.4.10–11). Plea bleeds into imperative in Isabella's cry for him to "Hear me, oh, hear me, here," the homophones underlining his responsibility to let her speak at this very moment, in this very place (5.1.35).

This is a scene to which Shakespearean drama often returns: a complainer, demanding justice from someone who has to give them a hearing and a response, here and now. The indignant Egeus hauls Hermia and her rival suitors before Theseus in the opening action of *A Midsummer Night's Dream* ("Full of vexation, come I, with complaint / Against my child, my daughter Hermia").[26] Before the Duke of Venice, Shylock demands the pound of flesh to which he is contractually entitled; a group of petitioners in *2 Henry VI* bear supplications for Duke Humphrey, Lord Protector that Queen Margaret intercepts and tears to pieces; Henry Bolingbroke brings Mowbray before Richard II and accuses him of conspiring against the state; Queen Catharine pleads to Henry VIII on behalf of his over-taxed subjects "in great grievance"; a sergeant complains to the rebel leader Jack Cade of his wife's rape ("Justice, justice, I pray you, sir, let me have justice of this fellow here"), only to have Cade order his legs and tongue cut off so he can no longer run or complain for justice.[27] Malvolio makes his complaint to Olivia— "Why have you suffered me to be imprisoned, /.../...Tell me, why?"—and vows revenge when she rules on behalf of the defendants, despite her lighthearted assurance that he would "be both the plaintiff and the judge / Of thine own cause."[28] Offstage in *Coriolanus*, Roman citizens "vent[ing] their complainings"

---

[25] *Measure for Measure*, 5.1.34, 22–8. With the exception of *Richard III*, all citations of Shakespeare's work are from *The Norton Shakespeare*.

[26] *A Midsummer Night's Dream*, 1.1.22–3.

[27] Respectively, these Shakespearean scenes are from *The Merchant of Venice*, Act 4, scene 1; the Folio edition of *2 Henry VI*, Act 1, scene 3; *Richard II*, Act 1, scene 1; *Henry VIII* 1.2.20; and the Quarto edition of *2 Henry VI*, 4.7. 71–2, the latter cited from the Norton Digital Edition.

[28] *Twelfth Night*, 5.1.329–32, 342–3.

70 THE DRAMA OF COMPLAINT

successfully petition the senate for tribunes to represent the people, while onstage Menenius distracts another group of aggrieved citizens by ploddingly recounting the fable of the belly that scornfully answers the complaints made against it by the "mutinous members" of the body.[29]

These scenes are variations on a basic formula. Each stages the presentation of a judicial cause: the making of an accusation to someone with the power to judge, the power to act, and the obligation to hear and respond.[30] Some are showcases for virtuoso performances of forensic rhetoric, known to Shakespeare and his contemporaries from texts such as the anonymous *Rhetorica ad Herennium* and Quintilian's *Institutio oratoria*, staples of the Tudor grammar school curriculum, and their distillations in English rhetorical treatises such as Thomas Wilson's *Arte of Rhetorique* (1553) and Henry Peacham's *Garden of Eloquence* (1577). All highlight forms of address that belong to the category of speech act that Peacham terms *querimonia*:

> This forme of speech as it riseth from the griefe which is suffered for injuries, so doth it tend by complaint & praier to seeke succour and redresse, by this forme billes of complaint are exhibited to the Courts of judgement, and supplications to Princes.[31]

The modes of complaining that Peacham describes—actions that were socially visible in early modern England and, unlike the kind of complaining we saw in the previous chapter, culturally sanctioned—are the social templates of the plaintive scripts of the Shakespearean scenes I have just described. Such acts include submitting bills of complaint to a court; presenting petitions to county magistrates, civic officials, Parliament, or the crown; and supplicating the powerful for relief or redress.[32] Included in this category, too, are those plaints for justice that could only be directed to a divine addressee and court: pleas for God's merciful judgment such as the Penitential Psalms, listed by Peacham as an example of *querimonia*; or the "earnest prayers" with "sobbes and teares to God" that the future King James I would describe in *The True Lawe of Free Monarchies* (1598) as subjects' only lawful recourse when faced with a lawless sovereign.[33]

---

[29] *Coriolanus*, 1.1.200, 140.

[30] For an account of Shakespeare's dramatic representations of the presentation of judicial causes, and the rhetorical traditions and training that inform these forensic speeches, see Skinner, *Forensic Shakespeare*.

[31] Peacham, *The Garden of Eloquence*, 66.

[32] Lorna Hutson, examining the records of the ecclesiastical courts, notes the "intensification of popular litigiousness" in the latter half of the sixteenth century. Hutson, *The Invention of Suspicion*, 4. On the conventions of legal bills of complaint and the processes they set in motion, see J.A. Guy, *The Court of Star Chamber*, and Meyer, "'Humblewise.'" On the form of the petition, and historical changes in this form over the course of the late sixteenth and early seventeenth century, see Patterson, *Reading between the Lines*, 57–79. For staged petitions, see Oldenberg, "The Petition on the Early English Stage."

[33] Peacham, *The Garden of Eloquence*, 66. James VI/I, *The True Lawe of Free Monarchies*, D3r, C1v.

ETHICAL DEMANDS 71

While this chapter draws on insights gleaned from scholarship on the historical genealogies, institutional norms, and social functions of legal complaint and petitionary discourse, my aim is neither to add to this body of work nor to further elucidate the relationship between early modern literary and legal discourses.[34] Rather, I suggest that these scenes demonstrate one of the ways in which (as Kevin Curran has argued) Shakespeare thinks *"with* or *through* law"* about philosophical—and specifically ethical—questions about selfhood.[35] As idealized and composite versions of the exchanges they evoke, I see these theatrical scenes of plaintive judicial address as more symbolically suggestive than mimetically precise, as Subha Mukherji has argued of the early modern theatrical representation of legal procedure more generally.[36] Following the lead of Mukherji, who suggests that theatrical enactments of trials signify "judicial power" above all else, I want to propose that Shakespearean scenes of judicial complaint emphasize issues of *responsibility*, and particularly the responsibility of the addressee to respond, and to respond well, to the complaint.[37] These scenes call attention to those responsibilities by compressing legal procedures spread across time, space, and a network of actors into a dyadic encounter between plaintiff and addressee.[38]

The responsibility to respond is also central to the legal and poetic forms of judicial complaint that inform those Shakespearean scenes. All stress a "radical asymmetry" of power which, as Leah Whittington suggests of ritual supplication, brings into focus the ethical burden of the privileged addressee.[39] The norms of supplication outlined by Whittington represent at its most extreme the power disparity similarly integral to petitioning and legal suits, in which disadvantaged plaintiffs rhetorically emphasize their addressees' obligation to God to discharge their obligations to those who complain to them for justice. A representative example of this rhetorical topos appears on the title page of "The Complaint of

---

[34] Among the many studies of Shakespeare's engagement with early modern legal discourse and culture are Hutson, *The Invention of Suspicion*; Wilson, *Theaters of Intention*; Mukherji, *Law and Representation*; Cormack, *A Power to Do Justice*; Syme, *Theatre and Testimony*; Curran, *Shakespeare's Legal Ecologies*; and Geng, *Communal Justice in Shakespeare's England*. On the intersections of petitionary discourse and literary complaint, see Kerrigan, *Motives of Woe*, 58–60. For studies of medieval and early Tudor intersections of legal, petitionary, and Parliamentary forms of complaint with literary complaint, see Scase, *Literature and Complaint* and Giancarlo, *Parliament and Literature*.

[35] Curran, *Shakespeare's Legal Ecologies*, 4, author's emphasis.

[36] See Mukherji, *Law and Representation*, 192.   [37] Mukherji, *Law and Representation*, 205.

[38] More specifically, these scenes compress discrete and prolonged investigatory procedures (the plaintiff's accusation, a defendant's replication, the testimonial evidence of witnesses, the judgment and sentencing) into one dramatic action, thus bringing the plaintiff and judge, into more intimate, concentrated, and dialogic relation than in any early modern court or trial setting. As Holger Schott Syme shows, in criminal trials under the common law, the plaintiff need not even be present in person during the trial, as his accusation could be read out loud by the clerk. See Syme, *Theatre and Testimony*, 29, 22.

[39] Whittington, *Renaissance Suppliants*, 16. In her account of the early modern afterlives of classical forms of ritual supplication, Whittington theorizes supplication as an asymmetrical but reciprocal structure of address, a notion that resonates in many ways with my notion of judicial complaint, although I am interested in asymmetries of power and obligation that correspond to institutional structures and offices.

72   THE DRAMA OF COMPLAINT

Roderick Mors," a mid-sixteenth century petition against enclosures and rising rents, which features a verse from the Psalms—"Oh Lord God, heare my prayer, & despyse not my complaynt"—that at once implies Parliament's godlike position and, less deferentially, reminds them of another arena in which the plaintiff's cry is certain to be heard. The petitionary rhetoric of humility and submission is often interlaced with such bursts of boldness, its frequent figures of *exclamatio*—defined in the *Ad Herennium* as "cry[ing] out to our hearers to listen attentively"—followed by warnings of judgment if this cry goes unheard.[40] *The Lamentable Complaint of the Communaltie* (1588), a supplication for ecclesiastical reform, warns Parliament that

> if we should not be heard and relieved at this time, God knoweth howe great a multitude of us might be lodged in hell, and there crie and curse without ceasing, in the midst of the flames of eternall fire remedilesse...if you depart with the neglect of this our petition concerning the glory of God and our safetie, a sting remaine in your consciences afterwards, and an incurable wound in your heartes in the day of your death.[41]

The writer projects the plaintive voice of the people demanding relief in the spatiotemporal presence of the scene of address ("this time") into a fiery hereafter in which—having been damned by Parliament's failure to provide a better ministry—that voice continues to cry out, now for vengeance. (Much like the "guiltless drops" of blood that Shakespeare's Henry V imagines being "every one a woe, a sore complaint / 'Gainst him whose wrongs gives edge unto the swords / That makes such waste in brief mortality" if his bishops lead him into an unjust war, or the mutilated "legs and arms and heads chopped off in a battle" that the English officer Williams imagines crying together for justice "at the latter day" if they "do not die well" in the King's unjust cause.)[42] As counterparts to the complaining voices of the damned, the writer of *The Lamentable Complaint* threatens a "sting" in the parliamentary addressees' consciences and an "incurable wound" in their hearts—traces of this ignored demand impressed upon their own souls, offering damning testimony to God.

And not only in the afterlife. Across early modern discourses, the refusal of vested authorities to give complaints a fair hearing epitomizes bad governance—poor stewardship at best, sovereign tyranny at worst—with dire consequences for the here and now. The violence that arises when complaint fails or is foreclosed is a standard trope of revenge tragedy, whose protagonists, as Peter Sacks notes, are

---

[40] Quoted in Skinner, *Forensic Shakespeare*, 76.
[41] *An humble petition*, N3r–5v. This is an augmented version of a supplication from 1585.
[42] *Henry V*, 1.2.25, 26–8; 4.1.126–7, 127–8, 134–5.

ETHICAL DEMANDS 73

often "unsuccessful plaintiffs" before they are revengers.[43] A commonplace held that complaints unheard by those in power would be answered by God in historical time. William Baldwin, the editor of the first edition of *A Mirror for Magistrates* (1559), suggests that rebellions constitute divine justice visited upon unjust monarchs, writing in his commentary on the rebel Jack Cade that

> Although the Devill raise them [rebels], yet God alwayes useth them to his glory, as a part of his justice. For whan Kinges and chiefe rulers suffer their under officers to misuse their subjectes, and will not heare nor remedy their peoples wronges whan they complaine, then suffereth God the rebell to rage, and to execute that part of his Justice, whiche the partiall Prince would not.[44]

Affirming this point is Cade's ghost, whose complaint monologue describes the cause of the Kentish rebellion Cade led against Henry VI thus: the men of Kent "their griefes unto the King complaine," and he "being deafe (as men say) on that eare /.../ Refused roughly our requestes to heare."[45] Baldwin returns to the power of unheard grievance in the passage of commentary that separates the complaint of the ghost of William Collingbourne, executed for writing a poem critical of Richard III, from the complaint of Richard's ghost. "The peoples grudge: the forerunner commonly of rulers destruction," he notes, "Vox populi, vox Dei, in this case is not so famous a proverbe, as true: the experience of all times doe approve it."[46] In a line especially resonant with the events of Shakespeare's play, Baldwin suggests of Richard III and his supporters that "They should also have bene warned of their owne sinnes, which call continually for Gods vengeaunce, which never faileth to fall on their neckes sodainly and horribly, unles it bee stayed with hearty repentaunce."[47] Here, wicked deeds are imagined to leave complaining traces that cry to a responsive divine addressee, much like the stinging consciences and wounded hearts of the unresponsive members of Parliament.

As these examples show, the image of justice that animates the forms on which Shakespearean scenes of judicial complaint were modeled—the idea that complaints *must* be heard—reflects the belief that the social order and its hierarchal relations are underpinned and guaranteed by divine law. This framework is especially relevant to *Richard III*'s engagement with the sixteenth-century historiographical narrative of Richard III's fall and Henry VII's rise as the divinely ordained conclusion to a long and lamentable English tragedy.[48] Scenes of judicial

---

[43] Sacks, "Where Words Prevail Not," 577.   [44] *The Mirour for Magistrates*, 159r.
[45] *The Mirour for Magistrates*, 157r–v.   [46] *The Mirour for Magistrates*, 229v.
[47] *The Mirour for Magistrates*, 229v.
[48] The classic articulation of this so-called Tudor Myth is E.M.W. Tillyard's in *Shakespeare's History Plays*, 321. This interpretation is (unsurprisingly) voiced by the newly crowned Henry VII in *Richard III*'s closing speech. On the ubiquity of this explanation in Shakespeare's historiographical sources, see Walsh, *Shakespeare*, 159.

74   THE DRAMA OF COMPLAINT

complaint in both *Richard II* and *Richard III*—the plays that respectively dramatize what Hall frames as the Original Sin of deposition and its redemption by the rise of the Tudors—directly reference the idea that God hears the complaints for justice that authorities will not hear. "Where then, alas, may I complain myself?" the Duchess of Gloucester asks John of Gaunt in the second scene of *Richard II*, angered at his refusal to take revenge on Richard for the murder of Gloucester, her "exclaims" notwithstanding; "To God," he responds.[49] The phrase is a stock formula for expressing the impossibility of procuring institutional justice in situations in which, as Gaunt puts it, "correction lieth in those hands / Which made the fault that we cannot correct."[50] The exchange maps the coming "correction"— Bolingbroke's rebellion—onto the space of silence where an answer to the Duchess's complaint should be. Similarly, in *Richard III*, Shakespeare frames Richard's attack of conscience as the long-deferred answer to a series of hitherto unanswered judicial complaints, including prayers and curses that invoke divine justice. Between the dramatic vocalization of these female-voiced complaints— Shakespeare's innovative addition to the Richard story—and the spectacular appearance of the ghosts, even some critics who generally see Shakespeare's history plays as exposing rather than echoing ideology have read *Richard III* as a less-than-critical treatment of the so-called Tudor myth.[51] Taking the opposite position, Brian Walsh and Lynne Magnusson argue that the play deconstructs its own seemingly providential conclusion by self-consciously calling attention to the human agency responsible for creating that end, from the theatrical labor that produces the ghosts to the potency of the speech acts that call for divine intervention.[52] My own reading of the connection between the complaints to God about Richard and the ghosts' visitation sits aslant both sides of the question of the play's relation to the matter of providential justice. While I would not argue that the play especially challenges the metaphysical framework that its characters assume, I do think that it remains in the conceptual and theatrical background of the ghost scene. The dramatic emphasis in all the play's scenes of judicial complaint falls heavily on the embodied dynamics of the dyadic encounters between Richard and the complainers. In staging Richard's experience of conscience as the answer to a chorus of complaining ghosts—in the context of a tragedy that has repeatedly signified Richard's tyranny through scenes of unanswered judicial complaints heavy with the expectation of an answer—Shakespeare frames the justice that his victims get as the justice that *their speaking* to him compels. This choice calls attention not to a transcendent, incorporeal power

---

[49] *Richard II*, 1.2.42, 2, 43.   [50] *Richard II*, 1.2.4–5.

[51] On Shakespeare's invention of the play's scenes of female complaint see Brooks, "*Richard III*, Unhistorical Amplifications." On *Richard III* and the Tudor Myth, see Rackin, *Stages of History*.

[52] Walsh, *Shakespeare*, 161. Magnusson, "Grammatical Theatricality in *Richard III*." Linda Charnes describes the ending as "hyperreal" and conspicuously overemplotted. See Charnes, *Notorious Identity*, 27.

behind the scenes of history but rather to the force of subjects speaking to each other, here and now.

2. Response and Responsibility in *Richard III*

Judicial complaint is vital to Shakespeare's construction of the relationship between Richard and his victims: it is the exemplary speech act assigned to the latter, and Richard is consistently represented as its cause and subject. This is exactly the role in which Richard casts himself in the first act of the play, as he accuses Queen Elizabeth and her kinsmen of having maligned him to Edward, all the while protesting his innocence with his characteristic theatrics:

> They do me wrong, and I will not endure it!
> Who is it that complains unto the King
> That I, forsooth, am stern and love them not?
>
> (1.3.42–44)

Characters injured by Richard consistently articulate their desire for justice as a demand for an answer to their complaints. Fittingly, the justice they receive in the ghost scene—Richard's experience of conscience—takes the form of a response that answers not only to the ghosts' complaints, but to the many unanswered judicial complaints that come before them.

From its beginning, the play situates Richard as the cause of complaints that cry out for justice to no avail. The first of the complaints performed against him, like the last, comes from a dead body. Lady Anne's funeral lament turns to forensic rhetoric as she commands Richard, in the presence of the other mourners, to gaze upon the inert corpse of Henry VI, which she presents as testamentary evidence:

> If thou delight to view thy heinous deeds,
> Behold this pattern of thy butcheries.
> —O gentlemen, see, see dead Henry's wounds
> Open their congealed mouths, and bleed afresh.
> —Blush, blush, thou lump of foul deformity,
> For 'tis thy presence that exhales this blood
> From cold and empty veins where no blood dwells.
> Thy deeds, inhuman and unnatural,
> Provokes this deluge most unnatural.
>
> (1.2.53–61)

Voicing the popular belief that wounds would weep blood in the presence of their perpetrator, Anne casts Henry's wounds as involuntary plaintiffs, their "congealed

76 THE DRAMA OF COMPLAINT

mouths" opening to accuse Richard—material "exhaled," forcibly drawn out, by his mere presence.[53] Her own complaint ventriloquizes theirs: "O God! Which this blood mad'st, revenge his death. / O earth! Which this blood drink'st, revenge his death" (1.2.62–63).[54] In claiming that Richard has "Filled [the earth] with cursing cries and deep exclaims," Anne imagines him as the father of complaints, verbal offspring that, along with their "unnatural" blood-brothers, prove his inhumanity (1.2.52). The bleeding wounds are soon joined by other plaintive expressions of injury: the curses of Queen Margaret ("The worm of conscience still begnaw thy soul"); the outcries of the Duchess of York, Clarence's children, and Queen Elizabeth ("not barren to bring forth complaints") for the deaths of Edward IV and Clarence; and the laments of the Duchess of York and Queen Elizabeth, who mourn the murder of the two young princes by complaining to God of "England's lawful earth, / Unlawfully made drunk with innocents' blood" (1.3.221; 2.2.67; 4.4.29–30).[55] These punctual performances create what the Duchess of York calls "scene[s] of rude impatience," as their impassioned speakers demand that the heavens make Richard answer for his crimes (2.2.38). The apparent bootlessness of these curses and laments will be recuperated by the ghosts' accusatory complaints, which retroactively endow them with a sense of efficacy, in a play uniquely interested in the potency of the speech acts of the (relatively) disempowered.[56]

Between the women's seemingly impotent lamentations and the ghosts' efficacious accusations the play stages an especially voluble scene of public complaining in which Richard's power is momentarily "intercept[ed]"—cut off, prevented, seized—by the Duchess and Elizabeth. Speaking in what Magnusson identifies as the language of forensic oratory, the women stop Richard with their "exclaims" as he marches with his men to meet Richmond.[57]

> DUCHESS ...be not tongue-tied. Go with me,
> And in the breath of bitter words let's smother
> My damned son, that thy two sweet sons smothered.
> > [*Trumpet sounds.*]
> The trumpet sounds. Be copious in exclaims.

---

[53] On wounds as legal evidence, see Mukherji, *Law and Representation*, 82–8.

[54] On *Richard III* and revenge, see Woodbridge, *English Revenge Drama*, 26–9, 75–80.

[55] On Margaret's curses see Bevington, "'Why Should Calamity be Full of Words.'" On Margaret's resemblance to the iconic figures of female lament in Greek drama, Tassi, "Wounded Maternity, Sharp Revenge."

[56] The extent to which female lamentation in Shakespearean drama suggests a lack of agency or constitutes a form of agency has generated much discussion in feminist criticism of the plays. On lamentation as exemplifying a decline in female agency in the tetralogies, see Howard and Rackin, *Engendering a Nation*, 120. Gina Bloom, by contrast, suggests that the laments of *Richard III*'s female characters possess force through their material link, via breath, to the curse. See Bloom, *Voice in Motion*, 94.

[57] See Magnusson, "Shakespearean Tragedy and the Language of Lament," 128.

> Enter KING RICHARD and his Train [including CATESBY],
> marching with drums and trumpets.
> KING RICHARD   Who intercepts me in my expedition?
> .....
> QUEEN ELIZABETH Hid'st thou that forehead with a
> golden crown
> Where should be graven, if that right were right,
> The slaughter of the prince that owed that crown
> And the dire death of my two sons and brothers?
> Tell me, thou villain slave, where are my children?
> DUCHESS Thou toad, thou toad, where is thy brother Clarence,
> And little Ned Plantagenet his son?
> QUEEN ELIZABETH Where is the gentle Rivers,
> Vaughan, Grey?
> DUCHESS Where is kind Hastings?
> KING RICHARD A flourish, trumpets! Strike alarum, drums!
> Let not the heavens hear these tell-tale women
> Rail on the Lord's anointed. Strike, I say! *Flourish. Alarums.*
> Either be patient and entreat me fair,
> Or with the clamorous report of war
> Thus will I drown your exclamations.
>
> (4.4.132–54)

This exchange beautifully illustrates what Bonnie Honig sees as the political nature of public grieving exemplified in Greek tragedy, in which mourning operates as a form of "resistance to injustice," and a means of seeking "rectification of wrong and vengeance for it"—a form of resistance that is particularly potent, she argues, when such grieving symbolically interrupts the normal routines of power.[58] In performance, an audience would likely recognize that the rhetorical questions the Duchess and Elizabeth have only just addressed to the absent dead ("Edward Plantagenet, why are you dead?" [4.4.19]) resurface here as accusations they demand that Richard answer. At once underlining the institutional bankruptcy of the law under Richard's rule and co-opting its procedures, as Alison Thorne has argued, the women improvise their own scene of judicial complaint.[59] Their speaking, as Cristina León Alfar points out, is an instance of parrhesia, as Foucault understands it, a form of speaking truth to power that Alfar argues is also "a form of care," predicated on the conviction that "the truth will serve an ethics of responsibility for others."[60] The potency of their complaining is rendered perceptible in Richard's response. He will literally *not hear* the women's complaints,

---

[58] Honig, *Antigone, Interrupted*, 120.   [59] Thorne, "'O, lawful let it be.'"
[60] Alfar, "Speaking Truth to Power," 789, 790.

78   THE DRAMA OF COMPLAINT

nor does he dare let those complaints be heard by heaven: the women must either "be patient"—which means not complaining, as Chapter 1 showed—or be drowned out by the trumpet and drum, the competing sounds of *his* power.[61] The long, radically incongruous verbal exchange with Elizabeth that follows this encounter, in which Richard persuades her to marry her daughter to him, reflects Richard's effort to regain control of the rhetorical situation following this humiliating public agon. The Duchess likens and links this war of words to actual battle through her parting curse: "take with thee my most grievous curse, / Which in the day of battle tire thee more / Than all the complete armour that thou wear'st" (4.4.188–90).

Among the remarkable things about the ghost scene is its inversion of the relational dynamics of the rest of the play, its continuation of what the Duchess and Elizabeth have started: here—against character—Richard is strikingly unable to command the stage or the rhetorical situation. It is the ghosts who steal the scene, in no small part because, to borrow Walsh's words, they "have a stage *presence*."[62] Their bearing is reminiscent of the vengeful ghosts of classical literature, and the conditions of their dramatic appearing recall the promise made by the speaker of Ovid's curse poem *Ibis* (here in a 1569 translation) who vows to return as a ghost who will

> seeme t'appeare to thee, to wake thee from thy sleepe
> And last what so thou dost, before thy face and eyes, I'll bee;
> And wyll complaine, so that no where, in quiet thou shalt bee.[63]

The scene is staged not only to emphasize the ghosts' externality from Richard, but also their singularity, the distinction of each ghost from the others, each with a personal grievance. Nine of the eleven—the Ghosts of Clarence, Rivers, Grey, Vaughan, the Princes Edward and Richard, Hastings, Lady Anne, Buckingham—have appeared earlier in the play as living characters, and are personated here by the same actors (they are joined and preceded in their complaints by the Ghosts of Prince Edward and his father King Henry VI, both killed by Richard in *3 Henry VI*). While, as John Jowett suggests, the lighting conditions of the Elizabethan theater may have made the ghosts "individually recognizable by face and costume," voice is the primary medium for communicating both their externality and their singularity.[64] Their bodies and voices are perfect examples of how the material characteristics of "signal-information" transmit "semantic information" in theatrical performance.[65] Appearing before Richard in the order of their

---

[61] For a corrective to readings that attribute the force of these female complaints to community and empathy—and that highlights instead the women's matching of Richard's own "self-serving...rhetorical power"—see DiGangi, "Competitive Mourning and Female Agency," 429.

[62] Walsh, *Shakespeare*, 155, author's emphasis.   [63] *Ovid his Invective against Ibis*, C2r.

[64] *The Tragedy of King Richard III*, ed. Jowett, 340, note to 5.4.96.1.

[65] Elam, *The Semiotics of Theatre and Drama*, 37. "This semanticization process extends beyond signal, message and channel to include the very *transmitters* or even, in certain performances, the *sources* of communication. The actor's voice and body, considered as signal-transmitters, are rendered

ETHICAL DEMANDS 79

deaths, each ghost speaks first to him, then to Richmond.[66] Each identifies him or herself and commands Richard to "Think on me," a phrase whose effect may be especially heightened if the stress is placed on that last word: "Think on *me*" (and *me*, and *me*, and *me*).

Shakespeare stages the ghosts' visitation of Richard as an interruption: they invade the privacy of his tent, where he is alone after having twice asked his men for solitude ("Leave me. /.../... Leave me, I say"), and as a vengeful chorus they break into his sleep, then awake him from it (5.3.76–78). The ghosts' complaints recount the nature of the injury, the date and location of its occurrence, and the perpetrator, evoking the format of legal bills of complaint. As if taking a page from Quintilian's advice to the prosecuting advocate to "make the charge seem as outrageous, or even, if possible, as pitiable as possible," their testimony highlights what Rebecca Lemon describes as Richard's characteristic "legal deformity," from his manufacture of evidence to his subversion of the rules of succession, his execution of subjects without trial to his ordered killing of children.[67] Fulfilling Anne's claim that his wounds would open their mouths to accuse Richard, the Ghost of Henry VI complains to Richard that "my anointed body / By thee was punched full of deadly holes" (5.3.124–25). The Ghost of Prince Edward also presents his stabbed body as evidence. And—in an echo of the Duchess's "tiring" curse that also gestures to the way they press around him—almost all the ghosts command Richard to "Let me sit heavy on thy soul tomorrow." I include their complaints in full here, to convey a sense of their weight:

> GHOST [of PRINCE EDWARD] (*to Richard*)
> Let me sit heavy on thy soul tomorrow.
> Think how thou stab'st me in my prime of youth
> At Tewkesbury. Despair, therefore, and die.
>
> ....
> GHOST [of HENRY VI] (*to Richard*)
> When I was mortal, my anointed body
> By thee was punched full of deadly holes.
> Think on the Tower and me. Despair and die.
> Harry the Sixth bids thee despair and die.
>
> ....

pertinent to the text in their materiality, since his personal stature, vocal qualities and physical idiosyncrasies, however incidental to the drama, will influence the spectator's perception and decoding of messages" (38, author's emphasis).

[66] As Jowett notes in his edition of the play, the exception to this order is Hastings, whose appearance between the Princes and Anne in Q suggests that the same boy actor may have played one of the princes and Anne. (In F, Hastings enters before the Princes.) See *Richard III*, ed. Jowett, 339, note to 5.4.96.1.

[67] Quintilian, *Institutio Oratoria*, 6.1.15, in *The Orator's Education, Volume III: Books 6–8*, 25. Lemon, "Tyranny and the State of Exception," 112.

80   THE DRAMA OF COMPLAINT

GHOST [of CLARENCE (*to Richard*)]
Let me sit heavy on thy soul tomorrow,
I, that was washed to death with fulsome wine,
Poor Clarence, by thy guile betrayed to death.
Tomorrow in the battle think on me,
And fall thy edgeless sword. Despair and die.

....

[GHOST of RIVERS (*to Richard*)]
Let me sit heavy on thy soul tomorrow,
Rivers that died at Pomfret. Despair and die.
[GHOST of] GREY [(*to Richard*)]
Think upon Grey, and let thy soul despair.
[GHOST of] VAUGHAN [(*to Richard*)]
Think upon Vaughan, and with guilty fear
Let fall thy lance. Despair and die.

....

GHOSTS [of PRINCES] (*to Richard*)
Dream on thy cousins smothered in the Tower.
Let us be lead within thy bosom, Richard,
And weigh thee down to ruin, shame and death.
Thy nephews' souls bid thee despair and die.

....

GHOST [of HASTINGS (*to Richard*)]
Bloody and guilty, guiltily awake,
And in a bloody battle end thy days.
Think on Lord Hastings. Despair and die.

....

GHOST [of ANNE] (*to Richard*)
Richard, thy wife, that wretched Anne, thy wife,
That never slept a quiet hour with thee,
Now fills thy soul with perturbations.
Tomorrow in the battle think on me,
And fall thy edgeless sword. Despair and die.

....

GHOST [of BUCKINGHAM] (*to Richard*)
O, in the battle think on Buckingham,
And die in terror of thy guiltiness.
Dream on, dream on, of bloody deeds and death.
Fainting, despair; despairing, yield thy breath.

(5.3.118–72)

Richard's conscience arrives on the scene in the form of his waking cry:
"O coward conscience, how dost thou afflict me!" (5.3.179). Shakespeare thus

positions his experience of conscience as a response—literally an answer—to the ghosts' complaints. An unmistakeable echo of Clarence's experience of conscience shortly before his death in Act 1, this moment directly inverts the earlier scene's representation of the causal relation between complaint and conscience. There, the imprisoned Clarence describes to his keeper a nightmare in which he has died and gone to the underworld, where he meets the complaining shades of his father-in-law Warwick, whom he betrayed, and Henry VI's son Prince Edward, whom he helped to kill, "shriek[ing]" for revenge (1.4.43–63). Nodding to the early modern commonplace that identified classical representations of ghosts haunting wrongdoers as poetic fictions for a guilty conscience *avant la lettre*, Shakespeare represents the complaining ghosts of Warwick and Prince Edward as the effects of Clarence's guilty conscience, evidence that he has "done these things, / That now give evidence against my soul" (1.4.66–67).[68] Moreover, these ghosts are doubly fictive: addressing Clarence from what he calls the place "which poets write of," they exist in a dream of a poetic fiction (1.4.46). What we see in Clarence's account of his dream, in short, is exactly the traditional logic of conscience—and the conventional dramatic form for staging conscience—that I am suggesting Shakespeare creatively rearranges in the ghost scene, which distinguishes the complaints of others from Richard's conscience, and places the ghosts (including the markedly embodied ghost of Prince Edward) outside the frame of Richard's dream. Rather than simply returning to the classical model of the vengeful complaining ghost highlighted in the *Ibis* or imagining those classical ghosts purely as metaphors for conscience, as in Clarence's dream, the ghost scene combines the two in a new way, making the complaining ghosts of classical revenge narratives the external cause of conscience.

Richard wakes into the judicial scene of complaint created by the ghosts. He repeats their accusations; he plays the part of the defendant, refuting the accusations; finally, he speaks as the judge, sentencing himself to despair:

> Is there a murderer here? No. Yes, I am.
> Then fly! What, from myself? Great reason why?
> Lest I revenge. What, myself upon myself?
> Alack, I love myself. Wherefore? For any good
> That I myself have done unto myself?
> O, no. Alas, I rather hate myself,
> For hateful deeds committed by myself.
> I am a villain. Yet I lie; I am not.
> Fool, of thyself speak well. Fool, do not flatter.
> My conscience hath a thousand several tongues,

---

[68] For this commonplace, see Woolton, *Of the Conscience*, E4r.

82   THE DRAMA OF COMPLAINT

> And every tongue brings in a several tale,
> And every tale condemns me for a villain.
> Perjury, perjury in the highest degree;
> Murder, stern murder, in the direst degree.
> All several sins, all used in each degree,
> Throng to the bar, crying all, 'Guilty, guilty!'
> I shall despair.
>
> (5.3.184–200)

In the ghosts' complaints and Richard's response, audiences may have recognized the inversion of a stock formula for the self-examination early modern magistrates were encouraged to conduct, searching their own consciences to discover "Whether such as he could not rightlie and lawfully oppresse and make dispatch of, hee have caused and procured by others to be trecherouslie accused, apprehended, wronged, hurt, or by anie manner of meane, brought within the compasse of daunger."[69] Here these are the accusations made against Richard by others. The dialogic rhetorical structure and bewildered tone of the speech registers the external origin of these complaints, tracking the way Richard, as the accused, not only comes to claim responsibility for his deeds, but also to assume—to take as his own—the ghosts' desire for vengeance, for as he will say, he "find[s] in myself no pity to myself" (5.3.203). Commanded to "guiltily awake," Richard finds himself guilty, in both the legal and emotional senses of the word (5.3.154). The soliloquy enacts that process, its climax a decision ("I shall despair") that repeats the language of the ghosts' demand ("Despair and die") as an echo, an answer that is also a trace of their vanished presence—his words a ghost of the ghosts' words, as it were.[70] In this final scene of judicial complaint, Richard is compelled at last to answer for his crimes by answering a long line of unanswered complaints made against him. The ghosts get what they demand: a response in the form of justice, and justice in the form of a response. It is in this scene of dramatically external address that Shakespeare situates Richard's experience of conscience and its ethical demand.

3. Conscience and the Voices of Complaint

I have been suggesting that Shakespeare represents Richard's experience of conscience as the response to unanswered judicial complaints. Now I want to consider the significance of the fact that that response takes the form of conscience, the fulcrum of early modern ethical subjectivity and responsibility. In routing

---

[69] [Andreas Hyperius], *The True Tryall and Examination*, D3v–D4r.
[70] See Ames, *Conscience, with the Power and Cases Thereof*, F3v.

ethical thought about conscience through the social dynamics of judicial complaint, and in reconfiguring the more typical relation between conscience and complaint that such scenes imagine, the play articulates new ways of thinking about ethical responsibility and the demand to which it responds.

As we have seen, conscience was more commonly conceptualized in early modern England through the figure of an internal or private scene of judicial complaint witnessed only by God. As Camille Wells Slights has argued, in the wake of the abolition of auricular confession and absolution, conscience became the privileged means by which one might know one's standing with God.[71] The most familiar imagined scenes of this faculty of the understanding common to "all reasonable creatures" were thus ones of self-examination and reflection, in which a person engages their conscience in dialogue to better know themselves (as Isabella, supplicating Angelo to pardon Claudio, asks him to "Go to your bosom, / Knock there, and ask your heart what it doth know / That's like my brother's fault").[72] Manuals like *The True Tryall and Examination of a Mans owne Selfe* (1586) instruct the reader to "diligently and carefully searcheth out, tryeth, groapeth, and inwardly rippeth up everie corner of his conscience," and to "enter into deep consideration with himselfe, and remember how and which way he hath offended, and brought his neighbour into any hazarde, perill, or daunger."[73] Not that conscience requires an invitation to speak its truth. "Your Consciences know you, though happily you be strangers to them," the minister Samuel Ward warns, "they compasse your paths, your lying downe, and accustomed wayes."[74] This is the figurative economy in which the trope of conscience as an internal voice of complaint circulates: when conscience is guilty, evil, or wicked—common descriptors for conscience metonymic for the condition of the person to whom it belongs—it complains, whether one asks to hear from it or not.[75]

Reflecting its status as "an other person within," neither identical with nor separable from the self, guilty conscience speaks in what were imagined to be two different but simultaneous scenes of private judicial complaint: as God's surrogate, it complains *to* the person in whom it resides, accusing them of wrongdoing, and as that person's consciousness of sin (a "notary," a "looking glass,"

---

[71] Slights, *The Casuistical Tradition*.

[72] Perkins, *A Discourse of Conscience*, 3. Shakespeare, *Measure for Measure* 2.2.137–9. At the same time, however, as Christopher Tilmouth has argued, Seneca, Montaigne, and other writers of moral philosophy encouraged readers to imagine their consciences as being exposed to the shame-inducing gaze of another person, too, to see themselves as they might be seen by other (human) judges. See Tilmouth, "Shakespeare's open consciences."

[73] [Hyperius], *The True Tryall*, A1v, D8r.

[74] Ward, *Balme from Gilead to Recover Conscience*, 70.

[75] Perkins describes the guilty conscience (whose "property" is "all the power it hath to accuse & condemne") as a corollary to the universal inheritance of Original Sin: whereas "in the estate of inno-cencie" Adam's conscience "did onely excuse & could not accuse him for any thing," he writes, now "All mens consciences since the fall are evill, and none are good but by grace." Perkins, *A Discourse of Conscience*, 150, 96, 97.

84   THE DRAMA OF COMPLAINT

a "witness"), it testifies *against* them before God.[76] Calvin illuminates the simultaneity of these two different judicial scenes in which the guilty conscience drives its accusations home:

> so when they [men] have a feeling of the judgement of God, as a witnesse joyned with them, which doth not suffer them to hide their sinnes but that they be drawen accused to the judgement seate of God, that same feeling is called Conscience. For it is a certaine meane betweene God and man, because it suffereth not man to suppresse in himselfe that which hee knoweth but pursueth him so farre till it bring him to giltines.[77]

Guilty conscience is both the accusation and the feeling of being accused, the voice that cries out to God at the same time that it pricks, stings, and gnaws the self. As reminders of the primordial and irrevocable bond to the moral law instantiated at creation, those proverbial pricks and stings—the affective counterparts of conscience's complaints—reenact the original wounding of the law's inscription and conscience's installation, when man's binding attachment to God was first formed. ("The law was once given to Adam and imprinted in his heart in his first creation... when his conscience was bound by the law, all were bound in him. And though this knowledge be lost by mans default, yet the bond remaines still on Gods part," Perkins writes.)[78] Early modern writers understand something to resound in conscience's accusatory address that is not simply a reminder of a specific transgression but of the ethical demand of that formative relational bond itself, which the wrongdoer has effectively denied but God remembers. Thus Calvin suggests that even the reprobate are forced to feel the pricks of conscience, not as instrumental spurs to repentance, but simply as a horrifying foretaste of their fate—for, as the petitionary discourse we examined earlier demonstrates, the double-facing private scenes of complaint and judgment that occur throughout the course of a person's lifetime are also previews of that final, all-too-public scene of judicial complaint, the Last Judgment.[79]

Conscience is always there, so to speak, as it was understood to be "inseperable from the soule, immoveable from the subject"—a thing one cannot be without—but what early modern clerics and poets emphasize is its phenomenological scenes of appearing and address, when the constitutive "division between the conscience and the man himselfe" is experienced as a felt reality.[80] These are

---

[76] Perkins, *A Discourse of Conscience*, 7. On the ubiquitous tropes of conscience as a notary and mirror, see Slights, "Notaries, Sponges, and Looking-glasses."

[77] Calvin, *Institution of Christian Religion*, Oo4v–Oo5r (3.19.15). On Calvin's pessimism about conscience's capacity to guide men aright, see Strohm, *Conscience: A Very Short Introduction*, 26–32.

[78] Perkins, *A Discourse of Conscience*, 29.

[79] Calvin, *A Commentarie upon...Romanes*, 88r.

[80] Ward, *Balme from Gilead*, 14. Perkins, *A Discourse of Conscience*, 96.

ETHICAL DEMANDS   85

moments of ethical pressure: moments when a choice pits desire against obligation, and conscience offers unwelcome counsel (as Lancelet Gobbo, arguing with his "hard conscience" about his wish to abandon Shylock, finds that "the fiend gives the more friendly counsel") or when a sin has been committed and conscience is compelled to complain.[81] Writers often depict the divided self in two representational figures, displacing the internal voice of conscience onto another body. Sometimes this is done imaginatively, as when Ward commands his congregants' consciences to "Follow them home therefore, cry aloud in their ears, and bosomes," sometimes in the mode of allegory, as in the morality play tradition, and sometimes in theatrical form—for instance, in the figure of a complaining ghost.[82] The archetypal Shakespearean ghost that is theatrical shorthand for a guilty conscience is the Ghost of Banquo, whose mere presence affirms Macbeth's tormented conscience.[83] The ghost of the murdered Duke Humphrey that Cardinal Beaufort sees by his deathbed in *2 Henry VI* need not even appear on stage: the Cardinal's ravings, couched in the language of the law—"Bring me unto my trial when you will /.../ Oh, torture me no more: I will confess"—are sufficient indices of its accusations.[84] The horror these Shakespearean characters experience chimes with Perkins' vivid description of the guilty conscience pursuing the fugitive sinner:

> An evill conscience is the greatest enemie a man can have, because it doth execute all the parts of judgement against him. It is the Lords sergeant. God neede not send out processe by any of his creatures for man: the conscience within man will arrest him, and bring him before God. It is the gayler to keepe man in prison in bolts & irons, that he may be forth-coming at the day of judgement. It is the witness to accuse him, the judge to condemne him, the hangman to execute him, and the flashings of the fire of hell to torment him.[85]

The more a wrongdoer denies its ethical demand, the more vehemently conscience asserts its presence.

As I noted earlier, the end of the historical Richard III's life was discussed in exactly these terms by sixteenth-century historians, clerics, and poets, for whom his dream served as an instructive object lesson about the tenacity with which conscience makes its accusing voice heard ("which prick of conscience although it strike not always," as Shakespeare's source Edward Hall admits).[86] Hall's remark cuts to the significance of the anecdote: despite the fact that some people seem to

---

[81] Shakespeare, *The Merchant of Venice*, 2.2.24, 25–6.
[82] Ward, *Balme from Gilead*, 70, 71. On the oratorical practice of invoking an addressee's conscience by ventriloquizing its voice, see Kuchar, "Ecstatic Donne." On conscience as a character in sixteenth-century texts, see Streeter, "The Beleaguered Virtue."
[83] Shakespeare, *Macbeth*, Act 3, scene 4.   [84] Shakespeare, *2 Henry VI*, 3.3.8–11.
[85] Perkins, *A Discourse of Conscience*, 165.   [86] Hall, *Union*, 53.

86   THE DRAMA OF COMPLAINT

never experience this "little god sitting in the middle of mens hearts"—the "deity in my bosom" that *The Tempest*'s Antonio claims he "feel[s] not"—the story affirms the bindingness of the moral law.[87] For these writers, the villainous Richard offers a compelling historical example of a formerly sleeping, benumbed, or seared conscience waking up and beginning to prick, the king's sudden and unwilled responsiveness to its complaints the form in which he is forced to acknowledge his responsibility.[88]

Shakespeare too treats Richard's experience of conscience as an exemplary scene of address that reveals, precisely as a limit case, the unbreakable bond that conscience incarnates. But instead of theatrically fleshing out the metaphor of the voice of conscience, Shakespeare uses theatrical form—namely, the template of the judicial complaint scene—to simultaneously reimagine the historical anecdote and remap the conventional scene of plaintive address associated with conscience. The scene is a prime example of how, as Curran suggests, "law afforded Shakespeare a conceptual language through which the self could be portrayed as part of a vital and interdependent world of things."[89] It also evinces what Patrick Gray has argued is Shakespeare's tendency to represent humans as *ethically* vulnerable—that is, "vulnerable to others' moral judgement of their character, just as they are vulnerable to being physically wounded," a kind of "interpellation" that makes the other's judgment "the ground of self-awareness."[90] In the theatrical experiment of the ghost scene we can see the outlines of a Shakespearean thought experiment: what if conscience were the *response to* a complaining voice, the *effect* of having been addressed? What if it is *through* and not *as* an address that conscience appears to consciousness? What if (as Freud would later suggest in another register) conscience is an experience that originates *outside* the self, in the external pressures of social relationality rather than the internal presence of the divine?

These are precisely the ideas that *Richard III* has broached even before the ghost scene, in the laymen's discourse on conscience between the two murderers hired to kill Clarence in Act 1, a conversation that, like Clarence's dream, reveals the extent of the play's interest in the experience of conscience. This early exchange offers a phenomenology of conscience that the ghost scene will echo

---

[87] Perkins, *A Discourse of Conscience*, 10. Shakespeare, *The Tempest*, 2.1.170–1. Early modern writers acknowledge that in its experiential dimensions conscience might well go unfelt until the end of a person's life—or even, in some cases, until the afterlife, when it gives its testimony at the Last Judgment. Hence Perkins' warning to "Atheists" that "they have that in them which will convince them of the truth of the godhead will they nill they, *either in life or death.*" Perkins, *A Discourse of Conscience*, 9, emphasis added.

[88] Perkins describes "benumbed," "sleeping," or "seared" consciences as all, to varying degrees, "dead," the general category for the conscience "which doeth not accuse for any sinne." Perkins, *A Discourse of Conscience*, 9, 152.

[89] Curran, *Shakespeare's Legal Ecologies*, 11.

[90] Gray, *Shakespeare and the Fall of the Roman Republic*, 222, 223. For Gray's resignification of the Althusserian term "interpellation" in the direction of horizontal relationality, see also Gray, "Shakespeare versus Aristotle."

ETHICAL DEMANDS 87

and deepen, for here—as there—it is a *word*, uttered out loud, that makes conscience appear. The second murderer, in a miscalculated verbal swagger, has crowed to the other murderer that Clarence will be unable to accuse his killers of cowardice "until the great Judgement Day" (1.4.103–4). But these words no sooner leave his mouth than they turn on their speaker, and press their way into him: "the urging of that word 'Judgement' hath bred a kind of remorse in me," he says, wonderingly (1.4.106–7). (This remorse grows into full-blown repentance by the end of the scene, nurtured by Clarence's plea for the murderers to listen to "that holy feeling in your souls" [1.4.249]). The murderer identifies this newly conceived remorse, propagated by a word, as the residual trace of conscience ("some certain dregs of conscience are yet within me" [1.4.121–22]). Hence his rueful complaint about living with conscience:

> I'll not meddle with it; it is a dangerous thing. It makes a man a coward: a man cannot steal but it accuseth him…'Tis a blushing, shamefaced spirit that mutinies in a man's bosom. It fills a man full of obstacles. It made me once restore a purse of gold that I found. It beggars any man that keeps it. It is turned out of all towns and cities for a dangerous thing, and every man that means to live well endeavours to trust to himself, and live without it.   (1.4.133–42)

The murderer describes conscience as a mutinous spirit in the bosom, an enemy within that must be excised if one is to "live well"—that is, with autonomy and without these dangerous "dregs" of this alien invader. In demonstrating how conscience returns, re-entering the city-self through "the urging of that word 'Judgement,'" the pressure of which breaches its gates, the scene suggests that that recurring breach in the self—an imprint of ethical pressure—is just what conscience is.[91]

In the ghost scene, too, conscience appears at the "urging" of a word, "several tale[s]" pleading for and demanding justice and threatening to dissolve Richard's fantasmatic autonomy. Ned Lukacher has claimed that in Shakespeare's plays, "conscience names a relation into which not every human being is called a priori," a felt relation with one's own alterity that one can only enter traumatically—as, I would suggest, we see in the case of *Richard III*'s second murderer.[92] But the particular form of entrance depicted in the ghost scene—and described in the

[91] My reading of Shakespearean conscience has affinities with William Hamlin's analysis of Shakespearean "god-surrogates"—speeches through which one character takes on the function of conscience for another character whose conscience has failed at its task of convicting them of their sin. Hamlin, however, explores Shakespeare's representation of the real effects of individual or cultural faith in conscience (insofar as it is this faith that motivates these god-surrogates to mimetically present conscience's truths), while I am interested in what Shakespeare takes "conscience" to be. See Hamlin, "Conscience and the god-surrogate," 244.

[92] Lukacher, *Daemonic Figures*, 16. This study, which argues for the place of Shakespearean tragedy in an intellectual genealogy of conscience as a figure for the traumatic alterity constitutive of being, focuses on *Hamlet* and *Macbeth*, with only a passing mention of *Richard III*.

88 THE DRAMA OF COMPLAINT

theological understanding of conscience—underscores the doubleness of the relation that conscience names: a relation both to internal alterity and to an external force that has created the subject by invading, cutting into and leaving its mark on it. Let's revisit the scene one last time, then, with an eye to what Shakespeare, reworking Hall's suggestion that Richard's dream was "no [mere] dream," locates *beyond* that dream, conceptually as well as spatially: the embodied ghosts, pressing around the king, complaining.

The thing to notice is that the ghosts' complaints both penetrate into and shatter the frame of Richard's dream. The last few ghosts to address Richard explicitly direct his dreaming, from the Ghost of Lady Anne, who tells Richard that she "Now fills thy sleep with perturbations," to the Ghosts of the Princes and the Ghost of Buckingham, who respectively order Richard to "Dream on thy cousins smothered in the Tower" and "Dream on, dream on, of bloody deeds and death" (5.3.161, 146, 171). Richard's responsiveness to their commands should be seen in light of two related early modern beliefs about the embodied mind: that the sleeping person was especially susceptible to being affected by irrational forces, and that passion could be transferred from one person to another—"pierc[ing] the eare, and thereby the heart," as the moral philosopher and Jesuit priest Thomas Wright puts it in *The Passions of the Minde* (1604)—through the acoustics of the human voice.[93] The complaining voice, Wright notes, is "apt to cut."[94] Indeed, these ghosts wake Richard with their clamor, just as the complaints of Warwick and Prince Edward's ghosts shatter the frame of Clarence's dream from within ("Such hideous cries, that with the very noise / I, trembling, waked" [1.4.60–61]). Notice that when Richard wakes, it is as one wounded:

> *Richard starteth up out of a dream.*
> KING RICHARD   Give me another horse! Bind up
>   my wounds!
> Have mercy, Jesu.—Soft, I did but dream.
> O coward conscience, how dost thou afflict me!
> ....
> Cold fearful drops stand on my trembling flesh.
> What do I fear? Myself? There's none else by.
>
>   (5.3.177–82)

As the apostrophe suggests, conscience is *there* when Richard awakes, a byproduct of the ghosts' complaints: the feeling that those words have bred in him, which *now* erupts on the scene.

---

[93] Wright, *The Passions of the Minde*, 175. Garrett A. Sullivan Jr. argues for the increased vulnerability of the sleeping body in *Sleep, Romance, and Human Embodiment*.
[94] Wright, *The Passions of the Minde*, 180.

Richard's recoil from the experience of conscience is evident in the way he immediately circumscribes its afflictions by locating them firmly within the dream ("Soft, I did but dream"). I would suggest that Shakespeare frames this explanation, which is the same interpretation that Hall and Woolton offer, as Richard's defense against the trauma of the external encounter and its ethical demand. It is a way of reassuring himself that his wound is merely imaginary ("Methought the souls of all that I had murdered / Came to my tent, and every one did threat / Tomorrow's vengeance on the head of Richard" [5.3.204–6]). The imminent wound he fears is a battlefield injury—hence the cry for the horse—but as he confesses to Ratcliffe, he is already wounded, even now:

> By the Apostle Paul, shadows tonight
> Have struck more terror to the soul of Richard
> Than can the substance of ten thousand soldiers
> Armed in proof, and led by shallow Richmond.
>
> (5.3.216–19)

Richard's reference to "shadows" is dismissive, like his description of the dream, a word intended to emphasize the difference between nothingness and substance, image and essence, illusion and reality. But those distinctions are undercut by the staging of the scene, which superimposes all the meanings of "shadow," each of which signifies one of the forms—dream, ghosts, actors—through which we have seen Richard "struck" by a plaintive address. As I have been arguing, in performance the theatrical scene draws attention to something that exceeds the mental phenomenon of Richard's dream, as well as the explanatory function that dream serves. In making the contingent of ghosts the orienting point of the scene's dramatic energy—amplifying their plaintive voices and their wounded bodies, centering their identities and experiences—Shakespeare readies the theatrical audience to recognize Richard's later proto-Nietzschean demystification of conscience as "but a word that cowards use, / Devised at first to keep the strong in awe" as yet another fantasmatic defense (5.3.309–10).[95] This defense, too, turns on dismissing the ghosts' complaints as merely "babbling dreams" (5.3.308).[96]

If Richard's initial explanation of the ghosts' complaints as the dream-work of conscience shields him from their external reality, in the light of day, as he prepares to go into battle, he distances himself from that interpretation too, ultimately suggesting that "conscience" was no cause of his affliction at all, but simply a word he uttered in a moment of cowardly weakness. This defense resonates with a

---

[95] On the similarity between what Richard says here and Nietzsche's notion of conscience, see Bonetto, "Coward Conscience and Bad Conscience."

[96] "Babble" suggests nonsensical sound, but as Cavarero argues (in terms especially relevant for theatrical performance), it is exactly the sonic substance of the voice that communicates the singularity and relationality of persons that Richard seeks to disavow. Cavarero, *For More than One Voice*, 177.

90   THE DRAMA OF COMPLAINT

moment from the end of *3 Henry VI*, in which Richard—who has just killed Henry VI and is now announcing his intention to set a trap for Clarence—articulates a fantasy of autonomy that hinges on banishing a particularly charged word from being "resident" in him. Having claimed that "I have neither pity, love nor fear," he imagines that what he lacks is what makes him whole:

> since the heavens have shaped my body so,
> Let hell make crooked my mind to answer it.
> I have no brother, I am like no brother;
> And this word 'love,' which greybeards call divine,
> Be resident in men like one another,
> And not in me. I am myself alone.[97]

In suggesting that he has not been marked with "this word 'love'"—a thing said to be divine—Richard proclaims his freedom from the moral law to which humans are bound through conscience, the law that "concernes duties of love partly to God & partly towards our neighbours...the very law of nature written in all mens heart."[98] This lack of putatively natural love was a hallmark of descriptions of the historical Richard III. Woolton marvels that he not only murdered his enemies but his "assistants" too, and "neyther spar[ed] his nephews king Edwarde sonnes nor his owne wife"; Thomas More's influential account sums up his character by noting that "Friend and foe was much what indifferent" to him; and Thomas Sackville's Ghost of Henry, Duke of Buckingham (speaker of a complaint poem first printed in the 1563 edition of *A Mirror for Magistrates*) accuses Richard of having been moved to pity by "neyther love, kindred, ne knot of bloud."[99] Like these writers, Shakespeare explicitly links Richard's notorious moral deformity to the "crooked" shape of his body. What I want to point out, however, drawing on others' diagnoses of Richard's narcissism, is how Shakespeare's Richard imagines those mirroring "deformities" as together forming a structural whole, a perfectly intact form in which no wounding word "love" has been carved.[100] The shape of his unloving mind "answers" the call of his unloved body, and thus he can see himself as "myself alone"—in relation with no one, and therefore complete, perfect. (And always already outside the relations from which he has been excluded on the basis of his bodily difference.)[101]

---

[97] Shakespeare, *3 Henry VI*, 5.6.69, 78–83.   [98] Perkins, *A Discourse of Conscience*, 14.

[99] Woolton, *Of the Conscience*, F1r; More, *The History of King Richard III*, 9; *The Mirour for Magistrates*, 218v.

[100] Useful here is Coppélia Kahn's description of what Freud identifies as Richard's narcissism. He is "unable to form or sustain bonds with others." Kahn, *Man's Estate*, 66–7. On Richard's horror of a contaminating feminine force that has infected him in the womb, see Adelman, *Suffocating Mothers*, esp. 3–4.

[101] On the ways Richard compensates for the meanings attached to his body, see Williams, "Enabling Richard."

ETHICAL DEMANDS 91

It is this avowed formal integrity that Richard's experience of conscience, and the complaints which spark that experience, threaten in *Richard III*'s ghost scene. Like his dismissal of "this word 'love'" in *3 Henry VI* as something that pertains only to "men like one another," his dismissal of conscience as "but a word" invented by men to set a limit on power works to suture the breach in the self that those words signify and cause, so that he can happily be "myself alone" once more. My point is not that those statements are false propositions, but rather that Shakespeare does not frame them as propositional statements at all. They are *wishes* ("Let hell make crooked my mind to answer it /.../ And this word 'Love'.../ Be resident in men like one another"; "Let not our babbling dreams affright our souls. / Conscience is but a word that cowards use"). These subjunctive expressions reveal Richard's fantasy of transcending the relationality that binds everyone else—a fantasy that plays out here as a rejection of the *language* of that relationality ("love," "conscience"). And thus what I find most striking about Richard's experience of conscience in the ghost scene is less his recognition of his guilt before the law than his profoundly uncharacteristic acknowledgment of despair at being excluded from the very same relations of love and pity that he has scorned: "I shall despair. There is no creature loves me, / And if I die, no soul will pity me" (5.3.200–1).[102] Wounded by the ghosts' words, Richard suddenly recognizes, in his exceptional exclusion from love and pity (and more precisely, the psychic "crookedness" shaped by that exclusion), the sign of his belonging to a social body. Just as the second murderer finds to his astonishment that "that word 'Judgement'" has an "urging" effect on him, so Shakespeare shows "love" and "conscience" to represent a pressing ethical demand that Richard, finally, feels too, both as obligation and as desire.[103] In those two lines, a minimal split opens between Richard and the villain he has been "determined to prove" as well as Richard and the overdetermined villain of Tudor history (1.1.30).[104] For just a

---

[102] Katharine Eisaman Maus also sees Richard as drawn back here into a web of relationality he has disdained, but through his reliance on the followers that abandon him. See Maus, *Inwardness and Theater*, 48, 53.

[103] I want to note the parallel to Shakespeare's sustained interrogation of conscience in *Henry VIII*, which also links the experience of conscience to words: in Henry's case, "certain speeches" by the Bishop of Bayonne on the ambiguous legitimacy of his marriage, which he says "entered" him

> with a splitting power, and made to tremble
> The region of my breast; which forced such way
> That many mazed considerings did throng
> And pressed in with this caution.
>
> (2.4.179, 180–83)

The play's running joke is that the suspiciously opportune "pricks" of Henry's conscience reflect his desire for Anne Boleyn. Obviously, the ease with which the King can translate his transgressive sexual desire into the vocabulary of an ethical obligation reflects the play's cynicism about the political or ethical authority of private conscience. But the overlaying of sexual desire and conscience also discloses the structural similarity between these polar opposites, each an unwilled responsiveness to proximate others that reveals a more fundamental relationality.

[104] On this overdetermination see Charnes, *Notorious Identity*, 20–49.

92 THE DRAMA OF COMPLAINT

moment, Shakespeare makes the monstrous king a creature among others. *Richard III*'s ghost scene renders perceptible, under the name of conscience, the ethical pressure of a human relationality that *even Richard* experiences.

The revelation of such relationality would not have been in and of itself surprising to early modern audiences, as many critics have explained: in early modern thought autonomy is a fantasy very often clearly marked as such, as it is here.[105] More remarkable is *Richard III*'s particular arrangement of a character's recognition of relationality, conscience, and the complaining voices of other people. Conscience, as all early modern treatises on the subject note, signifies a knowing-with; it is "that thing that combines two together, and makes them partners in the knowledge of one and the same secret"—these two being, of course, the person and God.[106] So too, Richard's experience of conscience, as I have been arguing, involves the awakening through a complaint to an occluded self-knowledge, as he comes to consciousness of a relationality he has disavowed, and to the ethical responsibility that follows from that relationality. What is note-worthy is that Shakespeare—as one of several early modern writers who theorizes conscience by recounting the historical Richard III's alleged dream of accusatory complaint—depicts this as a knowledge gained in the presence of other humans, through their actual and not metaphorical complaining voices, in an external rather than inward scene of judgment.

In refashioning the elements of those other narratives—making the ghosts real, linking their complaints to judicial complaints addressed to Richard by living characters throughout the play, showing Richard's dismissal of the ghosts as a dream to be a defense—Shakespeare tells a very different story about the way conscience appears in lived experience. At a historical moment when conscience signifies the dyadic relation between the self and God, within the framework of a Protestant ethics of self-examination and reflection, the play harnesses the affor-dances of theatrical judicial complaint to remap the internal drama of conscience as a social drama, a dialogic experience provoked by the plaintive address of embodied, injured others. *Richard III* represents the ethical pressure that "con-science" signifies as the felt experience of an opening to the human other to whose complaint for justice one must respond, and it accentuates the impossibility of evading the demands of this human relationality through the theatrical means by which it enacts the drama of conscience: the haunting voices of figures that are not fully comprehensible, but who are really there. I want to close by suggesting,

---

[105] On relationality as key to the period's conceptions of subjectivity, see Gray, *Shakespeare and the Fall of the Roman Republic*; Kuzner, *Open Subjects* and Curran, *Shakespeare's Legal Ecologies*. Indeed, Gray and Cox suggest that "the vision of the self most prevalent in Shakespeare's England, the 'com-monsense' default" is a relational one: a subject that "exist[s] in a state of constant, ever-changing engagement with the other, like a partner in a dance or an interlocutor in a conversation." See "Introduction: rethinking Shakespeare and ethics," 8–9.

[106] Perkins, *Discourse of Conscience*, 5.

then, that the play's mobilization of external, complaining voices to conceptualize the experience of conscience represents the complaints of the other as the paradigmatic ethical demand, investing them with what was, for early modern audiences, conscience's dignity and weight.[107] In this sense, *Richard III* might be a representative instance of what Curran, at the very close of his study, suggestively describes as a Shakespearean "ethics of exteriority" articulated in relation to law, an ethics he argues manifests in the ways in which certain plays "diagram a situated and relational form of being" that many phenomenological theorists "take as prerequisite to responsible living."[108] This is not to deny the obvious limits to the Richard story—the brevity of his experience of conscience, the retributive model of justice—as an exemplary tale of ethical responsibility. It is simply to identify the conceptual yield of the play's provocative turn away from the inner monologue of guilt to particular, external voices of complaint, voices whose claims of injury must be listened for and responded to.[109]

---

[107] On "the sovereignty of the individual conscience" in early modern thought see Braun and Vallence, *Contexts of Conscience*, xiv.

[108] Curran, *Shakespeare's Legal Ecologies*, 133.

[109] A more sustained discussion of the points of consonance and dissonance between the ethical thought developed in contemporary critical phenomenology and in Shakespearean drama (and particularly in the latter's scenes of judicial complaint, which link relationality and ethical responsibility to the moral law) would explore the extent to which Shakespeare sees recognition and justice for the injured other as depending on a commitment to some kind of normative ethics. On the resistance to all normative ethical commitments as a "bad habit" of critical theory, see Ruti, *Distillations*.

3

"Me and My Cause"

Spectral Complaints and Sublime Motives

Mark. Remember. Revenge. This chapter is about the peculiar poetic form of complaint that is the spectral complaint: a ghost's tale of grievance, punctuated with a command for the ghost's addressee to act. A conventional device of both narrative verse de casibus tragedy and dramatic revenge tragedy—in the former, a ghost orders a poet to tell and an audience to heed the story of its tragic fall, in the latter, it demands payback for that fall—the spectral complaint is often interpreted as a sign of early modern writers' aliveness to the political and poetic uses, or the traumatic residue, of the historical past.[1] My goal, by contrast, is to excavate the role that the form played in early modern conceptualizations of moral psychology, an explicit concern of de casibus tragedy that was also important to the ethical discourse about volition, reason, and passion that informed revenge tragedy. While a great deal of early modern literary complaints (including those discussed in the previous chapter) could be called spectral complaints in the sense that they are spoken by ghosts, I am using this rubric to bring together and isolate a smaller set of ghost-voiced complaints: those specific to works of tragedy concerned with accounting for the mysterious, curiosity-provoking causes of human action. For writers of de casibus and revenge tragedy, the spectral complaint, I will argue, was an especially apt poetic form for conceptualizing and representing a cause of action that was both irreducibly enigmatic as an object of philosophical thought and uniquely compelling as an embodied motive.

Hamlet persistently figures this strange cause as a sovereign command. In dramatizing how Hamlet comes to be commanded by it, the theatrical scene that initiates the play's revenge plot—the scene of spectral complaint—notably focalizes the workings of Hamlet's mind, the place where he promises that the Ghost's "commandment" will dwell (1.5.102). The Ghost claims that simply hearing its complaint will bind Hamlet to revenge.[2]

> GHOST   Mark me.
> HAMLET   I will.

---

[1] See, for instance, Schwyzer, *Literature, Nationalism and Memory* and Anderson, *Performing Early Modern Trauma.*

[2] On the Ghost as a plaintiff presenting a judicial cause, see Skinner, *Forensic Shakespeare*, 73.

The Drama of Complaint: Ethical Provocations in Shakespeare's Tragedy. Emily Shortslef, Oxford University Press.
© Emily Shortslef 2023. DOI: 10.1093/oso/9780192868480.003.0004

> ....
> GHOST Pity me not, but lend thy serious hearing
> To what I shall unfold.
> HAMLET   Speak, I am bound to hear.
> GHOST So art thou to revenge when thou shalt hear.
> ....
>   List, list, O list,
> If thou didst ever thy dear father love—
> HAMLET O God!
> GHOST   —Revenge his foul and most unnatural murder!
> HAMLET Murder!
> GHOST   Murder most foul—as in the best it is—
> But this most foul, strange and unnatural.
> HAMLET Haste me to know't that I with wings as swift
> As meditation or the thoughts of love
> May sweep to my revenge.
> GHOST   I find thee apt.
> And duller shouldst thou be than the fat weed
> That roots itself in ease on Lethe wharf
> Wouldst thou not stir in this. Now, Hamlet, hear[.][3]

Apt links Hamlet's capacity to act to his capacity for receiving, making sense of, and retaining the sense impressions that in the Aristotelian model of perception inform the mind.[4] His response to the Ghost's complaint affirms, in more material terms, this link between initial impression and future action:

> Yea, from the table of my memory
> I'll wipe away all trivial fond records,
> All saws of books, all forms, all pressures past
> That youth and observation copied there
> And thy commandment all alone shall live
> Within the book and volume of my brain
> Unmixed with baser matter.
>
> (1.5.98–104)

Hamlet's language stresses the ethical absoluteness of what he later calls the Ghost's "dread command," the awful sovereign mandate to revenge that obliterates the

---

[3] 1.5.2–34. References to the play are, unless otherwise noted, from the Second Quarto (1604) and are cited from *Hamlet*, eds. Thompson and Taylor. Hereafter cited parenthetically.

[4] *OED*, s.v. "apt": "2.b. of persons: fit, prepared, ready. 5. Susceptible to impressions; ready to learn; intelligent; quick-witted; prompt." On Shakespeare's recurring engagement with a "physics of impression," grounded in Aristotelian natural philosophy and developed in later medieval and early modern thought, see Crane, "Form and Pressure in Shakespeare," 28.

96   THE DRAMA OF COMPLAINT

moral precepts he has dutifully internalized (3.4.105). His promise to replace "all pressures past" with a new script for his future formalizes an assent already implied in his action, when, at the Ghost's first motion for him "to go away with it / As if it some impartment did desire / To you alone," he sets aside both his reason and decorum, threatening violence against anyone who stands in his way (1.4.58–60, 81). In the Ghost's form Hamlet claims to proleptically see his future ("My fate cries out" [1.4.81]), just as he will react to its revelation with an exclamation of retroactive recognition ("O my prophetic soul!" [1.5.40]). Here it is worth noting the hypothetical call that Horatio has imagined when he warns Hamlet that the Ghost might lead him to the "dreadful summit of the cliff" where he could not resist *l'appel du vide* ("The very place puts toys of desperation / Without more motive into every brain" that looks down and hears the "roar" of the sea [1.4.70, 75–76, 78]). The possibility that Hamlet would not merely lose his power of reason but suffer it to be deposed by an irrational, higher imperative would seem to be actualized when he overwrites all else in his mind with the spectral command ("unmixed with baser matter"). The pressure Hamlet experiences is distinct from external compulsion ("the sort of principle in which the agent, or rather the victim, contributes nothing," as per the *Nicomachean Ethics*).[5] And yet the scene's descriptions of a motive impressed on the brain and figured as both sovereign order and hylomorphic impression underline the force of an extra-volitional, intrusive command that "deprive[s] your sovereignty of reason" and pushes Hamlet forward "without more motive" (1.4.73, 76).

By the end of the scene, the Ghost's command has indeed become Hamlet's single cause and motive: his prompt to action and reason for acting, the catalyst and telos of his motion. From the ambiguity surrounding the Ghost's identity to the Ghost's cryptic warning to "Taint not thy mind" in enacting its command, the scene of spectral complaint provides the play's audience with ample reason to question the moral rightness of Hamlet's cause (1.5.85). But Shakespeare also highlights how completely Hamlet identifies with this injunction, a point underscored in the complaint he utters as he exits the stage: "The time is out of joint; O cursed spite / That ever I was born to set it right!" (1.5.186–87). The unfolding of the Ghost's story ends with Hamlet reconceiving his life around its charge: he is, in the logic of this rather astounding assertion, born again as an ethical subject. His guilty self-identification upon the Ghost's later reappearance in Gertrude's closet as "your tardy son.../ That, lapsed in time and passion, lets go by / Th'important acting of your dread command" affirms the pressure of that singular command (3.4.103–5).

The spectral complaint, I suggest, functions in the play as the primary figure for the enigmatic thing that motivates Hamlet, the motive impressed on his brain. Yet it isn't the only such figure. As I will show, *Hamlet* makes a leitmotif of the

---

[5] Aristotle, *Nicomachean Ethics*, 35.

phenomenon of being driven to act by a sublime motive—a motive that exceeds rational intention, strains the understanding, and calls attention to the bounds of reason—that Shakespeare links to an enigmatic, sovereign command that has animated its addressee.[6] The likeness between Hamlet and the play's other animated figures is especially obvious in those cases when Hamlet himself recognizes it—when, suddenly "unpregnant of my cause," the impressed form of the Ghost's command having dissolved in the "dull and muddy-mettled" matter of his brain, he observes in the actions of the Player and Fortinbras's soldiers a more fruitful relation to their informing motives, the irrationality of which astonishes him (2.2.503, 505). But the play is full of similar, sometimes quieter, echoes, such as Hamlet's description of the "compulsive ardour [that] gives the charge" to Gertrude, or the "fighting / That would not let me sleep" that he reports having felt "in my heart" onboard the ship bound for England (3.4.84, 5.2.4–5, 4). As in the scene of spectral complaint, in these scenes of animation Shakespeare figures the motive for action as a command that moves the addressee from within, as an alien thing that speaks with a voice more urgent than that of reason. Considered as a set, these scenes offer a new critical perspective from which to consider the perennial critical question of why Hamlet cannot do what he has "cause and will and strength and means" to do (4.4.44).[7] In these vignettes of irrational motion and motivation, Shakespeare insists on a quantum of senselessness that prevents a fully satisfactory answer to the complementary questions of what drives action and what "puzzles the will," perplexing the mind and obstructing intention: as we will see, the play's account of motivation repeatedly locates the *why* of inaction and action alike in the presence or absence of a vital but senseless animation (3.1.79).

I argue that these moments of ethically freighted stasis and motion—first introduced in the scene of spectral complaint and framed by Hamlet's many self-reproachful reflections on his "dull revenge"—are indices of the play's engagement with the tensions between Pauline theology, as interpreted by Calvin via Augustine, and the model of moral psychology derived from classical moral philosophy, which describes action as following from the mutual coordination of the rational powers of the will (the faculty of desiring, choosing, and commanding) and the understanding, its sovereign (4.4.32).[8] The first section of this chapter explains

---

[6] I find *animation*, which Sianne Ngai describes as a "zero-degree feeling," an "affective state" that "impl[ies] the most basic or minimal of all affective conditions: that of being, in one way or another, 'moved,'" an especially helpful word for discussing this phenomenon, which *Hamlet* represents in a figurative language of motion and stasis, quickness and dullness. Ngai, *Ugly Feelings*, 31, 91.

[7] For a recent book-length study that summarizes the long critical history of analyzing Hamlet's problem, and theorizes Hamlet's delay as a "tarrying"—a purposeful waiting for the right conditions that creates those conditions—see Cutrofello, *All For Nothing*.

[8] Pierre de La Primaudaye describes reason holding "the sovereignty amongst the powers, vertues, and offices of the soul," where it is "joyned with" the will "as a counsailer or director, to admonish and to conduct it." *The Second Part of the French Academie*, 204. Studies of the will in early modern literature that have informed this chapter include Schwarz, *What You Will*; Freinkel, *Reading Shakespeare's Will*; Sanchez, *Queer Faith*; and Whigham, *Seizures of the Will*.

98 THE DRAMA OF COMPLAINT

these tensions, with particular attention to how the spectral complaint, as Shakespeare inherited it, was implicated in this same matrix of ethical thought, as a tragic narrative device that focalizes the commanding force of the irrational, not only in Senecan revenge drama but also in *The Mirror for Magistrates*, the collection of de casibus verse tragedies narrated by ghosts who relate their falls in didactic complaint monologues they describe as "cases," forensic accounts of motive and cause.[9] Expanded, revised, reissued, and imitated numerous times between its first publication in 1559 and its final incarnation in 1610—one critic suggests it had "a career perhaps more complex and influential than that of any other Elizabethan book"—the *Mirror* constitutes the single most influential source of early modern spectral complaint.[10] The *Mirror*'s spectral complaints, which both highlight irrational motivation and deny the limitations of reason that this irrationality implies, exemplify what I describe as a broader cultural disavowal of Calvinist theology's account of the limits of the "I" as a purposive and rational moral actor. This disavowal—by which I mean the effective denial *in practice* of a culturally commonplace, *rhetorically affirmed* theological belief—is the backdrop against which I then turn to *Hamlet*'s scenes of spectral complaint and the scenes of animation patterned on it, which expose the theological idea that the will is commanded by something other than reason. The play reiterates this idea, attempting to capture the horror, and the moral scandal, of the notion that we are motivated by forces we do not understand, beyond what we may even know, to what we may not want, often to our ruin. Insisting on what other accounts of moral psychology pretend not to know, *Hamlet* presents this as an appalling truth that—like the Ghost—"horridly...shake[s] our disposition / With thoughts beyond the reaches of our souls," unsettling the orienting point of ethical subjectivity (1.4.55–56).

1. Volitional Excess and Spectral Complaint

Having exhausted the plausible reasons for his failure to take his revenge—cowardice, conscience, uncertainty about the Ghost's identity and intent, forgetfulness—Hamlet at last finds himself unable to account for his inaction:

---

[9] As John Kerrigan notes, the *Mirror*'s complaints combine an Aristotelian commitment to tracing effects to their causes with the forensic sense of *causa*: explaining how and why the plaintiff came to do as they did, they are concerned with the establishing of motive, the rationalizing of action, and the determining of responsibility. See Kerrigan, *Motives of Woe*, 27–9.

[10] Brooke, "The Renaissance," 398. First printed in 1559 and edited by William Baldwin, the *Mirror*'s life spanned new and expanded editions (1563, 1578), revised editions (1571, 1574), a reissue (1575), two supplementary collections pitched as prequels (one by John Higgins in 1574, another by Thomas Blenerhaset in 1578), two lengthy compilations of old, revised, and new complaints (one printed in 1587 and edited by Higgins; the other, edited by Richard Niccols, printed in 1610), and, throughout the 1590s, numerous verse tragedies for which it was a model. For an account of the bibliographic and editorial history of the various *Mirror* texts, see Archer, *Unperfect Histories*.

> I do not know
> Why yet I live to say this thing's to do,
> Sith I have cause and will and strength and means
> To do't.
>
> (4.4.42–45)

Hamlet's enumeration of all the things he has brings into relief an enigmatic deficit, *something else* that he needs but lacks. Earlier in the play he has figured this implied lack as a loss, describing himself after the Player's lively performance of passion as "unpregnant of my cause," once the bearer of something no longer there: the commandment he had promised the Ghost would "all alone...live / Within the book and volume of my brain, / Unmixed with baser matter" (2.2.503; 1.5.102–4).[11] In both instances, the contrast Hamlet draws between others' actions and his own inaction (here Fortinbras's army is marching through Denmark to the worthless plot of Polish land) is framed in the language of animation and inanimation, bodies enlivened and in motion versus bodies that are sluggishly slow or deathly still.[12] The Player is visibly moved, he is "dull and muddy-mettled"; the Norwegian soldiers "for a fantasy and trick of fame / Go to their graves like beds," while he, "hav[ing] a father killed, a mother stained, / Excitements of my reason and my blood," passively "let[s] all sleep" (2.2.502; 4.4.60–61; 4.4.56–57, 58). Ashamed and bewildered by his failure to be sufficiently moved, Hamlet asks, "How stand I then?"—a not-entirely-rhetorical question that plays on the double meaning of "standing," underlining both his inexplicable inertness and its uncertain moral implications (4.4.55). Why is he not sweeping to his revenge? How then does he stand, in relation to the commandment he has not kept?

Evoked in Hamlet's complaint is another famous complaint about being unable to do as one wills: "for what I wolde, that do I not...for to wil is present with me: but I finde no meanes to performe that which is good."[13] This, of course, is Paul's description in Romans 7 of his incapacity to fulfill the demands of the Law, an impotence whose corollary is his powerlessness to avoid doing what he wants *not* to do ("I do not the good thing, which I would, but the evil, which I would not, that do I" [v. 19]). And yet it is not exactly he himself who does it, he claims, for such evil acts do not follow from the desires he identifies as his own; on the contrary, they are done against what he calls the "law of my mind," which serves the Law of God (v. 23). Thus Paul concludes, in a now familiar formulation, "it is no more I, that do it, but sin that dwelleth in me" (v. 17). Transgressions of the Law reflect the commands of sin that rules in and over his flesh, enthralling him

---

[11] On this Shakespearean coinage as aligning tragic action with the very matter of the body, see Pollard, "Conceiving tragedy."

[12] On the play's highlighting of motion in its accounts of action, see Raman, "Hamlet in Motion."

[13] Romans 7: 15–18. All quotations from the Bible are from *The Geneva Bible: A Facsimile of the 1560 Edition*.

100 THE DRAMA OF COMPLAINT

to its own law. This is the same problem foregrounded in Augustine's account of his arduous conversion in the *Confessions*. He longs for his soul to rise up to heaven, "Yet I was not doing what with an incomparably greater longing I yearned to do."[14] He wonders why the mind can successfully command the body's limbs to move, but cannot successfully command itself to will its conversion ("The mind commands the body and is instantly obeyed. The mind commands itself and meets resistance... The mind orders the mind to will. The recipient of the order is itself, yet it does not perform it. What causes this monstrosity and why does this happen?" [147]). Augustine finds in Romans 7 both an articulation of this "monstrous situation" and an explanation of its root cause: "I was neither wholly willing nor wholly unwilling," he writes, "And so it was 'not I' that brought this about 'but sin which dwelt in me'" (148–9). For Augustine, the in-dwelling sin described by Paul divides the will so that it desires at once to follow the promptings of reason in pursuit of higher, eternal things and to pursue the (ultimately more compelling) sensual pleasures and temporal goods desired by the appetite. In the divided nature of the will, he discerns a horrifying truth. The will itself is not enough; something else is needed.

For Calvin, as for Augustine and Paul, that thing is grace, which Paul describes as beyond all human understanding and action ("it is the gifte of God, not of workes, lest any man shulde boaste him self"), and which Calvin says "dwell[s]" in the regenerated person as "no part of the fleshe."[15] Indeed, in Calvinist theology the will has no natural desire for the good. Original Sin is not merely an inclination toward evil that affects the appetite but an inherited disease that "possesseth both the understanding minde and heart," ruling over even the rational powers: "Whatsoever is man, even from the understanding to the will, from the soule to the fleshe, is corrupted and stuffed full with this concupiscence," he insists.[16] In claiming that "our nature is not onely bare and emptie of goodnesse, but also is so plenteous and fruitefull of all evilles, that it cannot bee idle," Calvin emphasizes the causal force of this concupiscence, imagining it as an active, material presence within.[17] As he writes in his own commentary on Romans 7, even the regenerate struggle for the remainder of their earthly lives with the "reliques" of such concupiscence, which "doeth alwaye followe his [man's] corrupte affections."[18] It is grace alone that accounts for the will, as well as the power, to obey the Law. Elaborating this point in the *Institutes*, Calvin describes "the liquor of grace" as an animating force: "by the breath of [God's] power he so breatheth divine life into

---

[14] Augustine, *Confessions*, 147. Hereafter cited parenthetically.
[15] Ephesians 2:8–9. Calvin, *A Commentarie upon the Epistle of Saint Paul to the Romanes*, 89v.
[16] Calvin, *Institution of Christian Religion*, 74v (2.1.9, 2.1.8).
[17] Calvin, *Institution of Christian Religion*, 74v (2.1.8). As Melissa Sanchez notes, in Reformed theology concupiscence signifies "a more general longing or striving" than sexual lust. *Queer Faith*, 92.
[18] Calvin, *A Commentarie...Romanes*, 88r.

us, that we are not now stirred by our selves, but ruled by his stirring & moving."[19] In short, then, Calvinist theology insists on both the impotence of what Paul calls the will that is "present with me"—the desires a person can claim as their own—and on the power of a force that both supersedes and is excessive to that will. This is the power either of immanent concupiscence ("sin which dwelt in me") or of transcendent divine grace—structural counterparts of sorts, the former inherited at birth and the latter granted to those who have been reborn into the life of the spirit. In either event, the command that sets the subject in motion comes from what is "in me" that is "not I."

I will return later to the parallel I am suggesting *Hamlet* draws between this command and that of the Ghost. For now I want to note the incommensurability of this understanding of moral psychology and the intellectualist paradigms of Aristotelian and Stoic moral philosophy.[20] Calvin frequently charges the classical philosophers, church fathers (Augustine excepted), and scholastics with neglecting "the corruption of our nature."[21] Arguing that human nature is fallen and utterly depraved—that all our affections, thoughts, and actions are infected by the "lurking disease" of concupiscence—he refutes the maxim that desire naturally aims at the good shown to it by the understanding.[22] The truth, as he sees it, is just the opposite. We can intend and choose nothing good of our own volition (indeed, "oft we fall with our good intent"), and our evil deeds exceed those sins we intentionally choose, our "purposed malice and frowardnesse."[23] While "the Philosophers" "subtilly place both vices and vertues in the mind," defining ethical subjectivity in relation to voluntary, conscious choice, Calvin maintains in his commentary on Romans 7 that intention and volition are wholly inadequate frames for conceptualizing moral responsibility for actions, or for explaining motivation.[24] Put differently, he denies the self-creation integral to the framework of Aristotelian virtue ethics, in which a person fashions their own moral character through habitual action guided by reason.[25] Just as reason cannot of itself enable us to do what is good, neither can it reveal to us the full extent of our distance from the good, he suggests, for reason cannot apprehend the evil concupiscence for which Paul maintains, against the philosophers, that we are "not excusable."[26] (This "faulte of concupiscence...never commeth into question, so long as men

---

[19] Calvin, *Institution of Christian Religion*, 173v (3.1.3).

[20] On Augustine and Reformed theology, see Visser, *Reading Augustine in the Reformation*.

[21] Calvin, *Institution of Christian Religion*, 74r (2.1.8). From his perspective, they wrongly ascribe to the will a freedom of choice lost at the Fall, and erroneously locate concupiscence in a sensual or appetitive part of the soul cordoned off from reason and from the will, except when the will, through incontinence or error, consents to be commanded by it. See Calvin, *A commentarie...Genesis*, 95.

[22] Calvin, *Institution of Christian Religion*, 74r (2.1.8); *A Commentarie...Romanes*, 84r.

[23] Calvin, *Institution of Christian Religion*, 84v (2.2.25).

[24] Calvin, *A Commentarie...Romanes*, 84r.

[25] See 2.1 (1103a–b) of the *Nicomachean Ethics*. On the tension between the ethical "self-fashioning" of Aristotelian thought and Reformed theology, see Streete, *Protestantism and Drama*, 15.

[26] Calvin, *A Commentarie...Romanes*, 84r.

102 THE DRAMA OF COMPLAINT

judge according to their sense," Calvin writes, but only in the light of a divine law that "pearceth unto the concupiscence, which is more secrete then the will.")[27] Thus he concludes that although "suche a description of humane witte there is amongst the Philosophers, the Scripture setteth downe a more deepe philosophie, because...it sawe nothing to remaine in the heart of man, besides perversitie or frowardnesse."[28]

The notion that without grace we can do nothing but sin was a commonplace of early modern English theological discourse, enshrined in the Thirty-Nine Articles ("Works done before the grace of Christ...for that they are not done as God hath willed and commanded them to be done, we doubt not but they have the nature of sin") and in the Catechism of the Book of Common Prayer ("My good childe knowe this, that thou art not able to doo these thinges of thy self, nor to walke in the commaundementes of God, and to serve him, without his special grace").[29] It was also echoed in popular religious writing such as the poem *The Complaint of a Christian Soule* (1610), whose speaker, echoing Paul, laments, "Thou knowst that which I would not, that I do: / And yet not I, but my corruptions."[30] A prayer from Thomas Becon's devotional manual *The Governance of Vertue* (1578) reminds readers that they are commanded either by sin or by grace:

> We are all grievous sinners, and can of our selves doe nothing but sinne. For all our imaginations, intents, and thoughtes are enclined, and disposed to evill from our youth up. Our damnation commeth of our selves, we our selves are not able to thinke a good thought. It is thou only that doest worke in us both the will and the deede.[31]

This is not to say, however, that early modern people went through their everyday lives and routines thinking themselves to be incapable of doing good, worrying that every action, thought, and affection was infected by concupiscence, or believing that sin or grace was the moving force behind all human action.[32] Adrian Streete argues that although "Reformed theology recalibrated the subject's attitude towards the relative theological and cultural import of the volitional impulse," Shakespeare's contemporaries surely did not "believe themselves incapable of

---

[27] Calvin, *A Commentarie...Romanes*, 84r.

[28] Calvin, *A Commentarie...Romanes*, 88r–v. On points of tension as well as continuity between the Augustinian-Calvinist ethical paradigm and the intellectualist traditions, see Bouwsma, "The Two Faces of Humanism."

[29] The Thirty-Nine Articles 1563, 72–3. Book of Common Prayer, Aaiiir.

[30] Muschet, *The Complaint of a Christian Soule*, B2v.

[31] Becon, *The Governaunce of Vertue*, 183v–184r.

[32] Anxieties about election, however, were rampant. On the self-scrutiny generated by these anxieties see Swann, "Nosce Teipsum." For a discussion of the complex and contradictory relation between Calvinist doctrine and the experience of despair in early modern England, see Ryrie, *Being Protestant*.

willed, volitional action."[33] Luke Wilson, in his study of early modern conceptions of intention, suggests that "Calvin's dismissal of human will in spiritual matters should not be extended very far into the social sphere."[34] Calvin himself acknowledges in the *Institutes* that reason "attaineth somewhat" in certain matters and spheres of action, namely the arts and sciences, as well as matters of political, civic, and household governance.[35] Indeed, he is not attempting to discredit moral philosophy or disparage reason ("wit"), but to highlight the point beyond which they cannot go by stressing the limitations of reason within the mind and the limits of moral philosophy as a discourse premised on reason's sovereignty. Where reason is insufficient, he notes, is in providing knowledge of "the rule to frame our life."[36]

Such knowledge, however, is precisely the aim of moral philosophy, the ambitions and foundational assumptions of which are at odds with the understanding of the self propounded by Reformed theology. This tension occasionally appears in moral compendia such as Pierre de La Primaudaye's *The French Academie* (1594) and Pierre Charron's *Of Wisdome* (1608), as well as treatises on the passions such as Thomas Wright's *The Passions of the Minde in Generall* (1604). These syncretic treatises promote intellectualist models of mind in which the will is naturally drawn toward and usually chooses the correct objects shown to it by "celestial and divine" reason, despite the pull of the sensual appetite.[37] Wright's dominant position, for instance, can be summed up in his claim that "The Will affecteth, for the most part, that [which] the understanding perswadeth to bee best."[38] Yet he also says exactly the opposite:

> the sensitive appetite often, yea and (for the most part) traleth and haleth the will to consent and follow her pleasures and delights…(I would to God it were not true) howe oft yeeldeth the will to the appetite, in procuring sensuall pleasures and pastimes, for no other ende, than to pleasure the unpleasable appetites, and lustes of the flesh.[39]

In such moments, the authors acknowledge that Original Sin complicates the models of moral psychology inherited from classical antiquity. The Protestant La Primaudaye, in particular, echoes the Reformed notion of concupiscence as an

---

[33] Streete, *Protestantism and Drama*, 15. Streete does note though that "Protestantism encouraged the subject produced within its purview to believe that such willed action was at best an indulgence, and at worst folly, a mere adjunct to broader matters of salvation" (15).

[34] Wilson, *Theaters of Intention*, 267n4.

[35] Calvin, *Institution of Christian Religion*, 80v (2.2.13).

[36] Calvin, *Institution of Christian Religion*, 80v (2.2.13).

[37] La Primaudaye, *The Second Part of the French Academie*, 598. On the transparently self-contradictory explanations of the relation between will and reason in early modern faculty psychology, see Schwarz, *What You Will*, especially Chapter 1.

[38] Wright, *The Passions of the Minde*, 58.   [39] Wright, *The Passions of the Minde*, 31.

104   THE DRAMA OF COMPLAINT

agitating internal excess when—having just described affections as God-given "pricks" of pleasure to encourage our desire for what is good—he warns that

> there is always some excesse even in the perfectest, and that being sinne, is properly called evil concupiscence, because it continually provoketh us to evil, and causeth us to goe beyond the bounds which God had set to our affections. Whereof it is come to passe, that that which shoulde be a benefite unto men in their naturall pleasures, is become hurtfull unto them.[40]

Similarly, he claims that "the will desireth or refuseth nothing, which reason hath not first shewed that it is to be desired or disdained"—but then reminds his readers that

> It is always requisite that the grace of God should governe our minde and will, to perswade them evermore to counsaile and to imbrace the best: otherwise we shall make choyce of the worst, and of evill rather than of good.[41]

My point is not that these accounts are internally contradictory. It is rather that they are not particularly *troubled by* these contradictions, which the authors neither mark as such nor attempt to smooth over. They do not deny—indeed, they acknowledge, if only briefly—the pivotal roles that evil concupiscence and divine grace play in the psychological drama of desiring, choosing, and acting. Then they carry on with their praise of reason and of moral philosophy, which La Primaudaye says gives

> most sure and certaine principles of knowledge, which shine in the minde as it were a light, which are the rules whereby the soule squareth out her actions...to the ende that all the actions thereof might agree with these rules, which are the beames of heavenly wisdom in our selves.[42]

---

[40] *The Second Part of the French Academie*, 218–19. It's worth noting the parallel between this theological understanding of an "evil concupiscence" that pushes desire beyond the "natural" bounds of pleasure and the libidinal energies that in psychoanalytic theory structure both unconscious desire and conscious intention. Lacan himself famously plays up this homology in his seminar on the ethics of psychoanalysis, where he elaborates the concept of the Thing (*das Ding*)—the void around which the libidinal economy is organized—by quoting from Romans 7, substituting the Thing for what Paul calls sin, and suggests that "Freud is telling us the same thing as Saint Paul, namely, that what governs us on the path of our pleasure is no Sovereign Good." Lacan, *Seminar VII*, 102–3, 118. On the continuities of Augustinian notions of the will and Freudian and Lacanian notions of libido, and their similarly vexed relation to Aristotelian ethics, see De Kesel, *Eros and Ethics*, 15–16. As Lisa Freinkel explains, Freud and Lacan were influenced by the current of thought about moral psychology that runs from Plato through Paul and Augustine to the theology of Calvin and Luther, with its insistence on "the inherent irrationality of the will itself." See Freinkel, *Reading Shakespeare's Will*, 245.

[41] La Primaudaye, *The Second Part of the French Academie*, 204, 208.

[42] La Primaudaye, *The Second Part of the French Academie*, 244.

It is as if he has forgotten what he has said about the "excess even in the perfectest" of desires that "causeth us to goe beyond the bounds which God had set."

The same general optimism about the directional capacities of reason and the instructiveness of moral philosophy characterizes *The Mirror for Magistrates* (whose first editor, William Baldwin, wrote the best-selling *A Treatise of Morall Phylosophie* [1548], a collection of commonplaces prefaced by a vigorous defense of the harmony between moral philosophy and the Scriptures). Written at moral philosophy's intersections with political counsel, history, and tragedy, the collaboratively authored and accretive *Mirror* offers instructive accounts of virtuous and wicked conduct from the lives of figures from English history and legendary British prehistory, stories that John Higgins, editor of the 1587 omnibus edition, promises will teach readers "not to excede the bands of measure, & to kepe Desire under the yoke of Reason."[43] The ghosts of these famous figures explain the causes of their tragic falls—causes being, as one notes, "the chiefest thinges / That should be noted of the story wryters"—to a mediator (in most cases either "Baldwin" or "Higgins") whom the ghosts command to "mark" their cases well so that the living may learn from their fatal mistakes (170v).[44] Across the varying historical circumstances of these falls, the moral cause of ruin remains the same: it is always desire unregulated by reason. This is how Higgins sums up the overarching lesson of the volume:

> To passe the measure of his [man's] degree, and to let will run at random is the only destruction of all estates. Else how were it possible, so many learned, polliticke, wise, renoumed, valiaunt, and victorious personages, might ever have come to such utter decay?   (A3v)

The function of the spectral complaint monologues that comprise the *Mirror* is to firmly link the "utter decay" of their speakers to unchecked will (a notoriously slippery word that can mean desire that has slipped reason's bounds, as well as the very faculty of mind itself). And indeed, its wicked ghosts unanimously attribute their fates to their enslavement by lust, vice, mischief, lewdness, pleasure, and ill—all, like will, signifiers for the kind of evil that the proper use of reason would prevent.

These spectral complaints are thus both forensic and didactic, often concluding with an admission of responsibility and blame:

---

[43] Quotations are from *The Mirour for Magistrates* (London, 1587). A3r. Hereafter cited parenthetically.

[44] This line is from the ghost of the Lord Tiptost, Earl of Worcester. I refer to the *Mirror*'s poems by their speakers' names, whose spelling I have regularized.

106 THE DRAMA OF COMPLAINT

> My selfe was for my woefull fall to blame.
> > (Ghost of King Emerianus, 63v)
>
> Blame my selfe I must.
> > (Ghost of Claudius Tiberius Nero, 86r)
>
> The case is clere, / ... blame I must my onely selfe therefore.
> > (Ghost of Domitius Nero, 90v)
>
> I must perforce my selfe accuse, / I was in fault I cannot it denye.
> > (Ghost of King Morgan, 38v)

Taken together, these complaints attempt to account for what would otherwise remain a mystery: how, as Higgins puts it, all those "learned, polliticke, wise, renoumed, valiaunt, and victorious personages, might ever have come to such utter decay." Some ghosts, for instance, argue that the existential chaos commonly attributed to Fortune, the conventional mover of de casibus tragedy, is in truth caused by disorderly human desire, rather than contingency and happenstance. "Fortune is the folly and plague of those / Which to the world their wretched willes dispose," declares the ghost of the rebel Jack Cade (157r). The ghost of Lord Irenglas concurs. "No fortune is so bad our selves ne frame," he argues, concluding:

> There is no destiny but is deserv'd,
> ....
> Let us not then complayne of Fortunes skill:
> For all our good descends from Gods good will,
> And of our lewdnes springeth all our ill.
>
> > (73r)

As we can see here, the *Mirror*'s complaints also attempt to parse the Calvinist paradox that in a universe determined by divine providence, humans freely choose sin and are thus fully to blame for their own damnation.[45] This is the point made by the ghost of Henry VI, who declares that the "chiefe cause" of all that happens is "the will devine, calde desteny and fate," yet argues that "our heavy haps" are *also* caused by "sinne through humours holpe," that is, sin that conspires with the body's very matter (176v). If we can only know how and why others fell, these complaints assume, we can avoid such falls ourselves.

And so these retrospective spectral complaints reconstruct the originary moment of choice, the fateful act by which their speakers first consented to be commanded by sin and, through the force of habit, thereafter lost their freedom to choose otherwise. The language of these complaints tends to frame that choice

---

[45] Timothy Rosendale explains how Reformed theologians reconcile causal determinism with moral responsibility. See Rosendale, *Theology and Agency*, esp. the Introduction (1–31) and Chapter 1, (32–77). For the relation between the *Mirror*'s representation of Fortune and providence, and the latter's dominance as a causal explanation, see Kiefer, "Fortune and Providence."

"ME AND MY CAUSE" 107

as an act of inversion: putting will in the place of reason, lust in the place of law, and then faithfully obeying the commands of this evil agency. Thus Richard II, in the words of the ghost of Robert Tresilian, his Chief Justice, "set his lustes for Lawe, and will had reasons place" (111v), while the ghost of Henry, Duke of Buckingham, admits of himself and Richard III that "Will was wisdom, our lust for law did stand" (217r). The ghosts describe this inversion as the cause of a psychic divide between (impotent) rational desire and (irresistible) irrational desire, a split expressed grammatically through objective, reflexive, and passive first-person pronouns. The ghost of Lord Mowbray laments that "mischief so through malice led my will," compelling him to do what "my harte abhored" (120r). The ghost of William de la Pole, Duke of Suffolk complains about the "vicious deedes which much possessed me" (153v), while the ghost of Richard II describes himself as helplessly driven by the "pricks" of pleasure ("As pleasure prickt, so needes obay I must" [122v]). The ghost of King Madan frames his ruin as a form of self-fashioning, achieved through the persistent repetition of "lewd" acts: "But I did still in laps of lewdnes runne, / At last my selfe to cruelty I bent" (25r). (One cannot help but think of Freud's description of the death drive's manifestation in repetition compulsion that makes its sufferers look as if they are "being pursued by a malignant fate or possessed by some 'daemonic' power.")[46]

Many of these spectral complaint poems are implicitly premised on the intellectualist assumption of a rational mind whose commands these particular men have disobeyed out of incontinence—too weak to follow their correct judgment of the good—or intemperance, having deliberately chosen a false good. But the *Mirror* also occasionally reflects the Calvinist notion of a mind that can obey reason—that can choose what is good, and avoid what is evil—only if it has been granted the grace to do so. This doctrine assumes a subject always already "addicted to sin," as Calvin puts it in his commentary on Romans, the will having made its free and irrevocable choice of evil in a primordial moment beyond all recall.[47] The problem, from this perspective, is not that we lose ourselves "when wee have our willes too much," but rather that if we do not have grace, we have *only* our wills (61r). As the ghost of King Madan laments,

> who so doth with will and pleasure fight,
> (Though all his force doe strive them to withstand)
> Without good grace they have the upper hand.
>
> (25r)

---

[46] Freud, *Beyond the Pleasure Principle*, 23.

[47] Calvin, *A Commentarie...Romanes*, 87r. Calvin argues that the will, having freely made that initial choice of evil, is now bound to choose that same evil, again and again. "We are pressed down with a yoke, but yet none other but of a certaine willing bondage, therefore by reason of our bondage we are miserable, by reason of our will wee are inexcusable, because will when it was free, made it selfe the bondservant of sinne." *Institution of Christian Religion*, 88v (2.3.5).

108　THE DRAMA OF COMPLAINT

On a more hopeful note, Madan acknowledges that "The giftes of grace may nature overcome, / And God may graunt the time when wee repent"—yet the possibility expressed by the modal verb was never realized for him (25r). Nor did that grace materialize for Richard Plantagenet, Earl of Cambridge, whose ghost wonders what might have been "If I had had the grace my wit to set" (131v), or for King Kimarus, whose ghost closes his tale of his "wilfull deedes" by noting that "Such wrecks in th'end to wretches all are rife, / Who may and will not call for grace before," his "may...not" a reflection of the hardline Calvinist position that without grace one cannot even have *the will to will* to receive it (60r). The despair of the graceless is encapsulated in the plaintive rhetorical question of the ghost of King Varianus, who, describing "gifts of grace," laments, "Where no good giftes have place, nor beare the sway, / What are the men, but wilful castaway?" (65r). An allusion to the shipwrecked man—a stock figure for someone ruined by Fortune—"castaway" also has specifically theological resonances: it is a signifier for the reprobate, whom God has rejected.

Even a single verse tragedy, that of the rebel Cade's ghost (whose way of thinking Baldwin wittily describes in his framing commentary as surprisingly "philosopher-like" and "like a divine") may simultaneously argue that reason can temper the mind's susceptibility to the lure of appetite *and* that reason is of no use without grace (159r). Cade urges readers to employ "the skill God hath in reason wrought" (156v) and tells those who wish to "bee not Fortunes slaves" that they must "Follow reason, [and] / Subdue their willes" (158v). Yet he also admits that they may not be able to do so, for

> though this skill bee geven to every man
> To rule the will, and keepe the minde aloft,
> For lacke of grace full fewe use it can.
>
> (156v)

Here the "lacke of grace"—a gift no one can choose to receive—incapacitates the universally granted "skill" of reason, which becomes powerless before a "will enclined to nought," bent on destruction (156v). The *Mirror's* practical didacticism pales in such textual moments, which locate virtue not in human action, but in the sublime *je ne sais quoi* of grace.

Compressed in Cade's complaint, then, are the tensions that traverse the *Mirror*, which occasionally admits an innate irrationality that only grace can supersede while also remaining committed to the idea of a fundamentally rational mind. The *Mirror's* identification of will as the cause of ruin is characterized by the same dynamic: even as its complaints sometimes locate the cause of tragedy in the sin-enslaved will itself, they more frequently emphasize the dangers of willfulness, or desire that has become irrational and excessive ("will run[ning] at random"), desire that should have been reined in by reason. Higgins himself gives voice to both possibilities. "Who so bathes in flickering Fortunes blisse, / Without Gods grace, I count ill fortune his," he says in one of his poetic envoys (58v)—then, reiterating the theme of his preface in the following envoy, declares that "The only causes why these Princes fell, / Are vices vile" (60v).

As with the other intellectualist accounts of moral psychology, it is not the fact of internal contradiction that is significant here (indeed, we should expect nothing less from the *Mirror*, given its multiple contributors and its ideological heterogeneity) but rather the way in which an overarching project of ethical instruction—a project to which reason is absolutely central—is not especially disrupted by such open admissions of reason's insufficiency.[48] I would suggest that in all these texts (and perhaps, as Streete and Wilson suggest, in everyday early modern life) these Calvinist truisms about the limits of reason, the irrationality of the will, and the evil concupiscence that infects all action are disavowed, in the sense that they are rhetorically affirmed as common knowledge even as they are effectively denied in practice. Calvin anticipates just such a reaction, which he attributes to the psychological difficulty of accepting this truth. It is bad enough to be told that we are infected with concupiscence, made "to acknowledge the diseases of [our] desires," he writes, but the hard Pauline truth that reason "is farre from sure directing" is even more painful.[49] He likens it to a theft of a valued object: Paul "taketh also this away from us, that we should not thinke that it can come in our mindes how any thing is to bee done well," and this deprivation "seemeth too hard to us, that do unwillingly suffer our selves to be spoyled of the sharpnesse of reason, which we accompt a most precious gift."[50] It isn't that early modern moral philosophy refuses to recognize the concupiscence that infects the whole person. But in leaving reason more or less unspoiled of its sharpness in its accounts of moral psychology, this discourse effectively denies what it knows: it carries on as if what its writers wish were not true were indeed not true.[51]

What *Hamlet* does, I argue, is the opposite: it fixates on this disavowed knowledge. Theology is, more generally, an insistent presence in the play, whose language is shot through with enigmatic but highly evocative theological signifiers—Wittenberg, purgatory, Cain's jawbone, the primal curse of a brother's murder, a heavenly audit, unconfessed sin, death by a serpent in an orchard, special providence and falling sparrows.[52] So too, at both ends of the narrative, the act of revenge is bracketed by explicitly soteriological concerns: first in the Ghost's

---

[48] On the religious and political diversity of the *Mirror*, see Archer and Hadfield, eds., *A Mirror for Magistrates in Context*.

[49] Calvin, *Institution of Christian Religion*, 84v (2.2.24, 2.2.25).

[50] Calvin, *Institution of Christian Religion*, 84v (2.2.25).

[51] Žižek, who frequently writes about this kind of "fetishistic disavowal" in everyday life under late capitalism, formulates its logic as "'I know, but I don't want to know that I know, so I don't know.'" Žižek, *Violence*, 53.

[52] On the informing presence of Calvinist theology in particular, see Hirschfeld, *The End of Satisfaction* and Gillies, "The Question of Original Sin in *Hamlet*."

110 THE DRAMA OF COMPLAINT

disclosure to Hamlet of the state of his soul, then in Laertes' request to "exchange forgiveness" with Hamlet so that their acts may "come not upon" them (5.2.313, 314). Indeed, for Hamlet to even think about acting is to run up against a theological problem that inhibits action: the divine law against self-slaughter, the fear of something after death, the "purging of [Claudius's] soul" in prayer (3.3.85). The theological film that covers all his reflections on action is especially visible in his curious (non)apology to Laertes, in which he "disclaim[s]" that his killing of Polonius was a "purposed evil" (5.2.218):

> Give me your pardon, sir. I have done you wrong,
> ....
> Was't Hamlet wronged Laertes? Never Hamlet.
> If Hamlet from himself be ta'en away
> And when he's not himself does wrong Laertes,
> Then Hamlet does it not; Hamlet denies it.
> Who does it then? His madness. If't be so,
> Hamlet is of the faction that is wronged—
> His madness is poor Hamlet's enemy.
>
> (5.2.204–17)

Wilson's comment on Hamlet's invocation of exculpatory topoi is especially helpful here. As he points out, "Despite endeavoring to insert an element of the accidental (and blameless because unaccountable) Hamlet seems compulsively to add qualifications and refinements that reinscribe personal agency," thereby undoing his own defense.[53] Notice, though, that this description of the "incoherence" of Hamlet's self-explanation within an early modern *legal* frame also indicates the *theological* frame within which, I would suggest, Hamlet's words do make a kind of sense:

> As a matter of law, there is no agent behind the act of a mad man; *but Hamlet nevertheless, cued apparently by a recollection of Romans 7.20, feels compelled to ask 'Who does it then?' as if unable to grasp the point of the exculpatory strategy he has embarked on, which should make this question unnecessary.* His answer subjectifies his madness as though it were a person who has victimized not only Laertes but Hamlet himself.[54]

As Wilson's reference to Romans 7 indicates, Hamlet's description of his madness follows the same logic as Paul's complaint about in-dwelling sin, Augustine's complaint about the "dissociation" that sin causes, and Calvin's description of the

---

[53] Wilson, *Theaters of Intention*, 61.   [54] Wilson, *Theaters of Intention*, 61–2, emphasis added.

concupiscence with which we are "stuffed full." The speech captures the horrible paradox of being responsible not only for "purposed evil[s]" but for actions caused by something evil *in* me that is *not* me—a very different kind of "madness" than the kind recognized by the law. Just as theological concerns shape Hamlet's own thoughts about action, then, so I would suggest that theology informs the way *Hamlet* thinks about motivation and action. Exposing what Melissa Sanchez refers to as the "irrationality that theology assiduously locates at the core of desire," *Hamlet*'s scenes of animation stage, in exaggerated form and in relation even to non-spiritual matters, the entwined ideas of being able to do nothing good of one's own and of being provoked from within by an evil concupiscence.[55] Through such scenes the play engages motivation and "madness"—those standard topoi of revenge tragedy—on the ethical terrain of Reformed moral psychology, distributing across its characters' actions what Senecan revenge drama and early modern moralists describe as the pathological irrationality of the revenger. The play both exploits the dramatic possibilities and explores the ethical implications of a Calvinist moral psychological framework that posits the relative impotence of reason and the motivating force of the irrational.

Hamlet's use of spectral complaint brings into relief the play's philosophical and aesthetic distance from the *Mirror* with regard both to its understanding of moral psychology and its approach to questions of tragic cause. The *Mirror*'s tragedies reflect an Aristotelian view of tragedy (albeit in the form of narrative verse rather than dramatic mimesis) insofar as they suggest that what is seemingly inexplicable can be rationalized—that frightful tragic falls stem from the moral disaster of a reckless will whose first bad choice can be pinned down and explained. Spectral complaint is the formal means of this sense-making, as a device that constructs a retrospective narrative of cause. By contrast, *Hamlet*'s treatment of motivation and its deployment of spectral complaint suggest that the desire for a legible cause of tragedy reflects a gap in knowledge where there is nothing but an ineradicable kernel of nonsense (an insight that Lee Edelman and Madhavi Menon describe as a point of intellectual continuity between Shakespearean tragedy and psychoanalytic theory).[56] The play dethrones reason in its account of causes. But more than simply revealing the flaws in reason or exposing its gaps, *Hamlet* vividly underlines an irrational, sublime, and ultimately unaccountable motive that the play suggests "shapes our ends" (5.2.10). The play entertains this idea in a way that formally echoes the accretive, repetitive, and universalizing logic of the *Mirror*, through repeating, periodic scenes of animation that follow the pivotal scene of spectral complaint in revolving around a sublime motive. Although I am not claiming that Shakespeare is responding specifically to the *Mirror*, I do want to suggest that the concept of a tragic narrative whose spectral complaints are "mirrors" that tell stories about motivation is important

---

[55] Sanchez, *Queer Faith*, 94.   [56] Edelman and Manon, "Queer Tragedy," 285–97.

112 THE DRAMA OF COMPLAINT

to the play. Together its scenes of spectral complaint and scenes of animation actualize *Hamlet*'s embedded ideal of a drama that "hold[s] as 'twere the mirror up to Nature," exposing truth—not for the corrective purposes that the mirror metaphor conventionally connotes, but to stun, to "amaze" and "appall," as Hamlet says of the Player's "horrid speech" (3.2.21–22, 2.2.502). Rather than telling its readers how to choose the good and shun the evil, the play confronts them with a baffling, recalcitrant desire for which it presents no cure. It's no coincidence that this kind of ruinous irrationality is exactly what Hamlet is trying to make sense of on each of the two occasions the Ghost appears to him.

2. Ghostly Excitations: *Hamlet*'s Dull Revenge

The first time Hamlet sees the Ghost, it interrupts him as he is expounding the enigma and the scandal of moral ruin. Keeping watch for the Ghost on the walls of Elsinore with Horatio, Marcellus, and Barnardo as Claudius and his men loudly toast below, Hamlet is complaining that such ritualized intemperance sullies the reputation of the Danish body politic. The Ghost materializes just as he is attempting to explain what corrupts "particular men" of "infinite virtue." The cause, he suggests, is "some vicious mole of nature":

> So oft it chances in particular men
> That, for some vicious mole of nature in them,
> As in their birth wherein they are not guilty
> (Since nature cannot choose his origin),
> By their o'ergrowth of some complexion
> Oft breaking down the pales and forts of reason,
> Or by some habit that too much o'erleavens
> The form of plausive manners—that these men,
> Carrying, I say, the stamp of one defect
> (Being Nature's livery or Fortune's star),
> His virtues else, be they as pure as grace,
> As infinite as man may undergo,
> Shall in the general censure take corruption
> From that particular fault: the dram of eale
> Doth all the noble substance of a doubt
> To his own scandal—
>   *Enter* GHOST.
>
>   (1.4.23–38)

Hamlet locates the corrosive workings of this "vicious mole"—a figure for Original Sin—in incontinent and intemperate acts alike. It manifests in excessive appetite, the "o'ergrowth of some complexion" (a term that evokes both the humoral theories and the racializing operations of early modern moral psychology) that "break[s] down the pales and forts of reason." It also manifests in the immoderate actions willfully repeated to the point of enthrallment, "some habit that too much o'erleavens / The form of plausive manners," deforming one's character. The enigmatic quality of this thing is emphasized by his repeated use of "some" as a modifier ("*some* vicious mole," "*some* complexion," "*some* habit"). What vexes Hamlet, as this speech's thorny syntax suggests, is the fact that an otherwise virtuous person can be held accountable for this "particular fault," this "stamp of one defect," this single "dram of eale"—this strange thing that, moreover, was impressed upon them by "nature" or "Fortune," and not (at least it would seem) by choice.

Through both the timing of the Ghost's entrance and the odd expression that Hamlet utters after it has vanished ("Well said, old mole, can'st work i'th' earth so fast?" [1.5.161]), the play creates an associative link between the Ghost and the "vicious mole of nature" that "break[s] down the pales and forts of reason." One of the qualities both share, as the epithet emphasizes, is their disruptive motions; indeed, Hamlet's description of the Ghost as "an old mole" already "work[ing]" beneath Elsinore renders perceptible the phenomenon of its unsettling of the earth. This turbulence links *Hamlet*'s Ghost to the complaining ghosts of the Senecan revenge tragedies *Troades* and *Thyestes*, translated into English by Jasper Heywood and respectively printed in 1559 and 1560. In Heywood's rendition, the revenge plot of *Troades* (*Troas*, in his titling) begins in Act Two when the ghost of Achilles comes to the upper world to demand the death of Polyxena, rising out of the earth with a "dreadfull sounde" that shakes both the surrounding environs and the messenger Talthybius, sole witness to the ghost's appearance ("My mynde is masde my tremblyng synnews quake and are afearde," Talthybius notes, referencing the trembling of the limbs that—as a conventional signifier of frightened shock—was a literary trope of spectral encounters).[57] A comparable ghostquake occurs in the first scene of *Thyestes*, when the Fury Megæra summons the ghost of Tantalus from the underworld to spread discord through the House of Atreus, "let[ting] furie blynde enflame / their myndes and wrathfull wyll."[58] The ghost enters and unsettles the house even as the Fury speaks:

> I followe thee: through all this house nowe rage and furie throwe.
> Let them be dryven so, and so let eyther thyrst to see

---

[57] Seneca, *Troas*, B5v. While Seneca's Talthybius merely reports the ghost's appearance, Heywood—citing "the want of some thynges" in the Senecan text—creates a speaking role for the Ghost of Achilles, comprised entirely of a ninety-one line complaint ("Achilles death shalbe revenged heare /...ible/ Nought els but thys may satisfye our ire, / Her will I have and her I you require"). Preface (unpaginated), B5r–B5v.

[58] Seneca, *Thyestes*, A2r.

114   THE DRAMA OF COMPLAINT

> Eche others blood. Full well hathe felte the cummyng in of thee
> This house: and all with wycked touche of thee begun to quake.
>
> (A4v)

The psychophysiological excitations figured by these environmental disturbances in Senecan tragedy are what Seneca identifies in the moral essay *De Ira* as the "first motions" of revenge.[59] He describes such stirrings of anger as involuntary reactions to stimuli, mere "agitations of the bodie" classified in *De Ira* with a list of other "first motion[s] of the minde we cannot avoide," such as the shaking of the limbs or the upstarting of the hair at a frightful sight (529). (The very reactions the Ghost predicts Hamlet would have to the story of his "prison-house," could he tell it [1.5.14].) In the Stoic ethical paradigm, a person is blameless until they consciously allow these motions to become the passion or affection of wrath, which Seneca defines as a desire for revenge to which the mind, having "treadeth downe reason," has assented in an error of judgment (529). "Wrath is a concitation of the minde, tending voluntarily and with judgement to revenge," he writes (530); "This is no motion that may incite it selfe without our will [*voluntate*]" (528). This knowing assent to irrational desire is exactly what *Thyestes* dramatizes. After the play's opening exchange between Megæra and the ghost of Tantalus, Atreus— incensed at his brother Thyestes for having committed adultery with his wife and stolen his throne—approves the motions of anger that perturb him, and decides to pursue some horrible "mischief" yet unknown:

> I graunte: a tomblyng tumulte quakes, within my bosomes loe,
> And rounde it rolles: I moved am and wote not whereunto.
> But drawen I am....
> So be it, so be it, let mischiefe suche be sought,
> As ye O gods wolde feare.
>
> ....
>
> What thyng it is I can not tell:
> But great it is. Be it so, my mynde now in this feate proceede[.][60]
>
> (B1v)

Reflecting the Stoic model of a unified mind that no "wicked touch" can drive to wrath or revenge without its consent, the Senecan revenger metabolizes the involuntary agitations his mind passively suffers ("the motions of such minds, as are willing to bee moved" [529]) into a motive through the intellective act of *voluntas*, encapsulated here in Atreus's "I graunte...Be it so."

---

[59] Seneca, *The Workes of Lucius Annaeus Seneca*, 530. Hereafter cited parenthetically.

[60] I have slightly modernized some of the spelling in this passage.

Shakespeare uses this same lexicon of psychophysiological animation to figure the revenger's motivation, linking Hamlet's decision to obey the beckoning Ghost ("Go on! I'll follow thee") to the effects of its call, which reaches into his innermost parts, "mak[ing] each petty artery in this body / As hardy as the Nemean lion's nerve" (1.4.86, 82–83). But in *Hamlet*'s theologically-informed account of moral psychology, such tropes are representational shorthand for a sublime motive *beyond* what the mind knowingly approves and wills, a volitional excess not fully metabolized by the intellect.[61] The Ghost—the cause of Hamlet's voluntary and involuntary motions—is an embodiment of this very excess, and is consistently framed by the play's language and dramaturgy in such a way as to call attention not only to its ambiguous identity as the dead king's spirit, but to its too-muchness, both as a force and as a phenomenon. The Ghost "shake[s]" the "disposition" of its onlookers, making them "burst in ignorance," just as it has "burst [its] cerements" and its sepulcher (1.4.55, 46, 48). The disruptive, shattering effects of "this thing" are clear from the first time it stalks on stage, just as Barnardo is telling the skeptical Horatio the tale of its most recent appearance (1.1.20). Recall that the Ghost simultaneously steps into the space of Barnardo's narrative and breaks its frame:

> BARNARDO Last night of all,
> When yond same star that's westward from the pole
> Had made his course t'illume that part of heaven
> Where now it burns, Marcellus and myself,
> The bell then beating one—
> *Enter* GHOST.
> MARCELLUS   Peace, break thee off, look where it comes again.
> (1.1.34–39)

The Ghost exceeds the interpretive paradigms available to the play's theatrical audience too. Early modern audiences would have initially recognized the Ghost's complaint as an iteration of a conventional tragic device, the standard generator of the revenge plot (and a tired theatrical bit, if we trust *A Warning for Fair Women*'s Comedie, who mocks Tragedie for her predictable scenario of "a filthie whining ghost" who "Comes skreaming like a pigge halfe stickt, / And cries

---

[61] Before they assent to the involuntary agitations they suffer, the protagonists of Senecan tragedy remark on the experience of alterity caused by these agitations in language very similar to Romans 7 (for instance, before she succumbs to the stirrings of lust for her stepson Hippolytus, Phaedra says, "I call all you gods to witness that this thing I want—I do not want." See Seneca, *Phaedra*, 2.605). I am grateful to the anonymous reader of this manuscript who alerted me to this passage. One might say that if Senecan tragedy dramatizes the way in which an involuntary agitation becomes fully integrated into a passionate, willed motive, *Hamlet* focalizes a kind of animation that remains distinct from a passionate, willed motive.

116   THE DRAMA OF COMPLAINT

Vindicta, revenge, revenge").[62] Yet the play also endows the Ghost with an eerie reality in its play-world that no Senecan ghost possesses. (Certainly not the ghost of Achilles, whom the Chorus of *Troades* explicitly identifies as a poetic fiction— the notion of souls surviving the death of their bodies being but "fayned lies"—or the Ghost of Don Andrea in Thomas Kyd's *The Spanish Tragedy* [1592], whose plaintive dialogue with the allegorical character of Revenge serves as a metatheatrical frame narrative, an obvious pretext for the play's main revenge narrative.)[63] In contrast to these precedents, *Hamlet*'s Ghost is a "portentous figure" whose enigmatic quality never resolves into legibility for characters or audiences, a "questionable shape" with no answer (1.1.108, 1.4.43).[64] The confessional faultlines in early modern post-Reformation theology offer one frame for understanding the persistence and the affective power of that enigma.[65] Another, as I am suggesting, is the Reformed theological understanding of moral psychology. From this angle, the play's refusal to make sense of the Ghost reflects the Ghost's figural representation of excess—an unknown motivating variable—that cannot be made sense of. Viewed through this interpretive lens, Shakespeare's placement of the Ghost within a purgatorial afterlife takes on a different significance: rather than (only) indexing post-Reformation cultural anxieties about the place of the dead, the Ghost, embedding its command in Hamlet's heart, appears as a figure of *unpurged sin*—what Calvin calls the ineradicable "relics of the flesh," in the flesh.

While the play's exploration of the motivating force of an irrational excess (an excess we might think of as an analogue to evil concupiscence or divine grace) ranges beyond the act of revenge commanded by the Ghost, it is also at the forefront of *Hamlet*'s two representations of successful revenge, each of which features a revenger motivated by a notably concupiscent force distinct from what he identifies as his will. In taking revenge on Hamlet, Laertes is an instrument for a will in excess of his own, having agreed to "be ruled" by Claudius as long as he "might be the organ" of revenge (4.7.66–68). The phrase figures Laertes as a body part doing as the mind commands, an image supported by Claudius's suggestion that Laertes "put me in your heart for friend": the logic of the conceit transplants the king's will into Laertes' heart, the will's traditional seat, where it commands from inside this "organ" (4.7.2). Laertes' announcement of himself to Hamlet as having a "motive in this case [that] should stir me most / To my revenge" recalls this surplus motive soldered onto his—a motive, born of Claudius's lust, that remains opaque to Laertes to the end (5.2.222–23). In contrast to its figuration of this motive as a command internalized in Laertes' heart, *Hamlet*'s second-order representation of revenge in the Player's speech highlights the difference between

---

[62] *A Warning for Fair Women*, lines 54, 57–8.   [63] Seneca, *Troas*, Chorus to Act 2, C5r.

[64] On the uniqueness of Hamlet's Ghost and the ambiguity in early modern culture as to whether ghosts are supernatural emissaries or figments of the imagination, see Belsey, "Beyond reason."

[65] See especially Greenblatt, *Hamlet in Purgatory*.

Pyrrhus's "will and matter"—his desire and reason for revenge—and a commanding force located outside his body and his control, in his sword (2.2.419). The first thing the sword does is thwart Pyrrhus's intention ("Pyrrhus at Priam drives, in rage strikes wide" [2.2.410]). Then, distracted by the falling towers, it freezes, mid-blow, "seem[ing] i'th' air to stick"—with the consequence that "Pyrrhus stood / Like a neutral to his will and matter, / Did nothing" (2.2.417, 418–20). The sword's inattention to revenge, its disregard for Pyrrhus's will, renders Pyrrhus impotent, making him a mirror of Priam, whose "antique sword, / Rebellious to his arm, lies where it falls, / Repugnant to command" (2.2.406–8). (I trust that the phallic resonance of the sword needs no gloss, but it is worth recalling Augustine's identification of the erection as the exemplary instance of a libidinal movement that the will has no power over, rising or falling only at the commands of lust.)[66] Pyrrhus returns to his revenge only at the order of a "roused vengeance" that sets the sword in motion:

> A roused vengeance sets him new a-work,
> And never did the Cyclops' hammers fall
> On Mars's armour, forged for proof eterne,
> With less remorse than Pyrrhus' bleeding sword
> Now falls on Priam.
>
> (2.2.426–30)

In an inversion of the pause at which his will and the sword are volitionally unhinged, here at the moment of action Pyrrhus is fully identified with the sword, grammatically speaking, his motions its. As he moves mechanically and the sword becomes remorseless, they meld into a hybrid human-thing revenger, their seamlessness visible against the backdrop of that fleeting moment in which—wielding a sword that had lost its thirst for blood—Pyrrhus was stuck with nothing but his will to revenge.

In similar terms, the play suggests that the would-be revenger's inaction—Hamlet's inaction—is a matter of a senseless inanimation distinct from (and opposed to) his will to act. Hamlet's reflections on his inanimation only highlight its senselessness. This is not to say that there are no good reasons for him not to enact his revenge, only that the play shows that none of them *are* the reason. From the beginning, his inaction is strangely unmotivated, plot-wise: he is buoyant when the Ghost vanishes at the end of Act 1, but the very next time he is alone, following the Player's painfully lively performance, he is already complaining about a failure to act that he describes in terms of an absence of animation:

---

[66] Augustine, *City of God*, 389 (14.24). Here Augustine speculates that before the Fall, "those parts of the body that are now moved only by lust should have been moved only by the will."

118 THE DRAMA OF COMPLAINT

> What would he do
> Had he the motive and that for passion
> That I have? He would drown the stage with tears
> And cleave the general ear with horrid speech,
> Make mad the guilty and appal the free,
> Confound the ignorant and amaze indeed
> The very faculties of eyes and ears. Yet I,
> A dull and muddy-mettled rascal, peak
> Like John-a-dreams, unpregnant of my cause,
> And can say nothing. No, not for a king
> Upon whose property and most dear life
> A damned defeat was made. Am I a coward?
>
> (2.2.498–506)

Hamlet likens himself to an actor who has forgotten his part "and can say nothing," who remains still in response to the "motive and cue" of the Ghost's command, a stillness he struggles to explain.[67] His overproduction of causes is telling: maybe he is a coward, or maybe it is the "dread of something after death," or maybe he has too keen a sense of conscience (3.1.77). Each of these explanations is a shot in the dark. This includes what has become in the wake of new historicism the most compelling explanation, his uncertainty concerning the Ghost's identity. Having professed his faith in the Ghost to Horatio at the end of Act 1 ("It is an honest ghost—that let me tell you"), Hamlet's doubt surfaces as he reacts to the Player's animation, a context that links that doubt both to his shame and to his attempt to rationalize his inaction (1.5.137). Thus his hunt for a reason passes through cowardice ("For it cannot be / But I am pigeon-livered and lack gall") to land on the problem of the messenger: "The spirit that I have seen / May be a de'il, and the de'il hath power / T'assume a pleasing shape. Yea, and perhaps..." (2.2.511–12, 533–35). The desire for more knowledge appears as a symptom, rather than the cause of—or the solution to—his inaction.[68] After "The Mousetrap," his epistemological uncertainties evaporate ("O good Horatio, I'll take the Ghost's word for a thousand pound"); indeed, when the Ghost appears again, Hamlet immediately identifies himself as "your tardy son" (3.2.278–79, 3.4.103). Yet he still does not act, and more importantly, he keeps saying that he does not know why he has not done so.[69] His absolute ignorance about the cause of his inaction is especially pointed in his final complaint about it, where he attributes it to

---

[67] This formulation ("the motive and the cue") is only in F.

[68] Cf. Levy, who suggests that Hamlet's inaction stems from a lack of knowledge that he must remedy as far as it possible to do so. Levy, "'Things Standing Thus Unknown.'"

[69] A useful contrast is the delayed revenge of Hieronimo, the revenger of *The Spanish Tragedy*, who laments that his son's murder remains unavenged but never wonders *why* he has waited (he must first ascertain the identities of the murderers).

"Bestial oblivion or some craven scruple / Of thinking too precisely on th'event"—as if the possibility that he has totally forgotten his obligation seems as likely as the possibility that he has thought too conscientiously about it (4.4.39–40). At last he admits

> I do not know
> Why yet I live to say this thing's to do,
> Sith I have cause and will and strength and means
> To do't.
>
> (4.4.42–45)

Hamlet finally, ironically, succeeds in pinpointing the answer: all the things he has are just not enough.[70]

Like his explanation to Laertes of his role in Polonius's death, Hamlet's incoherent accounts of why he has not acted echo the "monstrous situation" that Augustine bemoans in his conversion story, and that Paul complains about in Romans 7: I do not do as I will, but as something "not I" wills. "Mind commands, I say, that it should will," Augustine writes, but "The willing is not wholehearted, so the command is not wholehearted...the will that commands is incomplete, and therefore what it commands does not happen" (147, 148). The repeated prayer of the *Confessions*—"Grant what you command, and command what you will"—makes clear that spiritual action depends on following a divine command that fills out that self-divided, "incomplete" will (202). Indeed, Augustine recounts that what makes the difference in his conversion struggle is an overheard chant ("Pick up and read, pick up and read") that he interprets "as a divine command...to open the book" of Romans (152, 153). The command enters him: "At once, with the last words of this sentence, it was as if a light of relief from all anxiety flooded into my heart" (153). This is the same language that early modern writers use when describing how grace motivates and empowers its bearers to seek the good. Calvin suggests that "the liquor of God's grace" fills the elect, so that they are "ruled by his stirring & moving...made his members."[71] La Primaudaye suggests that in an ideal scenario, the human will may be "as it were wholly swallowed up" by the love of God, its desires determined by the in-dwelling divine will:

---

[70] One might ask if what I'm referring to as Hamlet's inanimation is another term for his self-identified melancholy. Discussions of melancholy typically identify Hamlet's excessive affective investment in one object (the dead father) as the cause of his inability to invest libidinal energy in other objects (revenge, Ophelia, etc.). Though I too am describing Hamlet's failure to cathect to the object of revenge, I am not offering a determinate cause for this failure (or, in my terminology, his lack of animation), as I maintain that it's precisely that lack of a reason that the play emphasizes. Drew Daniel describes Hamlet's melancholy as an affective excess and epistemological lack that itself ceaselessly elicits interpretation in *The Melancholy Assemblage*, 120–54.

[71] Calvin, *Institution of Christian Religion*, 173v (3.1.3).

120   THE DRAMA OF COMPLAINT

> And if we place God in the highest degree of love, as the soveraigne good, with
> whose love we ought to be as it were wholly swallowed up, we will love nothing
> but in him and by him, and for his sake: and consequently we will desire nothing
> but according to his Will, because we can Will or desire nothing but that which
> we shall love...we beseech him to guide & govern us, to reforme us daily more
> & more after his own image and similitude, to the end we may be made con-
> formable to him both in mind & will, & become true temples for him to
> dwel in.[72]

This force transforms the mind's desires, bending them to its own ends, so that we
want the "soveraigne good" we would not want without it. Here, what moves (in)
the subject, pursuing what it wants, is a divine supplement to the will.

Drawing from a similar rhetorical and figurative repertoire, *Hamlet* represents
action as the effect of an animating command that seems to fill the mind's inter-
stices and direct desire to particular objects in the world. By keying the fleeting
phenomenon of Hamlet's own animation to the Ghost's physical presence,
Shakespeare underlines that the Ghost's command is the thing that *has to be there*
for Hamlet to be animated: Hamlet cannot obey the command to revenge when
that command speaks from his will alone; only *its* articulation of the command
will do. His inability to be animated to revenge in the absence of the Ghost is
especially evident when he comes upon the kneeling Claudius, draws his sword,
and decides not to strike:

> Now might I do't. But now 'a is a-praying.
> And now I'll do it [*Draws sword.*]—and so 'a goes to heaven,
> And so I am revenged! That would be scanned:
> ....
>   And am I then revenged
> To take him in the purging of his soul
> When he is fit and seasoned for his passage?
> No. [*Sheathes sword.*]
>
>   (3.3.73–87)

Hamlet offers a rationale for not acting: he would not be revenged if he were to
send the king to his death but not his damnation. The language through which he
arrives at this conclusion ("Why, this is base and silly, not revenge") links Hamlet's
inaction to the sudden appearance, in the light of reason's "scanning," of a gap
between *revenge*—the sublime object commanded by the Ghost—and the act of
killing Claudius, an act that now seems mundane, sordid, base, "not revenge"

---

[72] La Primaudaye, *The Second Part of the French Academie*, 210–11.

(3.3.79). With its wish not only for a more desirable opportunity in the future but for a mind more excited, Hamlet's apostrophe to his sword for it to stay sheathed until it can "know thou a more horrid hent" emphasizes, again, that animation is what fills in that gap (3.3.87).

As Hamlet's revenge fizzles, *Hamlet* exposes irrational motivation elsewhere, its language and actions directing the audience's gaze to enigmatic animating commands, as with Laertes, "ruled" by Claudius in his heart, and Pyrrhus, "set a-work" by a vengeance that grips his sword.[73] In a recent study of revenge tragedy, Derek Dunne classifies *Hamlet* as "an anomaly in the revenge genre" for its relative disinterest even in the action of revenge, let alone its sociopolitical causes and effects.[74] I have been pulling at one of the play's many philosophical threads by showing how, in the conventional locus of revenge's cause—the scene of spectral complaint—Shakespeare constructs a more generalized image of motivation. This image reflects theological understandings of the mind that diverge from the moral psychology that underpins Senecan revenge drama, which assumes the intellective, voluntary act of consenting to the passion of wrath, an error of judgment that Neostoic moral philosophers suggest could be prevented by the right use of reason. By contrast, *Hamlet*'s scenes of spectral complaint, and its scenes of animation, repeatedly stress reason's categorical insufficiency, not only to prevent or motivate revenge, but to motivate action and to construct a satisfactory account of motivation. In these scenes, the play exposes a "madness" that is hardly unique to the revenger, that no act of volition can digest, that no narrative makes sense of, and that early modern moral philosophy disavows. It is not to identify the Ghost itself as good or evil, but rather to accentuate this enigmatic and vital motive, a motive beyond reason and nonidentical with the will, that the play implies a subtle analogy between the "dread command" that Hamlet internalizes in the scene of spectral complaint and the sublime commands of "supernaturall grace" and evil concupiscence.[75]

To what purpose? An answer is suggested by *Hamlet*'s play-within-a-play. Unlike its bloody precedent in *The Spanish Tragedy*, designed by Hieronimo as a vehicle for enacting his revenge, "The Mousetrap" aims to expose and upset its audience. Having remembered a story of "guilty creatures sitting at a play" spontaneously moved to confess their crimes ("For murder, though it have no tongue, will speak / With most miraculous organ"), Hamlet dreams of making Claudius's "occulted guilt /... itself unkennel"—of playing for him a play that will "tent him

---

[73] I concur with John Kerrigan that Shakespeare does not frame Hamlet's killing of Claudius as revenge for his father's death: the act is unplanned, Hamlet does not claim to have achieved revenge, he never confronts Claudius with his deeds or exposes them publicly (he calls Claudius "incestuous" and "murderous," but the latter refers more obviously to Claudius's responsibility for the poisoned drink and envenomed rapier), and the Ghost never reappears. See Kerrigan, *Revenge Tragedy,* 187–8.

[74] Dunne, *Shakespeare, Revenge Tragedy and Early Modern Law*, 97.

[75] Calvin, *Institution of Christian Religion*, 74v (2.1.9).

122   THE DRAMA OF COMPLAINT

to the quick" and make him "blench" by publicly staging his secret (2.2.524, 528–29; 3.2.76–77; 2.2.532).[76] His description of mimesis that pokes at a sore spot and uncovers what has been hidden recalls Sidney's praise of tragedy in *The Defence of Poesy* (1595) as "open[ing] the greatest wounds, and show[ing] forth the ulcers that are covered with tissue."[77] Hamlet will again voice this theory of theater that inspires his staging of "The Mousetrap" when he pompously reminds the Players before their performance that "the purpose of playing... was and is to hold as 'twere the mirror up to Nature to show Virtue her feature, Scorn her own image, and the very age and body of the time his form and pressure" (3.2.20–24). Theater, in this view, is a powerful moral instrument—a "miraculous organ"— precisely insofar as it is a mirror, showing its audiences an image of themselves they would keep veiled from sight. For *Hamlet* as for Hamlet, I want to suggest, the ethical impact of theatrical drama is identical with its confrontational and revelatory capacities. Shakespeare's play attempts to force, if not a confession, an acknowledgment from its audiences of a known but disavowed truth about motivation.

Spectral complaint, as I have been arguing, is vital to how *Hamlet* reveals this sight meant to startle, for it simultaneously focalizes the irrational motivation of a "dread command" and elicits wonder in its staging of an unusually enigmatic, compelling Ghost, which I have been reading as both an inexplicable phenomenon in the play-world and a figure for something excessive in motivation and necessary to action. This doubled significance is dramatically pronounced in the second scene of spectral complaint—the Ghost's final appearance—in Gertrude's closet, as Hamlet is continuing his work of exposure after Claudius's flight has interrupted "The Mousetrap." Here he stages another hidden sight for his captive audience of one, again trying to compel acknowledgment through horror:

> Come, come, and sit you down. You shall not budge.
> You go not till I set you up a glass
> Where you may see the inmost part of you.
> ....
> —Leave wringing of your hands. Peace, sit you down
> And let me wring your heart.
>
> (3.4.17–33)

As Hamlet is attempting to decipher the enigma of Gertrude's desire for Claudius by making her see and reveal to him her "inmost part," the Ghost reappears to "whet" his "almost blunted purpose," once more interrupting a rant about

---

[76] A similar anecdote is recounted in *A Warning for Fair Women*, which Shakespeare's company performed in 1599, and in Thomas Heywood's *Apology for Actors* (1612), G1v–G2r. Interestingly, in Heywood's account it is a stage ghost—that of a murdered man who haunts his guilty wife—that prompts a woman in the audience to confess to just such a murder.

[77] *Sir Philip Sidney: The Major Works*, 230.

"ME AND MY CAUSE" 123

something Hamlet can hardly stomach but wants to get to the heart of (3.4.107, 105). I'll return to the spectral complaint—and the famous crux—of the closet scene momentarily. First, it is necessary to see the companion scenes of animation the play holds up to it.

3. Scenes of Animation: *Hamlet*'s Dread Commands

"Who commands them, sir?" (4.4.12). Like the play's first line ("Who's there?"), the query of one guard to another on Elsinore's walls, the question of who commands—a question posed by Hamlet to the Captain who seeks permission for Fortinbras and his soldiers to cross through Denmark to Poland—bears a surplus meaning that ripples out over the play (1.1.1). *Hamlet*, as we have seen, represents motivation and action as a matter of being commanded by something enigmatic, questionable. In the final section of this chapter, I want to show how the play's exploration of the question of who or what commands across its scenes of animation constitutes a cumulative conceptual disorientation of ethical subjectivity. These scenes focalize an operative command that is decidedly not the universal demand of the good, mediated through reason, but something singular and sublime, beyond reason, that seizes the will of a particular person. The play exposes its audiences to this command through Hamlet, whose reactions are at once a mirror and a conduit for the agitation that that exposure is meant to excite.

Among the many things that are affective flashpoints for Hamlet are other people's irrational motivation. Think of his reaction to the Player's passion, to the Norwegian army's death march, and to Gertrude's desire—all forms of animation that Shakespeare figures as obedience to a sublime, enigmatic command. What astonishes Hamlet about the Player and the army is not simply that these men can act, but that their action attests to strange commands that have overruled their reason, enigmatic commands inferior to—but in their exceeding of rational desire, not unlike—his own. "Prompted to my revenge by heaven and hell," he remains motionless, his transcendent cue notwithstanding (2.2.519). By contrast the Player, whose ability to "force his soul so to his own conceit" Hamlet envies, is animated by nothing more than the authoritative order of his own imagination, which "in a fiction, in a dream of passion," neutralizes his reason so that he can be moved by that fiction (2.2.488, 487). It is this ability to force himself to effectively believe in his own lie, and not the fictive nature of that passion's object, Hecuba, that Hamlet finds so "monstrous" about the Player's performance:

> Is it not monstrous that this player here,
> But in a fiction, in a dream of passion,
> Could force his soul so to his own conceit
> That from her working all the visage waned

124 THE DRAMA OF COMPLAINT

> —Tears in his eyes, distraction in his aspect,
> A broken voice, and his whole function suiting
> With forms to his conceit—and all for nothing—
> For Hecuba?

(2.2.486–93)

In the Player's performance of Aeneas's speech to Dido, Hamlet sees a character animated by an actor's motions, and an actor animated by a character's imagined passion. Commanding his soul at an ecstatic remove from himself, what "works" in the Player is a "motive...for passion"—a motive for his action—that is not exactly *his*, though it has no life apart from him either (2.2.496). This, of course, is simply what theatrical performance is. It is only Hamlet's horrified reaction that lets the play's audience know that they have witnessed, in *Hamlet*'s embedded representation of a skillful dramatic performance, something "monstrous."

The same is true for the Norwegian army, marching across the stage in a unified motion whose contrast with his own stillness Hamlet invites the theatrical audience to "witness":

> Witness this army of such mass and charge,
> Led by a delicate and tender prince
> Whose spirit with divine ambition puffed
> Makes mouths at the invisible event
> Exposing what is mortal and unsure
> To all that fortune, death and danger dare
> Even for an eggshell. Rightly to be great
> Is not to stir without great argument
> But greatly to find quarrel in a straw
> When honour's at the stake. How stand I then
> That have a father killed, a mother stained,
> Excitements of my reason and my blood,
> And let all sleep; while to my shame I see
> The imminent death of twenty thousand men
> That for a fantasy and trick of fame
> Go to their graves like beds, fight for a plot
> Whereon the numbers cannot try the cause,
> Which is not tomb enough and continent
> To hide the slain? O, from this time forth
> My thoughts be bloody or be nothing worth.

(4.4.46–65)

The same themes that characterize Hamlet's reaction to the Player's passion reappear here. The army's action is for "nothing," as the Captain readily admits:

they "go to gain a little patch of ground / That hath in it no profit but the name" (4.4.17–18).[78] The motive could hardly be more irrational, a point the play makes by stressing its sheer incommensurability with the mundane numerical accounting of lives and ducats and acreage ("The numbers cannot try the cause"). Thus Hamlet compares the matter to "th'impostume . . . / That inward breaks and shows no cause without / Why the man dies": the cause of the soldiers' fatal action is as imperceptible as an abscess that destroys from within (4.4.26–28). What Hamlet recognizes is that the cause is not in the land itself, but in the command that propels the men toward it—and that command, like an abscess, is within but not identical with the corporate body the soldiers comprise. Hamlet's characterization of Fortinbras as "a delicate and tender prince" is incongruous (as editors often note), if taken as a literal description of the man. But the phrase makes sense as part of a conceit meant to emphasize the astounding slightness of the command that enlivens—and exposes to death—an "army of such mass and charge." In this figurative logic, the prince is the minimally material soul (the "spirit with divine ambition puffed") that animates and wills a large, mortal body to move, stirring it to pursue an intrinsically worthless object.

Couched in the same language of animation, vitality, and motion, Hamlet's anguished question—"How stand I then?"—expresses his shame at failing to carry out a superior charge, "Excitements of my reason and my blood." The soldiers go to their deathbeds, he sleeps; they move, he stands. To stand, in the play's vocabulary, is to be inanimate, and more specifically impotent in relation to one's own will, as "Pyrrhus stood" or Claudius "stand[s] in pause" as his "stronger guilt defeats [his] strong intent" and "inclination . . . as sharp as will" to kneel (3.3.42, 40, 39). Simultaneously suggesting an unsatisfactory "standing" in relation to an obligation—a law, a debt, a duty—Hamlet's question also brings to a head the specifically ethical pressure of the Ghost's as-yet unfollowed command. That pressure, which first emerges in the original scene of spectral complaint, becomes palpable again in the scene of spectral complaint framed by the closet scene. The mere appearance of the Ghost is enough to spark Hamlet's admission of guilt in relation to the Ghost's "dread command," his neglecting of its "important acting." He even imagines and preempts the Ghost's scolding words:

> *Enter* GHOST.
> Save me and hover o'er me with your wings,
> You heavenly guards! What would your gracious figure?
> QUEEN   Alas, he's mad!
> HAMLET   Do you not come your tardy son to chide
> That, lapsed in time and passion, lets go by

---

[78] On the irrationality of these pursuits, see Baldo, " 'His form and cause conjoin'd.' "

126   THE DRAMA OF COMPLAINT

> Th' important acting of your dread command?
> O say!
> GHOST   Do not forget! This visitation
> Is but to whet thy almost blunted purpose.

(3.4.100–7)

The Ghost's visit, with its reiteration of its command ("Do not forget!") does indeed reanimate Hamlet, however briefly, as Gertrude testifies:

> Forth at your eyes your spirits wildly peep,
> And as the sleeping soldiers in th'alarm
> Your bedded hair like life in excrements
> Start up and stand on end.

(3.4.115–18)

Notice, here, Hamlet's soldier-like readiness to do as he is commanded, the standing at attention.

What cannot but puzzle *Hamlet*'s audiences is that these indexical traces are all Gertrude sees of a "gracious figure" that never materializes within her field of vision, despite Hamlet's direction of her eye:

> QUEEN   Whereon do you look?
> HAMLET   On him, on him! Look you how pale he glares,
>   His form and cause conjoined preaching to stones
>   Would make them capable.
> ....
> HAMLET   Do you see nothing there?
> QUEEN   Nothing at all, yet all that is I see.
> HAMLET   Nor did you nothing hear?
> QUEEN   No, nothing but ourselves.
> HAMLET   Why, look you there! Look how it steals away—
>   My father in his habit as he lived.
>   Look where he goes even now out at the portal!
> QUEEN   This is the very coinage of your brain.
>   This bodiless creation ecstasy
>   Is very cunning in.

(3.4.120–37)

How do we account for the discrepancy between what Hamlet and Gertrude see? The simplest explanation is Gertrude's: that in his "ecstasy" Hamlet sees things where there is "nothing at all." Yet the scene seems designed to complicate this interpretation, and not only because the wide eyes and raised hairs that Gertrude describes track perfectly with the conventional reactions to ghosts in early modern literature. By aligning the audience's perspective with Hamlet's, Shakespeare places the ready explanation at a remove: one might conclude that Gertrude is correct, but the question of what has captivated Hamlet has had to be asked. The significance of the crux qua crux comes into focus through the consonance between the question that the bewildered Gertrude poses to Hamlet ("how is't with you, / That you do bend your eye on vacancy") and Hamlet's astonishment at the animation of the Player and the army, similarly fixed on objects of "nothing" (3.4.112–13). In confronting the audience with the coexistence of incompatible perspectives, this scene of spectral complaint, I would suggest, emphasizes an animation that can only look like madness to the "objective" observer.

In this sense the timing of the Ghost's return dramatizes, to startling effect, the very phenomenon Hamlet has just been raving about, for its appearance interrupts his haranguing of Gertrude for her own senseless animation, evident in her desire for Claudius:

> Ha, have you eyes?
> You cannot call it love, for at your age
> The heyday in the blood is tame, it's humble
> And waits upon the judgement, and what judgement
> Would step from this to this? Sense, sure, you have—
> Else could you not have motion. But sure, that sense
> Is apoplexed, for madness would not err
> Nor sense to ecstasy was ne'er so thralled
> But it reserved some quantity of choice
> To serve in such a difference. What devil was't
> That thus hath cozened you at hoodman-blind?
> Eyes without feeling, feeling without sight,
> Ears without hands or eyes, smelling sans all,
> Or but a sickly part of one true sense
> Could not so mope.
>
> (3.4.65–79)

Invoking the Aristotelian model of the tripartite soul in which the relation between the rational powers of understanding and willing is analogous to that between the sensible powers of apprehending and moving, Hamlet argues that in "batten[ing] on this moor"—the verb explicitly links physical motion to appetite for a putatively undesirable, racialized object—Gertrude proves herself devoid of sense, in both meanings of the word (3.4.65). Not only has her will overruled her reason, he suggests, but even her inferior judgment, that of the senses, must be "apoplexed." Her desire is so senseless, so without "quantity of choice," that it is sheer motion, random and distracted, as the blindfolded person "mopes"

128   THE DRAMA OF COMPLAINT

(wanders aimlessly), a point Hamlet punctuates by confronting her with the portraits of her two husbands. The patent impossibility of his "seeing" what she does in Claudius finds its more startling counterpart in the futility of his attempt to make her see the Ghost. He and Gertrude each look where the other's eye bends and insists that there is no apparent cause for the other's motions.

The cause of Gertrude's desire for Claudius, Hamlet concludes, is not in Claudius but rather in herself: "compulsive ardour gives the charge" (3.4.86). It is Gertrude's animation that is—along with Hamlet's inability to obey the Ghost's command—the senseless textual phenomenon that gestures most explicitly to the Calvinist conception of moral psychology. While *Hamlet* implies a certain structural resemblance between the Ghost's command and divine grace, the play is more emphatic still about the parallel between the command that animates Gertrude and the evil concupiscence limned by Calvin. This "compulsive ardour" is vital to the story the Ghost tells, a story that not only casts that ardour as a manifestation of Original Sin, but also imagines Gertrude's turn to Claudius as a repetition of the Fall itself, a tragic "falling off," in the Ghost's words, that leaves (so Hamlet claims) "a mother stained" (1.5.47, 4.4.56). Wondering at how Claudius "won.../ The will of my most seeming-virtuous Queen," the Ghost locates the cause in concupiscence, the voraciousness of which knows no reason: "Lust, though to a radiant angel linked, / Will sate itself in a celestial bed / And prey on garbage" (1.5.45–46, 55–57). The line recalls Calvin's description of humans as "stuffed full with concupiscence," host to a force that never stops consuming, driven to eat solely by its own appetitive nature—a lust that however it sates itself remains hungry.[79]

As scenes of unwilled motivation, *Hamlet's* scenes of animation capture the irrational nature of desire more broadly, which the play figures as a disturbing, quasi-alien part of the self. The causes I have been describing in terms of sublimity, Shakespeare represents as fatally corrosive—and disgusting—corporeal excesses: the abscess within Fortinbras's army that "inward breaks and shows no cause without why the man dies" (4.4.27); the "ulcerous place" in Gertrude's soul from which "rank corruption mining all within / Infects unseen" (3.4.145, 146–47); the "black and grieved spots / As will leave there their tinct" that she says she sees in her soul (3.4. 87–88); the "vicious mole of nature" so suggestively aligned with the Ghost (1.4.24); the "stamp of nature" (3.4.166) that Hamlet tells Gertrude habitual good actions ("use") "almost can change," underscoring its indelibility (3.4.166). All are metaphors for forces that in one way or another confound reason: the abscess and ulcer produce effects that seem to have no cause, the spots reflect the senseless choices of concupiscence, the mole "break[s] down the pales and forts of reason" (1.4.28). Gertrude's nominally sovereign reason cannot judge

---

[79]   Calvin, *Institution of Christian Religion*, 74v (2.1.9, 2.1.8).

aright ("reason pardons will" [3.4.86]), so ruled is she by the "monster Custom," those "habits devil" that Hamlet suggests "eat[s]" all sense (3.4.159, 160, 159). These are also all familiar early modern figures for Original Sin, in line with Calvin's warning about the human heart ("grievous diseases do reigne there"), Sidney's epigrammatic description of the will ("our erected wit maketh us know what perfection is, and yet our infected will keepeth us from reaching unto it"), and Augustine's lament for "the morbid condition of the mind."[80] But even Hamlet's awed description of the lofty "divine ambition" that "puff[s]" the spirit that moves Fortinbras's army, causing "the imminent death of twenty thousand men" for the sake of "an eggshell," is tinged with a certain horror (4.4.48, 59, 52). In each of these cases, the orienting point of desire is a command that pushes its bearer to an object that reason would direct them away from (the land, Hecuba, Claudius, revenge).

These scenes of animation are mirrors for an intrinsic and ineradicable irrationality that *Hamlet* suggests might appall us, were we to see it—a reaction that the play does not just try to provoke, but also stages, in Hamlet's own responses to these sights. The affect that circulates in the scenes of spectral complaint and in the scenes of animation I have been describing is markedly excessive, out of proportion to its objective correlatives, to use T. S. Eliot's memorable language. So too, the play exaggerates, overstates, its point. This, I would suggest, is an intentional overcorrection to the disavowal of such irrationality, and to the praise of reason, in moral philosophy, in which ethical subjectivity comes down to the will—the "part of the reasonable soule...whereby we are made and called good or wicked," in Charron's words.[81] As he explains, "A man is neither good nor wicked, honest nor dishonest, because he understandeth and knoweth those things that are good, and faire, and honest, or wicked and dishonest, but because he loveth them, and hath desire and will towards them" (69). Classical moral philosophy assumes that desire to be informed by reason—the husband to the will, in Charron's metaphor—and oriented, naturally, toward the good, as it pushes the subject out to, and joins him to the objects of, the world ("By the will...the soule goeth foorth of it selfe, and lodgeth and liveth elswhere in the thing beloved, into which it transformeth it selfe" [69]). What *Hamlet* suggests, by contrast, is that desire is irrational, that the will is divided and incomplete, and that its choice of objects is not entirely conscious or considered. This calls into question the excellence of reason too, if it is insufficient to guide the will.

When Hamlet repeats the standard moral philosophical truisms about reason, it is with a sense of irony, as in his sardonic praise of "man" to Rosencrantz and Guildenstern as "a piece of work...noble in reason;...infinite in faculties, in form

---

[80] Calvin, *A commentarie...Genesis*, 95; Sidney, *Defence of Poesy*, in *Sir Philip Sidney: The Major Works*, 217; Augustine, *Confessions*, 148.

[81] Charron, *Of Wisdome*, 69.

130   THE DRAMA OF COMPLAINT

and moving" (2.2.269–71), or when, as he reproaches himself for his senseless failure to take revenge, he suggests that it is only the capacity to use reason and act on its counsel that distinguishes humans from beasts, whose "chief good" is "but to sleep and feed" (4.4.33, 34). That reason might "fust"—become moldy and rotten as it sits "in us unused"—is a possibility he invokes precisely as an impossibility, something that surely cannot be:

> Sure he that made us with such large discourse,
> Looking before and after, gave us not
> That capability and godlike reason
> To fust in us unused.

> (4.4.35–38)

As Hamlet is shaken elsewhere by the appearance of the irrational, in these instances we see him astounded by the sudden dawning of the insufficiency, the incapability, of reason. This same reaction is at play in his initial questioning of the Ghost, when he asks this thing that "mak[es] the night hideous" what it wants, why it has appeared to "we fools of nature / So horridly to shake our disposition / With thoughts beyond the reaches of our souls" (1.4.54, 54–56). The question foregrounds the agitation of the "disposition"—the mind, not the limbs—at being brought to the very limits of its understanding, its concepts and categories strained to their breaking point. What the mind encounters there is a "horrid" truth about its limitations as well as the strangeness of the desires and thoughts that grip it.

Hamlet will repeat this articulation of reason's limit and its structural "beyond" in his response to Horatio's assessment of the spectral visitation as "wondrous strange," when he suggests that "There are more things in heaven and earth, Horatio, / Than are dreamt of in your philosophy" (1.5.163, 165–66). The most immediate reference is to a metaphysical framework inadequate to explain supernatural phenomena. But as other critics have noted, Horatio's philosophy is represented in the play as a (Stoic) moral philosophy too.[82] Horatio is one "whose blood and judgment are so well co-meddled / That they are not a pipe for Fortune's finger / To sound what stop she please"—a man who lives by reason, who "is not passion's slave" (3.2.65–67, 68). These are the reasons Hamlet gives for singling Horatio out as his confidant and friend, and they are the reasons that, as I'd like to suggest in closing, Shakespeare also singles him out: he is the character whose philosophy will be punctured over the course of the play, and the one who survives to absorb the disavowed ethical truth to which it has been exposing its audience. In Act 1, we have seen how the metaphysical framework that

---

[82] See Hui, "Horatio's Philosophy in *Hamlet*." On Horatio's importance, see also Warley, "Specters of Horatio."

"ME AND MY CAUSE"   131

(in Barnardo's words) has lent Horatio "ears / . . . so fortified against our story" is shaken by the sight of the Ghost, which he admits "harrows me with fear and wonder" (1.1.30–31, 43). In Act 5, Horatio's reigning ethical paradigm is similarly harrowed—broken up, distressed—by witnessing the motivating force of a sublime command both senseless and singular. But this time, it is no Ghost that exposes him to this irrationality. Instead, it is Hamlet's address.

Act 5, which begins with Hamlet's unexpected return from the voyage to England, is generally agreed to represent a major shift in the play, a shift that corresponds to the noticeable sea change Hamlet himself has undergone since his last appearance. The Hamlet of Act 5 is animated by what he describes to Horatio as a "special providence," a phrase that alludes to the Calvinist notion of a divine will that directs each life (a will that Calvin describes as active in the "particular movings" of every individual thing).[83] Hamlet's belief in "heaven ordinant" in his action stems from his improbable shipboard escape, a story he has foreshadowed in his letter to Horatio only as "words to speak in thine ear [that] will make thee dumb," and which, in the telling, he frames in the language of animation (5.2.48, 4.6.23–24). What he describes to Horatio is a mysterious stirring in his heart that made him toss and turn in his bed like a prisoner in chains, eventually making him rise ("Sir, in my heart there was a kind of fighting / That would not let me sleep. Methought I lay / Worse than the mutines in the bilboes" [5.2.4–6]). He recounts this same force driving him without thought to Rosencrantz and Guildenstern's cabin, pushing him to rifle through their things, and to hastily, almost mindlessly (before he "could make a prologue to my brains") compose a new commission to replace the one he discovers (5.2.30). Hence his iconoclastic praise of "rashness," a term used in moral philosophical discourse to signify the irrational as well as the impulsive, and in either case, acts that are not good:

> HAMLET   Rashly—
> And praised be rashness for it—let us know
> Our indiscretion sometime serves us well
> When our deep plots do fall—and that should learn us
> There's a divinity that shapes our ends,
> Rough-hew them how we will.
> HORATIO   That is most certain.
>
> (5.2.6–11)

The sentiment Hamlet expresses here is one he has heard in *Hamlet*'s own play, in the Player King's reminder to his protesting Player Queen that "Our wills and

---

[83] Calvin, *Institution of Christian Religion*, 56r (1.16.1). Calvin describes this will as "susteyning, cherishing and caring for, with singular providence everie one of those thinges that hee hath created even to the least sparowe" 57r (1.16.3).

132   THE DRAMA OF COMPLAINT

fates do so contrary run / That our devices still are overthrown, / Our thoughts are ours, their ends none of our own" (3.3.205–7). The sententious quality of those lines finds an echo in Horatio's rote affirmation of Hamlet's words ("That is most certain"). The idea of incomplete—unfinished, imperfect, open—plots and thoughts that require further shaping from something "none of our own" is a truism of Calvinist theology. Along with his subsequent allusion to "special providence," Hamlet's praise of "a divinity that shapes our ends, / Rough-hew them how we will" has sparked many critical conversations about the play's position with regard to the philosophical questions of agency and free will that Calvinist theology inevitably raises but that were unlikely to have compelled early modern people to believe themselves incapable of freely willed action.[84] What is remarkable here, then, is simply that in this moment Shakespeare represents this commonplace idea as a truism that Hamlet *takes seriously*. That is, he acts as if he really believes that the divine force that shapes his end is present in his "particular movinges." This is evident in his rationale for refusing Horatio's offer to make an excuse to get him out of the match with Laertes. Instead—as if recalling Calvin's description of those who are "superstitiously fearefull" because they lack faith in "the will of God, which is wont to bring thinges doubtfull and confused to a certaine ende"—Hamlet surrenders up his life to the providence that works through what (to the ignorant) looks like happenstance.[85]

HORATIO   If your mind dislike anything, obey it. I will forestall their repair hither and say you are not fit.

HAMLET   Not a whit. We defy augury. There is special providence in the fall of a sparrow. If it be, 'tis not to come. If it be not to come, it will be now. If it be not now, yet it will come. The readiness is all, since no man of aught he leaves knows what is't to leave betimes. Let be.   (5.2.195–202)

The takeaway here is the dramatic fact of Hamlet's irrational animation, his willingness to die or not die, as providence wills. This is what Shakespeare represents as the animating effect, as it were, of Calvinist ideology. Rather than "obey[ing]" his *mind* as Horatio urges, Hamlet obeys this higher command, just as in the scene of spectral complaint he has let himself be led by the Ghost, following the cry of his "fate," Horatio's warnings notwithstanding. Here, as there, Horatio—the play's embodiment of reason, its amateur moral philosopher—is confronted with a senseless animation that motivates Hamlet to do something seemingly mad.

This is why it matters that *Hamlet*'s last scene of animation is Horatio's. When the dying Hamlet leaves Horatio with a weighty charge, commanding him to "report me and my cause aright" to those who will be wonderstruck by what they

---

[84] See Sinfield, "Hamlet's Special Providence"; Mallette, "From Gyves to Graces."
[85] Calvin, *Institution of Christian Religion*, 57v (1.16.3).

have witnessed, he describes "this chance" as a theatrical spectacle that generates wonder and fear at the irrational:

> I am dead, Horatio. Wretched Queen, adieu.
> You that look pale and tremble at this chance,
> That are but mutes or audience to this act,
> Had I but time (as this fell sergeant Death
> Is strict in his arrest)—O, I could tell you—
> But let it be. Horatio, I am dead.
> Thou livest: report me and my cause aright
> To the unsatisfied.
>
> (5.2.317–24)

Hamlet's singling out of Horatio to take up his cause calls back the Ghost's singling out of Hamlet in the scene of spectral complaint. With Hamlet's repeated insistence that "I am dead," and his command for Horatio to tell his strange story, and particularly the cause of his fall, to an unknowing, wondering world, it also evokes the spectral complaints of the *Mirror*, and their addresses to "Baldwin" or "Higgins." Repeatedly addressing Horatio by name, Hamlet, like the Ghost, appeals to love:

> O God, Horatio, what a wounded name,
> Things standing thus unknown, shall I leave behind me!
> If thou didst ever hold me in thy heart
> Absent thee from felicity awhile
> And in this harsh world draw thy breath in pain
> To tell my story.
>
> (5.2.328–33)

Earlier Hamlet has told Horatio that "Since my dear soul was mistress of her choice / And could of men distinguish her election / Sh'ath sealed thee for herself," that his soul has put its impression on Horatio, marking Horatio as its own and therewith incorporating him into its own recesses, to "wear him / In my heart's core—ay, in my heart of heart" (3.2.59–61, 68–69). Now Hamlet asks Horatio to hold him in *his* heart, a presence that estranges Horatio from himself, creating a "psychic caesura," in James Kuzner's striking phrase.[86] Recall that Horatio's desire is to die, in what he frames as obedience to the Stoic code of honor with which he identifies ("I am more an antique Roman than a Dane" [5.2.325]). For Horatio to do as Hamlet wills—to go on living—is to forsake his

---

[86] Kuzner, *Shakespeare As a Way of Life*, 18.

134 THE DRAMA OF COMPLAINT

pursuit of "felicity," the happiness that in the Aristotelian ethical paradigm is the *summum bonum* of human life. Hamlet thus asks Horatio to turn away from two classical ethical ideals, one Greek, one Roman: to absent himself from felicity, and to choose life "in this harsh world" over death. And Horatio does so, "without more motive" than Hamlet's command (1.4.76). It is a conversion of sorts, a turning through which the play emphasizes, once again, both the limits of Horatio's philosophy and a motive that exceeds reason. It also repeats the dynamic at the very heart of the scene of spectral complaint: the way the ghost's desire—formulated as a complaint—becomes transferred to the addressee, in whom it takes up a spectral life as a force that commands and drives their action, into the future.

Like the Ghost's complaint, Hamlet's command is a singular ethical imperative—a new sovereign good around which Horatio must configure his way of being in the world. This is what the spectral complaint form captures, and what *Hamlet* has been repeatedly revealing through its various scenes of animation: the motive that the actor relates to from a minimal distance, as neither exactly his nor not his. This final scene of animation, like its precedents, is meant to evoke wonder, to make "You that look pale and tremble at this chance, / That are but mutes or audience to this act" acknowledge, again, the sublimity of the motive that drives action. But in closing with an ethical commitment motivated by a love that outweighs normative ethical codes, *Hamlet*, which has consistently exposed irrational and idiosyncratic motives through its scenes of spectral complaint and its scenes of animation, turns from the destructive, ruinous effects of that motivation to its creative and enlivening potential. Here the play makes its audience entertain the idea that such a motive might constitute a worldly form of revitalization, an investment in life—and that it might be theater, rather than moral philosophy, that captures the irrational desire at the heart of what we are.

4
Lamentable Objects
Good Audiences and the Art of Female Complaint

Unseen, unknown, I here alone complain
To rocks, to hills, to meadows, and to springs,
Which can no help return to ease my pain,
But back my sorrows the sad echo brings.
Thus still increasing are my woes to me,
Doubly resounded by that moanful voice,
Which seems to second me in misery,
And answer gives like friend of mine own choice.
Thus only she doth my companion prove,
The others silently do offer ease:
But those that grieve, a grieving note do love.
  —Mary Wroth, *The Countess of Montgomery's Urania*

Urania wants her complaints not only to be heard, but to be answered, and to be answered with echoes. This affirmative sympathetic reception is the fundamental demand of female complaint, a term that critics of early modern literature generally use to refer to forms of complaint that imitate or evoke those of Ovid's *Heroides*.[1] Spoken by female characters—though often written by men, performed by male characters or boy actors imitating women, or mediated through the voices of male narrators—these complaints are concerned with grievances marked by gender, usually a lover's abandonment or death, lost chastity, or sexual violence; expressed in impassioned language and actions coded as feminine, such as tears, sighs, and appeals for pity; and characterized by an especially acute self-consciousness about their status as rhetorical performances designed for someone's ear, someone's eye.[2]

---

[1] On the relation between early modern female complaint and the *Heroides*, see the essays in *The Rhetoric of Complaint*, ed. Wiseman; Clarke, "'Form'd into words by your divided lips': Women, Rhetoric, and the Ovidian Tradition"; Enterline, "'Past the Help of Law': Epyllia and the Female Complaint." On women writers of Ovidian-style female complaint, see Smith, O'Callaghan, and Ross, "Complaint."

[2] On the extensiveness of female complaint in early modern literature, see Kerrigan, *Motives of Woe*. On the construction of gender in the female complaint, see Harvey, *Ventriloquized Voices*; Enterline, *The Rhetoric of the Body from Ovid to Shakespeare*; Clarke, "'Signifying, but not sounding': Gender and Paratext in the Complaint Genre"; and Bates, "Shakespeare and the Female Voice in Soliloquy."

The Drama of Complaint: Ethical Provocations in Shakespeare's Tragedy. Emily Shortslef, Oxford University Press.
© Emily Shortslef 2023. DOI: 10.1093/oso/9780192868480.003.0005

136   THE DRAMA OF COMPLAINT

The pathos of female grief was proverbial, as was its reputed capacity to compel sympathy.[3] While critical readings of female complaint often focus on the construction of the complainer's gender, in this chapter I want to show how this poetic form, in print and on the stage, imagines a distinctly feminized form of reception modeled on the ideal of an especially impressionable subject ready to mirror or echo another person's demonstrable sorrow. This reflection is in fact built into scenes of female complaint: it appears either as a represented phenomenon—as when, in Shakespeare's most noted example, Lucrece stands before the painting of Troy, with its "thousand lamentable objects," and laments for the grief-stricken Hecuba—or as the object of the complainer's desire, the thing she says she wants.[4] It is the consistent representation of sympathetic reception as a structural feature of scenes of female complaint, rather than the nature of sympathy itself, that I will be concerned with here. Whereas other scholars have shown how early modern literature offers insights into how sympathy was understood in the period, I will be considering how these depictions of sympathy as an aesthetic emotion (in Sianne Ngai's concise definition, "feelings unique to our encounters with artworks") illuminate early modern conceptions of literature's ethical force and effects.[5] I will suggest that in their coupling of plaintive performances with acts of sympathetic reception, early modern scenes of female complaint are forms of poetic self-reflection and audience instruction through which writers theorized the virtue—the power and the moral goodness—of literature and its audiences. More specifically, I will argue that their gendered depictions of the reception of "lamentable objects," or lamenting things that claim to merit the lamentation of onlookers, conceptualize the experience of reading or viewing literary art in a way that registers two related historical phenomena: the emergence of early modern aesthetic theory, and a shift in ethical paradigms of literary reception.

The dominant paradigm is familiar. Reception was the primary concern of early modern literary theory, and it was understood as a matter of ethical subjectivity, of the good or the ill that literature ("poetry," in sixteenth-century parlance) does in the lives of its readers, and, through them, in the world.[6] Conjoining Plato's critiques with invocations of the Bible, poetry's detractors emphasized its deleterious effects, citing its distortions of the truth, its stirring up of lust and excessive passion, and its encouragement of "idleness."[7] Early modern writers,

---

[3] See Pollard, "Conceiving tragedy."

[4] *The Rape of Lucrece*, line 1373. Unless otherwise noted, citations of Shakespeare's work are from *The Norton Shakespeare*.

[5] Ngai, *Ugly Feelings*, 6. For an overview of the rich conceptual history of sympathy, see *Sympathy: A History*, ed. Schliesser.

[6] For accounts of early modern literary theory's focus on reception, see Craik and Pollard, "Introduction: Imagining Audiences" and Whitney, "Ante-aesthetics." On the inescapably ethical implications of reading in the period, see the essays in *Reading Renaissance Ethics*, ed. Grossman.

[7] On early modern accounts of literature's ethical value, see Ferguson, *Trials of Desire* and Matz, *Defending Literature*. On antitheatrical and antipoetic sentiment in the period, see Barish, *The Antitheatrical Prejudice* and Herman, *Squitter-wits and Muse-Haters*.

editors, and translators of fiction were equally concerned to emphasize the ethical value of their work. In the "Induction" to the 1587 edition of *The Mirror for Magistrates*, for instance, John Higgins reminds readers of the moral riches contained in earlier editions, affirming its worth as a resource for ethical formation:

> Examples there, for all estates you finde
> ....
> The rich and poore, and ev'ry one may see,
> Which way to love, and live in due degree.[8]

Defending theatrical performance against charges that it corrupts its audiences, Thomas Heywood's *Apology for Actors* (1612) praises "lively and well-spirited action" for its "power to new mold the harts of the spectators and fashion them to the shape of any noble and notable attempt."[9] For Higgins and Heywood, poetry doesn't simply do no harm; rather, it produces virtuous character.

While rhetorical battles waged over whether literature was a force for good or evil, what would seem almost unthinkable in early modern England is the idea that literature lacks transformative power, that the experience of reading a poem or seeing a play has no discernable ethical effect. Recently, however, Corey McEleney has interrogated both the historically persistent defense of literature's moral utility and the historicist claim that there exists no noninstrumental conception of literary art prior to the eighteenth century by tracing what he calls a "'futilitarian' impulse" in early modern literature. A term that "designates the troublesome quality of literature... namely, the prospect that poetic pleasure may be pointless at best, poisonous at worst, and profitless either way," the futilitarian names a possibility that McEleney argues some early modern writers entertain, albeit only temporarily; in the texts he examines, literary pleasure that is not in the service of the good must ultimately, after a period of dalliance, be rejected as harmful.[10] This indulged-and-disavowed futilitarian impulse, he suggests, "reveals... a literary culture unable to commit either to rigid standards of poetic utility or to an aestheticist project of pure futility, and incapable of reconciling those two choices as well."[11] Although it is not the thrust of his argument, what I find suggestive about his account of this ambivalence is its revelation of the faultlines that were beginning to form in the dominant early modern conception of literature as morally profitable and efficacious, an ethical paradigm of reception that we might call (with reference only to the "futilitarian" intimations identified by McEleney and not to the philosophical position) "utilitarian."

These faultlines correlate with what Hugh Grady, Victoria Kahn, and Rachel Eisendrath, among others, have argued is an inchoate but emerging early modern

---

[8] *The Mirour for Magistrates*, C3v. [9] *An Apology for Actors*, B4r.
[10] McEleney, *Futile Pleasures*, 4. [11] McEleney, 5.

138   THE DRAMA OF COMPLAINT

aesthetic theory that stresses the manifestly artificial form of literary art, its distance (however minimal) from immediate empirical reality, and the distinctive judgments and modes of perception that it invites.[12] At the core of this unevenly articulated aesthetic theory, Grady suggests, is the idea of an "aesthetic space"—the stage, for example—"created for the inscription of specific contents organized into artful forms."[13] Early modern aesthetic space is relatively "'autonomous,' existing in a world of its own," not in the sense that it is wholly untethered from the moral, political, or religious ends that art was acknowledged to serve in the period, but in the sense that it is "radically differentiated from 'the real'"—the world of everyday experience and empirical knowledge.[14] As such, it ushers an audience into what Grady describes as "a more contemplative mode of reception" attentive to the "artificiality and shaping" of the objects framed by that space.[15]

It is no coincidence that the mode of aesthetic experience underpinned by this aesthetic theory was conceptualized in female complaint, a form of complaint that was both notably artful and notoriously futile. Nor is it surprising that in imagining new ways of experiencing literary art, scenes of female complaint were sites in which a new ethical paradigm for literary reception was articulated. In this chapter's first section, I explore scenes of female complaint that I suggest function as microcosms of aesthetic space. As I will show, these plaintive performances model a feminized sympathetic reception, in which the audience's virtuousness lies in their affirmation of the lamentable quality of the complaint. In the second section, I develop this argument in relation to several interconnected historical verse tragedies written as poems of female complaint in the early to mid 1590s, all of which depart from the utilitarian ethical paradigm of reading tragic history by stressing instead the virtue of attending sympathetically to the lamentable poem. Together these two sections chart, in scenes of female complaint, the transfer of ethical significance from literature's capacity to transform the self to the audience's capacity to respond sympathetically to the object. These scenes of female complaint, I argue, idealize a notably bounded sympathy whose parameters coincide with an aesthetic space distinct from the world of everyday reality, a

---

[12] See Grady, *Shakespeare and Impure Aesthetics*; Kahn, *The Future of Illusion*; and Eisendrath, *Poetry in a World of Things*. See also Pye, *The Storm at Sea*; Robson, *The Sense of Early Modern Writing*; and *The Insistence of Art*, ed. Kottman. It must be noted that Shakespeare and his contemporaries are writing before the historical appearance of a fully-fledged philosophical notion of the aesthetic, a word (from the Greek *aisthesthai*, to sense) that does not exist until the mid-eighteenth century, and a concept generally said to be tied to the epistemic fragmentation of culture into the distinct spheres of ethics, science, and art; the Cartesian split between subject and object; the rise of the liberal state; the dominance of the capitalist mode of production; Enlightenment rationality; and other hallmarks of modernity. Yet, as these critics argue, it is the prematurity of early modern aesthetic thought that allows for the jettisoning of certain components of Kantian aesthetic thought, particularly the disinterestedness of aesthetic judgment, the formal unity and beauty of artworks, and the idea that the knowledge art offers is strictly non-cognitive. See Grady's introduction for a theorization of "impure" aesthetics.

[13] Grady, *Shakespeare and Impure Aesthetics*, 28.   [14] Grady, 28.

[15] Grady, 29, author's emphasis.

sympathy virtuous only in relation to the scene's internal ethical logic, that is, without necessary effect or immediate meaning outside of the delimited aesthetic space. This claim will obviously require unpacking, but for now I want just to suggest that these scenes are intent on stressing both the distinctiveness of aesthetic experience and the formal difference of its ethical logic, and that they emphasize the artifice and creativity integral to that difference in a way that gives the audience a modicum of critical distance from their own activity of reception. The final section of this chapter reads *Richard II*'s well-known thematic preoccupation with sympathy, and its appropriation of the sensibility of female complaint, as a Shakespearean engagement with this new paradigm of ethical reception. At once the most conspicuously plaintive, poetic, and aestheticized of Shakespeare's tragic history plays, as well as the most politically volatile, *Richard II* simultaneously capitalizes on the internal ethical logic that female complaint foregrounds and introduces ethical anxiety into sympathetic reception.

1. Idle Art: Female Complaint and Sympathetic Reception

Bidding his last farewell to his Queen as she departs for France and he for prison, Shakespeare's Richard II instructs her to sit down and stage, on some winter's night to come, a scene of female complaint:

> Good sometimes queen, prepare thee hence for France.
> Think I am dead, and that even here thou tak'st,
> As from my death-bed, thy last living leave.
> In winter's tedious nights sit by the fire
> With good old folks, and let them tell thee tales
> Of woeful ages long ago betid.
> And ere thou bid good night, to quite their griefs,
> Tell thou the lamentable tale of me
> And send the hearers weeping to their beds.
> For why the senseless brands will sympathize
> The heavy accent of thy moving tongue
> And in compassion weep the fire out;
> And some will mourn in ashes, some coal-black,
> For the deposing of a rightful king.[16]
>
> (5.1.37–50)

This imagined scene of plaintive fireside performance and mutual mourning is commonly read as an idealized *mise en abyme* of the staging of *Richard II*, a

---

[16] 5.3.323. All citations are from *Richard II*, ed. Charles R. Forker. Hereafter cited parenthetically.

140   THE DRAMA OF COMPLAINT

"lamentable tale" crafted from the historical account of Richard's reign offered in Holinshed's expanded *Chronicles* (1587) and its poetic treatments in the *Mirror* as well as Samuel Daniel's epic poem *The Civil Wars* (1595), the latter Shakespeare's likely source for this unhistorical representation of the royal couple's parting.[17] Richard's vision is clearly a partisan one, and critics have long debated the extent to which Shakespeare himself represents sympathy as the right response to Richard's fall.[18] The question arises precisely because Richard is so insistent that he should be perceived as full of grief and received with tears—an insistence that finds expression not only in this speech but in several other moments throughout the tragedy in which Richard and the Queen attempt to make him appear lamentable by lamenting for him themselves. It is in the context of such performances that the full significance of Richard's injunction to "Think I am dead" comes to light: more than realistic pessimism or tragic foreknowledge, it is an excited prompt to the Queen's imagination that echoes Quintilian's advice for creating pathos (with what infectious sadness would she speak of him if he were dead!).[19] Such passion, performed skillfully through the pliable instrument of the voice, would virtually compel its hearers to "sympathize"—in early modern usage, "to be affected in consequence of the affection of some one or something else."[20]

But what a limited kind of sympathy it is that Richard imagines. His wish is that the Queen's story of "the deposing of a rightful king" would stir up sympathizers who neither come to his assistance nor promise revenge, but—as "good old folks" and literal firebrands—do nothing but weep with her. This strikingly impotent sympathy contrasts sharply with the plot to restore Richard to the throne that is taking shape in the play even now, unbeknownst to Richard. (Lending additional, if retrospective, irony to Richard's branding of his deposition as matter for a mere winter's tale is its repeated invocation as a political cause by characters in the subsequent history plays of the second tetralogy, as well as the nebulous association of *Richard II* with Essex's 1601 rebellion, which would seem to confirm the deposition's potency as a political exemplar, albeit as inspirational historical precedent rather than tragic transgression.)[21] But Richard seems wholly unconcerned with

[17] On the play's relation to Daniel's poem, see Forker, Introduction to *Richard II*, 140–4.

[18] On this critical debate, and the notorious problem of sympathy in the play, see Meek, "'Rue e'en for ruth': *Richard II* and the Imitation of Sympathy."

[19] "When pity is needed, let us believe that the ills of which we are to complain have happened to us, and persuade our hearts of this... the student should be moved by his subject and imagine it to be real." *Institutio Oratoria*, 6.2.35–36, *The Orator's Education*, 63.

[20] *OED*, s.v. "sympathize." The meaning of "sympathy" is in transition in the period: for most of the sixteenth century, the term refers to a natural, intrinsic, and esoteric likeness, affinity, or correspondence between physical things that allows them to be affected by the same thing or by each other. See Floyd-Wilson, *Occult Knowledge*. By the end of the century, "sympathy" also refers to a consonance of feeling or disposition. In the early seventeenth century, it begins to denote the moral virtue of fellow-feeling, and was used more or less interchangeably with "pity" and "compassion." See Lobis, *The Virtue of Sympathy*.

[21] On the day before Essex's rebellion his supporters gave Shakespeare's company forty shillings to revive a play on the deposition of Richard II. For a recounting of this event and its aftermath, as well as the multiple allegorical alignments of Elizabeth with Richard in the period, see Forker, Introduction, 5–10.

sparing his life, restoring his kingship, or securing a posthumous revenge for his grievances. Instead the speech encapsulates what I would suggest is the fantasy of sympathy manifest in all of Richard's many complaints: it imagines a virtuous audience whose tears affirm that Richard's artfully mediated suffering is indeed lamentable.

Refigured in this particular vision of sympathetic reception is a truism about what pleases those who demonstrably grieve. "All extreme heavinesse, and vehement sorowes [...] seeke a mourner that woulde take parte with them" in "a felowship of sorowe," Thomas Wilson's *Arte of Rhetorique* (1553) instructs.[22] As the narrator of *The Rape of Lucrece* (1594) puts it,

> Grief best is pleased with grief's society:
> True sorrow then is feelingly sufficed
> When with like semblance it is sympathized.[23]

Shakespeare returns several times in scenes of complaint composed in temporal proximity to *Richard II* (in or around 1595), to the notion of a "like semblance" of grief that is sufficiently good, as a form of reception, because it "suffices" to please the complainer—a virtuous correspondence that he often terms "sympathy."[24] This correspondence is what Venus finds in the "idle sounds" of the caves that "seeming troubled, / Make verbal repetition of her moans, / Passion on passion deeply…redoubled" when she sings a plaintive song after Adonis abandons her for the hunt.[25] It occurs when Lucrece's maid, seeing her mistress weeping, becomes the "poor counterfeit of her complaining" without even knowing the reason for Lucrece's tears.[26] And it is this mirroring "sympathy of woe" that Titus imagines when he asks the weeping, mutilated Lavinia, his "speechless complainer," whether it would ease her grief if the Andronici were to fill a fountain with their tears, bite out their tongues, or "cut away our hands like thine."[27] The visual likeness he envisions between complainer and co-mourners recalls the sympathetic reception he has earlier imagined when, lying in the dust and bemoaning the tribunes' refusal to hear his plea for his sons' lives, he has defended his "vain" laments to the disapproving Lucius thus:

> I tell my sorrows bootless to the stones
> Who, though they cannot answer my distress,

---

[22] *The Arte of Rhetorike*, 67.   [23] *The Rape of Lucrece*, lines 1111–13.

[24] Forker notes that in Shakespeare's lexicon, "sympathy" always means a correspondence between things that makes them similarly affected, rather than the moral virtue of fellow-feeling or compassion. See 4.1.n34 in *Richard II*. What I'm suggesting is that Shakespeare ascribes virtue to the perceptible, external correspondence, the "sympathy" or "like semblance," between a mourner and her witness.

[25] *Venus and Adonis* (1593), lines 848, 830–2.   [26] *The Rape of Lucrece*, lines 1229, 1269.

[27] *Titus Andronicus*, 3.1.147; 3.2.39, 3.1.129, cited from the Folio edition printed in the Norton Digital Edition.

142 THE DRAMA OF COMPLAINT

> Yet in some sort they are better than the tribunes
> For that they will not intercept my tale.
> When I do weep, they humbly at my feet
> Receive my tears, and seem to weep with me[.][28]

Titus's wet stones are akin to the "senseless," weeping brands whose black ashes Richard imagines as mourning garments, both more capable of sympathy than certain human audiences (the "tribunes more hard than stones," the "bad men" that deny the Queen's tearful request for Richard to accompany her into exile [5.1.71]).[29] The same is true of the "neighbor caves" that flatteringly echo Venus's complaints, more receptive listeners than Adonis, who has scorned the "idle over-handled theme" of her plaintive plea for him to remain with her and expressed shame at having listened to her at all ("Mine ears that to your wanton talk attended / Do burn themselves for having so attended").[30] And the sympathetic tears that flow from the maid at the mere sight of Lucrece's weeping eyes—a dynamic the narrator likens to the reflexive bedewing of the earth after the sun has set—are an unmistakable contrast to that earlier scene of complaint in which Tarquin's "heart granteth / No penetrable entrance to her plaining," his lust only "harden[ed]" by Lucrece's tears.[31] One hardly needs to spell out the logic of such contrasts and their invocation of nature. Only a person who is unfeeling and unnatural—inhuman—could fail to be moved by the complainer's display of sorrow, which moves the good person not simply to feel a corresponding passion, but to "passionate": to perform passion along with the complainer. The plaintive echoes of the natural world, in this ethical logic, are not simply fanciful stand-ins for the friend or the neighbor; rather, as Sarah C. E. Ross has suggested in her reading of female complaint, the friend or neighbor is imagined on the model of the echo.[32]

It is the "passioning" role of the witness, rather than the complainer, that offers a point of identification for the reader or viewer of these scenes. Variously imagined as a passive condition of being involuntarily affected by something, an intentional act of mirroring, and the effect of having consented to be moved, what is consistent about the sympathetic reception delineated as an ethical ideal in all these examples is that it is distinctly performative. By this I mean that it is described as a perceptible, externalized reaction to another's display of grief, as opposed to an inward, private feeling "which passes show."[33] So too, it is undertaken for the sake of the complainer's good, her well-being, her desire: generally

---

[28] *Titus Andronicus*, 3.1.27, 36–41.   [29] *Titus Andronicus*, 3.1.44.
[30] *Venus and Adonis*, lines 770, 809–10.   [31] *The Rape of Lucrece*, lines 558–9, 560.
[32] Ross argues that the figure of Echo—often interpreted in terms of the attenuation of the female voice—functions in female-voiced complaint poetry as a model of the "answering voices...through which a female community is constructed." See Ross, "Complaint's Echoes," 187.
[33] *Hamlet*, 1.2.85.

speaking, such scenes do not even address the question of what good this sympathy does for the sympathetic spectator.[34] As I have already noted, many scenes of complaint represent this sympathetic reception as an integral part of the passionate performance. Take, for instance, the narrator's description of Lucrece and the maid weeping in harmony together, Lucrece for the wrong she has suffered, the maid as she is "enforced by sympathy":

> A pretty while these pretty creatures stand,
> Like ivory conduits coral cisterns filling:
> One justly weeps, the other takes in hand
> No cause but company of her drops spilling.[35]

My interpretation of sympathetic reception as a corresponding response to lamentable art may not seem to pertain to the maid's tears, insofar as Shakespeare does not frame Lucrece's laments as specifically artful objects—that is, skillfully constructed and performed things like Venus's songs, or the Queen's hypothetical "lamentable tale." And yet the scene does feature an artful lamentable object, in the form of a conspicuously aestheticized and objectified complaining subject. Notice how the narrator describes the maid's perception of Lucrece: "Lucrece' cheeks unto her maid seem so / As winter meads when sun doth melt their snow," the maid "durst not ask of her audaciously / Why her two suns were cloud-eclipsèd so."[36] The maid sees Lucrece through the frame of conventional Petrarchan similes, while the narrator's similarly aestheticizing perspective on these "pretty creatures" weeping together flickers between the red-and-white of Petrarchan tropes and the architectural images of Roman ruins, beautiful in their melancholy. Constructed around the symmetry of a complainer and a spectator who joins in the performance, this scene is an exemplary instance of the early modern articulation of sympathetic reception as an ethically meaningful *aesthetic* telos—the good response to lamentable art—and an aestheticized *ethical* telos: the pleasing response of the virtuous audience, who weep for "no cause"—for no reason and to no end—"but company" of the complainer.

It makes sense that female complaint would be one of the discursive sites where the virtuousness of sympathetic reception was articulated with particular energy, for the form was already associated in the early modern cultural imagination with

---

[34] For instance, these scenes do not typically suggest that the spectator moved to tears experiences something like catharsis (in any of the four potential Aristotelian meanings of the term, as explained by Patrick Gray: moral purification, medical purgation, emotional moderation, intellectual clarification). This may be because the *Poetics* was not translated into English until 1623, although it was available from the early sixteenth century onward in Italian translations and was familiar to some writers, including Sidney. On catharsis and its relation to the ethical ends of Shakespearean tragedy, see Gray, "Seduced by Romanticism."

[35] *The Rape of Lucrece*, lines 1233–6.   [36] *The Rape of Lucrece*, lines 1217–18, 1223–4.

144   THE DRAMA OF COMPLAINT

the artful representation of grief and the power to move audiences to tears. Linked to a rich poetic tradition that included Book 4 of the *Aeneid*, the *Metamorphoses*, the *Heroides*, and Euripidean and Senecan tragedy, the form was embedded in the practices of the early modern grammar school, where school-boys not only studied but were required to imitate the passionate complaints of figures such as Hecuba and Dido, as Lynn Enterline has shown.[37] (She links "the sudden flowering of 'female complaint' in the 1590s" to exactly these curricular practices.)[38] This type of imitation is the subject of the scene in *The Two Gentleman of Verona* in which Julia, forsaken by Proteus for Silvia and now disguised as the boy Sebastian, tells Silvia how "he," in a Whitsun "pageant of delight," once performed the "lamentable part" of Ariadne and made Julia cry:

> And at that time I made her weep a-good,
> For I did play a lamentable part.
> Madam, 'twas Ariadne, passioning
> For Theseus' perjury and unjust flight,
> Which I so lively acted with my tears
> That my poor mistress, movèd therewithal,
> Wept bitterly.[39]

In the imaginary scenario that "Sebastian" sketches, the virtuous Julia weeps for his Ariadne, just as in Shakespeare's scene, Silvia herself, moved by Sebastian's artful description, begins to weep for the abandoned Julia, a response that leads Sebastian/Julia to conclude that Sylvia is "a virtuous gentlewoman, mild and beautiful!"[40] It is only one of many early modern literary examples in which a performance of complaint by a female character commands a sympathetic recep-tion that is itself marked as feminine and virtuous. Such receptiveness to external phenomena is the alleged quality of women's minds that *Lucrece*'s narrator offers as the reason for the maid's sympathy. "Their gentle sex to weep are often willing," he notes, launching into an extended simile that likens women's minds to wax, more susceptible than masculine marble to "th'impression of strange kinds" stamped upon them "by force, by fraud, or skill."[41] What is "female" about female complaint, then, is not simply the constructed gender of the speaker, but the correlative trope of an audience particularly vulnerable to the artfulness ("force, fraud, and skill") of the complaints to which they are exposed. The ideal reception

---

[37] Enterline, *Shakespeare's Schoolroom*, especially Chapter 5, 120–52.

[38] Enterline, 125–6. So too, she suggests that the female complaint's characteristic "fantasy of address, audience, and judgment" restages the psychic dynamics of the instructional scenes of the Tudor grammar school, where schoolboys were trained to imitate the complaints of classical female figures for the approval of their schoolmasters. Enterline, 133.

[39] *The Two Gentleman of Verona*, 5.1.154, 160–6.   [40] *The Two Gentleman of Verona*, 5.1.175.

[41] *The Rape of Lucrece*, lines 1237, 1242, 1243.

LAMENTABLE OBJECTS **145**

scenario of female complaint is summed up in the metaphor of the impression, which suggests an effect that is the simulacrum of its cause—and indeed, the one kind of efficacy consistently credited to female complaint is the power to produce replicas of its speaker's passion.

To illustrate how early modern writers conceptualized aesthetic experience through the female complaint form and its conventional reception script, I'd like to turn to an especially rich scene from Francis Beaumont and John Fletcher's *The Maid's Tragedy* (1619), performed by The King's Men around 1611. Abandoned by her lover when the King forces him to marry another woman, Aspatia identifies with the female complainants of the *Heroides*. Desiring to see images of her sorrow, she conscripts her maids into making lamentable art with her ("Come, let's be sad, my girls" [2.2.27]). First she makes Olympias pose as one after another Ovidian figure, from Oenone to Dido ("Now a tear, / And then thou art a piece expressing fully / The Carthage queen" [2.2.31–33]). Then, displeased by the insufficiently miserable Ariadne that Antiphila has created in her needlework, Aspatia orders Antiphila to craft a new, more plaintive Ariadne, with herself as the model. I quote the passage at some length, because—from Aspatia's command to "Come, let's be sad, my girls" to the scene's conclusion, reproduced below—the whole scene is an extraordinary microcosm of aesthetic experience:

> ASPATIA Do it again by me, the lost Aspatia,
> And you shall find all true but the wild island.
> And think I stand upon the sea breach now,
> Mine arms thus, and mine hair blown with the wind,
> Wild as that desert, and let all about me
> Tell that I am forsaken. Do my face
> (If thou hadst ever feeling of a sorrow)
> Thus, thus, Antiphila. Strive to make me look
> Like Sorrow's monument; and the trees about me,
> Let them be dry and leafless; let the rocks
> Groan with continual surges, and behind me
> Make all a desolation; look, look, wenches,
> A miserable life of this poor picture!
> OLYMPIAS   Dear madam—
> ASPATIA   I have done. Sit down, and let us
> Upon that point fix all our eyes, that point there.
> Make a dumb silence, till you feel a sudden sadness
> Give us new souls.   [*They sit.*]
>   *Enter Calianax.*
> CALIANAX ....
>   —Well, how now, huswives?
> What, at your ease? Is this a time to sit still?

146 THE DRAMA OF COMPLAINT

Up, you young, lazy whores, up, or I'll swinge you.

....

You'll lie down shortly. Get you in and work!
What, are you grown so resty?
ANTIPHILA   My lord, we do no more than we are charged.
It is the lady's pleasure we be thus in grief[.]

(2.2.65–93)

There are two things I want to note about the aesthetic experience that this scene simultaneously represents, conceptualizes, and enables. First, the scene underlines that sympathetic reception—a perceptible correspondence with the complainer's sorrow—is also a productive way of seeing, a response that in *affirming* the lamentable quality of the object effectively *creates* it as such. Ngai's suggestion that affect "suture[s] ... into a spontaneous experience" what she describes as the "two sides" of an aesthetic category ("the judgment we utter, a way of speaking; [and] the form we perceive, a way of seeing") is useful here.[42] In regard to lamentable art, sympathy—implicit in which is a subjective judgment that something is lamentable, a judgment "uttered" in these examples in the form of tears—confers that quality on the object, as if it were a positive feature of it. What sympathy responds to are perceived cues from the object, cues highlighted as such in this particular scene of complaint. As she describes the way Antiphila's Ariadne should look, Aspatia also directs her on- and offstage audiences as to how they should look at her. They are to see her as an incarnation of Ariadne ("a miserable life of this poor picture"), and as "Sorrow's monument," grief objectified. Like Aspatia's maids, the theatrical audience is implicated in this performance not simply as passive spectators of her sorrow but as active participants, collaborators in the scene of complaint she is creating: they are the "groan[ing]" rocks that Aspatia orders to materialize all about and behind her, the landscape that would "tell that I am forsaken," the live backdrop to her live Ariadne. Their woeful faces are thus the likely referents of the unspecified sight on which Aspatia—inverting the usual roles played by actors and audience members in the theatrical structure of plaintive performance—directs her maids to fix their eyes as the women, sitting together, stare at something that she suggests will fill them with a "sudden sadness."

Just as audiences are cued to perform sympathetic reception, so too are they alerted to the spatiotemporal distinctiveness of this aesthetic experience and the boundedness of the sympathy it focalizes. The difference between the women's activity and the actions of "real life" is marked at the instant their play is broken up, when Aspatia's father enters and orders the women to get up and get to work: "What, at your ease? Is this a time to sit still?" (Like Aspatia's directions to her

---

[42] Ngai, *Theory of the Gimmick*, 1.

maids, his scolding address extends to the audience, who may have recognized its echoing of the antitheatricalist charge of idleness.) The internal ethical logic of the scene is articulated in Antiphila's defense: "We do no more than we are charged. / It is the lady's pleasure we be thus in grief." The key point is the ethical pressure to respond in kind to a display of grief for the mere sake of pleasing the complainer (a pressure in tension with the competing ethical imperative to be productive). In observing this retroactive delimiting of an idle stretch of time marked by a recursive grief that is simultaneously virtuous (powerful, good) and vain (useless, self-indulgent), we might think back to the description of Lucrece and her maid standing together, tears running down their faces, for what the poem's narrator tellingly calls "a pretty while," an ambiguous phrase that suggests both (patronizing) approbation and (leering) disapproval.[43]

Aspatia's complaint indicates the stakes of the relationship I am suggesting between the bounded zones of plaintive performance and sympathetic reception that scenes of female complaint represent, on the one hand, and, on the other, the developing early modern notion of the aesthetic as "a special kind of cultural zone or space, exempt from the truth-claims implied by ordinary discourse" that "induct[s] the audience into a different mode of perception from that of ordinary life."[44] That relationship is analogical, but—as seen here—it can also be synecdochic: from the inside of poems and plays that are themselves framed as aesthetic spaces, scenes of female complaint cordon off miniaturized zones in which writers theorize aesthetic experience by self-reflexively depicting it. These zones are both created and dissolved through a rhetoric of commands and gestures ("Come, let's be sad," "Sit down"; "Well, how now, huswives," "Up, you young, lazy whores, up!") that demarcate entrances into, and exits from, particular ways of seeing. These zones are feminized, not only by their settings and their participants, but also through a sexist rhetoric that is variously sentimentalizing, dismissive, mocking, scolding, or sexualizing. That language predictably appears when external observers of these scenes, and sometimes the participants themselves, suggest that the experience they contain is fond, silly, and vain, an observation made just as the scene dissolves.[45] If, as I am suggesting, these scenes stress the difference between aesthetic experience and other kinds of experience, they suggest that that difference has to do with the former's lack of obvious utility: it seems only to produce a sympathy that stays contained, stuck in a feedback loop between

---

[43] On the ambivalence of idleness and its association with aesthetic experience, see Nandi, "The Dangers and Pleasures of Filling Vacuous Time" and Scherer, "The 'Sweet Toyle' of Blissful Bowers."

[44] Grady, *Shakespeare and Impure Aesthetics*, 30.

[45] The scene of plaintive performance and sympathetic reception between Lucrece and the maid, for instance, breaks up when Lucrece impatiently tells the maid that her weeping "small avails" her, and sends her to find a messenger to carry her letter to Collatine. Here, in contrast with *The Maid's Tragedy*, the demands of the real world and its activity erupt from within. *The Rape of Lucrece*, line 1273.

148 THE DRAMA OF COMPLAINT

the lamentable object and the sympathetic spectator that persists until it happens to be broken.

Read as reflections on early modern aesthetic experience, these scenes may seem to exemplify the ambivalence that McEleney sees in poets' oscillation between recognizing and repudiating the pleasures of poetic futility (a repudiation which, he persuasively argues, displaces the negativity that futility represents onto queer and feminized figures).[46] I would suggest, however, that the articulation of aesthetic experience through female complaint has less to do with disavowing a profitless and harmful poetic pleasure than acknowledging, from the outset, an aesthetic experience that has no use and then crafting a new concept of power, and a new ethical logic, proper to that experience. The affordance of female complaint—a form virtually synonymous with "bootless" speech—is that it is always already freed from the expectation of utility. As the exception to that bootlessness, one might take the passion that the female complaint reliably impresses on some reflecting surface as a mere consolation prize for its lack of force in the world, as much an epitome of futility as a form of success. But as Enterline notes, in the Tudor schoolroom, the "transfer of feeling" from performer to audience was precisely what constituted success in the performance of female grief.[47] In the familiar form of female complaint, then, early modern writers possessed a template for imagining the production of an impotent passion as both a virtue of art and an end in itself—and, moreover, for imagining sympathy as itself a sufficiently virtuous reception, what we might call a *good enough* response. Thus female complaint seems an exception to the oppositional structure McEleney identifies in early modern literary theory: the form is a site for conceptualizing aesthetic experience as idle and profitless and vain— different from other kinds of experience, and not morally useful—but for all that not *not good.*

There is no better illustration of the internal ethical logic of aesthetic experience than the iconic scene in *The Rape of Lucrece* that conjoins ekphrasis, a device that Eisendrath calls a "model in miniature of aesthetic experience," with female complaint.[48] The scene centers on an act of sympathetic reception at once futile and powerful. After a night of profitless complaint in the aftermath of her rape ("In vain I rail at Opportunity, / At Time, at Tarquin, and at uncheerful Night"), Lucrece—"pausing for means to mourn some newer way"—finds her way to a "well-painted piece" of the Fall of Troy (lines 1023–24, 1365, 1443). Gazing on the painting's "thousand lamentable objects / [that] in scorn of nature, art gave lifeless life" (1373–74), Lucrece's eyes gravitate to that paragon of female complaint: Hecuba, ravaged by grief as she looks on the bleeding Priam. In Hecuba's face

---

[46] McEleney, *Futile Pleasures*, 11.   [47] Enterline, *Shakespeare's Schoolroom*, 121.
[48] Eisendrath, *Poetry in a World of Things*, 4.

> the painter had anatomized
> Time's ruin, beauty's wrack, and grim care's reign.
> Her cheeks with chops and wrinkles were disguised:
> Of what she was no semblance did remain.
> Her blue blood changed to black in every vein,
> Wanting the spring that those shrunk pipes had fed,
> Showed life imprisoned in a body dead.
>
> (1450–56)

Here Shakespeare takes the inherent limitations of painting as an occasion for underlining the performative—the perceptible and the productive—nature of sympathetic reception. As she weeps for the painted Hecuba ("shap[ing] her sorrow to the beldam's woes"), Lucrece recognizes that Hecuba's is a doubly "lifeless life": the painter ("well-skilled" but "no god") "did [Hecuba] wrong / To give her so much grief, and not a tongue" (1458, 1374, 1461, 1462–63). Her complaint must be projected, imagined, by the spectator. Lucrece goes a step further and actually voices Hecuba's soundless complaint, her own tongue the instrument through which life flows through Hecuba's "shrunk pipes" again (1455):

> "Poor instrument," quoth she, "without a sound,
> I'll tune thy woes with my lamenting tongue,
> And drop sweet balm in Priam's painted wound,
> And rail on Pyrrhus that hath done him wrong,
> And with my tears quench Troy that burns so long,
> And with my knife scratch out the angry eyes
> Of all the Greeks that are thine enemies.
>
> (1464–70)

Having restored life to Hecuba through her plaints, Lucrece "throws her eyes about the painting round, / And who she finds forlorn she doth lament" (1499–1500). But she also bestows another kind of tears on the painting's "lamentable objects," tears that enact justice for a wrong done. Recall what she does to the figure of Sinon, the captive Greek soldier who deceives Priam into bringing the Trojan horse into the city:

> Here, all enraged, such passion her assails
> That patience is quite beaten from her breast.
> She tears the senseless Sinon with her nails,
> Comparing him to that unhappy guest
> Whose deed hath made herself herself detest.
> At last she smilingly with this gives o'er:
> "Fool, fool," quoth she, "his wounds will not be sore."
>
> (1562–68)

150   THE DRAMA OF COMPLAINT

Embedding her tears in the painting, Lucrece's sympathetic reception becomes a part of the painting's scene of female complaint in the most material of senses. It is a perfect illustration of how sympathetic reception simultaneously affirms and creates the lamentable object. It also a perfect illustration of futility. Lucrece recognizes that what she has been doing is "foolish"—laughable to imagine that it is anything but a surface phenomenon—and yet there is an unmistakable ethical logic that has governed it. "Set a-work" by passion, she has made and passed judgment, giving characters what she decides they want or deserve in the form of her tears (1496). She has invested the act of reception with ethical energy, treating her experience of the painting as a space in which she can exercise a certain power and do a certain kind of good, for a time, in a manner that the poem insists has no real effect beyond that space.

The extravagant futility of Lucrece's aesthetic experience differs markedly from those instances Heather James has elaborated in which Shakespeare sketches the disruptive, cascading social effects of a sympathy sparked by an encounter with artfully told sad stories.[49] Here, quite literally, it is only the painting that is transformed. One might suggest that while Lucrece's sympathetic reception has no effect on her relations with the world outside the painting, she at least benefits from it herself: Michael Schoenfeldt has argued, for instance, that her encounter with the painting attests to "a significant, if temporary, analgesic effect achieved in compassionately viewing the suffering of others in art."[50] But the primary benefit the poem shows Lucrece receiving from her experience is simply that it passes time. The period that she "with painted images hath spent" concludes the long night of futile complaint ("idle words," "unprofitable sounds," a "helpless smoke of words") that stands between her and the suicide that she understands as the "remedy indeed to do me good" (1577, 1016, 1017, 1027, 1028). It is because she is killing time until the arrival of morning and Collatine that she goes to the painting in the first place ("The weary time she cannot entertain" [1361]). Lamenting for these lamentable objects, "time doth weary time with her complaining": meanwhile, the morning, which "all this time hath overslipped her thought," arrives when time itself has slipped her mind (1570, 1576). Making a virtue out of what moralists considered a vice, the real power that the poem attributes to aesthetic experience— and specifically to lamentable aesthetic objects—is the power to waste time.[51]

The knowing smile that punctuates the end of Lucrece's aesthetic experience and her "giv[ing] o'er" of both her tears and her complaints coincides with the appearance of morning—and with it, *The Rape of Lucrece's* narrative return from the rhetorical excursus of her vain complaints to its political plot. Capped off by

---

[49] James, "Dido's Ear." For other literary representations of characters transformed by their sympathetic identifications, see the essays in *Shakespearean Sensations*, eds. Craik and Pollard.

[50] Schoenfeldt, "Shakespearean Pain," 197.

[51] Alison Chapman argues that the painting offers Lucrece an escape from the flow of linear time into which she has been "embedded" against her will by the rape. See Chapman, "Lucrece's Time," 179.

this miniaturized scene of aesthetic experience, the poem's lengthy scene of female complaint (67 of its 265 stanzas) constitutes a space of exception within its own narrative logic. Before Lucrece begins to complain, the poem's focus is on moral deliberation (Tarquin's extended internal debate, his will torn between reason and lust; Lucrece's futile appeals to his better self); at the close of her complaint, the narrator shifts to the political substance of the story, in Lucrece's revelation of Tarquin's wrong, her suicide, her kinsmen's revenge and the people's expulsion of the Tarquins from Rome. Its scene of female complaint is a set-piece extraneous to the story the poem tells (the origin myth of the Roman Republic), an extraneousness accentuated by its notably different narrative pacing. If Lucrece's aesthetic experience makes her fictive clock time pass quickly, these stanzas dilate narrative time as they turn Lucrece into a lamentable object for the reader's gaze, Shakespeare's equivalent of the painted Hecuba: a "lifeless life," suspended between life and death. The poem draws an implicit analogy between Lucrece and the painting, on the one hand, and the reader and the complaining Lucrece on the other. These coinciding framed spaces of exception, both of which allow an observer to contemplate a lamentable object in a way that differs from how they engage what is "outside" that space (before and after that experience), supports Grady's claim that Shakespeare is a "proto-theorist of the aesthetic" who "presents...acute conceptualizations of what will later be called 'the aesthetic.'"[52] Here Shakespeare stresses a formal difference, an incommensurability of ethical logics, of measures of time, of representational strategies, all of which underscore a fundamental distinction between aesthetic space and empirical reality.

This difference is even more pronounced in *Richard II*'s scenes of female complaint. Embedded in larger narratives, scenes of female complaint may invite audiences to respond with sympathy to a character represented in far less sympathetic terms elsewhere in the text. Such scenes in *Richard II* (the only Shakespearean text to contain more references to "grief" and its cognates than *Lucrece*) certainly articulate an ethical logic at odds with how Richard is otherwise represented.[53] These scenes not only offer audiences a different way of seeing Richard, but construct a model for seeing with sympathetic eyes via the Queen, who laments for Richard in each of her three appearances in the play, and wants company in her mourning.[54] As Richard Meek suggests, audiences "may feel ambivalent about Richard but may nevertheless find themselves feeling 'rue' for the Queen."[55] Like Lucrece before the painting of Troy, the lamenting Queen is both a complainant of her own sorrows and a sympathetic spectator of another's.

---

[52] Grady, *Shakespeare and Impure Aesthetics*, 41.
[53] See Wells, "The Lamentable Tale of 'Richard II.'"
[54] On performances of weeping as cues to the theatrical audience to weep, see Steggle, *Laughing and Weeping in Early Modern Theatres*. The lamenting Queen's three appearances are in Act 2, scene 2; Act 3, scene 4; and Act 5, scene 1.
[55] Meek, "'Rue e'en for ruth,'" 140.

152   THE DRAMA OF COMPLAINT

In Act 5, she orders her ladies to "rest" with her and look on Richard as he is led to the Tower:

> Here let us rest, if this rebellious earth
> Have any resting for her true king's queen.
>   *Enter* [KING] RICHARD *and Guard.*
> But soft, but see, or rather do not see
> My fair rose wither. Yet look up, behold,
> That you in pity may dissolve to dew
> And wash him fresh again with true-love tears.
> Ah, thou, the model where old Troy did stand,
> Thou map of honour, thou King Richard's tomb,
> And not King Richard! Thou most beauteous inn,
> Why should hard-favoured Grief be lodged in thee[?]
>
>   (5.1.5–14)

The Queen instructs her women to see Richard as she does, through "true-love tears" that simultaneously witness his "withering" and "wash him fresh again." Here, as in other scenes of female complaint, the virtue of sympathy is the power to create—and, more specifically, in the play's figurative economy, to give life. Figures of organic renewal and resurrection combine to suggest that it is through their sympathetic gaze that he is made anew as the beautiful, sorrowful thing she apostrophizes: "not King Richard," he is now "King Richard's tomb," a "beauteous inn" occupied by grief, an image of Troy in ruins. With its evocation of such iconic precedents as Hecuba mourning for Priam and the women mourning for Christ, the Queen's lament, spoken at "rest," and possibly as she sits on the ground, frames the tearful Richard as a lamentable object—just as Richard imagines that the "heavy accent" of her "moving tongue" will do, as she tells his story to an audience sitting around a fireside, whiling away a winter's night by swapping "tales / Of woeful ages long betid" (5.1.45, 41–42). In fantasizing his metamorphosis into sorrowful legend through the Queen's artistic labor, his story circulating among and exchangeable with other stories like it (indeed, he describes it as aesthetic currency with which she can "quite [the] griefs" of her companion storytellers) Richard imagines an aesthetic otherlife that evokes a set of tragic historical poems contemporary with Shakespeare's play (5.1.43). These poems, too, turn to female complaint to turn ruined historical subjects into lamentable objects, able to elicit and ready—dying—to receive a good audience's virtuous sympathy.

2. Virtuous Tears: Tragic History as Female Complaint

Among the many poetic experimentations of the 1590s was what critics have described as a hybrid of the de casibus tragedies of spectral complaint made famous by the *Mirror* and Ovidian complaint, amorous, impassioned, and female-voiced.[56] These poems, with which *Lucrece* is typically classified despite its complainer not being a ghost, are Samuel Daniel's *Complaint of Rosamond* (1592); Thomas Churchyard's augmented version of *Shore's Wife* (1593), first printed in the 1563 edition of the *Mirror*; Thomas Lodge's *Tragicall Complaint of Elstred* (1593); and Michael Drayton's *Matilda* (1594). Although its speaker is male, critics often group Drayton's *Peirs Gaveston* (1593/4) with these poems, as it is written in the same style, and similarly features a complainant who was the object of a king's desire.[57] Family resemblances, as well as intertextual citations, link these poems: narratives that blend the accusatory style of the *Heroides* with the sexual violence thematized in the *Metamorphoses*, describing the speaker's seduction, coercion, or rape by a lustful king; highly ornamental language dense with rhetorical figures and epic similes; similar metrical patterns of either sestets or rhyme royal; and an emphasis on the sensuous beauty of their speakers and the sadness of their stories, offset against their questionable reputations. (Rosamond—like Shore's Wife and Elstred, a king's mistress—complains that Shore's Wife "passes for a Saint," Churchyard's poem having "justifie[d] her foule attaint"; the virginal Matilda makes a point of emphasizing that among Shore's Wife, Rosamond, and Elstred, she is the only one who cannot be accused of being unchaste.)[58]

Along with Drayton's *Englands Heroicall Epistles* (1597), these female complaint poems instantiate a new mode of writing English history as tragedy, instructing readers in the ethical paradigm of sympathetic reception. Although these poems are not widely studied, their significance has been recognized by several critics. Georgia Brown and Richard Helgerson have each suggested that the female complaint (which he contrasts with chronicle history, and she with epic) opens historical poetry to new, feminized perspectives, as well as to the world of private experience in the form of passion and sexual desire.[59] As I will show, these poems also imagine and invite a kind of reception different from the utilitarian paradigm that was especially important to tragic historical literature, in which the ethical value of literature lies in the lessons that one can apply to one's own everyday life. These poems' explicitly articulated desire for the reader's sympathy, and the framing of this sympathy as the reader's sole ethical duty with regard to the poem, distinguishes them from the complaints of the *Mirror* on which they are modeled. This framing of sympathy has to do with an Ovidianism

---

[56] Critical accounts of female complaint as a subgenre of historical complaint distinct from the poems of the *Mirror* (and in dialogue with each other) include Smith, *Elizabethan Poetry*; Dubrow, "A Mirror for Complaints"; and Swärdh, "From hell: *A Mirror for Magistrates* and the Late Elizabethan Female Complaint."

[57] See Quinn, "Mastering Complaint: Michael Drayton's 'Peirs Gaveston' and the Royal Mistress Complaints." No date is listed on the poem's title page, but it was registered in December 1593.

[58] *Delia... with the complaint of Rosamond*, H3v. For a thorough account of the intertextuality of these poems, see Finn, "'Of Whom Proud Rome Hath Boasted Long': Intertextual 'Conversations' in Early Modern England."

[59] Brown, *Redefining Elizabethan Literature*, 187; Helgerson, "Weeping for Jane Shore."

154   THE DRAMA OF COMPLAINT

that goes beyond rhetorical style and theme. With its accounts of one after another woman transformed by a vengeful or sympathetic god, or by the sheer power of her grief, into a lamenting thing—a plaintive feature of the natural landscape and, through Ovid's craft, an object of art—the *Metamorphoses* is the *locus classicus* for a model of female complaint as the form in which those who have died to one form of life survive, in a manner of speaking, in another, as objects. This romanticized notion of female complaint animates the poems of Daniel, Churchyard, Lodge, and Drayton, which suggest that it is because these figures have become aesthetic objects—and because it is to those objects that the reader's sympathy responds—that they can evoke sympathy, despite the vexed reputations of the historical figures themselves.

The universal, generic reader that these poems envision is sympathetic and feminine, a point underscored by the fact that those with female speakers are dedicated to noblewomen (and prospective patrons) whose discernment the poets praise, and whom they invite to treat the poems kindly.[60] This request for sympathy repeats across the poems. The writer of one of the epideictic poems that prefaces "Matilda," for instance, asks readers to with "Tears in your eyes, and passions in your hearts, / With mournful grace vouchsafe Matilda's story"—a request that Matilda's ghost herself repeats when she appears at the start of Drayton's poem and, expressing "hope of some compassion" from her audience, asks that "eyes may lend me teares to wash my wound."[61] Having wistfully imagined that Delia (Daniel's dedicatee, Mary Sidney, Countess of Pembroke) "may happe to deygne to read our story, / And offer up her sigh," Rosamond's ghost suggests that "That indulgence would profit me the best."[62] The "profit" she asks for comes from the reader and falls to the complainer, while the term "indulgence" gives ethical significance to the reader's pleasurable sympathy. Indeed, Rosamond describes herself as stuck in Purgatory unless she can garner "sighes on earth," comparing herself enviously to Shore's Wife, whose "well-told tale did such compassion finde, / That she is pass'd, and I am left behinde."[63] This is a transformation of the age-old trope of the life-renewing poem: here, what gives life from death is not simply the well-crafted poem, but the sympathy with which the reader receives it. Rosamond will figure this sympathy as "grace" for her graceless state, Matilda as "balm" for her wound, and Elstred as "life" that overturns her death sentence.[64]

---

[60] Daniel's *Complaint of Rosamond* is appended to his sonnet sequence *Delia*, dedicated to Mary Sidney, Countess of Pembroke; Lodge's *Tragicall Complaint of Elstred* is appended to his sonnet sequence *Phillis*, dedicated to the Countess of Shrewsbury. Churchyard's augmented *Shore's Wife* is prefaced with a dedicatory poem to Lady Mounteagle in *Churchyards Challenges*, the 1593 miscellany in which it is printed. The first edition of Drayton's *Matilda* is dedicated to Lucy Harington, the future Countess of Bedford.

[61] *Matilda*, B1r.   [62] *Rosamond*, H4r.   [63] *Rosamond*, H3r, H3v.

[64] *Rosamond*, H3v, K2v; *Matilda*, H1r; B1r; *Phillis... where-unto is annexed, the tragicall complaynt of Elstred*, L4r.

Each of these poets presents his poem as the artful object in and through which the complainer has received a new form of life. The historical Matilda—described by her ghost as the "glasse where heaven her-selfe may well behold"—becomes "Matilda," Drayton's "heaven-inchanting lay."[65] This playful conflation of (beautiful) historical subject and (beautiful) poem, already suggested by the poems' titles, is endemic to their narratives. This is particularly evident in Churchyard's 1593 revision of the decades-old *Shore's Wife* in the wake of Daniel's *Rosamond*. Several of the twenty-one stanzas that Churchyard adds to the poem—additions he describes in a dedicatory epistle as undertaken for the sake of "beautifying" the poem—are descriptions of the physical beauty of Shore's Wife, who claims that "Rosamond the faire / . . . / For beauties boast, could scarce compare with me / . . . / A piece of worke, should please a princes eie."[66] The poem reflects the beauty of its subject, who describes him or herself as having been, while living, strikingly poem-like. The face of Matilda was a "gift my Maker had assigned," a "worke [that] might shew the Arts-mans praise."[67] At his prime, Gaveston was the very picture of a well-wrought poem:

> If cunning'st pensill-man that ever wrought
> By skilfull arte of secret sumetry,
> Or the divine Idea of the thought
> With rare descriptions of high poesy,
> Should all compose a body and a mind,
> Such a one seem'd I, the wonder of my kind.[68]

As Drayton especially emphasizes, the poet possesses a godlike power to create life and beauty. But whereas the divine creator endowed these subjects with a beauty that unfortunately set aflame a king's desire, the poet—resurrecting them from the dead in the form of the complaint poem—turns them into lamentable objects whose beauty compels only a pleasing sympathy, an aesthetic emotion. Indeed, Rosamond's ghost says that she has "come here to plain" in order that Daniel's narrator-poet may in his "wofull Song / . . . forme my case, and register my wrong," so that "I through beautie made the wofullest wight, / By beautie might have comfort after death."[69] Like Lucrece, supplementing the fictional painter's "well-painted piece" to reanimate the "lifeless life" of Hecuba, these readers are

---

[65] *Matilda*, C2r, B2r.

[66] *The Tragedie of Shores wife*, in *Churchyard's Challenge*, 129–30. In the dedicatory epistle to the augmented poem, Churchyard mentions his admiration of, and pointedly masculine rivalry with, Daniel: "because Rosimond is so excellently sette forth (the actor whereof I honour) I have somewhat beautified my Shores wife, not in any kind of emulation, but to make the world knowe, my device in age is as ripe & reddie, as my disposition and knowledge was in youth" (126).

[67] *Matilda*, B3v, B3r.   [68] *Peirs Gaveston Earle of Cornwall*, B4r.

[69] *Rosamond*, H3r, H3v.

156   THE DRAMA OF COMPLAINT

offered the opportunity to give life through their sympathetic reception of the poet's life-giving labor.

As the religious language suggests, such sympathy is a sign and exercise of the reader's virtue: their goodness and their power. The poems invite readers to prove themselves better audiences than the markedly unvirtuous historical audiences described in the stories that all of these speakers tell—audiences whose lack of virtue manifests in the lack of sympathy with which they responded to the speakers' complaints. The poems comprise an aesthetic space in which that sympathy is scripted as the right judgment, conforming to the internal ethical logic of the poems. In Lodge's *Elstred*, which begins and ends with a melancholy narrator alone by the banks of the Severn, the watery emergence of the ghosts of Elstred and her daughter Sabrine, paired with their submergence into the water once they have told their stories, mark the limits of that zone. At the center of this chiasmic structure is a scene of failed judicial plaint: as Elstred explains, after her lover Locrinus's death, she and Sabrine were brought before Locrinus's wife Gwendolen, and at her order—their "plaints ha[ving] little force"—"cast at once into the wofull wave" of the Severn.[70] This scene of judgment has a counterpart beyond the boundaries of the poem, in Lodge's Induction to *Phillis*, the sonnet sequence to which *Elstred* is appended. There, addressing his dedicatee the Countess of Shrewsbury, Lodge describes the poem as "these little loves but lately hatched" as "Who from the wrestling waves have made retreat, / To pleade for life before thy judgement seate."[71] Within the poem, the women's ghosts make this plea themselves: before returning to the water, they promise that "if the Gods or men compassion have, / Compassion that with tender hearts nere sleepeth, / We both shall live."[72] Thus Lodge offers his readers the chance to be more virtuous audiences than the "marble-breast[ed]" Gwendolen—to give god-like, life-giving tears.[73] The prime example of such a sympathetic figure, of course, is the poet himself, whom each of the ghosts praise for having singularly heard, pitied, and told their stories.

None of this is to suggest that the sympathy these poems elicit cannot have further effect or consequence: indeed, as Helgerson has argued, readers' sympathies can be leveraged into a critique of sovereign tyranny. The point, rather, is that the poems depict sympathetic reception as a virtuous end in itself. Lending support to the idea that sympathetic reception is the telos of the female complaint form is a parodic poem appended to Giles Fletcher's sonnet sequence *Licia* (1593).[74] Entitled *The Rising to the Crowne of Richard the Third, Written by him selfe*, the poem is spoken by the ghost of Richard III, who complains that the falls of Shore's Wife, Rosamond, and Elstred are less tragic than his, and that he is

---

[70] *Elstred*, L3r, L4r.   [71] *Elstred*, A4r.   [72] *Elstred*, L4r.   [73] *Elstred*, L3r.
[74] *Licia* follows the same format as Daniel's *Delia* and Lodge's *Phillis*: a sonnet sequence with an appended female complaint, addressed to a noblewoman (here, Lady Mollineux). Kerrigan discusses these as analogues to Shakespeare's *A Lover's Complaint*, which was appended to the *Sonnets* (1609).

prepared "To play the fourth" part of a tragedy—provided that he, a male monarch, can summon up the right lamenting tone. Hence his invocation: "Sorrow sit downe, and helpe my muse to sing, / For weepe he may not, that was cal'd a King."[75] Fletcher's self-conscious imitation of the historical female complaint poem, applied to a famously villainous king, demonstrates an awareness of the implications of the ethical paradigm attached to the female complaint form and the lamentable objects it created.

What Fletcher's poem treats as a joke—the idea that the female complaint form, associated with the victims of tyrannous kings, could render even a tyrannous male king sympathetic—Shakespeare engages seriously in *Richard II*. Like *The Rape of Lucrece*, the play demonstrates an understanding of female complaint as the artful form that converts the historical subject into an aesthetic object for which good audiences might weep. Its use in *Richard II* reflects the complexities of the tragedy's historical subject, a king who inflicts and then becomes the victim of sovereign violence; a negative moral exemplar curiously Christ-like in his passion; an object of political critique felled by what Shakespeare's sources described as the most horrible of political acts. Scenes of female complaint are key to what I will suggest is the play's simultaneous adoption and critique of the ethical logic of sympathetic reception. That critique emerges from the very thing emphasized in the poems we have just seen: sympathy as collaboration with the vision and craft of the poet. Such artfulness is thrown into relief by Shakespeare's collapsing of the lamentable aesthetic object and the poet in the figure of the plaintive Richard, who, like Fletcher's Richard III, self-consciously attempts to make a lamentable object of himself.

3. Becoming Lamentable in *Richard II*

Richard's parting injunction to the Queen illustrates how Shakespeare has built into his character a recognition of the potential of female complaint to offer an aesthetic escape from the tragic events of historical time into the literature of historical tragedy. Recapitulated in Richard's "Think I am dead" is a request to be seen both as he will be in the play's fictional timeline and as he already is, in the time of *Richard II* (5.1.38). This is a demand he has been pressing upon his onstage and theatrical audiences since his return to England from Ireland in Act 3, scene 2, the pivotal moment in the play at which his fortunes turn. There the historical narrative of the king's fall, deposition, and death morphs into the tragedy of subjectivity: in being reduced to his mortal self, Richard does not become

[75] Giles Fletcher, *Licia... whereunto is added the Rising to the Crowne of Richard the third*, L2r.

158 THE DRAMA OF COMPLAINT

like other men but less than them, deprived of his sublime kingly body, and with it, his identity.[76] Hence his post-deposition lament:

> I have no name, no title—
> ....
>   Alack the heavy day
> That I have worn so many winters out
> And know not what name to call myself.
> O, that I were a mockery king of snow,
> Standing before the sun of Bolingbroke,
> To melt myself away in water-drops!
>
>   (4.1.255–62)

This speech exemplifies Richard's most characteristic plaint pattern: a declaration of his undoing as a subject, coupled with a fantasy of having become a lamentable object. These complaints blend mournful nostalgia with a future-oriented wistfulness, a desire often expressed, as it is here, through the grammar of the wish ("O, that I were a mockery king of snow"). While Jeremy Lopez has rightly observed that Richard's language exemplifies "a desire, and inability, to disappear," I would suggest that that very recalcitrance, that inability to disappear, is also desired by Richard: he wants to be *and* not to be.[77] In the narrative time between Richard's symbolic and physiological deaths, as his subjectivity dissolves, Shakespeare dramatizes his self-dramatizing attempt to remake himself as a lamentable object—a thing resurrected to a form of life, and to social significance and circulation, in the domain of the aesthetic.[78] Tearful complaints are the means through which Richard imagines that he simultaneously melts himself away and is recomposed, dying and reemerging from death as "the lamentable tale of me"— and, as such, an object worthy of the aesthetic emotion of sympathy (5.1.44).

The historiographical narrative that Shakespeare inherited is, to put it mildly, more complicated.[79] Its contradictions and ambivalence are reflected in the play, whose polyvocality allows for a range of conflicting perspectives on Richard. As Meek suggests, "much of *Richard II* is self-consciously concerned with the

---

[76] I am alluding here, of course, to Ernst Kantorowicz's formative interpretation of the play in *The King's Two Bodies: A Study in Medieval Political Theology*, the touchstone for all political and political-theological readings of the play.

[77] "Introduction," 34–5.

[78] In this regard Shakespeare's Richard invites comparisons to Cleopatra, whom Patrick Gray argues Shakespeare represents as an "artist, staging her own demise," fantasizing that she can control how she is seen—and not seen—by others who will judge her. (It's worth noting, though, that Cleopatra fears precisely what I think Richard wants—to be an aesthetic object.) See Gray, "Seduced by Romanticism," 519, and *Shakespeare and the Fall of the Roman Republic*, 220–58.

[79] On the ambivalence of early modern historiographical accounts of Richard's reign and deposition, their "divergent and competing interpretations of Richard and Bolingbroke," and Shakespeare's reflection of this ambivalence, see Forker, Introduction, 23–50, 23.

question of whether we should feel pity for Richard."[80] Another way to put this would be to say that Shakespeare—rather than deciding that Richard should or should not be sympathetic, and attempting to persuade us accordingly—shifts onto the audience the obligation to make this judgment. The burden, framed as a choice of ethical significance, is a palpably heavy one. Indeed, in pressing the question of whether sympathy for Richard is the right response, the play trains the audience's eyes as much on sympathetic reception itself as on Richard: Richard is the object for whom one might lament or not, but the object of ethical judgment is one's own sympathy, or lack thereof.

Female complaint teaches the audience to see Richard with sympathy. Just like the Queen in Daniel's *Civil Wars*, in Shakespeare's play the function of Richard's companionate Queen is to observe and lament the suffering of Richard, to be in her complaints a lamentable object herself, as well as a point of identification for the ideal sympathetic spectator.[81] It is through the Queen's sorrowful gaze that the play first frames Richard as a lamentable object, in fact. In Act 2, scene 2, following Richard's departure for Ireland, the Queen laments to Bushy that her "inward soul / With nothing trembles. At something it grieves / More than with parting from my lord the King" (2.2.11–13). Bushy says that she merely sees Richard's absence through "Sorrow's eyes," which have the power to make many fanciful images of sorrow from one true "substance of a grief" (2.2.14):

> For Sorrow's eyes, glazed with blinding tears,
> Divides one thing entire to many objects,
> Like perspectives, which, rightly gazed upon,
> Show nothing but confusion; eyed awry,
> Distinguish form. So your sweet majesty,
> Looking awry upon your lord's departure,
> Find shapes of grief more than himself to wail,
> Which, looked on as it is, is naught but shadows
> Of what it is not. Then, thrice-gracious Queen,
> More than your lord's departure weep not. More is not seen,
> Or if it be, 'tis with false Sorrow's eye,
> Which for things true weeps things imaginary.
>
> (2.2.16–27)

Like the person who views an anamorphic image "awry" and thus "distinguish[es] form" where from another perspective "nothing but confusion is," the Queen

---

[80] Meek, "'Rue e'en for ruth,'" 145.

[81] The fact that in the preface to the 1609 edition of *The Civil Wars* Daniel explains his decision to deviate from historical truth in his invention of the Queen (whose historical counterpart was only eleven years old) suggests that *The Civil Wars* was Shakespeare's source for *Richard II*, rather than vice versa. See Forker, Introduction, 11.

160   THE DRAMA OF COMPLAINT

weeps for a kaleidoscopic array of sorrowful images ("shapes of grief") that appear in the void where Richard once was. Her perspective, Bushy argues, fills her with a sadness that is "nothing but conceit" (2.2.33), the product of her own imagination, whereas if Richard's absence were "rightly gazed upon," all she would see is what is really there, which is nothing but the shadow-image of a missing Richard ("naught but shadows / Of what it is not"). The Queen's rebuttal to Bushy puns on his description of the absent Richard as a "nothing" that casts a shadow: "*nothing* hath begot my something grief, / Or something hath the nothing that I grieve" (2.2.36–37). Like Richard's "Think I am dead," her words suggest a tragic foreknowledge about the events that will unfold in linear time while also highlighting the sorrow produced, even now, by the fanciful play between her imagination and an image that is *not Richard*. Here, as in her later framing of Richard as "King Richard's tomb, / And not King Richard!" (5.1.12–13), the Queen models a way of seeing through "Sorrow's eye(s)" that is simultaneously receptive and creative, that enables the "something" of a lamentable object to emerge from "naught."

In both instances, the Queen's laments locate the origin of this object in a passage through death, absence, and nothingness, a lack that is the premise of the lamentable object and the creative matrix of female complaint. I would suggest that it is because of the form's conventional objectifying capacity that Richard's own complaints for himself—which have been described as ornate, tearful, histrionic, self-dramatizing, metapoetic, and, of course, effeminate—are modeled on female complaint. Critics have long alternated between reading these complaints as stereotypical signifiers of Richard's effeminacy, political inefficacy, and queerness, or as a clever rhetorical tactic to manipulate his audiences into sympathizing with his cause.[82] More recently, Maggie Vinter, Donovan Sherman, and Alice Dailey have read Richard's laments as self-conscious performances of non-self-identity that crystallize various conceptual and representational concerns engaged by Shakespeare, rather than reflections of the interiority of a coherent dramatic character.[83] I join them in seeing Richard's laments as performances that are, like his character, slightly unhinged from the play's fictional narrative, evincing a "temporal dislocation" that I, like Dailey, link to the play's concern with the aesthetic.[84] That concern is mediated through a self-reflexive Richard who sees himself as the aesthetic object that Shakespeare's play has made him. With their verbal and visual rhetoric of becoming nothing—vanishing, dying, being undone, melting, "pin[ing] away"—Richard's complaints have the effect of emphasizing the distinction between the mortal person and the immortal office of a king

---

[82] See McMillin, "*Richard II*: Eyes of Sorrow, Eyes of Desire"; and Vaught, "'Sad Stories of the Deaths of Kings': Lyric and Narrative Release from Confining Spaces in Shakespeare's *Richard II*."

[83] See Vinter, *Last Acts*, 88; Sherman, "'What more remains?': Messianic Performance in *Richard II*"; Dailey, "Little, Little Graves: Shakespeare's Photographs of Richard II."

[84] Vinter, *Last Acts*, 89. Dailey, "Little, Little Graves," 143.

(3.2.209). But they also highlight that their speaker is "not King Richard": not a king, but an actor's construction of a king. This metatheatricality reminds the play's audience that whatever sympathy these complaints elicit is an aesthetic emotion, generated by an artificial object created through poetic labor.

Shakespeare represents that labor as Richard's. The play showcases Richard's attempts to make himself into a lamentable object to be judged aesthetically—on the basis of how sad he appears—rather than morally or politically. From the very moment he returns from Ireland, Richard begins not simply to mourn for his fate but to demarcate, through his complaints, an aesthetic space with himself as the object of attention at its center. Hearing of Bolingbroke's invasion and the dispersal of his forces, Richard suggests that his men should see him as already dead ("Have I not reason to look pale and dead?"), his tears writing his epitaph (3.2.79):

> Of comfort no man speak!
> Let's talk of graves, of worms and epitaphs,
> Make dust our paper and with rainy eyes
> Write sorrow on the bosom of the earth.
>
> (3.2.144–47)

As Jean Howard notes, "Richard is a self-conscious weeper...call[ing] conspicuous attention to his tears in ways that reveal an awareness of the spectacle he creates in performing them."[85] Fittingly turning to a theatrical metaphor, Richard suggests that a king is no more than an actor, playing on borrowed time lent by that "grinning" sovereign-author Death, who watches him in amusement, "Allowing him a breath, a little scene," and then "Comes at the last and with a little pin / Bores through his castle wall, and farewell, king!" (3.2.163, 164, 169–70). Yet Death's existential stage direction for the actor-king's exit cues the latter's reentrance on another stage, for the more sympathetic gaze of another audience. From death, as Richard imagines it, comes a new form of life. Farewell king, hello sad story:

> For God's sake let us sit upon the ground
> And tell sad stories of the death of kings—
> How some have been deposed, some slain in war
> Some haunted by the ghosts they have deposed,
> Some poisoned by their wives, some sleeping killed—
> All murdered.
>
> (3.2.152, 155–60)

---

[85] Howard, "Monarchs Who Cry," 458.

162 THE DRAMA OF COMPLAINT

As Paul Budra argues, Richard is evoking the de casibus tragedies of the *Mirror* here.[86] But crucially, Richard is also resignifying the collective meaning of those stories, imposing an editorial aesthetic unity on disparate narratives by categorizing them as "sad stories"—stories that should make one weep—rather than moral exemplars. By inserting his own story into this lineage, he reframes the *Mirror's* account of Richard II, summed up in the title of Richard's ghost's complaint: "How King Richard the Second was for his evill governaunce deposed from his seate, in the yeare 1399, and murdered in prison the yeare following."[87] By this point in the play, audiences have seen *Richard II* give voice to some of the same proofs of "evil governance" (Richard's choice of flatterers as councilors; his indulgence of his appetites; his over-taxation of his subjects and leasing of lands to pay for his luxuries; his perversions of justice). Here, though, Shakespeare's Richard imagines that his story might nevertheless be reduced—as he himself has been—to his suffering and sorrow, which requires its audiences to recognize an ethical logic different from, and even incommensurable with, that of the *Mirror*.

The language of this scene-within-a-scene, with Richard forbidding "comforting" speech and commanding his men to "sit upon the ground," is the conventional language that marks aesthetic space, and particularly that of plaintive performance and sympathetic reception. The imaginative, poetic flights in which Richard describes himself as dead and as a thing of grief are consistently marked by commentary (from himself as well as others) that emphasizes the foolishness of his speech: he is "talk[ing] but idly" (3.3.171); "speak[ing] fondly like a frantic man" (3.3.185); and "pratt[ling] ... tedious[ly]" (5.2.26). Imitating the speakers of female complaint, Richard remakes himself as a lamentable aesthetic object by describing himself in language that is not only poetic in its "verbal opulence"—rich in figures and elaborate conceits, rhetorically ornate—but in its fancifulness and its pragmatic inefficacy.[88] Indeed, this language is willfully counterproductive with regard to the situation that his character is in, a point highlighted in the words with which this particular scene of complaint comes to a close, as the Bishop of Carlisle turns to the rhetoric of complaint-shaming to get Richard on his feet: "My lord, wise men ne'er sit and wail their woes, / But presently prevent the ways to wail" (3.2.178–79). In calling attention to the folly of Richard's response to his own plight, Carlisle's speech recalls a resonant moment from *3 Henry VI* in which Warwick, weary from battle, rouses himself and his companions by criticizing their inaction:

---

[86] Budra, *A Mirror for Magistrates and the de casibus Tradition*, 90.

[87] *The Mirour for Magistrates*, Fol. 122r.

[88] Forker, Introduction, 4. On Richard's eloquence, and the play's interest in poetic language, see Bolam, "*Richard II*: Shakespeare and the languages of the stage."

> Why stand we like soft-hearted women here,
> Wailing our losses whiles the foe doth rage,
> And look upon, as if the tragedy
> Were played in jest by counterfeiting actors?[89]

Here, as in Richard's performances of complaint, Shakespeare limns aesthetic space negatively, as a place apart from the here-and-now of reality. Aesthetic emotion is treated in similar terms, as a response that is appropriate for particular subjects (women) in relation to particular objects (the "jest" of a theatrical tragedy), but wholly inappropriate for real men to experience in relation to real objects. Richard's gambit, however, is to aestheticize himself wherever he is, whatever else is happening. As with Rosamond, Shore's Wife, Elstred, and Gaveston, he can be pleasurably lamented as a sad story, rather than judged as a person, if he is recognized as only an aesthetic object.

Between Richard's anticipation of death and his actual death in the play is the drama that enacts it in miniature: the deposition, an undoing followed by a reconstitution as an object of grief (the whole thing a "woeful pageant," in the Abbot's suggestive phrase [4.1.321]). Here Richard's undoing and becoming are enacted through the gestures of transferring the crown and shattering the mirror, actions accompanied by a language of grief through which Richard objectifies himself—as, in one especially memorable image, a sinking bucket that fills with the tears into which his kingship dissolves while Bolingbroke's bucket rises ("That bucket down and full of tears am I, / Drinking my griefs" [4.1.188–89]). In the deposition scene, the complaint that accompanies Richard's transfer of the crown to Bolingbroke rhetorically entwines his un-kinging ("I must nothing be. /.../ Now mark me how I will undo myself") with his assumption of a new identity as a thing of grief (4.1.201–3). Thus, before handing the crown to Bolingbroke, Richard calls attention to the grief he still possesses: "but still my griefs are mine. / You may my glories and my state depose, / But not my griefs; still am I king of those" (4.1.191–93). Relinquishing the crown in a speech comprised almost entirely of performative utterances ("My acts, decrees, and statutes I deny"), he says, again in subjunctive language, "Make me, that nothing have, with nothing grieved" (4.1.213, 216). It is his grief that gives him a modicum of substance, his grief that forms the kernel of his new life as a lamentable aesthetic object.

This grief is not "in" Richard, but produced in an exchange between his performance of sorrow and the audience's perception and affirmation of that sorrow. Shakespeare makes this especially clear in the "sport" of the mirror scene, a scene devoted to the matter of how to see Richard, figuratively and literally (4.1.290). Having asked for a mirror so that he may "see the very book indeed / Where all

---

[89] *3 Henry VI*, 2.3.25–8.

164   THE DRAMA OF COMPLAINT

my sins are writ, and that's myself"—seemingly, to recollect his sins before reading aloud the confession Bolingbroke's men have written for him—Richard then uses the mirror as a mirror, to "show me what a face I have" (4.1.273–74, 266).

> *Enter one with a glass.*
> Give me that glass, and therein will I read.
> > [*Takes looking-glass.*]
> No deeper wrinkles yet? Hath Sorrow struck
> So many blows upon this face of mine
> And made no deeper wounds?
>
> > (4.1.276–79)

Richard's play with the looking glass, I would suggest, explicitly figures the replacement of the ethical paradigm encapsulated in the metaphor of the mirror: here, a utilitarian model of reading centered on moral judgment and introspection is discarded (and its ethical logic mocked) in favor of a model of sympathetic reception that begins with contemplating a lamentable object. So too, what Richard recognizes when he looks in the mirror is not a moral failure, but an aesthetic shortcoming embodied by the actor: his face just looks too good. Here Shakespeare points to the limitations of the living images of theatrical representation, as in *Lucrece* he has emphasized the limitations of the medium of painting: the material reality of a live face that can be only so ravaged by grief poses a hard limit to the vivid descriptions of sorrowing, death-like faces one finds in female complaint poetry (as in *A Lover's Complaint*, where the narrator describes the complaining woman's face as "the carcass of a beauty spent and done").[90] Richard's live face requires a supplement to be the lamentable object he wants (us) to see. By shattering the mirror, he amends his face, each fragment a visual synecdoche of the face wounded by sorrow: "As brittle as the glory is the face! [*Shatters glass.*] / For there it is, cracked in an hundred shivers" (4.1.290–91). Richard's lost glory materializes in the broken mirror, its shattered pieces the lamentable object(s) that represent his wrecked face to the audience ("there it is"). When Richard tells Bolingbroke, now Henry IV, what it means ("Mark, silent King, the moral of this sport, / How soon hath sorrow destroyed my face") Henry corrects him: "The shadow of your sorrow hath destroyed / The shadow of your face" (4.1.290–1, 292–93). Ventriloquizing, with a "ha!", Henry's suggestion that these "external manner of laments" are but the images of a more substantial "unseen grief" that lies within, Richard sarcastically thanks the new king for "not only giv[ing] / Me cause to wail, but teach[ing] me the way / How to lament the cause" (4.1.296, 297, 300–2). Henry is the spectator who in reaching for a deeper meaning misses the

---

[90] Shakespeare, *A Lover's Complaint*, line 11.

point. Yet, rather like Bushy's chiding of the fanciful Queen, Henry's insistence that Richard is looking at nothing but "shadows" emphasizes that the "Richard" who appears before the theatrical audience is but a lamentable object distributed between the stuff of theater: an actor's face and the prop of the broken mirror, its fragmented "shivers" and their own embodied (even *shivering*) passionate response.

We have seen how scripts for virtuous reception, conventional to the female complaint form, frame lamentable aesthetic objects as the products of creative collaboration between the skillful performance of the complainer and the sympathetic reception of a participatory audience. One of the most pointedly metatheatrical moments in the play indicates that Richard's status as a lamentable object hangs in the balance, and that sympathy, in its presence or absence, is the unavoidable frame for his reception. Narrating Richard's entry into London behind Henry IV, York weeps as he describes the unsympathetic Londoners, whose hearts he suggests must have been "steeled" by God "for some strong purpose," or "barbarism itself [would] have pitied him" (5.2.34, 36):

> As in a theatre the eyes of men,
> After a well-graced actor leaves the stage,
> Are idly bent on him that enters next,
> Thinking his prattle to be tedious,
> Even so, or with much more contempt, men's eyes
> Did scowl on gentle Richard.
>
> (5.2.23–28)

Insofar as it draws a line between aesthetic space and empirical reality, and the modes of judgment appropriate to each, this speech is more than the critique of a "barbaric" lack of sympathy that York intends. Shakespeare certainly highlights the theatricality of political power in York's description of the crowd, who judge Richard and Henry as if they were actors of differing skill, needing to move audiences by their performances, rather than divinely appointed king and usurper. But more simply, York's horror—it is as if the people were watching *actors!*—cannot but remind the play's audience that they are doing just that: sympathizing with the man whose performance, in the context of a space of relative idleness and prattle, is the most "well-graced." York's lament for the failures of natural sympathy has the paradoxical effect of thoroughly denaturalizing that sympathy, underscoring its status as an aesthetic emotion that responds to the performance of the actor that plays Richard.

Switching idioms slightly, I want to close by suggesting that each of Richard's scenes of complaint dramatize his unanswered desire to find an audience who, by showing sympathy, will *play along with* him, an audience who will consent to his fantasy of himself as a lamentable object and locate themselves within that scene. The idea of play dominates Richard's final complaint, performed in his prison cell

166   THE DRAMA OF COMPLAINT

immediately before he is murdered. Figuring his lonely cell as a microcosm, he imagines that by making his "brain…the female to my soul, / The soul the father" he might "hammer…out" yet more unhappy thoughts, "none contented"—conceptions that will "people this little world," providing him with like-minded company (5.5.6–7, 5, 9). Included in this scene of complaint, unlike his others, is a performance of sympathetic reception. Having declared that if he thinks himself "unkinged," he finds that "[I] straight am nothing" (5.5.37, 38), Richard begins to mournfully philosophize, when he is interrupted by an invisible musician:

> But whate'er I be,
> Nor I nor any man that but man is
> With nothing shall be pleased till he be eased
> With being nothing.   *The music plays.*
>   Music do I hear?
>
>   (5.5.38–41)

The music turns Richard's attention to the moral imperative of "keep[ing] time" in "the music of men's lives," and his neglect of this charge ("I wasted time, and now doth Time waste me" [5.5.42, 43, 49]). Time wastes him, leaving him nothing but his sorrowful face. Yet the intricate conceit through which he elaborates this claim stresses—in contrast to a penitent soul—the sorrowfulness of his face, showing, as in the mirror scene, how Time is impressed on his form. His passioning body is Time's "numb'ring clock" (5.5.50). His eyes are the numbers ("the outward watch") to which his finger, "cleansing them from tears," gestures "like a dial's point" (5.5.52, 54, 53). His sighs express his thoughts, which are minutes, and his "clamorous groans" are the sounds of the clock's bell, his heart: "So sighs, and tears, and groans / Show minutes, times, and hours" (5.5.56, 57–58). The music that has been accompanying this lament comes to a stop when Richard, suddenly recognizing that "my time / Runs posting on in Bolingbroke's proud joy / While I stand fooling here," commands it to "sound no more" (5.5.58–60, 61). This is the same dynamic that we have seen in other scenes of female complaint, where the aestheticized co-mourning of a complainer and a sympathetic observer breaks up with an acknowledgment of its idle foolishness. As in the scene with Lucrece and the painting of Troy, here Shakespeare sets the time of the lamentable object—a figure for aesthetic experience more generally, as I have been suggesting—against the historical clock time of pragmatic action, mastered by Bolingbroke.[91] If the foolish laments to which Richard devotes his diminishing clock time imaginatively order that time by turning his lamenting body into Time's clock,

---

[91] On Bolingbroke's control of time, see Sherman, "Messianic Performance."

such play does no lasting good: the conceit, like the music, is just the "nothing" that pleases Richard in the moments before he will be "eased" by death.

Nevertheless, like the other scenes of female complaint this chapter has explored, this scene calls attention to its own internal ethical logic, casting the musician as someone who has done well in accompanying Richard's complaints. After the music stops at his order, Richard makes a point of expressing gratitude to the anonymous musician:

> Yet blessing on his heart that gives it me,
> For 'tis a sign of love; and love to Richard
> Is a strange brooch in this all-hating world.

(5.5.64–66)

As a metaphor for sympathetic reception, the "strange brooch," a rare jewel, figures a performative aesthetic emotion, a "love" (dis)played as a mark of distinction. In the performance of the music, the play gives an example of someone "playing along with" Richard's laments, harmonizing with him. Interestingly, this sympathetic spectator is someone the audience never sees. He is more cipher than character, one about whom we know nothing at all—nothing but his skill at playing along.

In this chapter, I have traced how the poetic form of female complaint was co-articulated with a new ethical paradigm of reception for early modern theatergoers and readers of literature. Retraining audiences who were, as Grady puts it, taught "always to seek 'applications' of cultural productions to their personal lives, to invest the self into works of the imagination," the sympathetic reception foregrounded in scenes of female complaint reimagines what it means to be a good audience, at a historical moment when conceptions of what literature is and does were shifting.[92] Such scenes cultivate attachments to a practice of virtuous reception whose ethical logic is internal: while the paradigm of sympathetic reception I have been exploring does not foreclose moral utility or real-world effects, it renders these beside the point, suggesting instead that it is *good enough* for the subject to give the lamentable object the show of passion it wants.

Although early modern female complaint has elicited many incisive analyses of the poetics and politics of gender, the form's intimacy with early modern aesthetic theory has received little attention. This is unfortunate, because female complaint—as I have been suggesting—is a site where literary and philosophical thought about the intersections of aesthetics and ethics has been rendered in particularly direct ways, especially in its combinations with other forms. This chapter has largely, though not exclusively, described its presence in tragedy, the genre that "must have passions that must move the soule /.../ Extorting teares out of

---

[92] Grady, *Shakespeare and Impure Aesthetics*, 42.

168   THE DRAMA OF COMPLAINT

the strictest eyes"—and the genre that Lynne Magnusson suggests was identified with no speech act so much as the "passionate lament."[93] Because it foregrounds a passion of dubious utility, some writers have treated female complaint as a crystallization of their concerns about the boundedness of tragic sympathy. Augustine professes shame for having wept as a boy for Dido's sufferings and not the state of his own soul, and having later loved the futile grief generated by tragic theatrical shows ("What quality of mercy is it in fictitious and theatrical inventions? A member of the audience is not excited to offer help, but invited only to grieve").[94] Taking the opposite position, Philip Sidney defends the morally transformative force of such tragic fictions in *The Defence of Poesy* (1595) by relating an anecdote from Plutarch's *Lives* about the tyrant Alexander Phaeraeus, whose tears for Hecuba and Andromache at a performance of Euripides' *Trojan Women* could and should have moved him to be ashamed of the real-life "tragedies" he himself had inflicted—although, as Sidney awkwardly admits, they did not.[95] The aesthetic emotion of sympathy would be recuperated and made morally respectable by the sentimental theory of the eighteenth century, which would situate sympathy as the basis of moral judgments and—positing that sympathy in relation to tragic art bears on the capacity for sympathetic identification in other spheres of life—would place a moral and aesthetic premium on art that elicits sympathy.[96] There are clear connections between the subject matter and style of the *Mirror*-style female complaints and the sentimental melodramatic tragedies of the eighteenth century, as Götz Schmitz has shown, and in some ways the ethical logic I have attributed to early modern female complaint seems to anticipate the prioritizing of sympathy in this later reception paradigm.[97] But early modern scenes of female complaint, as I have been suggesting, do not quite make these connections between the sympathy that responds to lamentable objects of art and self-improvement. On the contrary, some of these scenes seem to underscore the boundedness of that sympathy, its confinement to the aesthetic space. While some early modern texts are, as Heather James shows, acutely attuned to the putatively detrimental—that is, subversive—effects of sympathy with regard to moral, social, and political norms, I would argue that in many other early modern texts the morally beneficial social implications of virtuous sympathetic reception

---

[93] These lines are spoken by the figure of Tragedie in *A Warning for Fair Women*, lines 44–6. Magnusson, "Shakespearean Tragedy and the Language of Lament," 121.

[94] Augustine, *Confessions*, 36. For Dido, see 15–16.   [95] *The Defence of Poesy*, 231.

[96] On sentiment and sympathy in eighteenth-century thought see, for instance, Marshall, "Adam Smith and the Theatricality of Moral Sentiments" and *The Surprising Effects of Sympathy*; Mullan, *Sentiment and Sociability*; Driver, "Moral Sense and Sentimentalism."

[97] Schmitz, *The Fall of Women in Early English Narrative Verse*. These female complaint poems might be said to belong to the same genealogy as the sentimental and melodramatic early twentieth-century mass-marketed genres of "female complaint" that Lauren Berlant explores, which Berlant suggests cultivate "juxtapolitical" forms of belonging. See Berlant, *The Female Complaint*.

look, in retrospect, like something *not yet there* (as for Sidney, it is not quite there in his example, though he wants it to be).

The scenes of female complaint this chapter has examined refuse the imperative associated with the utilitarian paradigm of reception: the imperative that art be transformative of the self, and that its lessons be applied to action in the real world. The representations of breathtakingly impotent sympathy in some of these scenes—Lucrece tearing the painting, Richard idealizing the weeping firebrands—even seem to mock that notion. In imagining a sympathy that responds to what strikes the senses in the moment of plaintive performance, the paradigm of sympathetic reception embraces the "sottish and feminine pitie" that Pierre Charron criticizes for "not respecting the depth and merit of the cause, but the present fortune, state and condition" (a sympathy he contrasts to an admirable compassion that responds only to undeserved suffering, which a man can offer without "effeminating his owne nature").[98] More audaciously, by the terms of their own internal ethical logic the scenes of female complaint in which this paradigm is articulated suggest that this kind of sympathy is *good*.

To return to *Richard II*, the play, I have argued, both accepts and stakes out a distance from the ethical paradigm of sympathetic reception and its internal ethical logic by putting the complaints for sympathy in the mouth of the transparently manipulative Richard. The play does not reject the ethical paradigm of sympathetic reception whose emergence it registers, but it does inject a certain ethical anxiety into it. This anxiety comes especially to the fore in the closing speech. Here Henry IV, taking over the Queen's role as the plaintive sympathetic spectator, asks his on- and offstage audiences to mourn with him "for what I do lament," the lamentable object of Richard's body:

> Lords, I protest, my soul is full of woe
> That blood should sprinkle me to make me grow.
> Come, mourn with me for what I do lament
> And put on sullen black incontinent.
> I'll make a voyage to the Holy Land
> To wash this blood off from my guilty hand.
> March sadly after; grace my mournings here
> In weeping after this untimely bier.
>
> (5.6.45–52)

The speech highlights a certain coerciveness that hovers over the ideal of sympathetic reception articulated in scenes of female complaint. The conventional closing call to communal mourning, in a play that consistently poses the question

---

[98] Charron, *Of Wisdome*, 99.

170 THE DRAMA OF COMPLAINT

of whether to recognize Richard as lamentable, suggests that the lamentable object is created through a sovereign command to see it as such, to consent to mourning for it. Here at the moment that announces the vanishing of the aesthetic space, the closing of its frame—the play has ended, the actors are leaving the stage—Shakespeare adds a self-reflexive step to sympathetic reception, a movement in which the spectator's conscious contemplation of the object doubles back on itself, to how it has been shaped by the artist's vision and cues. In the end, then, *Richard II* makes sympathetic reception a matter of complicity with some form of power, whether it is political or poetic.

What is more, in presenting Henry's woe for Richard as an enigma—evidence of what we might alternately interpret as the character's genuine sorrow, his fear of divine justice, or his strategic pretense—Shakespeare directs the audience's attention from the question of Richard's sympathetic qualities to the question of the meaning of Henry's performance of sympathy for Richard. The play thus enacts in its own narrative a perspectival shift by which sympathetic reception becomes not only an ethical good but also an object of ethical judgment. While contemporary tragic historical poems of female complaint imagine aesthetic space as a domain in which to exercise ethical virtue, *Richard II* introduces anxiety into that exercise, making aesthetic space a site of concentrated ethical self-scrutiny. The *good enough* audience performs sympathy. But the *good* audience, the play suggests, is one who knows what their sympathy says, not only about the lamentable object, but about themselves, the subjects who lament for it.

5

"Nobody, I Myself"

Deathbed Complaint and the Authority of Happiness Scripts

The ethical paradigms whose conjunctions with complaint this book has been exploring can be described as what Sara Ahmed calls happiness scripts: cultural roadmaps that chart a path toward happiness, that telos of ethics and perennial subject of philosophical inquiry, by marking certain objects of desire as good, "happy objects"—causes of happiness—and others as bad, "unhappy objects," causes of unhappiness.[1] What happiness scripts deliver, Ahmed suggests, is "the promise of happiness," or the promise that "if you have this or have that, or if you do this or do that, then happiness is what follows"—in short, that happiness is "what you get for desiring well" and acting in accordance with that desire.[2] We have seen how poetic forms of complaint, with their signature dramas of desire, participate in the construction of various early modern happiness scripts that tell audiences how (and how not) to live, what (and what not) to want and do. I have been arguing that Shakespearean tragedy modifies these scripts: that scenes of existential complaint demonstrate appropriate and inappropriate ways of speaking feeling to authority that are challenged in *King Lear*; that the internal drama of conscience figured in scenes of judicial complaint is remapped as an external and relational drama in *Richard III*; that *Hamlet*'s scenes of spectral complaint emphasize the irrationality disavowed when those scenes theorize moral psychology elsewhere, an irrationality that calls into question the subject's capacity to follow those happiness scripts in the first place; and that *Richard II* introduces a note of anxiety into an emerging paradigm of virtuous literary reception foregrounded in scenes of female complaint.

This final chapter explores how early modern domestic tragedies take up happiness scripts that aim to reproduce the norms pertaining to the "natural" order of the household, norms whose violation—and the unhappiness that follows—the genre famously takes as its subject. In the first section, I show how these scripts

---

[1] Ahmed, *The Promise of Happiness*, 38.

[2] *The Promise of Happiness*, 29, 37. Ahmed's analysis of these scripts critiques this promise as an ideological fantasy that works to replicate existing social hierarchies and reinforce dominant norms, and to cast certain subjects—who don't desire the right things, or do desire the wrong things—as the causes of others' unhappiness.

The Drama of Complaint: Ethical Provocations in Shakespeare's Tragedy. Emily Shortslef, Oxford University Press.
© Emily Shortslef 2023. DOI: 10.1093/oso/9780192868480.003.0006

172 THE DRAMA OF COMPLAINT

are authorized in domestic tragedies through the deathbed complaint, my term for the speeches conventionally performed at the conclusions of such plays, in which the character whose transgression the tragedy has dramatized confesses their sin and repents, expressing regret for their actions. Deathbed complaints are doubly didactic: at the same time that they explicitly underline the bad choices and unhappy objects that audiences are to avoid, they also, more implicitly, extol the value of the happy object (the marriage, the family) the speaker has lost. Spoken from the retrospective perspective of the deathbed, from which the complainer passes on a lesson learned too late, such complaints do not simply recapitulate but more precisely attest to the validity of the happiness scripts that inform those plays.

The second section of the chapter turns to *Othello*, commonly considered Shakespeare's "nearest approach to domestic tragedy."[3] There I examine the play's engagement with the racist happiness script propounded in its source, Cinthio's *Gli Hecatommithi* (1565), in which Disdemona says as her death draws near, "I fear greatly that I shall be a warning to young girls not to marry against their parents' wishes; and Italian ladies will learn by my example not to tie themselves to a man whom Nature, Heaven, and manner of life separate from us."[4] In *Othello*, one of the many direct echoes of this script, which suggests that unhappiness— both misfortune and sadness—must follow from an "unnatural," interracial marriage, appears in Brabantio's exclamation on learning of Desdemona's elopement with Othello: "O unhappy girl!— / With the Moor, say'st thou?"[5] But though the play sets up the possibility, and even creates the expectation, that Desdemona will come to repent her marriage, she never says that she does, not even on her deathbed. On the contrary, as Ayanna Thompson notes, "Desdemona, unlike Disdemona, dies protecting Othello and continuing to pledge her love for him": by staging her death in a way that "hardly lends itself to a clear moral narrative," Shakespeare's play "resists [the] simplistic moral thrust" of Cinthio's novella.[6] What I want to show is how this sense of moral complexity or ambiguity follows from Shakespeare's formal experimentation with the conventional scene of deathbed complaint. The play fragments Desdemona's deathbed complaint, rendering it

---

[3] Orlin, "Domestic Tragedy," 391. On the play's proximity to domestic tragedy see also Benson, *Shakespeare, Othello, and Domestic Tragedy*; and Whipday, *Shakespeare's Domestic Tragedies*.

[4] Quoted from *Othello*, ed. Honigmann, p. 389. This chapter's understanding of race as a socially constructed, protean, unstable conceptual system for categorizing, assigning significance to, and distributing power and privilege across one or more types of difference (including, but not limited to, skin color, religion, culture, geographical origin, lineage, and nationality) is indebted to a large body of work by scholars of premodern critical race studies. For a formulation of the tenets and goals of this scholarship—and a refutation of the claim that race is an anachronistic analytical category with regard to early modernity—see Peter Erickson and Kim F. Hall, "'A New Scholarly Song': Rereading Early Modern Race."

[5] 1.1.161–2. All citations of the play are from *Othello*, ed. Honigmann. Hereafter cited parenthetically.

[6] Thompson, "Introduction," *Othello*, 14.

"NOBODY, I MYSELF"   173

enigmatic and parceling its parts out among several characters, in a set of gestures that ultimately, I suggest, displace ethical authority onto the audience.

1. Deathbed Complaint and the Happiness Scripts of Domestic Tragedy

Unkindness, in the fullest sense of the word, is the horror explored by the plays that critics have come to call domestic tragedy, their plots driven by transgressions committed by a member of the family or close community—a neighbor, a father, a wife, a servant—against another, in defiance of all "natural" bonds. These plays are, as one of their Chorus-figures suggests, "home-borne Tragedie[s]," not only in that many were based on real-life incidents in England recounted in pamphlets and broadside ballads, but because their represented evils begin within the bounds of the home.[7] Concerned with the physical space, material objects, and everyday routines of the non-aristocratic English household, as well as the intimate, volatile, and hierarchized relationships of the household's members and its proximate others, these plays vibrate with cultural anxieties about companionate marriage, social mobility and changing class relations, and the increasingly permeable boundaries of the community on local, regional, and national scales.[8] Hence the reparative gestures of their conclusions, which pair the punishment of the transgressors with a move toward the restoration of order—gestures marked by a flurry of didactic platitudinous speech, foremost among which is the deathbed complaint. Such speech is at once forensic and apotropaic, retrospectively explaining the cause of these unhappy events in an attempt to prevent their replication in another household, another community.

The critic Henry Hitch Adams, author of one of the first studies of the genre, described these explicitly moralizing (and, in his judgment, "inferior") dramas not only as "domestic tragedy" but as "homiletic tragedy" for their plainspoken articulation of conventional theological and moral truths.[9] Although the pathbreaking accounts offered by Lena Cowen Orlin, Frances Dolan, and others of domestic tragedy's intersections with oeconomic discourse and conversancy with matters of everyday early modern life have opened new perspectives on these plays' cultural work, it is their explicit didacticism that I want to emphasize. This is not to echo Adams' dismissive conclusions about the "subordinate" aesthetic status of the genre, or his assessment that these plays are "concerned with the

---

[7] Quoted from line 26 of Tragedie's Epilogue in *A Warning for Fair Women*. Lines from the play are hereafter cited parenthetically.

[8] Critical studies of domestic tragedy include Adams, *English Domestic or, Homiletic Tragedy*; Orlin, *Private Matters and Public Culture*; Dolan, *Dangerous Familiars*; Comensoli, "Household Business"; and Whipday, *Shakespeare's Domestic Tragedies*. See also Bengtsson, "True and Home-Born."

[9] Adams, *English Domestic or, Homiletic Tragedy*, vii.

174 THE DRAMA OF COMPLAINT

things of the next world rather than with the things of this."[10] I agree with Orlin that these plays cannot be reduced to what she suggests Adams characterizes as "their monotonous moralizing formula: sin is committed, it is discovered, and the sinners repent, are punished, and seek divine mercy."[11] And yet Adams is not incorrect to identify their moralizing drive or describe it as following a formulaic plot arc that moves from transgression to repentance and punishment.

It is along that familiar, moralizing plot arc that domestic tragedies unfold their conventional happiness scripts. The happiness scripts that inform domestic tragedy reflect what critics unanimously identify as the genre's preoccupation with domestic ideology—the naturalizing of the religious moral norms that dictated the proper relations between men and women, husbands and wives, masters and servants, parents and children, the family and the wider society—as well as its investment in the "early modern theories of order" that supported and were supported by those norms.[12] "There is a way of ordering the familie aright, and there is a misgoverning of it," Robert Cleaver's *A Godlie Forme of Householde Government: For the Ordering of Private Families* (1598) instructs.[13] The well-governed family or household held up as an ethical ideal in the period's domestic conduct books is one in which each member obediently performs the duties appertaining to their position within its hierarchy. Ubiquitously described as a "little common wealth" both analogous to the body politic in its structure and beneficial to it in its own internal "comeliness or decencie," the family is constructed in domestic discourse as a happy object that brings other happy objects—and thus happiness itself—closer to hand.[14] "A householde is as it were a little common wealth, by the good government wherof, Gods glorie may be advaunced [and] the common wealth which standeth of severall families, benefited," Cleaver writes; "A familie is a little Church, and a little commonwealth, at least a lively representation thereof," William Gouge suggests in *Of Domesticall Duties* (1622), "who knoweth not that the preservation of families tendeth to the good of Church and commonwealth?"[15] If the master and the mistress of a household "preserve" the family by maintaining proper discipline, order, and duty, Cleaver promises, good things must follow: "And so no doubt, God will poure his blessings on them, and theirs, in this life, and everlasting happinesse on them in the life to come."[16]

Domestic conduct manuals—and domestic tragedies too—trace unhappiness to failures of governance, both of oneself and one's household. "Most men enter into this estate, and being entred complaine therof," William Whately says of marriage

---

[10] Adams, *English Domestic or, Homiletic Tragedy*, 189–90.
[11] Orlin, "Domestic Tragedy," 392.   [12] Comensoli, "Household Business," 16.
[13] Cleaver, *A Godlie Forme of Householde Government*, 15.
[14] Cleaver, *A Godlie Forme of Householde Government*, 13, 16.
[15] Cleaver, *A Godlie Forme of Householde Government*, 13. Gouge, *Of Domesticall Duties*, 18.
[16] Cleaver, *A Godlie Forme of Householde Government*, A5r.

in his prefatory epistle to *A Bridebush, or A Direction for Married Persons* (1623), going on to assure readers that this unhappiness can only be an effect of "liv[ing] in matrimony not after Gods direction, but the rules (crooked rules they be) of thine owne lusts."[17] The co-implicated happy objects of domestic ideology— female chastity, the loving marital couple, the well-governed family, the godly community—are as precarious as they are precious, vulnerable to internal and external forces of disintegration. Domestic conduct manuals prescribe rules and principles for obtaining and preserving these objects. Domestic tragedies, by contrast, dramatize the conditions of their loss, through the transgressions of thieving outsiders and/or rebellious insiders (usually women, servants, and men who are at the margins of the household or community in question), transgressions that point to dire failures of governance on the part of husbands, fathers, and other figures of male authority.

To the extent that the well-governed family appears in their narratives as an unrealized ideal, domestic tragedies can be said to expose the illusoriness of this happy object. But while they underscore the difference between ideal and reality, the dogma of domestic ideology and its embodiment in lived experience, domestic tragedies also shore up the normative objects as well as the norms of conduct that are transgressed, violated, and subjected to pressure in their narratives. The promise of happiness attached to normative happy objects is ultimately affirmed—if never exactly fulfilled—in their plots. My argument is that the conventional form that I am calling the scene of deathbed complaint is the primary site where these scripts are validated. This formulaic scene constitutes the emotional climax and conclusion of a domestic tragedy. A figurative term, the scene of deathbed complaint (sometimes, but not necessarily, set around an actual bed) focalizes a character readying themselves to die, speaking words weighted with significance because they will be their last. The complainer's death is prefaced with a last message for a community that survives, a community for whom the complainer's confession, repentance, and belated recognition of error can still do some good. With the authority of one who now knows better, the unhappy complainer stresses the surety and the desirability of the happiness promised in the script from which they strayed.

For a representative example, we might look at the scene of deathbed complaint that concludes *A Yorkshire Tragedy* (1608), a domestic tragedy now generally attributed to Thomas Middleton. The scene is set immediately outside a household, as the character simply called Husband is being led by officers to his execution, having killed his two sons and nearly their mother, Wife. As they pass the house, Wife comes out, and Husband repents, kissing the bodies of his sons:

---

[17] Whately, *A Bridebush*, A3r.

176 THE DRAMA OF COMPLAINT

>   HUSBAND I am right against my house, seat of my ancestors.
>   ....
>   WIFE Unkindness strikes a deeper wound than steel.
>   You have been still unkind to me.
>   ....
>   HUSBAND Now glides the devil from
>   Me, departs at every joint, heaves up my nails!
>   Oh, catch him! New torments that were ne'er invented!
>   Bind him one thousand more, you blessed angels,
>   In that pit bottomless! Let him not rise
>   To make men act unnatural tragedies,
>   To spread into a father, and in fury,
>   Make him his children's executioners,
>   Murder his wife, his servants, and who not!
>   For that man's dark where Heaven is quite forgot.
>   WIFE Oh, my repentant husband!
>   HUSBAND My dear soul, whom I too much have wrong'd,
>   For death I die, and for this I have long'd.
>   WIFE Thou shouldst not—be assured—for these faults die,
>   If the law could forgive as soon as I.
>   ....
>   HUSBAND I'll kiss the blood I spilt and then I go:
>   My soul is bloodied, well may my lips be so.
>   [*He kisses the children.*]
>   Farewell, dear wife, now thou and I must part;
>   I of thy wrongs repent me with my heart.
>   ....
>   Let every father look into my deeds,
>   And then their heirs may prosper while mine bleeds.[18]

Here, in the presence of house, wife, and children, Husband remembers the "Heaven" he has "forgot," recognizing only now—in their departure from him—both the devil whom he suggests has made him act this "unnatural tragedy" and what he has lost by doing so. His deathbed complaint articulates the normative validity as well as the value of "kind fatherhood," the lost happy object of patrilineal descent and inheritance emblematized in the ancestral house and the bodies of his dead sons.

Such scenes appear at the close of every one of the extant plays labeled by modern critics as domestic tragedies, their arcs moving from the transgression to the performance of the deathbed complaint, with its expression of repentant

---

[18] Scene 8, lines 1–60. *A Yorkshire Tragedy.*

mourning for a lost happiness known too late: *Arden of Faversham* (1592), *A Warning for Fair Women* (1599), *2 Edward IV* (1599), *Two Lamentable Tragedies* (1601), *A Woman Killed with Kindness* (1607), and *The Witch of Edmonton* (1621).[19] The remainder of this section will discuss the deathbed complaints of three domestic tragedies that resonate with Iago's concocted story of Desdemona's infidelity. Two are narratives in which a wife's sexual transgression leads to a criminal act. The anonymous *Arden of Faversham*, the earliest extant English domestic tragedy, is a fictionalized rendering of an event related in Holinshed's *Chronicles* (1587), the murder in 1551 of a Kentish landowner, Thomas Arden, by his wife Alice and her lover Mosby, along with several accomplices who aid in the murder and its cover-up. *A Warning for Fair Women*, also of unknown author-ship, depicts the 1573 murder of George Saunders, a merchant tailor, a murder plotted by his wife Anne, her lover George Browne, her neighbor Mistress Drury, and Mistress Drury's servant Roger. In both plays, the murderers are eventually discovered by civic-minded citizens and local authorities, the adulterous motives revealed, and the guilty parties punished by death—not, though, before the wife has the opportunity to confess, repent, and express a desire to be reconciled to her husband.

Alice Arden's profession of repentance occurs under the guard of the watch. First, led to the place where her husband's body lies, she is urged by the Mayor to "Confess this foul fault and be penitent." Addressing Arden's dead body, bleeding in her presence, she admits her guilt, and pleads for forgiveness:

> MAYOR   See, Mistress Arden, where your husband lies.
> Confess this foul fault and be penitent.
> ALICE   Arden, sweet husband, what shall I say?
> The more I sound his name, the more he bleeds.
> This blood condemns me and, in gushing forth,
> Speaks as it falls and asks me why I did it.
> Forgive me, Arden! I repent me now;
> And, would my death save thine, thou shouldst not die.
> Rise up, sweet Arden, and enjoy thy love,
> And frown not on me when we meet in heaven!
> In heaven I love thee, though on earth I did not.[20]

Alice's impossible plea for Arden to "rise up" and "enjoy" her—a wish that creates the image of an embrace—idealizes the unbroken marital couple from the per-spective of its ruin. A further confession of her newfound love for her dead

---

[19] On the domestic tragedy canon, and on the lost plays whose titles suggest their alignment with these others, see Orlin, "Domestic Tragedy."

[20] *Arden of Faversham*, 16.1–11. Quoted from *English Renaissance Drama*. Hereafter cited parenthetically.

178   THE DRAMA OF COMPLAINT

husband is her renunciation of Mosby as they are led away by the watch to their
places of execution:

> Ah, but for thee I had never been strumpet.
> What cannot oaths and protestations do
> When men have opportunity to woo?
> I was too young to sound thy villainies,
> But now I find it and repent too late.
> ....
> Let my death make amends for all my sins!

(18.14–33)

Alice's complaint is at once addressed to Mosby, whom she accuses; an unspecified audience for whose benefit she speaks her moralizing rhetorical question;
and to God, to whom she utters a prayer for redemption. Like her wish that Arden
will "frown not on me when we meet in heaven," her turn to "meditate upon my
Savior Christ, / Whose blood must save me for the blood I shed" articulates a
hope that happiness awaits her elsewhere, though her repentance, like her love,
comes "too late" on earth (18.10–11).

If the happy object whose loss Alice mourns is a marital "enjoyment" she imagines in intimate, eroticized terms, in the equivalent scene of deathbed complaint
at the end of *A Warning for Fair Women*, Anne Saunders laments that the "wilfulle
sin" of her "wicked lust" has not only stained her marriage but "griev'd" and
"abusde" an entire public ("al my friends and kinred wheresoever," "al men and
women in the world") (2621–22, 2676–80). Deciding on the day of her execution
to stop proclaiming her ignorance of the murder plot, she confesses to the clergyman who has been visiting her: "Here I confesse I am a grievous sinner / And
have provok't the heavy wrath of God / ... / But now I do repent and hate my selfe"
(2618–23). In her deathbed complaint, addressed to her children as they bid her
farewell, she describes herself as an unhappy object, the cause of everyone else's
unhappiness as well as her own:

> But could my husband and your father heare me,
> Thus humbly at his feete would I fal downe,
> And plentifull in teares bewayle my fault.
> Mercy I aske of God, of him, and you,
> And of his kindred which I have abusde,
> And of my friends and kinred wheresoever,
> Of whom I am ashamed and abasht,
> And of al men and women in the world,
> Whome by my foule example I have griev'd,

Though I deserve no pity at their hands,
Yet I beseech them all to pardon me,
And God I thanke that hath found out my sin,
And brought me to affliction in this world,
Thereby to save me in the world to come.
Oh children learne, learne by your mothers fall
To follow vertue, and beware of sinne.

(2672–87)

Having emphasized her own wretchedness, Anne leaves her children with a literal happiness script, copies of the *Meditations* of the Protestant clergyman John Bradford, burned at the stake in 1555:

Here I give to each of you a booke
Of holy meditations, *Bradfords* workes,
That vertuous chosen servant of the Lord,
Therein you shall be richer than with gold,
Safer than in faire buildings: happyer
Than all the pleasures of this world can make you.
Sleepe not without them when you go to bed,
And rise a mornings with them in your hands.
So God send downe his blessing on you al:
Farewel, farewel, farewel, farewel, farewel.
[*She kisses them one after another.*]
Nay stay not to disturbe me with your teares,
The time is come sweete hearts, and we must part,
That way go you, this way my heavie heart. *Exeunt.*

(2702–14)

The physical parting of ways that concludes the scene of deathbed complaint and the dramatic narrative is metaphorical as well. When Anne hands Bradford's books to her children she bequeaths to them as their rightful inheritance the possibility of the happiness she lost, a happiness promised to them if they follow the script outlined within and choose the path she forsook. Along with its "warning to fair women," then, the scene—juxtaposing the just deserts of wickedness to the rewards of virtue—advertises a happiness script for all, a script guaranteed to lead to pleasure and blessedness.

Thomas Heywood's *A Woman Killed with Kindness* (1607)—the domestic tragedy often described as especially resonant with *Othello*—begins with the wedding of John and Anne Frankford, a union that promises "much joy" until it is interrupted by Anne's adultery with Frankford's friend Wendoll, a gentleman to whom

180   THE DRAMA OF COMPLAINT

the more prosperous Frankford has given a room and a servant in his house, as well as authority over it when he is away.[21] Critical discussions of this play invariably note that the adultery seems an almost inevitable consequence of Frankford's decision to share his place in the household with Wendoll, whose intimacy with Frankford is described in terms evocative of the marital bond itself, their hearts "joined and knit together" (vi, 50). After Frankford catches the adulterous pair in bed, he chases Wendoll from the house, and banishes the despondent Anne from it, in a divorce *a mensa et thoro*, sending her to live in another of his manors. Thus the woman idealized in the play's opening lines ("She's beauty and perfection's eldest daughter, / Only found by yours, though many a heart hath sought her" [I, 23–24]) and praised by Frankford as the happiest of his happy objects—"Chief / Of all the sweet felicities on earth" (iv, 9–10)—is, by the close, a living emblem of unhappiness, "the woefullest wretch on earth, / A woman made of tears" (xvi, 82–83). It is as such that Anne describes herself as an object lesson, telling an imagined crowd of women, "you that have yet kept / Your holy matrimonial vow unstained," to "Make me your instance" (xiii, 137–38, 139). In her penitent grief, put to shame by Frankford's "kindness" to her ("I thank him; he is kind and ever was") she vows to take no food and water, and thus, though her transgression is not a criminal act, she—like Alice Arden and Anne Saunders—dies for it anyway (xvi, 30–31).

In this play, the arc from transgression to repentance is also the arc from divorce to the re-formation of the marital couple whose sad fracturing has been lamented by Wendoll himself ("Oh, God, I have divorced the truest turtles / That ever lived together, and being divided / In several places, make their several moan" [xvi, 51–53]). The site of this re-formation is the deathbed. In the play's closing scene, Frankford, having come to his dying wife's bedside where she lies surrounded by their servants and extended family, clasps hands with Anne as she supplicates for his pardon:

> ANNE   Will you vouchsafe,
> Out of your grace and your humanity,
> To take a spotted strumpet by the hand?
> FRANK.   That hand once held my heart in faster bonds
> Than now 'tis gripped by me. God pardon them
> That made us first break hold.
> ANNE   Amen, amen.
> ....
>   Oh, good man,
> And father to my children, pardon me.

---

[21] Scene i, 13, 70. Heywood, *A Woman Killed with Kindness*. Hereafter cited parenthetically. The composition and first performance dates of both *A Woman Killed with Kindness* and *Othello* are uncertain, but each was likely written between 1602 and 1604.

Pardon, Oh, pardon me! My fault so heinous is
That if you in this world forgive it not,
Heaven will not clear it in the world to come.
....
FRANK.   My wife, the mother to my pretty babes,
Both those lost names I do restore thee back,
And with this kiss I wed thee once again.
Though thou art wounded in thy honored name,
And with that grief upon thy deathbed liest,
Honest in heart, upon my soul, thou diest.
ANNE   Pardoned on earth, soul, thou in Heaven art free;
Once more thy wife dies thus embracing thee. [*Dies.*]
FRANK.   New married and new widowed! Oh, she's dead,
And a cold grave must be our nuptial bed.

(xvii, 77–124)

In its reenactment of the wedding with which the play began—now in the mode
of grief, rather than joy—and its restaging of the first marital embrace as a final
parting, the scene of deathbed complaint drives home both the tragedy of "the
first break" and the pathos of the marital couple. These doubled partings doubly
assert the value of the marriage, which appears as a happy object briefly possessed
and lost, then fleetingly recaptured and lost again ("New married and new
widowed!").[22] The bed, site of Anne's transgression, becomes the site of her
reconciliation with her husband, and the place from which the play articulates the
power of "kindness" to both chastise and restore the sinner included in its reach.

I have been arguing that the scenes of deathbed complaint conventionally
staged at the end of domestic tragedies highlight the value of the happy objects
whose loss the plays have dramatized, that they reiterate the guarantee of happiness promised to those who follow the normative ethical scripts for marriage and
for household governance, and that they do so largely by drawing such clear and
direct lines between their speakers' unhappiness and their deviation from these
norms. Insofar as deathbed complaints are spoken from an especially authoritative spatial location, they resemble the genre of the "ballad-lament," described by
Katharine Craik as "a new subset of complaint, seemingly written or uttered by
female criminals on the verge of death."[23] (The ballad-laments entitled "Complaint
and Lamentation of Mistress Arden" and "The Wofull Lamentacion of Mistress
Anne Saunders" suggest that early moderns recognized that resemblance between
theatrical speeches of deathbed complaint and the ballad-laments too.) In her

---

[22] This ending is similar to that of Part Two of Heywood's *Edward IV* (1599), which concludes with
a scene of deathbed complaint in which the King's former mistress Jane Shore is reconciled with her
estranged husband Matthew, who dies alongside her, both lamenting.

[23] Craik, "Shakespeare's *A Lover's Complaint*," 446.

182   THE DRAMA OF COMPLAINT

account of how "the formal properties of Renaissance complaint were appropriated and adjusted by the authors of ballad-laments precisely in order to elicit female repentance by ventriloquizing enraptured confession," Craik argues that these ballads imagine confession less as a religious speech act aimed at "private spiritual absolution" than a "public spectacle of contrition" in which the speaking subject is made to produce ideological truth claims couched as personal testimony.[24] The same, I have been suggesting, is true of the deathbed complaints of domestic tragedy, which repeat the normative truths of domestic ideology, from the firsthand, retrospective perspective of one who has learned too late the value of the happy object she lost. It is a critical commonplace that domestic tragedy "confront[s] its audiences with the disorder that ideology could never sufficiently contain," as Orlin puts it, a disorder that exceeds the "heavy-handed moralizing" of their conventional conclusions.[25] But that doesn't mean these plays don't try. At the emotional climax of their narratives, the closing scene of deathbed complaint attempts to contain disorder not simply by depicting the punishment of transgressors, but by making order an object of desire. With its multiple rhetorical elements—the complainer's expression of unhappiness, their confession of wrongdoing, their profession of repentance, their acceptance of their punishment—the complaint enacts a set of symbolic sutures at the level of the narrative, reconciling the complainer to the person they have wronged, and reintegrating them into the community fractured by the transgression. I want to stress that it is here, in the same speech of complaint through which the transgressor reaffirms their broken marital vow or familial bond, that these tragedies signal most explicitly their own commitment to, their own validation of, the happiness scripts whose violations they have depicted.

In his own staging of a domestic tragedy, Shakespeare plays self-consciously with the tropes of the genre, actualizing one of its conventional plotlines—a husband's murder of his wife and subsequent suicide—through the specter of another conventional plotline that operates in the play precisely as a fiction, a "horrible fancy": the story of Desdemona's adulterous coupling with Cassio invented by Iago to "abuse Othello's ear" (4.2.26, 1.3.394). Like the plays we have been examining, *Othello* ends with a deathbed complaint in which Othello reflects on the tragic error he has made, and—speaking in the third person—makes some attempt to direct how he will be spoken of, before stabbing himself and falling on the bed where Desdemona lies already dead:

> OTHELLO Soft you, a word or two before you go.
> I have done the state some service, and they know't:
> No more of that. I pray you, in your letters,
> When you shall these unlucky deeds relate,

---

[24] Craik, "Shakespeare's *A Lover's Complaint*," 439.   [25] Orlin, "Domestic Tragedy," 394, 395.

> Speak of me as I am. Nothing extenuate,
> Nor set down in malice. Then must you speak
> Of one that loved not wisely, but too well;
> Of one not easily jealous, but, being wrought,
> Perplexed in the extreme; of one whose hand,
> Like the base Indian, threw a pearl away
> Richer than all his tribe; of one whose subdued eyes,
> Albeit unused to the melting mood,
> Drops tears as fast as the Arabian trees
> Their medicinable gum. Set you down this,
> And say besides that in Aleppo once,
> Where a malignant and a turbanned Turk
> Beat a Venetian and traduced the state,
> I took by th' throat the circumcised dog
> And smote him—thus!   *He stabs himself.*
> LODOVICO O bloody period!
> GRATIANO   All that's spoke is marred.
> OTHELLO I kissed thee ere I killed thee: no way but this,
> Killing myself, to die upon a kiss.
>   [*Kisses Desdemona, and*] *dies.*
>
>   (5.2.336–57)

Othello's own unhappiness is underlined in the simile that likens his "subdued eyes," dropping otherwise uncharacteristic tears, to "Arabian trees" that weep gum. Notice, though, the logic of the other exoticized figures through which Shakespeare has Othello describe himself as someone who has done something terrible and lost something precious. By explicitly likening himself to "the base Indian" who "threw a pearl away," and implicitly aligning himself with "a malignant and a turbanned Turk" who "Beat a Venetian and traduced the state," a "circumcised dog," he describes himself as a distinctly racialized unhappy object *to Desdemona.* In other words, at the same time that Othello's deathbed complaint, punctuated with his suicide and dying kiss, concludes the conventional domestic tragedy arc of transgression, repentance, and punishment that the play sets up for him by framing him as "One that loved not wisely, but too well," it also implicates him in another happiness script (one that we might say purports to offer "a warning to fair women").[26] His complaint demonstrates how Shakespeare has formally distributed the content of Cinthio's happiness script across his own characters'

---

[26] Recently Cora Fox has also explored *Othello* through the lens of Ahmed's work on happiness. Suggesting that Shakespeare shows how Othello is excluded from the happiness "associated with narratives of being Venetian and being married," Fox reads *Othello* as a document in what Ahmed calls an "unhappiness archive"—that is, as a text that shows how some subjects are barred from happiness and cast as the causes of others' unhappiness. See Fox, "Othello's Unfortunate Happiness."

184 THE DRAMA OF COMPLAINT

speeches, a happiness script central to which is *Desdemona's* repentance of what Shakespeare's source describes as *her* transgression: not marital infidelity, but her marriage to Othello.

2. *Othello* and the Fragmented Deathbed Complaint

From the outset, the marriage at the heart of *Othello* is rendered as a violation of domestic order. The play opens outside a house just "robbed" of its daughter by "an erring Barbarian," as Iago reveals to Desdemona's father a sexual transgression whose racial stakes he makes immediately clear ("Zounds, sir, you're robbed! For shame put on your gown! / Your heart is burst, you have lost half your soul, / Even now, now, very now, an old black ram / Is tupping your white ewe!" [1.3.356, 1.1.84–88]). Joyce Green MacDonald suggests that Brabantio "is perhaps even more distressed that Desdemona has chosen a black man who will degrade his lineage than he is that she has dared to choose for herself," an interpretation supported by his order, on confirming Desdemona's absence from the house, to "Raise all my kindred" (1.1.165).[27] Similarly certain that news of the marriage will "incense her kinsmen," Iago has urged Brabantio to "Awake the snorting citizens," as if this "theft" might be seen not only as an affront to Brabantio and his kin but as an assault on Venice itself (1.1.68, 89).[28] The rhetorical conflation of citizen and kin around their mutual exclusion of Othello reaches its apex in Brabantio's conviction, in vowing to complain to the Duke, that his "brothers of the state," his fellow Senators figured here as members of the same family, will recognize his grievance as a "wrong" done to them all, with grievous consequences for the social order:

> Mine's not an idle cause, the duke himself,
> Or any of my brothers of the state,
> Cannot but feel this wrong as 'twere their own.
> For if such actions may have passage free
> Bond-slaves and pagans shall our statesmen be.
>
> (1.2.95–99)

---

[27] MacDonald, "Black Ram, White Ewe," 210.

[28] This scene also foregrounds cultural anxieties about the precarious integrity of the Venetian commonwealth, a type of precarity that has long been historically figured in terms of a sexually open, vulnerable, or violated (and, as Kim F. Hall, Margo Hendricks, and others have argued, distinctly *white*) female body. See Hall, *Things of Darkness*; Hendricks, "A word, sweet Lucrece." In *Shakespeare Jungle Fever*, Little argues that the play's plot, spanning Othello's commission to the outpost of Cyprus to his sacrificial suicide after Desdemona's murder, tracks the dynamics of cultural repair, laying bare the way in which a body politic shores up a fantasmatic sense of its own purity and integrity by rendering monstrous and expelling from itself the "cultural outsiders" whose "materials and laboring bodies" it has used, disavowing its formative entanglements with alterity (69). For Little, Shakespeare's Venice is a figure for early modern England, whose attempts to deport black people from its borders works toward the construction of a "cultural and racial whiteness" (69).

The Senators do not in fact find the match entirely "preposterous," and the Duke rules in favor of the couple after hearing their testimony (1.3.63). But if the first act of *Othello* has a comic structure in the couple's triumph over the disapproving father, it ends on a troubled note not unlike that which many critics find at the close of Shakespeare's comedies, for Brabantio's description of the marriage as a falling off from an ideal is not so much refuted as echoed, in more muted terms, in the Duke's advice that he cease to "mourn a mischief that is past and gone," seeing that "remedies are past," and "take up this mangled matter at the best" (1.3.205, 203, 173). Even as the Duke pronounces the situation resolved, that is, his language suggests a thing mutilated, corrupted, damaged.[29] Michael Neill and Arthur L. Little, Jr. have both explored how the idea of the "corrupted" marriage continues to resonate in the play. Noting that adultery, in its etymological association with "pollution or corruption," is fundamentally "a violation of the natural order of things," Neill has suggested that Iago "produc[es] Othello's abduction of Desdemona as an act of racial adulteration, violating the natural laws of kind."[30] Thus, he proposes, "In the cruel system of paradox created by this play's ideas of race and adultery, Othello as both stranger and husband can be *both* . . . adulterer and cuckold."[31] Little argues that this racial fantasy of an intrinsically adulterous *marriage* positions Desdemona and Cassio as the "play world's most natural pair," a "courtly and proper couple [that] is effectively displaced into the sexual and improper couple of Othello and Desdemona."[32] To translate their ideas into the terms of my own analysis, I would suggest that if two stock figures of domestic tragedy are mapped onto Othello—the cuckolded husband as well as the man who takes his place—the same is true for Desdemona: the play positions her at once as the adulterous woman who *breaks* her marital vow and as a woman who has transgressed in the very *making* of that "adulterous" vow. Shakespeare makes it clear that it is only in Iago's false narrative—and eventually, Othello's imagination—that Othello is a cuckold and Desdemona an unfaithful wife. But the play keeps alive, for the play's audience as for Othello himself, the possibility actualized in Cinthio's novella, the possibility that the marriage might (as Brabantio and Iago suggest it must) become an unhappy object to Desdemona, a choice to repent.

Consider the significant emphasis that Act 1 places on Desdemona's *choice* of Othello. Her volition is underscored by her testimony to the Duke, in which she refutes Brabantio's accusations of witchcraft and confesses that she was in fact "half the wooer" (1.3.176). Brabantio speaks of that choice as an irrational one by which Desdemona has lost the happiness promised by another object: the marriage that might have been, the marriage between Desdemona and a Venetian man. (Any Venetian man, it would seem: having only just told Roderigo,

---

[29] *OED*, s.v. "mangled": "mutilated, damaged; lacerated, torn apart; spoiled, corrupted."
[30] Neill, "Unproper Beds," 408, 399.   [31] Neill, "Unproper Beds," 411, author's emphasis.
[32] Little, Jr., *Shakespeare Jungle Fever*, 81, 82.

186   THE DRAMA OF COMPLAINT

"My daughter is not for thee," Brabantio, having learned of the elopement, now says, "O, would you had had her!" [1.1. 96–97, 173]). In the immediate aftermath of Brabantio's discovery this unrealized marriage is repeatedly described as the "natural" object of Desdemona's desire, an object she has tragically forsaken by having, as Roderigo puts it,

> made a gross revolt,
> Tying her duty, beauty, wit and fortunes
> In an extravagant and wheeling stranger
> Of here and everywhere.
>
> (1.1.131–34)

Echoing the warnings in domestic conduct manuals, Brabantio's language like-wise homes in on the seemingly unnatural motion evinced both in Desdemona's attachment to such a "stranger" and her "gross revolt" from a proper marital tra-jectory. "Refer[ring]" himself "to all things of sense," he asks Othello whether anyone might believe that "a maid so tender, fair and happy, / So opposite to mar-riage" (1.2.64, 66–67) would of her own volition have

> shunned
> The wealthy, curled darlings of our nation,
> ...t'incur a general mock,
> Run from her guardage to the sooty bosom
> Of such a thing as thou? to fear, not to delight.
>
> (1.2.67–71)

Brabantio's summative phrase—"to fear, not to delight"—captures the absurdity ("t'incur a general mock") of the idea that Desdemona could be drawn to the wrong object ("such a thing as thou"): to an object that should rightly cause fear, not delight; an object that promises unhappiness.[33] Brabantio returns to this theme in his complaint to the Duke, arguing that "for nature so preposterously to err," Desdemona must have been bewitched:

> she, in spite of nature,
> Of years, of country, credit, everything,
> To fall in love with what she feared to look on?
> It is a judgement maimed and most imperfect

---

[33] Here racial ideology is articulated through the tenets of moral psychology examined in Chapter 3, including the assumptions that some objects are naturally attractive and others naturally repulsive, that these objects are respectively good and evil, that reason naturally knows the difference, and that the will naturally follows reason's judgments. On the racialization of sexual norms in early modern discourse, see Sanchez, *Queer Faith*, especially Chapter 2.

That will confess perfection so could err
Against all rules of nature.

(1.3.97–102)

His certainty notwithstanding, Brabantio is decisively proven wrong. In his bitter parting words, his last in the play, he ultimately accepts that his daughter has in fact freely chosen to (as he sees it) "err / Against all rules of nature," and he warns Othello that she may at some point turn from her husband as she has turned from her father, that she may stray from her marital household as she strayed from her familial one: "Look to her, Moor, if thou hast eyes to see: / She has deceived her father, and may thee" (1.3.293–94). Even before Iago announces the "engendering" of his plot, then, the play raises the specter of Desdemona changing her mind, desiring a new object (1.3.402). What has been chosen may be repented.

After the marriage has been affirmed by the Duke, Iago plays on both of these themes, his insistence that Desdemona must "repent" her marriage a thread running through his more lurid speculations to Othello about her coupling with Cassio. When Othello, made anxious by Iago's insinuations, recalls the errancy decried by Brabantio, Iago urges him to "smell in such a will" something "rank," something "unnatural":

OTHELLO And yet how nature, erring from itself—
IAGO Ay, there's the point: as, to be bold with you,
Not to affect many proposed matches
Of her own clime, complexion and degree,
Whereto we see, in all things, nature tends—
Foh! One may smell in such a will most rank,
Foul disproportion, thoughts unnatural.

(3.2.232–37)

What Iago seizes upon in the idea of Desdemona's incorrectly oriented will is the surety of course correction. She *may* turn to Cassio, Iago says, because she *must* turn from Othello. The unrealized "proposed match" to "the darlings of our nation" that Desdemona has been "opposite to" will appear as a counterfactual past that must be fulfilled in the future—the thing that Desdemona must eventually turn toward. Indeed, Iago consistently imagines Desdemona's turn to Cassio as a return, a natural correction of an unnatural error: the motion of "Her will, recoiling to her better judgement" (3.3.240).[34] To Roderigo he describes this willful change as both appetite *and* reason, a return to her senses: "when she is sated

---

[34] The fact that Cassio is a Florentine and not a Venetian only reiterates that the important difference at stake here is not that between Venetian and non-Venetian men, but between whiteness and blackness.

188 THE DRAMA OF COMPLAINT

with his body she will find the error of her choice; she must have change, she must"; "her delicate tenderness will find itself abused, begin to heave the gorge, disrelish and abhor the Moor—very nature will instruct her in it and compel her to some second choice" (1.3.351–52, 2.1.229–33). To Othello he makes the same point. He describes Desdemona's infidelity both as a reflection of the "country disposition" of shameless Venetian women, well-accustomed to adultery, *and* the effect of being guided by her "better judgement" to "repent" her shameful choice, as she compares Othello against "her country forms":

> I may fear
> Her will, recoiling to her better judgement,
> May fall to match you with her country forms,
> And happily repent.

(3.3.239–42)

This evocation of the "hap," the chance, of her repentance implies the good fortune of such an event. To "poison [Othello's] delight," then, Iago not only suggests the likelihood of Desdemona's penitence, but more subtly suggests that such repentance would be a happy object, a thing for her good (1.1.66).

Othello's audiences know, of course, what Othello does not: that Iago is lying about Desdemona and Cassio. Yet the play forces no equivalently definitive distance between their expectations and Iago's prediction that Desdemona will, in some form, repent the marriage: for all they know, she may indeed do so. A declaration of penitent regret from Desdemona would in fact affirm what Heather Hirschfeld describes as a common early modern cultural narrative about marriage. While marriage was popularly considered "the scene of potential wrongdoing and thus an *occasion for* repentance," and had been understood in its sacramentalized, pre-Reformation form as a means of penitence, Hirschfeld argues that post-Reformation ethical discourse and fiction tended to represent marriage as "an *object* of penitence…frequently cast[ing] wedlock as a choice and condition that could be repented as a grave spiritual error."[35] As *Othello*'s early modern audiences knew very well, "to talk of marriage in this period…was to talk about repentance."[36] (Recall Whately's observation that "Most men enter into this estate, and being entred complaine therof.") The play lets its audience entertain the idea that Desdemona's and Othello's norm-defying marriage might become such an object of repentance, especially in light of Iago's plot to destroy it. As the tragedy approaches its climax, it increasingly flirts with affirming Cinthio's happiness script by emphasizing Desdemona's unhappy misfortune (a fate anticipated in her very name, Greek for "unfortunate") and by making Othello, in his jealousy,

---

[35] Hirschfeld, *The End of Satisfaction*, 125, author's emphases. She suggests that in the play jealousy, for Othello, is the "singular symptom" of this repentance (128).

[36] Hirschfeld, *The End of Satisfaction*, 122.

"NOBODY, I MYSELF" 189

assume the properties of the unhappy object, the cause of her unhappiness. After he strikes her and accuses her of being a whore, treating her with what she calls an "unkindness [that] may defeat my life / But never taint my love" (4.2.162–63), she becomes demonstrably wretched, weeping before Iago and Emilia:

> IAGO Do not weep, do not weep: alas the day!
> EMILIA   Hath she forsook so many noble matches,
> Her father, and her country, and her friends,
> To be called whore? would it not make one weep?
> DESDEMONA It is my wretched fortune.
>
> (4.2.126–30)

Emilia's words invoke those other potentially more happy objects, the "many noble matches" that Desdemona "forsook," thereby imagining an alternative life of marital happiness that echoes Iago's earlier ominous conditional: "If she had been blest she would never have loved the Moor" (2.1.250–51). An explanation of Desdemona's tears (how could she not weep, after having given up so much for this love?), Emilia's rhetorical question—"would it not make one weep?"—also picks up a language of exemplarity that makes individual characters, their choices, and their actions become object lessons for others. Like her counterparts in other domestic tragedies, Desdemona, in Emilia's framing, exemplifies an unhappiness caused by her own choices. Her tears and admission of "wretched fortune" may thus seem the harbingers of a fuller repentance to come, a repentance that would validate the happiness script against interracial marriage that several characters have articulated from the outset of the play.

That moment never arrives, however. On the contrary, Desdemona's deathbed complaint—the form that validates the happiness scripts that circulate in domestic tragedies, through its first-person testimony of a lesson learned—denies her personal affirmation of that happiness script, and thereby frustrates the expectation that the play will in any definitive, explicit sense validate that script either. Just as this didactic work would typically operate at the level of form (the content of the complaint is no less important than the fact that it is spoken by the transgressor, from the deathbed, at the end of the narrative, and in a compressed speech made up of several standard components), so too in *Othello* the play's swerve from overt didacticism is also enacted through form. The play's scene of deathbed complaint is extended across two different theatrical scenes, connected through the image of the marital bed: the scene of mourning in which Desdemona performs the willow song as she undresses for bed (4.3) and the scene of confession and farewell as she dies on that bed (5.2).[37] The speech of complaint itself is similarly broken up, its typical components—the transgressor's expression of unhappiness, their

---

[37] The willow song scene, which is often cut from performance, is present only in the 1623 Folio edition of the play, and not the 1622 Quarto.

190 THE DRAMA OF COMPLAINT

confession of wrongdoing, their expression of repentance, their acceptance of their punishment—distributed among the three figures present: Desdemona, Emilia, and Othello. This formal fragmentation, I am suggesting, has the effect of evacuating didactic authority both from Desdemona herself and from the play.

The willow song establishes Desdemona's unhappiness, aligning her with the forlorn speakers of erotic ballad-complaints who lament being betrayed or otherwise injured by their lovers. Indeed, she attributes the song—a contemporary ballad-complaint, with its gender roles reassigned—to her mother's maid, Barbary, who "was in love, and he she loved proved mad" (4.3.25). Shakespeare's choice of name for the maid seems designed to make an audience think at this moment of Othello, earlier denigrated by Iago as a "Barbary horse" who would "cover" Desdemona (1.1.110) and an "erring Barbarian" with whom she, the "super-subtle Venetian," has made a "frail vow" (1.3.356–57). But Desdemona does not talk of her own unhappiness in love. Her many expressions of unhappiness in this scene are conspicuously secondhand, at a remove: it is as if we are being instructed to see her both as a figure of unhappiness and as someone who will not identify herself as such, someone who will not claim the unhappiness she talks and sings about as her own. The scene begins with *Emilia* wishing that Desdemona had "never seen" Othello, a wish that Desdemona immediately denies:

> EMILIA Would you had never seen him!
> DESDEMONA So would not I: my love doth so approve him
> That even his stubbornness, his checks, his frowns
> —Prithee unpin me—have grace and favour.
>
> (4.3.16–19)

Desdemona does not rescind her "approval" of Othello. Throughout this scene, it is only through unconscious and mediated forms of expression (the song stuck in her mind, a mistake she makes while singing it, a bodily symptom) that assertions of unhappiness are made. For instance, she preemptively dismisses as the notion of a "foolish mind" her identification of her marital sheets as her death shroud:

> EMILIA I have laid those sheets you bade me on the bed.
> DESDEMONA All's one. Good faith, how foolish are our minds!
> If I do die before thee, prithee shroud me
> In one of those same sheets.
> EMILIA   Come, come, you talk.
>
> (4.3.20–23)

Desdemona describes the willow song, too, as something that comes into her mind unbidden, for a reason she does not know. Though she notes that the song "expressed her fortune" (4.3.27)—the fortune of Barbary, that is, whom Desdemona says "died singing it" (4.3.28)—she does not suggest that it might express her own fortune, only that she must sing it:

> That song tonight
> Will not go from my mind. I have much to do
> But to go hang my head all at one side
> And sing it like poor Barbary.
>
> (4.3.28–31)

Even as Desdemona becomes a figure of pathos in the act of performing the willow song, the song's lyrics doubly distance her from her unhappiness, for its speaker is not the "poor soul" who "sat sighing by a sycamore tree." This complainer is described in the third-person, from a distance, as if the song's speaker is the observer of *someone else's* sadness:

> DESDEMONA [*Sings.*]
> The poor soul sat sighing by a sycamore tree,
> Sing all a green willow:
> Her hand on her bosom, her head on her knee,
> Sing willow, willow, willow.
> The fresh stream ran by her and murmured her moans,
> Sing willow, willow, willow:
> Her salt tears fell from her and softened the stones,
> Sing willow, willow, willow.
> [*Speaks.*] Lay by these.
> Willow, willow—
> [*Speaks.*] Prithee hie thee: he'll come a'non.
> Sing all a green willow must be my garland.
> Let nobody blame him, his scorn I approve—
> [*Speaks.*] Nay, that's not next. Hark, who is't that knocks?
> EMILIA   It's the wind.
> DESDEMONA [*Sings.*]
> I called my love false love; but what said he then?
> Sing willow, willow, willow:
> If I court moe women, you'll couch with moe men.
> [*Speaks.*] So, get thee gone; good night. Mine eyes do itch,
> Doth that bode weeping?
> EMILIA   'Tis neither here nor there.
> DESDEMONA I have heard it said so.
>
> (4.3.39–59)

192 THE DRAMA OF COMPLAINT

Notice that Desdemona's shift to a first-person pronoun is a mistake: the line ("Let nobody blame him, his scorn I approve") has come too soon, it is "not next." The question about the knocking with which she follows that mistake reads as an interruption, a way to avoid continuing down the path that—precisely by saying "Let nobody blame him"—broaches the possibility of blaming her lover. By "interruption" I do not mean that Desdemona stops herself, as if there is some knowledge she is, as it were, trying not to know. What I mean, more simply, is that here the *play* conspicuously approaches and then just as conspicuously retreats from saying something. This is the dynamic of the entire scene: it clearly shows that Desdemona is unhappy *and* refrains from saying in any direct way that she is.[38]

This indirection is a stark contrast to the death scene in 5.2, in which Desdemona, now on her deathbed, does confess quite plainly to a "sin"—a sin she names, importantly, as her love for Othello. The language of this scene, with its legal rhetoric, recalls that of the confession scenes in domestic tragedies, in which a confession of wrongdoing is demanded from the transgressor. Though Othello is at this moment an impassioned husband who believes himself to have been cuckolded, he speaks to himself and to Desdemona as the impassive agent of a lawful punishment, someone who must carry out justice, regardless of his personal wishes ("Yet she must die, else she'll betray more men" [5.2.6]). Compare his demand that she confess her sins—"Thou art on thy death-bed. /.../ Therefore confess thee freely of thy sin"—to the speeches of authority figures who urge the transgressor to such confessions in early modern domestic tragedies, as the Mayor in *Arden of Faversham* urges Alice Arden to "Confess this foul fault and be penitent," or *A Warning for Fair Women*'s clergyman presses Anne Saunders to do the same ("The houre is nowe at hand.../ At length acknowledge and confesse your fault").[39] Like those women, Desdemona confesses, and like them, her "sin" is a sexual one, love:

---

[38] Another example of this dynamic involves the seemingly unmotivated exchange Desdemona and Emilia share about Lodovico immediately before Desdemona begins to sing:

> EMILIA Shall I go fetch your night-gown?
> DESDEMONA No, unpin me here.
> EMILIA This Lodovico is a proper man. A very hand some man.
> DESDEMONA He speaks well.
> EMILIA I know a lady in Venice would have walked barefoot to Palestine
> for a touch of his nether lip.

(4.3.32–38)

Here, I would suggest, is how the happy object Desdemona has lost by choosing Othello—the match to a "proper" Venetian man—surfaces in this scene, not as the object of *Desdemona's* desire but of some other woman's desire ("a lady in Venice"). Interestingly, the speech prefix in the Folio assigns "This Lodovico is a proper man" to Desdemona, yet editors often reassign it to Emilia precisely because it seems incongruous with Desdemona's character. See *Othello*, 295n34–5.

[39] *Arden of Faversham*, 16.2; *A Warning for Fair Women*, 2613–14.

OTHELLO   If you bethink yourself of any crime
Unreconciled as yet to heaven and grace,
Solicit for it straight.
DESDEMONA Alack, my lord, what may you mean by that?
....
OTHELLO   Think on thy sins.
DESDEMONA   They are loves I bear to you.
OTHELLO   Ay, and for that thou diest.
DESDEMONA   That death's unnatural that kills for loving.
....
OTHELLO   Sweet soul, take heed,
Take heed of perjury. Thou art on thy death-bed.
DESDEMONA   I?—but not yet to die!
OTHELLO   Yes, presently.
Therefore confess thee freely of thy sin,
For to deny each article with oath
Cannot remove nor choke the strong conception
That I do groan withal. Thou art to die.
DESDEMONA Then Lord have mercy on me.
OTHELLO   I say amen.

(5.2.26–57)

The play puts in Othello's mouth the link between Desdemona's confessed love
and her death, her punishment: "Ay, and for that thou diest." The words are puz-
zling from the perspective of the cuckoldry plot he believes himself to be in, as
editors often note.[40] The line makes sense, though, if we imagine that here Othello
is talking less as himself than as the voice of the happiness script that has been
circulating in the play, identifying Desdemona's love as the cause of her death.
The crucial thing, again, is that it is not Desdemona who does so.

Nor, famously, does she do so—at least not plainly—when she briefly revives
after being smothered. Here, as Emilia draws back the curtains that Othello has
closed to reveal Desdemona, dying on the bed, and implores her to "speak,"
Shakespeare sets the stage for Desdemona's deathbed complaint. But this expected
moment of disclosure and revelation turns out to be deeply enigmatic, particularly when read against the plainspoken complaints of other domestic tragedies.
Desdemona says that she dies a "guiltless death," that she has been "falsely murdered." Yet she also claims a certain responsibility for her own death, just like the
speakers of those complaints:

---

[40] Honigmann suggests that perhaps Shakespeare wrote "bore" instead of "bere": if Desdemona's
assertion of love is in the past tense, "then Othello would mean 'you die because you have stopped
loving me.'" See *Othello*, 312n40.

194 THE DRAMA OF COMPLAINT

> DESDEMONA O falsely, falsely murdered!
> EMILIA O lord, what cry is that?
> OTHELLO That? what?
> EMILIA Out and alas, that was my lady's voice:
> > [*She draws the bed-curtains.*]
> > Help, help, ho, help! O lady, speak again,
> > Sweet Desdemona, O sweet mistress, speak!
> DESDEMONA A guiltless death I die.
> EMILIA   O, who hath done
> > This deed?
> DESDEMONA   Nobody. I myself. Farewell.
> > Commend me to my kind lord—O, farewell! *She dies.*
> > > (5.2.115–23)

"Nobody. I myself": in response to Emilia's question as to "who hath done / this deed," Desdemona doesn't simply refuse to implicate Othello, but actually says that she herself has done it. What are we to make of this assertion of responsibility? Is "I myself" just a filler phrase to modify "Nobody"? Are we to think that Desdemona is suggesting that she is actually to blame? And if so, for what? For angering Othello? For arousing his suspicions? Is she implying that she has made an error in having chosen him in the first place, and is now reaping the consequences of her choice? Is Shakespeare underlining her selflessness? Her naivety? Her guilt? What seems most salient is precisely the irreducibly enigmatic nature of the complaint: "I myself" is, in this context, an indeterminate rhetorical signifier of responsibility. It elicits but also frustrates interpretation. Unlike the speeches of Cinthio's Disdemona, or those of Alice Arden, Anne Saunders, and Anne Frankford, there is no clear lesson to be learned. Desdemona does resemble the female protagonists of domestic tragedy, however, in the thing that distinguishes her most from her counterpart in Cinthio's novella: she asks to be commended to her "kind lord," Othello and their marriage appearing to her from the perspective of her death as twinned happy objects. Indeed, her continued attachment to Othello is the clearest message communicated by her complaint.[41] This is important precisely because that assertion of attachment is exactly the opposite of the profession of repentance that other characters have predicted for her. Put differently, it is the *denial of repentance* (and not the self-sacrificing goodness of Desdemona's

---

[41] A message that feminist readers and artists have long found troubling, as it would seem to reassert the sexual and gender norms that Desdemona has boldly transgressed, as Thompson explains:

> It is after all a play about a woman who breaks away from the expected conventions of her Venetian family and society to marry and then follow into battle a foreign mercenary: in this respect Desdemona looks both empowered and empowering. But it is also the tale of a woman who willingly protects the identity of her physical assailant, refusing to place culpability on the Moor: in this respect Desdemona looks both disempowered and complicit.
>
> ("*Desdemona*: Toni Morrison's Response to *Othello*," 494)

character or the strength of her love) that I would argue the play means to signal by her "Nobody" and her "kind lord."

If, as I am suggesting, Shakespeare keeps repentance out of Desdemona's mouth and gives her only an opaque admission of responsibility ("I myself") for her death, he also has other characters supply these absent meanings. Together, Emilia and Othello offer moralizing glosses on Desdemona's death, elaborating its lesson. Emilia's epitaph for Desdemona, spoken angrily to Othello, emphasizes her fatal commitment to her choice of lover: "She was too fond of her most filthy bargain!" (5.2.153). Here the chaste Desdemona comes to seem like the "spotted strumpets" of domestic tragedy, ruined by her desire, but unrepentant to the end.[42] The task of performing Desdemona's renunciation of this "filthy bargain" falls to Othello, who—in the presence of the representatives of the Venetian state gathered around the deathbed—sets this scene of repentance in the afterlife. Lamenting over Desdemona's cold, white body, he declares that when they meet again, she will "hurl my soul from heaven":

> Now: how dost thou look now? O ill-starred wench,
> Pale as thy smock. When we shall meet at compt
> This look of thine will hurl my soul from heaven
> And fiends will snatch at it. Cold, cold, my girl,
> Even like thy chastity. O cursed, cursed slave!
> ....
> O Desdemon! dead, Desdemon. Dead! O, O!
>
> (5.2.270–79)

In an echo of the moment in Book VI of the *Aeneid* where Dido's shade turns away from Aeneas, here Othello imagines his ejection from heaven, his soul's damnation, in terms of Desdemona's rejection. She does not even need to speak her repentance: with her very "look," he imagines, she will "hurl" away the unhappy object she has recognized too late.

3. Interpreting the Scene of Complaint

This chapter's reading of *Othello* has taken as its premise Thompson's observation that Shakespeare's play "resists [the] simplistic moral thrust" of its source text, Cinthio's *Gli Hecatommithi*, in which the character of Disdemona declares that "Italian ladies will learn by my example not to tie themselves to a man whom Nature, Heaven, and manner of life separate from us."[43] I have been tracing the

[42] Anne Frankford calls herself a "spotted strumpet" in *A Woman Killed with Kindness*, xvii, 79.
[43] "Introduction," *Othello*, 13.

196 THE DRAMA OF COMPLAINT

formal strategies through which the happiness script validated in Disdemona's speech—the warning against interracial marriage—is diffused and stripped of such definitive authority in *Othello*. We have seen that the play fragments the deathbed complaint, the signature form for conveying a moral truth in domestic tragedies. Here there is no compressed, straightforward, first-person expression of unhappiness, confession of wrongdoing, declaration of repentance, and acceptance of punishment. Rather, the rhetorical elements that comprise this form are distributed across *Othello's* characters and scenes. These pieces include a conspicuously mediated, indirect alignment of Desdemona with figures of unhappiness in the willow song scene; her deathbed confession of a sexual "sin" ("loves I bear to you") and deeply enigmatic admission of responsibility for her death ("I myself"); and multiple expressions of her repentance, all noticeably *projected* by other characters, and none voiced by her. Instead of presenting the audience with a character who explains the lesson she has learned the hard way, the play presents us with a character who makes no attempt to draw a moral from her death. The absence of such an authoritative speech has the effect of creating ambiguity around the question of the play's relation to the happiness script that that speech would, ordinarily, affirm and validate.

What the play does not *tell* it may, of course, *show*. The mere absence of any explicit expression of repentance from Desdemona does not mean that it rejects or refutes the validity of that racist happiness script. The very fact of the murder—an act of eroticized violence that the play visually and verbally racializes—lends itself to affirming multiple racist scripts, as premodern critical race scholars have long argued. As Little notes, the murder evokes a scene of racist fantasy ("mak[ing] visible the horror of the black man raping the white woman") materialized again and again in the play's pictorial and theatrical afterlives.[44] Calling attention to the fact that historical audiences have found in the play a validation not only of injunctions against interracial marriage but of racist stereotypes more generally, MacDonald suggests, "I would argue that *Othello* has retained its power to reach audiences precisely because it uncannily seems to play out what they think they already know, what they have been taught, about race and sex: about black men's fundamental irreconcilability to the values of civilized society and about what happens to nice young (white) girls who defy their fathers' wishes."[45] It is abundantly clear that such responses to the play are not foreclosed by the lack of a conventional deathbed complaint from Desdemona, nor by the play's transparency about Iago's villainy. For these reasons, among others, Thompson has made the thought-provoking and oft-quoted suggestion that *Othello* "resists recuperation" as a performance text.[46] These arguments direct us, importantly, beyond

---

[44] Little, *Shakespeare Jungle Fever*, 91.   [45] MacDonald, "Black Ram, White Ewe," 214.

[46] Here I am citing "Shakespeare and Race," a 2018 episode of the Globe Theatre podcast *Such Stuff* in which Thompson is interviewed by Farah Karim-Cooper. There Thompson explains the layered

the question of Shakespeare's intentions and the play-text itself to the wealth of cultural histories that inform audience interpretations, and to the social worlds in which those interpretations have real effects.[47] They also direct us to our own positionality as critical interpreters.[48]

Ultimately, I would suggest, the formal innovation with regard to deathbed complaint that this chapter has been arguing for does not tell us anything about what Shakespeare thinks about the content of the happiness script articulated through that fragmented form. Nor does it tell us what to think. I would propose, however, that the fragmenting of the deathbed complaint, the distribution of its parts across the play and its characters, does open a certain space *for thinking*— that is, for interpreting. (It seems likely that the conversations that scholars have about the play would be quite different if Desdemona did have a didactic speech like that of Cinthio's Disdemona, or the dying complaints of Alice Arden, Anne Saunders, and Anne Frankford.) My sense is that Shakespeare does not write this kind of speech for Desdemona because he does not want the play to speak with that kind of ethical authority. One way to relinquish that authority, in an early modern domestic tragedy, is to turn the genre's signature authorizing form into a ghost of itself, by converting the authoritative speech of one person into the dialogue of many characters, and scattering it across the play rather than compressing it into one exemplary moment. *Othello*'s formal experimentation with deathbed complaint displaces the authority of the complainer and the text for which the complainer speaks, relocating that authority in an audience who must become active participants in the construction of meaning. Witnesses become interpreters, with all the risk and responsibility that entails.

*

The Drama of Complaint has argued that in their arrangement and rearrangement of familiar poetic forms of complaint, Shakespeare's scenes of complaint seize attention, excite thought, and spark desire. The plays to which these scenes belong are not didactic, and they make no clear moral appeals to audiences. I hope to have shown, however, that those tragedies play with some of the most

---

histories that contribute to making *Othello* such a problematic play to stage, from its explicitly racist performance and reception histories, to its connection to the minstrelsy tradition in the United States, to its comic structure, which as she notes aligns the theatrical audience with Iago. Her point is that staging the play in an antiracist, ethically responsible way requires an immense amount of "scaffolding" that most theater companies are unequipped to offer, however good their intentions may be.

[47] For a powerful discussion of these issues, see Grier, "Are Shakespeare's Plays Racially Progressive?"

[48] Discussing unconscious, culturally conditioned racial bias, Ian Smith suggests that to ask "how such bias influences acts of reading and interpretation within a profession whose scholars are, to use [Toni Morrison's] memorable formulation, ideologically conditioned or 'positioned as white'" is in fact to take up and extend an inquiry of *Othello* itself, insofar as the play repeatedly calls attention to processes of seeing and interpreting, and to the ways in which moral meaning is projected onto blackness and whiteness, "turning a physiological fact into a racial idea expressing the collective cultural thinking." Smith, "Seeing Blackness," 419, 408.

commonplace truisms of everyday early modern ethical thought; that such experimentation is especially concentrated in their now iconic scenes of complaint; and that for the early modern theatergoer as well as the twenty-first century critic these scenes are invitational points of entry to participate in these creative ways of thinking differently. I want to close with one of the unlikely origin points of this project: an offhand, mildly disparaging remark in a mid-century study of late medieval and early modern complaint and satire that speaks to the compelling qualities of complaint. Having defined as art those literary works that display "the capacity, roughly, to leave the reader's mind at rest," the literary scholar John Peter claims that while satire can rise to these heights, "Complaint cannot: it is continually nagging at us to do something or be something other than, left to ourselves, we should have done or been."[49] About art, he is wrong; but as a description of complaint, this is exactly right.

[49] Peter, *Complaint and Satire*, 55–6.

Bibliography

Primary Sources

Ames, William. *Conscience, with the Power and Cases Thereof*. London, 1639.

Arden of Faversham. In *English Renaissance Drama*, edited by David Bevington, Lars Engle, Katharine Eisaman Maus, and Eric Rasmussen. New York: Norton, 2002.

Aristotle. *Nicomachean Ethics*. Translated by Terence Irwin. Indianapolis, IN: Hackett, 2019.

Augustine. *City of God*. Vol. IV. Translated by Philip Levine. Loeb Classical Library. Cambridge, MA: Harvard University Press, 1966.

Augustine. *Saint Augustine: Confessions*. Translated by Henry Chadwick. Oxford: Oxford University Press, 2008.

Beaumont, Francis, and John Fletcher. *The Maid's Tragedy*. In *English Renaissance Drama*, edited by David Bevington, Lars Engle, Katharine Eisaman Maus, and Eric Rasmussen. New York: Norton, 2002.

Becon, Thomas. *The Governaunce of Vertue*. London, 1578.

Becon, Thomas. *The Sicke Man's Salve*. London, 1568.

Bernard, Richard. *Christian See to Thy Conscience*. London, 1630.

The Book of Common Prayer. London, 1572.

[Butts, Thomas]. *Commonplace book*. MS HM 8, Huntington Library, San Marino, CA.

Calvin, John. *A commentarie of John Calvine, upon the first booke of Moses called Genesis*. Translated by Thomas Tymme. London, 1578.

Calvin, John. *Institution of Christian Religion*. Translated by Thomas Norton. London, 1582.

Calvin, John. *A Commentarie upon the Epistle of Saint Paul to the Romanes*. Translated by Christopher Rosdell. London, 1583.

Calvin, John. *Sermons of Maister John Calvin, upon the Booke of Job*. Translated by Arthur Golding. London, 1584.

Certaine select Prayers, gathered out of S. Augustines Meditations. London, 1574.

Charron, Pierre. *Of Wisdome*. Translated by Samson Lennard. London, 1608.

Chaucer, Geoffrey. *The Riverside Chaucer*. 3rd edition. Edited by Larry Benson et al. Boston, MA: Houghton Mifflin, 1986.

Churchyard, Thomas. *Churchyards Challenge*. London, 1593.

Cleaver, Robert. *A Godlie Forme of Householde Government: For the Ordering of Private Families*. London, 1598.

A Complaynt agaynst the wicked enemies of Christ. London, 1564.

Daniel, Samuel. *Delia . . . with the complaint of Rosamond*. London, 1592.

Daniel, Samuel. *The First Fowre Bookes of the civile wars between the two houses of Lancaster and Yorke*. London, 1595.

Donne, John. *John Donne: The Major Works*, ed. John Carey. Oxford: Oxford University Press, 2000.

Drayton, Michael. *Matilda the faire and chaste Daughter of the Lord Robert Fitzwater*. London, 1594.

Drayton, Michael. *Peirs Gaveston Earle of Cornwall*. London [1593/4].

200 BIBLIOGRAPHY

English Renaissance Drama: A Norton Anthology. Edited by David Bevington, Lars Engle, Katharine Eisaman Maus, and Eric Rasmussen. New York: Norton, 2002.

Fletcher, Giles. *Licia...whereunto is added the Rising to the Crowne of Richard the third*. London, 1593.

Gascoigne, George. *The Droomme of Doomes Day*. London, 1576.

Gascoigne, George. *The Whole Woorkes of George Gascoigne Esquyre*. London, 1587.

The Geneva Bible: A Facsimile of the 1560 Edition. Edited by Lloyd E. Berry. Madison, WI: University of Wisconsin Press, 1969.

Goodman, Godfrey. *The Fall of Man, Or the Corruption of Nature*. London, 1616.

Gouge, William. *Of Domesticall Duties*. London, 1622.

[Greene, Robert.] *Selimus, Emperor of the Turks*. In *Three Turk Plays from Early Modern England*, edited by Daniel J. Vitkus. New York: Columbia University Press, 2000.

Hall, Edward. *The Union of the Two Noble and Illustre Famelies of Lancastre and Yorke*. London, 1548.

Hall, Joseph. *Virgidemiarum*. London, 1602.

Hall, Joseph. *Two Guides to a Good Life*. London, 1604.

Hall, Joseph. *Meditations and Vowes, Divine and Morall*. London, 1605.

Hall, Joseph. *Characters of Vertues and Vices*. London, 1608.

Hall, Joseph. *Salomons Divine Arts, of Ethickes, Politics, Oeconomicks*. London, 1609.

Herbert, George. *The English Poems of George Herbert*. Edited by Helen Wilcox. Cambridge: Cambridge University Press, 2007.

Heywood, Thomas. *Apology for Actors*. London, 1612.

Heywood, Thomas. *A Woman Killed with Kindness*. In *Renaissance Drama: An Anthology of Plays and Entertainments*, edited by Arthur F. Kinney. Malden, MA: Blackwell, 2005.

Holbrooke, William. *Loves Complaint, For Want of Entertainement*. London, 1609.

An humble petition of the communaltie to their nost [sic] renowned and gracious soveraigne, the Lady Elizabeth... The lamentable complaint of the communaltie by way of supplication to the high court of Parliament for a learned ministerie, renued and augmented. A petition made to the Convocation house, 1586. [Middelburg], 1588.

[Hyperius]. *The True Tryall and Examination of a Mans owne Selfe*. Translated by Thomas Newton. London, 1586.

James VI/I. *The True Lawe of Free Monarchies*. London, 1603.

Kingsmill, Thomas. *A Complaint against Securitie in these perillous times*. London, 1602.

Kyd, Thomas. *The Spanish Tragedy*. In *English Renaissance Drama*, edited by David Bevington, Lars Engle, Katharine Eisaman Maus, and Eric Rasmussen. New York: Norton, 2002.

[Kyd, Thomas]. *The Tragedye of Solyman and Perseda*. London [1592].

The Lamentable Tragedy of Locrine. Edited by Jane Lytton Gooch. New York: Garland Publishing, 1981.

Lane, John. *Tom Tel-Troth's Message, and His Pens Complaint*. London, 1600.

[Lipsius, Justus]. *Two Bookes of Constancie*. Translated by John Stradling. London, 1595.

Lodge, Thomas. *Phillis... where-unto is annexed, the tragicall complaynt of Elstred*. London, 1593.

Marlowe, Christopher. *Tamburlaine the Great, Part 1*. In *English Renaissance Drama*, edited by David Bevington, Lars Engle, Katharine Eisaman Maus, and Eric Rasmussen. New York: Norton, 2002.

[Middleton, Thomas]. *A Yorkshire Tragedy*. In *Thomas Middleton: The Collected Works*, edited by Gary Taylor and John Lavagnino. Oxford: Oxford University Press, 2007.

Milton, John. *Paradise Lost*. Edited by David Scott Kastan. Indianapolis, IN: Hackett, 2005.

The Mirour for Magistrates. London, 1587.

Montaigne, Michel de. "Of the Resemblance of Children to Fathers." In *The Complete Essays of Montaigne*. Translated by Donald M. Frame. Stanford, CA: Stanford University Press, 1998.

More, Thomas. *The History of King Richard III*. Edited by Richard S. Sylvester. New Haven, CT: Yale University Press, 1976.

Muschet, George. *The Complaint of a Christian Soule*. Edinburgh, 1610.

Nashe, Thomas. *Christs Teares Over Jerusalem*. London, 1593.

Norton, Thomas and Thomas Sackville. *The Tragedie of Gorboduc*. London, 1565.

Ovid. *Ovid his Invective against Ibis*. Translated by Thomas Underdown. London, 1569.

Peacham, Henry. *The Garden of Eloquence*. London, 1593.

Perkins, William. *A Discourse of Conscience*. London, 1596.

Perkins, William. *A salve for a sicke man*. London, 1600.

Plutarch. *The Philosophie, commonlie called, the Morals written by the learned philosopher Plutarch of Chaeronea*. Translated by Philemon Holland. London, 1603.

Powel, Gabriel. *The Resolved Christian, exhorting to Resolution*. London, 1600.

Primaudaye, Pierre de La. *The French Academie*. Translated by T. B. London, 1586.

Primaudaye, Pierre de La. *The Second Part of the French Academie*. Translated by T. B. London, 1594.

Puttenham, George. *The Art of English Poesy*. Edited by Frank Whigham and Wayne A. Rebhorn. Ithaca, NY: Cornell University Press, 2007.

Quintilian. *The Orator's Education*. 4 vols. Edited and translated by D. A. Russell. Loeb Classical Library. Cambridge, MA: Harvard University Press, 2002.

Robinson, Richard. *The Rewarde of Wickednesse*. London, 1574.

Robinson, Richard. *The Vineyarde of Vertue* (London, [1579]).

Sabie, Francis. *Adams Complaint*. London, 1596.

Scott, William. *The Model of Poesy*. Edited by Gavin Alexander. Cambridge: Cambridge University Press, 2013.

Seneca. *The Sixt Tragedie…entituled Troas*. Translated by Jasper Heywood. London, 1559.

Seneca. *The Seconde Tragedie of Seneca entituled Thyestes*. Translated by Jasper Heywood. London, 1560.

Seneca. *The Workes of Lucius Annaeus Seneca, Both Morrall and Naturall*. Translated by Thomas Lodge. London, 1614.

Seneca, *Phaedra*. Translated by John G. Fitch. Loeb Classical Library. Cambridge, MA: Harvard University Press, 2018.

Shakespeare, William. *Hamlet*. Edited by Ann Thompson and Neil Taylor. London: Bloomsbury Arden, 2006.

Shakespeare, William. *King Lear*. Edited by R. A. Foakes. London: Bloomsbury Arden, 1997.

Shakespeare, William. *Richard II*. Edited by Charles R. Forker. London: Bloomsbury Arden, 2002.

Shakespeare, William. *Hamlet: The Texts of 1603 and 1623*. Edited by Ann Thompson and Neil Taylor. London: Bloomsbury Arden, 2006.

Shakespeare, William. *Richard III*. Edited by James R. Siemon. London: Bloomsbury Arden, 2009.

Shakespeare, William. *The Norton Shakespeare*. Edited by Stephen Greenblatt, Walter Cohen, Suzanne Gossett, Jean E. Howard, Katharine Eisaman Maus, and Gordon McMullan. New York: Norton, 2016.

Shakespeare, William. *Othello*. Edited by E. A. J. Honigmann, new introduction by Ayanna Thompson. London: Bloomsbury Arden, 2016.

Sidney, Philip. *The Countess of Pembroke's Arcadia*. Edited by Maurice Evans. London: Penguin, 1987.

202 BIBLIOGRAPHY

Sidney, Philip. *The Countess of Pembroke's Arcadia (The Old Arcadia).* Edited by Katherine Duncan-Jones. Oxford: Oxford University Press, 1999.

Sidney, Philip. *The Major Works.* Edited by Katherine Duncan-Jones. Oxford: Oxford University Press, 2008.

Spenser, Edmund. *The Shorter Poems.* Edited by Richard A. McCabe. London: Penguin, 1999.

Standish, Arthur. *The Commons Complaint.* London, 1611.

The Thirty-Nine Articles 1563. In *Religion and Society in Early Modern England: A Sourcebook,* edited by David Cressy and Lori Anne Ferrell. 2nd edition. New York: Routledge, 2005.

The True Tragedie of Richard the third. London, 1594.

W., T. *The Lamentation of Melpomene, for the death of Belphœbe our late Queene.* London, 1603.

Ward, Samuel. *Balme from Gilead to Recover Conscience.* London, 1618.

A Warning for Fair Women. Edited by Charles D. Cannon. Paris: Mouton, 1975.

Webbe, William. *A Discourse of English Poetrie.* London, 1586.

Webster, John. *The Duchess of Malfi.* In *English Renaissance Drama,* edited by David Bevington, Lars Engle, Katharine Eisaman Maus, and Eric Rasmussen. New York: Norton, 2002.

Whately, William. *A Bridebush, or A Direction for Married Persons.* London, 1623.

Whetstone, George. *The Rocke of Regard.* London, 1576.

Wilson, Thomas. *The Arte of Rhetorike.* London, 1584.

Woolton, John. *Of the Conscience.* London, 1576.

Wotton, Henry. *The Life and Letters of Sir Henry Wotton.* Vol. II. Edited by L. P. Smith. Oxford: Clarendon Press, 1907.

Wright, Thomas. *The Passions of the Minde in Generall.* London, 1604.

Secondary Sources

Adams, Henry Hitch. *English Domestic or, Homiletic Tragedy 1575 to 1642.* New York: Columbia University Press, 1943.

Adelman, Janet. *Suffocating Mothers: Fantasies of Maternal Origin in Shakespeare's Plays, Hamlet to The Tempest.* New York: Routledge, 1992.

Ahmed, Sara, *The Promise of Happiness.* Durham, NC: Duke University Press, 2010.

Ahmed, Sara. *Complaint!* Durham, NC: Duke University Press, 2021.

Akhimie, Patricia. *Shakespeare and the Cultivation of Difference: Race and Conduct in the Early Modern World.* New York: Routledge, 2018.

Alfar, Cristina León. "Speaking Truth to Power as Feminist Ethics in *Richard III.*" *Social Research* 86, no. 3 (2019): 789–819.

Anderson, Thomas P. *Performing Early Modern Trauma from Shakespeare to Milton.* Burlington, VT: Ashgate, 2006.

Archer, Harriet, and Andrew Hadfield, eds. *A Mirror for Magistrates in Context: Literature, History and Politics in Early Modern England.* Cambridge: Cambridge University Press, 2016.

Archer, Harriet. *Unperfect Histories: The Mirror for Magistrates, 1559–1610.* Oxford: Oxford University Press, 2017.

Arthur, Jake, and Rosalind Smith. "Women's Complaint, 1530–1680: Taxonomy, Voice, and the Index in the Digital Age." In *Early Modern Women's Complaint: Gender, Form, and Politics,* edited by Sarah C. E. Ross and Rosalind Smith, 291–36. London: Palgrave Macmillan, 2020.

BIBLIOGRAPHY 203

Austin, J. L. *How to Do Things with Words*. Cambridge, MA: Harvard University Press, 1975.

Bailey, Amanda. "Speak What We Feel: Sympathy and Statecraft." In *Affect Theory and Early Modern Texts: Politics, Ecologies, and Form*, edited by Amanda Bailey and Mario DiGangi, 27–46. New York: Palgrave Macmillan, 2017.

Baldo, Jonathan. "'His form and cause conjoin'd': Reflections on 'Cause' in *Hamlet*." *Renaissance Drama* 16 (1985): 75–94.

Barish, Jonas A. *The Antitheatrical Prejudice*. Berkeley, CA: University of California Press, 1981.

Bates, Catherine. "The Enigma of *A Lover's Complaint*." In *A Companion to Shakespeare's Sonnets*. Edited by Michael Schoenfeldt, 426–40. Malden, MA: Wiley-Blackwell, 2007.

Bates, Catherine. "Shakespeare and the Female Voice in Soliloquy." In *Shakespeare and the Soliloquy in Early Modern English Drama*, edited by A. D. Cousins and Daniel Derrin, 56–67. Cambridge: Cambridge University Press, 2018.

Belsey, Catherine. "Beyond Reason: *Hamlet* and Early Modern Stage Ghosts." In *Gothic Renaissance: A Reassessment*, edited by Elisabeth Bronfen and Beate Neumeier, 32–54. Manchester: Manchester University Press, 2014.

Bengtsson, Frederick. "True and Home-Born: Domestic Tragedy on the Early Modern English Stage." PhD dissertation. Columbia University, 2014.

Benjamin, Walter. *The Origin of German Tragic Drama*. Translated by John Osborne. London: Verso, 2009.

Benson, Sean. *Shakespeare, Othello, and Domestic Tragedy*. London: Continuum, 2012.

Berlant, Lauren. *The Female Complaint: The Unfinished Business of Sentimentality in American Culture*. Durham, NC: Duke University Press, 2008.

Bevington, David. "'Why Should Calamity be Full of Words': The Efficacy of Cursing in *Richard III*." *Iowa State Journal of Research* 56, no. 1 (1981): 9–18.

Bloom, Gina. *Voice in Motion: Staging Gender, Shaping Sound in Early Modern England*. Philadelphia, PA: University of Pennsylvania Press, 2007.

Bolam, Robyn. "*Richard II*: Shakespeare and the languages of the stage." In *The Cambridge Companion to the Shakespearean History Play*, edited by Michael Hattaway, 141–57. Cambridge: Cambridge University Press, 2002.

Bonetto, Sandra. "Coward Conscience and Bad Conscience in Shakespeare and Nietzsche." *Philosophy and Literature* 30, no. 2 (2006): 512–27.

Bouwsma, William J. *A Usable Past: Essays in European Cultural History*. Berkeley, CA: University of California Press, 1990.

Braden, Gordon. *Renaissance Tragedy and the Senecan Tradition: Anger's Privilege*. New Haven, CT: Yale University Press, 1985.

Braun, Harald E., and Edward Vallence, eds. *Contexts of Conscience in Early Modern Europe, 1500–1700*. London: Palgrave Macmillan, 2004.

Bristol, Michael D. ed. *Shakespeare and Moral Agency*. London: Continuum, 2010.

Brooke, Tucker. *The Renaissance (1500–1660)*. Vol. 2 of *A Literary History of England*, edited by Albert C. Baugh. 4 vols. New York: Appleton-Century-Crofts, 1948.

Brooks, Harold F. "*Richard III*, Unhistorical Amplifications: The Women's Scenes and Seneca." *Modern Language Review* 75, no. 4 (1980): 721–37.

Brown, Georgia. *Redefining Elizabethan Literature*. Cambridge: Cambridge University Press, 2004.

Budra, Paul. *A Mirror for Magistrates and the de casibus Tradition*. Toronto: University of Toronto Press, 2000.

Bushnell, Rebecca. "The Fall of Princes: The Classical and Medieval Roots of English Renaissance Tragedy." In *A Companion to Tragedy*, edited by R. Bushnell, 289–306. Malden, MA: Blackwell, 2005.

204 BIBLIOGRAPHY

Butler, Judith. *Giving an Account of Oneself*. New York: Fordham University Press, 2005.

Cadman, Daniel. *Sovereigns and Subjects in Early Modern Neo-Senecan Drama: Republicanism, Stoicism and Authority*. New York: Routledge, 2016.

Cadman, Daniel, Andrew Duxfield, and Lisa Hopkins, eds. *The Genres of Renaissance Tragedy*. Manchester: Manchester University Press, 2019.

Cavarero, Adriana. *For More than One Voice: Toward a Philosophy of Vocal Expression*. Translated by Paul A. Kottman. Stanford, CA: Stanford University Press, 2005.

Cavell, Stanley. "The Avoidance of Love." In *Disowning Knowledge in Seven Plays of Shakespeare*, 39–123. Cambridge: Cambridge University Press, 2003.

Cavell, Stanley. *Philosophy the Day After Tomorrow*. Cambridge, MA: Harvard University Press, 2005.

Chapman, Alison A. "Lucrece's Time," *Shakespeare Quarterly* 64, no. 2 (2013): 165–87.

Charnes, Linda. *Notorious Identity: Materializing the Subject in Shakespeare*. Cambridge, MA: Harvard University Press, 1995.

Clarke, Danielle. "'Form'd into words by your divided lips': Women, Rhetoric, and the Ovidian Tradition." In *"This Double Voice": Gendered Writing in Early Modern England*, edited by Danielle Clarke and Elizabeth Clarke, 61–87. Basingstoke: Macmillan, 2000.

Clarke, Danielle. "'Signifying, but not sounding': Gender and Paratext in the Complaint Genre." In *Renaissance Paratexts*, edited by Helen Smith and Louise Wilson, 133–50. Cambridge: Cambridge University Press, 2011.

Clemen, Wolfgang. *English Tragedy Before Shakespeare: The Development of Dramatic Speech*. Translated by T. S. Dorsch. London: Methuen, 1961.

Clody, Michael C. "The Mirror and the Feather: Tragedy and Animal Voice in *King Lear*." *ELH* 80, no. 3 (2013): 661–80.

Cochran, Elizabeth Agnew. *Protestant Virtue and Stoic Ethics*. London: Bloomsbury T & T Clark, 2018.

Cohen, Stephen. "Between Form and Culture: New Historicism and the Promise of a Historical Formalism." In *Shakespeare and Historical Formalism*, edited by Stephen Cohen, 17–41. New York: Routledge, 2007.

Combe, Kirk. "The New Voice of Political Dissent: The Transition from Complaint to Satire." In *Theorizing Satire: Essays in Literary Criticism*, edited by Brian A. Connery and Kirk Combe, 73–94. New York: St. Martin's Press, 1995.

Comensoli, Viviana. *"Household Business": Domestic Plays of Early Modern England*. Toronto: University of Toronto Press, 1996.

Coodin, Sara. "What's Virtue Ethics Got to Do With It? Shakespearean Character as Moral Character." In *Shakespeare and Moral Agency*, edited by Michael D. Bristol, 184–99. London: Continuum, 2010.

Cormack, Bradin. *A Power to Do Justice: Jurisdiction, English Literature, and the Rise of Common Law, 1509–1625*. Chicago, IL: University of Chicago Press, 2007.

Cox, John D. *Seeming Knowledge: Shakespeare and Skeptical Faith*. Waco, TX: Baylor University Press, 2007.

Craik, Katharine A. "Shakespeare's *A Lover's Complaint* and Early Modern Criminal Confession." *Shakespeare Quarterly* 53, no. 4 (2002): 437–59.

Craik, Katharine A., and Tanya Pollard, "Introduction: Imagining Audiences," in *Shakespearean Sensations: Experiencing Literature in Early Modern England*, edited by Katharine A. Craik and Tanya Pollard, 1–25. Cambridge: Cambridge University Press, 2013.

Crane, Mary Thomas. "Form and Pressure in Shakespeare." *Philological Quarterly* 98, nos. 1–2 (2019): 23–45.

Cressy, David. "Demotic Voices and Popular Complaint in Elizabethan and Early Stuart England." *Journal of Early Modern Studies* 2 (2013): 47–6.

Critchley, Simon. *Infinitely Demanding: Ethics of Commitment, Politics of Resistance.* London: Verso, 2007.

Curran, Kevin. *Shakespeare's Legal Ecologies: Law and Distributed Selfhood.* Evanston, IL: Northwestern University Press, 2017.

Cutrofello, Andrew. *All For Nothing: Hamlet's Negativity.* Cambridge, MA: MIT Press, 2014.

Dailey, Alice. "Little, Little Graves: Shakespeare's Photographs of Richard II." *Shakespeare Quarterly* 69, no. 3 (2018): 141–66.

Daniel, Drew. *The Melancholy Assemblage: Affect and Epistemology in the English Renaissance.* New York: Fordham University Press, 2013.

De Kesel, Marc. *Eros and Ethics: Reading Jacques Lacan's Seminar VII.* Translated by Sigi Jöttkadnt. Albany, NY: SUNY Press, 2009.

Diaz, Joanne. "Grief as Medicine for Grief: Complaint Poetry in Early Modern England, 1559–1609." PhD dissertation. Northwestern University, 2008.

DiGangi, Mario. "Competitive Mourning and Female Agency in *Richard III*." In *A Feminist Companion to Shakespeare*, edited by Dympna Callaghan, 428–39. Malden, MA: Wiley-Blackwell, 2016.

DiGangi, Mario. "Entangled Agency: The Assassin's Conscience in *Richard III* and *King John*." In *The Oxford Handbook of Shakespeare and Embodiment*, edited by Valerie Traub, 385–99. Oxford: Oxford University Press, 2016.

Dionne, Craig. *Posthuman Lear: Reading Shakespeare in the Anthropocene.* Goleta, CA: Punctum Books, 2016.

Dolan, Frances E. *Dangerous Familiars: Representations of Domestic Crime in England, 1550–1700.* Ithaca, NY: Cornell University Press, 1994.

Dollimore, Jonathan. *Radical Tragedy.* Durham, NC: Duke University Press, [1984] 2004.

Driver, Julia. "Moral Sense and Sentimentalism." In *The Oxford Handbook of the History of Ethics*, edited by Roger Crisp, 358–76. Oxford: Oxford University Press, 2013.

Dubrow, Heather. "A Mirror for Complaints: Shakespeare's *Lucrece* and Generic Tradition." In *Renaissance Genres: Essays on Theory, History, and Interpretation*, edited by Barbara Kiefer Lewalski, 399–417. Cambridge, MA: Harvard University Press, 1986.

Dubrow, Heather. "Guess Who's Coming to Dinner?: Reinterpreting Formalism and the Country House Poem. *Reading for Form.* Special issue, *Modern Language Quarterly* 61, no. 1 (2000): 59–77.

Dunne, Derek. *Shakespeare, Revenge Tragedy and Early Modern Law: Vindictive Justice.* New York: Palgrave Macmillan, 2016.

Edelman, Lee, and Madhavi Menon. "Queer Tragedy, or Two Meditations on Cause." In *The Oxford Handbook of Shakespearean Tragedy*, edited by Michael Neill and David Schalkwyk, 285–97. Oxford: Oxford University Press, 2016.

Eisendrath, Rachel. *Poetry in a World of Things: Aesthetics and Empiricism in Renaissance Ekphrasis.* Chicago, IL: University of Chicago Press, 2018.

Elam, Keir. *The Semiotics of Theatre and Drama.* 2nd edition. New York: Routledge, 2002.

Elton, William. *King Lear and the Gods.* Lexington, KY: University of Kentucky Press, 1988.

Engle, Lars, Patrick Gray, and William M. Hamlin, eds. *Shakespeare and Montaigne.* Edinburgh: Edinburgh University Press, 2021.

Enterline, Lynn. *The Rhetoric of the Body from Ovid to Shakespeare.* Cambridge: Cambridge University Press, 2000.

Enterline, Lynn. *Shakespeare's Schoolroom: Rhetoric, Discipline, Emotion.* Philadelphia, PA: University of Pennsylvania Press, 2012.

BIBLIOGRAPHY

Enterline, Lynn. "'Past the Help of Law': Epyllia and the Female Complaint." In *Early Modern Women's Complaint: Gender, Form, and Politics*, edited by Sarah C. E. Ross and Rosalind Smith, 315–27. London: Palgrave Macmillan, 2020.

Erickson, Peter, and Kim F. Hall. "'A New Scholarly Song': Rereading Early Modern Race." Special issue, *Shakespeare Quarterly* 67, no. 1 (2016): 1–13.

Felch, Susan M. "Anne Lock and the Instructive Complaint." In *Early Modern Women's Complaint: Gender, Form, and Politics*, edited by Sarah C. E. Ross and Rosalind Smith, 29–46. London: Palgrave Macmillan, 2020.

Ferguson, Margaret. *Trials of Desire: Renaissance Defenses of Poetry*. New Haven, CT: Yale University Press, 1983.

Finn, Kavita Mudan. "'Of Whom Proud Rome Hath Boasted Long': Intertextual 'Conversations' in Early Modern England." In *Conversational Exchanges in Early Modern England*, edited by Kristen Abbott Bennett, 70–100. Newcastle-upon-Tyne: Cambridge Scholars Publishing, 2015.

Floyd-Wilson, Mary. *Occult Knowledge, Science, and Gender on the Shakespearean Stage*. Cambridge: Cambridge University Press, 2013.

Fox, Cora. "Othello's Unfortunate Happiness." In *Race and Affect in Early Modern English Literature*. Edited by Carol Mejia LaPerle. Tempe, AZ: ACMRS Press, 2021. https://asu.pressbooks.pub/race-and-affect/chapter/10-othellos-unfortunate-happiness/ (last accessed January 18, 2023).

Freinkel, Lisa. *Reading Shakespeare's Will: The Theology of Figure from Augustine to the Sonnets*. New York: Columbia University Press, 2002.

Freud, Sigmund. *Beyond the Pleasure Principle*. Edited by James Strachey. New York: Norton, 1990.

Garrett, Aaron. "Seventeenth-Century Moral Philosophy: Self-Help, Self-Knowledge, and the Devil's Mountain." In *The Oxford Handbook of the History of Ethics*, edited by Roger Crisp, 229–79. Oxford: Oxford University Press, 2013.

Geng, Penelope. *Communal Justice in Shakespeare's England: Drama, Law, and Emotion*. Toronto: University of Toronto Press, 2021.

Giancarlo, Matthew. *Parliament and Literature in Late Medieval England*. Cambridge: Cambridge University Press, 2007.

Gil, Daniel Juan. *Shakespeare's Anti-Politics: Sovereign Power and the Life of the Flesh* Basingstoke: Palgrave Macmillan, 2013.

Gillies, John. "The Question of Original Sin in *Hamlet*." *Shakespeare Quarterly* 64, no. 4 (2013): 396–424.

Gold, Moshe, Sandhor Goodhart, eds., with Kent Lehnhof. *Of Shakespeare and Levinas: "To See Another Thus."* West Lafayette, IN: Purdue University Press, 2018.

Goodland, Katharine. *Female Mourning and Tragedy in Medieval and Renaissance English Drama: From the Raising of Lazarus to King Lear*. Aldershot: Ashgate, 2005.

Grady, Hugh. "*Hamlet* as Mourning-Play: A Benjaminesque Interpretation." *Shakespeare Studies* 36 (2008): 135–65.

Grady, Hugh. "Presentism, Walter Benjamin, and the Search for Meaning in *King Lear*," *Shakespeare* 5, no. 2 (2009): 145–61.

Grady, Hugh. *Shakespeare and Impure Aesthetics*. Cambridge: Cambridge University Press, 2009.

Gray, Patrick, and John D. Cox, "Introduction: Rethinking Shakespeare and Ethics." In *Shakespeare and Renaissance Ethics*, edited by Patrick Gray and John D. Cox, 1–34. Cambridge: Cambridge University Press, 2014.

Gray, Patrick. *Shakespeare and the Fall of the Roman Republic: Selfhood, Stoicism and Civil War*. Edinburgh: Edinburgh University Press, 2019.

Gray, Patrick. "Seduced by Romanticism: Re-imagining Shakespearean Catharsis." In *The Routledge Companion to Shakespeare and Philosophy*, edited by Craig Bourne and Emily Caddick Bourne, 510–24. London: Routledge, 2019.

Gray, Patrick. "Shakespeare versus Aristotle: *Anagnorisis*, Repentance, and Acknowledgment," *Journal of Medieval and Early Modern Studies* 49, no. 1 (2019): 85–111.

Greenberg, Mitchell. "The Concept of 'Early Modern.'" *Journal for Early Modern Cultural Studies* 13, no. 2 (2013): 75–9.

Greenblatt, Stephen. *Shakespearean Negotiations: The Circulation of Social Energy in Renaissance England*. Berkeley, CA: University of California Press, 1988.

Greenblatt, Stephen. *Hamlet in Purgatory*. Princeton, NJ: Princeton University Press, 2001.

Grier, Miles. "Are Shakespeare's Plays Racially Progressive? The Answer Is in Our Hands." In *The Cambridge Companion to Shakespeare and Race*, edited by Ayanna Thompson, 237–53. Cambridge: Cambridge University Press, 2021.

Griswold, Jeffrey B. "Human Insufficiency and the Politics of Accommodation in *King Lear*." *Renaissance Drama* 47.1 (2019): 73–94.

Grossman, Marshall, ed. *Reading Renaissance Ethics*. New York: Routledge, 2007.

Guy, J. A. *The Court of Star Chamber and Its Records to the Reign of Elizabeth I*. London: HMSO, 1985.

Hall, Kim F. *Things of Darkness: Economies of Race and Gender in Early Modern England*. Ithaca, NY: Cornell University Press, 1995.

Hamlin, Hannibal. "The Patience of Lear." In *Shakespeare and Religion: Early Modern and Postmodern Perspectives*, edited by Ken Jackson and Arthur F. Marotti, 127–60. Notre Dame, IN: University of Notre Dame Press, 2011.

Hamlin, William. "Conscience and the god-surrogate in Montaigne and *Measure for Measure*." In *Shakespeare and Renaissance Ethics*, edited by Patrick Gray and John D. Cox, 237–60. Cambridge: Cambridge University Press, 2014.

Hammill, Graham, and Julia Reinhard Lupton, eds. *Political Theology and Early Modernity*. Chicago, IL: University of Chicago Press, 2012.

Harvey, Elizabeth D. *Ventriloquized Voices: Feminist Theory and English Renaissance Texts*. London: Routledge, 1992.

Helgerson, Richard. "Weeping for Jane Shore." *South Atlantic Quarterly* 98, no. 3 (1999): 451–76.

Hendricks, Margo. "'A word, sweet Lucrece': Confession, Feminism, and *The Rape of Lucrece*." In *A Feminist Companion to Shakespeare*, edited by Dympna Callaghan, 121–36. Malden, MA: Wiley-Blackwell, 2016.

Herman, Peter C. *Squitter-wits and Muse-haters: Sidney, Spenser, Milton and Renaissance Antipoetic Sentiment*. Detroit, MI: Wayne State University Press, 1996.

Hirschfeld, Heather. "Hamlet's 'first corse': Repetition, Trauma, and the Displacement of Redemptive Typology." *Shakespeare Quarterly* 54, no. 4 (2003): 424–48.

Hirschfeld, Heather. *The End of Satisfaction: Drama and Repentance in the Age of Shakespeare*. Ithaca, NY: Cornell University Press, 2014.

Holderness, Graham. *Shakespeare: The Histories*. New York: St. Martin's Press, 2000.

Honig, Bonnie. *Antigone, Interrupted*. Cambridge: Cambridge University Press, 2013.

Howard, Jean E. and Phyllis Rackin. *Engendering a Nation: A Feminist Account of Shakespeare's English Histories*. New York: Routledge, 1997.

Howard, Jean E. "Monarchs Who Cry: The Gendered Politics of Weeping in the English History Play." In *A Feminist Companion to Shakespeare*, edited by Dympna Callaghan, 457–66. Malden, MA: Wiley-Blackwell, 2016.

Hoxby, Blair. "Passions." In *Early Modern Theatricality*, edited by Henry S. Turner, 556–86. Oxford: Oxford University Press, 2013.

Hoxby, Blair. *What Was Tragedy? Theory and the Early Modern Canon.* Oxford: Oxford University Press, 2015.

Hughes, Daniel E. "The 'Worm of Conscience' in *Richard III* and *Macbeth*." *English Journal* 55, no. 7 (1965): 845–52.

Hui, Andrew. "Horatio's Philosophy in *Hamlet*." *Renaissance Drama* 41, nos. 1–2 (2013): 151–71.

Hutson, Lorna. *The Invention of Suspicion: Law and Mimesis in Shakespeare and Renaissance Drama.* Oxford: Oxford University Press, 2007.

Jackson, MacDonald P. *Determining the Shakespeare Canon: Arden of Faversham and A Lover's Complaint.* Oxford: Oxford University Press, 2014.

James, Heather. "Dido's Ear: Tragedy and the Politics of Response." *Shakespeare Quarterly* 52, no. 3 (2001): 360–82.

Johnson, Toria. "'To Feel What Wretches Feel': Reformation and the Re-naming of English Compassion." In *Compassion in Early Modern Literature and Culture: Feeling and Practice*, edited by Kristine Steenbergh and Katherine Ibbett, 219–36. Cambridge: Cambridge University Press, 2021.

Joughin, John J. "*Lear's* Afterlife." In "*King Lear* and its Afterlife," edited by Peter Holland. *Shakespeare Survey* 55 (2002): 67–81.

Jowett, John. Introduction. *The Tragedy of King Richard III*, edited by John Jowett, 1–132. Oxford: Oxford University Press, 2000.

Kahn, Coppélia. *Man's Estate: Masculine Identity in Shakespeare.* Los Angeles, CA: University of California Press, 1991.

Kahn, Victoria. *Wayward Contracts: The Crisis of Political Obligation in England, 1640–1674.* Princeton, NJ: Princeton University Press, 2004.

Kahn, Victoria. *The Future of Illusion: Political Theology and Early Modern Texts.* Chicago, IL: University of Chicago Press, 2014.

Kantorowicz, Ernst. *The King's Two Bodies: A Study in Medieval Political Theology.* Princeton, NJ: Princeton University Press, 1957.

Kearney, James. "'This is above all strangeness': *King Lear*, Ethics, and the Phenomenology of Recognition." *Criticism* 54, no. 3 (2012): 455–67.

Kerrigan, John. *Motives of Woe: Shakespeare and "Female Complaint".* Oxford: Oxford University Press, 1991.

Kerrigan, John. *Revenge Tragedy: Aeschylus to Armageddon.* Oxford: Oxford University Press, 1997.

Kiefer, Frederick. "Fortune and Providence in the *Mirror for Magistrates*." *Studies in Philology* 74 (1977): 146–64.

Kietzman, Mary Jo. "'Means to Mourn Some Newer Way': The Role of the Complaint in Early-Modern Narrative." PhD dissertation. Boston College, 1993.

Kietzman, Mary Jo. "'What is Hecuba to Him or [S]he to Hecuba?': Lucrece's Complaint and Shakespearean Poetic Agency." *Modern Philology* 97, no. 1 (1999): 21–45.

Kottman, Paul. *A Politics of the Scene.* Stanford, CA: Stanford University Press, 2008.

Kottman, Paul. *Tragic Conditions in Shakespeare: Disinheriting the Globe.* Baltimore, MD: Johns Hopkins University Press, 2009.

Kottman, Paul, ed. *The Insistence of Art: Aesthetic Philosophy after Early Modernity.* New York: Fordham University Press, 2017.

Kraye, Jill. "Moral Philosophy." In *The Cambridge History of Renaissance Philosophy*, edited by Charles B. Schmitt et al., 303–86. Cambridge: Cambridge University Press, 1988.

Kuchar, Gary. "Ecstatic Donne: Conscience, Sin, and Surprise in the *Sermons* and the Mitcham Letters." *Criticism* 50, no. 4 (2008): 631–54.

Kuchar, Gary. *The Poetry of Religious Sorrow in Early Modern England*. Cambridge: Cambridge University Press, 2011.

Kuzner, James. *Open Subjects: English Renaissance Republicans, Modern Selfhoods and the Virtue of Vulnerability*. Edinburgh: Edinburgh University Press, 2011.

Kuzner, James. *Shakespeare As a Way of Life: Skeptical Practice and the Politics of Weakness*. New York: Fordham University Press, 2016.

Lacan, Jacques. *The Seminar of Jacques Lacan: Book VII: The Ethics of Psychoanalysis, 1959–1960*. Edited by Jacques-Alain Miller. Translated by Dennis Porter. London: Routledge, 2008.

Laplanche, Jean. *New Foundations for Psychoanalysis*. Translated by David Macey. Oxford: Basil Blackwell, 1989.

Lehtonen, Kelly. "The Intelligence of Negative Passion and the Collapse of Stoicism in *King Lear*." *SEL* 59, no. 2 (2019): 259–80.

Lemon, Rebecca, "Tyranny and the State of Exception in Shakespeare's *Richard III*." In *Richard III: A Critical Reader*, edited by Annaliese Connolly, 111–28. London: Bloomsbury Arden, 2013.

Lemon, Rebecca. *Addiction and Devotion in Early Modern England*. Philadelphia, PA: University of Pennsylvania Press, 2018.

Levinas, Emmanuel. *Totality and Infinity*. Translated by Alphonso Lingis Pittsburgh, PA: Duquesne University Press, 1969.

Levinas, Emmanuel. *Ethics and Infinity*. Translated by Richard A. Cohen. Pittsburgh, PA: Duquesne University Press, 1985.

Levine, Caroline. *Forms: Whole, Rhythm, Hierarchy, Network*. Princeton, NJ: Princeton University Press, 2015.

Levinson, Marjorie. "What Is New Formalism?" *PMLA* 122, no. 2 (2007): 558–69.

Levy, Eric P. "'Things Standing Thus Unknown': The Epistemology of Ignorance in *Hamlet*." *Studies in Philology* 97, no. 2 (2000): 192–209.

Lewis, Rhodri. *Hamlet and the Vision of Darkness*. Princeton, NJ: Princeton University Press, 2017.

Little, Jr., Arthur L. *Shakespeare Jungle Fever: National-Imperial Re-Visions of Race, Rape, and Sacrifice*. Stanford, CA: Stanford University Press, 2000.

Lobis, Seth. *The Virtue of Sympathy: Magic, Philosophy, and Literature in Seventeenth-Century England*. New Haven, CT: Yale University Press, 2015.

Loewenstein, David. "Agnostic Shakespeare?: The Godless World of *King Lear*." In *Shakespeare and Moral Agency*, edited by Michael D. Bristol, 155–71. London: Continuum, 2010.

Loewenstein, David, and Michael Witmore. "Introduction." In *Shakespeare and Early Modern Religion*, edited by Loewenstein and Witmore. 1–19. Cambridge: Cambridge University Press, 2015.

Long, Zackariah C. "Toward an Early Modern Theory of Trauma: Conscience in 'Richard III.'" *Journal of Literature and Trauma Studies* 1, no. 1 (2012): 49–72.

Lopez, Jeremy. "Introduction." In *Richard II: New Critical Essays*, edited by Jeremy Lopez, 1–50. New York: Routledge, 2012.

Lorenz, Philip. *The Tears of Sovereignty: Perspectives of Power in Renaissance Drama*. New York: Fordham University Press, 2013.

Luis-Martínez, Zenón. "Shakespeare's Historical Drama as *Trauerspiel*: *Richard II*—and After." *ELH* 75, no. 3 (2008): 673–705.

Lukacher, Ned. *Daemonic Figures: Shakespeare and the Question of Conscience*. Ithaca, NY: Cornell University Press, 1994.

Lupton, Julia Reinhard. "Creature Caliban." *Shakespeare Quarterly* 51, no. 1 (2000): 1–23.

210 BIBLIOGRAPHY

Lupton, Julia Reinhard. *Thinking with Shakespeare: Essays on Politics and Life*. Chicago, IL: Chicago University Press, 2011.

Lupton, Julia Reinhard. "The Wizards of Uz: Shakespeare and the Book of Job." In *Shakespeare and Religion: Early Modern and Postmodern Perspectives*, edited by Ken Jackson and Arthur F. Marotti, 163–87. Notre Dame, IN: University of Notre Dame Press, 2011.

MacDonald, Joyce Green. "Black Ram, White Ewe: Shakespeare, Race, and Women." In *A Feminist Companion to Shakespeare*, edited by Dympna Callaghan, 206–25. Malden, MA: Wiley-Blackwell, 2016.

Macpherson, Sandra. "A Little Formalism." *English Literary History* 82, no. 2 (2015): 385–405.

Magnusson, Lynne. "Grammatical Theatricality in *Richard III*: Schoolroom Queens and Godly Optatives." *Shakespeare Quarterly* 64, no. 1 (2013): 32–43.

Magnusson, Lynne. "Shakespearean Tragedy and the Language of Lament." In *The Oxford Handbook of Shakespearean Tragedy*, edited by Michael Neill and David Schalkwyk, 120–34. Oxford: Oxford University Press, 2016.

Mallette, Richard. "From Gyves to Graces: 'Hamlet' and Free Will." *The Journal of English and Germanic Philology* 93, no. 3 (1994): 336–55.

Manley, Lawrence. *Literature and Culture in Early Modern England*. Cambridge: Cambridge University Press, 1995.

Marcus, Leah S. "*King Lear* and the Death of the World." In *The Oxford Handbook of Shakespearean Tragedy*, edited by Michael Neill and David Schalkwyk, 421–36. Oxford: Oxford University Press, 2016.

Marshall, David. "Adam Smith and the Theatricality of Moral Sentiments." *Critical Inquiry* 10, no. 4 (1984): 592–613.

Marshall, David. *The Surprising Effects of Sympathy: Marivaux, Diderot, Rousseau, and Mary Shelley*. Chicago, IL: University of Chicago Press, 1988.

Matz, Robert. *Defending Literature in Early Modern England: Renaissance Literary Theory in Social Context*. Cambridge: Cambridge University Press, 2000.

Maus, Katharine Eisaman. *Inwardness and Theater in the English Renaissance* (Chicago, IL: University of Chicago Press, 1995)

McEleney, Corey. *Futile Pleasures: Early Modern Literature and the Limits of Utility*. New York: Fordham University Press, 2017.

McKeithan, D. M. "*King Lear* and Sidney's *Arcadia*." *Studies in English* 14 (1934): 45–9.

McMillin, Scott. "*Richard II*: Eyes of Sorrow, Eyes of Desire." *Shakespeare Quarterly* 35, no. 1 (1984): 40–52.

Meek, Richard. "'Rue e'en for ruth': *Richard II* and the Imitation of Sympathy." In *The Renaissance of Emotion: Understanding Affect in Shakespeare and His Contemporaries*. Edited by Richard Meek and Erin Sullivan, 130–52. Manchester: Manchester University Press, 2015.

Meyer, Liam J. "'Humblewise': Deference and Complaint in the Court of Requests." *Journal of Early Modern Studies* 4 (2015): 261–85.

Mikics, David. *A New Handbook of Literary Terms*. New Haven, CT: Yale University Press, 2007.

Mousley, Andy. "Care, Scepticism, and Speaking in the Plural: Posthumanisms and Humanisms in *King Lear*" in *Posthumanist Shakespeares*, edited by Stefan Herbrechter and Ivan Callus, 97–113. New York: Palgrave Macmillan, 2012.

Mukherji, Subha. *Law and Representation in Early Modern Drama*. Cambridge: Cambridge University Press, 2006.

Mullan, John. *Sentiment and Sociability: The Language of Feeling in the Eighteenth Century.* Oxford: Clarendon Press, 1988.

Mullaney, Steven. "'Do You See This?': The Politics of Attention in Shakespearean Tragedy." In *The Oxford Handbook of the History of Ethics*, edited by Roger Crisp, 151–66. Oxford: Oxford University Press, 2013.

Nandi, Miriam. "The Dangers and Pleasures of Filling Vacuous Time: Idleness in Early Modern Diaries." In *Idleness, Indolence and Leisure in English Literature*, edited by Monica Fludernik and Miriam Nandi, 40–59. London: Palgrave Macmillan, 2014.

Neill, Michael. "Unproper Beds: Race, Adultery, and the Hideous in *Othello*." *Shakespeare Quarterly* 40, no. 4 (1989): 383–412.

Ngai, Sianne. *Ugly Feelings*. Cambridge, MA: Harvard University Press, 2005.

Ngai, Sianne. *Theory of the Gimmick: Aesthetic Judgment and Capitalist Form*. Cambridge, MA: Harvard University Press, 2020.

Nussbaum, Martha. *The Therapy of Desire: Theory and Practice in Hellenistic Ethics*. Princeton, NJ: Princeton University Press, 1994.

Nuttall, A. D. *Shakespeare the Thinker*. New Haven, CT: Yale University Press, 2007.

O'Callaghan, Michelle. "A Mirror for Magistrates: Richard Niccols' *Sir Thomas Overburies Vision* (1616)." In *A Mirror for Magistrates in Context: Literature, History and Politics in Early Modern England*, edited by Harriet Archer and Andrew Hadfield, 181–96. Cambridge: Cambridge University Press, 2016.

Ojakangas, Mika. *The Voice of Conscience: A Political Genealogy of Western Ethical Experience*. New York: Bloomsbury, 2013.

Oldenberg, Scott. "The Petition on the Early English Stage." *SEL* 57, no. 2 (2017): 325–47.

Orlin, Lena Cowen. *Private Matters and Public Culture in Post-Reformation England*. Ithaca, NY: Cornell University Press, 1994.

Orlin, Lena Cowen. "Domestic Tragedy: Private Life on the Public Stage." In *A New Companion to Renaissance Drama*, edited by Arthur. F. Kinney and Thomas Warren Hopper, 388–402. Malden, MA: Wiley-Blackwell, 2017.

The Oxford Companion to English Literature. 7th ed. Edited by Diana Birch. Oxford: Oxford University Press, 2009.

Parvini, Neema. *Shakespeare's Moral Compass*. Edinburgh: Edinburgh University Press, 2018.

Paster, Gail Kern. "The tragic subject and its passions." In *The Cambridge Companion to Shakespearean Tragedy*, edited by Claire McEachern, 142–59. Cambridge: Cambridge University Press, 2003.

Paster, Gail Kern. *Humoring the Body: Emotions and the Shakespearean Stage*. Chicago, IL: University of Chicago Press, 2004.

Paster, Gail Kern. "'Minded Like the Weather': The Tragic Body and Its Passions." In *The Oxford Handbook of Shakespearean Tragedy*, edited by Michael Neill and David Schalkwyk, 202–17. Oxford: Oxford University Press, 2016.

Patterson, Annabel. *Shakespeare and the Popular Voice*. Cambridge, MA: Blackwood, 1989.

Patterson, Annabel. *Reading Between the Lines*. Madison, WI: University of Wisconsin Press, 1993.

Patterson, Lee. *Acts of Recognition: Essays on Medieval Culture*. Notre Dame, IN: University of Notre Dame Press, 2009.

Perry, Curtis. *Shakespeare and Senecan Tragedy*. Cambridge: Cambridge University Press, 2021.

Peter, John. *Complaint and Satire in Early English Literature*. Oxford: Clarendon Press, 1956.

Pigman, G. W. *Grief and English Renaissance Elegy*. Cambridge: Cambridge University Press, 1985.

BIBLIOGRAPHY

Pollard, Tanya. "Conceiving tragedy." In *Shakespearean Sensations: Experiencing Literature in Early Modern England*, edited by Katharine A. Craik and Tanya Pollard, 85–100. Cambridge: Cambridge University Press, 2013.

Pollard, Tanya. *Greek Tragic Women on Shakespearean Stages*. Oxford: Oxford University Press, 2017.

Prendergast, Maria Teresa Micaela. *Railing, Reviling, and Invective in English Literary Culture, 1588–1617: The Anti-Poetics of Theater and Print*. Burlington, VT: Ashgate, 2012.

Princeton Encyclopedia of Poetry and Poetics. 4th edition. Edited by Roland Greene et al. Princeton, NJ: Princeton University Press, 2012.

Quinn, Kelly. "Mastering Complaint: Michael Drayton's 'Peirs Gaveston' and the Royal Mistress Complaints." *English Literary Renaissance* 38, no. 3 (2008): 439–60.

Rackin, Phyllis. *Stages of History: Shakespeare's English Chronicles*. Ithaca, NY: Cornell University Press, 1991.

Raman, Shankar. "Hamlet in Motion." In *Knowing Shakespeare: Senses, Embodiment and Cognition*, edited by Lowell Gallagher and Shankar Raman, 116–36. Basingstoke: Palgrave, 2010.

Raman, Shankar. "Protesting Bodies: *King Lear*." *Upstart: A Journal of English Renaissance Studies* (August 2015).

Rasmussen, Mark David, ed. *Renaissance Literature and Its Formal Engagements*. New York: Palgrave, 2002.

Reiss, Timothy J. "Renaissance theatre and the theory of tragedy." In *The Cambridge History of Literary Criticism: Volume 3, The Renaissance*, edited by Glyn P. Norton, 229–48. Cambridge: Cambridge University Press, 1999.

Reiss, Timothy J. *Mirages of the Selfe: Patterns of Personhood in Ancient and Early Modern Europe*. Stanford, CA: Stanford University Press, 2003.

Richardson, Catherine. *Domestic Life and Domestic Tragedy in Early Modern England: The Material Life of the Household*. Manchester: Manchester University Press, 2006.

Robson, Mark. *The Sense of Early Modern Writing: Rhetoric, Poetics, Aesthetics*. Manchester: Manchester University Press, 2006.

Rosendale, Timothy. *Theology and Agency in Early Modern Literature*. Cambridge: Cambridge University Press, 2018.

Ross, Sarah C. E. "Complaint's Echoes." In *Early Modern Women's Complaint: Gender, Form, and Politics*, edited by Sarah C. E. Ross and Rosalind Smith, 183–202. London: Palgrave Macmillan, 2020.

Ross, Sarah C. E. "Hester Pulter's Devotional Complaints." *Journal for Early Modern Cultural Studies* 20, no. 2 (2020): 99–119.

Ross, Sarah C. E., and Rosalind Smith, "Beyond Ovid: Early Modern Women's Complaints." In *Early Modern Women's Complaint: Gender, Form, and Politics*, edited by Sarah C. E. Ross and Rosalind Smith, 1–26. London: Palgrave Macmillan, 2020.

Ruti, Mari. *Distillations: Theory, Ethics, Affect*. London: Bloomsbury, 2018.

Ryrie, Alec. *Being Protestant in Reformation Britain*. Oxford: Oxford University Press, 2013.

Sacks, Peter. "Where Words Prevail Not: Grief, Revenge, and Language in Kyd and Shakespeare." *ELH* 49, no. 3 (1982): 576–601.

Salzman, Paul. "The Politics of Complaint in Mary Wroth's *Love's Victory* and *The Second Part of The Countess of Montgomery's Urania*." In *Early Modern Women's Complaint: Gender, Form, and Politics*, edited by Sarah C. E. Ross and Rosalind Smith, 137–55. London: Palgrave Macmillan, 2020.

Sanchez, Melissa. *Erotic Subjects: The Sexuality of Politics in Early Modern English Literature*. Oxford: Oxford University Press, 2011.

Sanchez, Melissa. *Queer Faith: Reading Promiscuity and Race in the Secular Love Tradition.* New York: New York University Press, 2019.

Santner, Eric L. *On Creaturely Life: Rilke, Benjamin, Sebald.* Chicago, IL: University of Chicago Press, 2006.

Scase, Wendy. *Literature and Complaint in England, 1272–1553.* Oxford: Oxford University Press, 2007.

Scherer, Abigail. "The 'Sweet Toyle' of Blissful Bowers: Arresting Idleness in the English Renaissance." In *Idleness, Indolence and Leisure in English Literature,* edited by Monica Fludernik and Miriam Nandi, 60–85. London: Palgrave Macmillan, 2014.

Schliesser, Eric, ed. *Sympathy: A History.* Oxford: Oxford University Press, 2015.

Schmitz, Götz. *The Fall of Women in Early English Narrative Verse.* Cambridge: Cambridge University Press, 1990.

Schoenfeldt, Michael C. *Bodies and Selves in Early Modern England: Physiology and Inwardness in Spenser, Shakespeare, Herbert, and Milton.* Cambridge: Cambridge University Press, 1999.

Schoenfeldt, Michael C. "Shakespearean pain." In *Shakespearean Sensations: Experiencing Literature in Early Modern England,* edited by Katharine A. Craik and Tanya Pollard, 191–207. Cambridge: Cambridge University Press, 2013.

Schwarz, Kathryn. *What You Will: Gender, Contract, and Shakespearean Social Space.* Philadelphia, PA: University of Pennsylvania Press, 2011.

Schwyzer, Philip. *Literature, Nationalism and Memory in Early Modern England.* Cambridge: Cambridge University Press, 2004.

Scott-Baumann, Elizabeth, and Ben Burton, eds. *The Work of Form: Poetics and Materiality in Early Modern Culture.* Oxford: Oxford University Press, 2014.

Shannon, Laurie. *The Accommodated Animal: Cosmopolity in Shakespearean Locales.* Chicago, IL: University of Chicago Press, 2013.

Sherman, Donovan. "'What More Remains?': Messianic Performance in *Richard II.*" *Shakespeare Quarterly* 65, no. 1 (2014): 22–48.

Shortslef, Emily. "Second Life: *The Ruines of Time* and the Virtual Collectivities of Early Modern Complaint." *Journal for Early Modern Cultural Studies* 13, no. 3 (2013): 84–104.

Shuger, Debora. *Habits of Thought in the English Renaissance: Religion, Politics, and the Dominant Culture.* Berkeley, CA: University of California Press, 1990.

Sinfield, Alan. "Hamlet's Special Providence." *Shakespeare Survey* 33 (1980): 89–98.

Skinner, Quentin. *Forensic Shakespeare.* Oxford: Oxford University Press, 2014.

Slights, Camille Wells. *The Casuistical Tradition in Shakespeare, Donne, Herbert and Milton.* Princeton, NJ: Princeton University Press, 1981.

Slights, Camille Wells. "Notaries, Sponges, and Looking-glasses: Conscience in Early Modern England." *English Literary Renaissance* 28, no. 2 (1998): 231–46.

Smith, Hallett. *Elizabethan Poetry.* Cambridge, MA: Harvard University Press, 1952.

Smith, Ian. "Seeing Blackness: Reading Race in *Othello.*" In *The Oxford Handbook of Shakespearean Tragedy,* edited by Michael Neill and David Schalkwyk, 405–20. Oxford: Oxford University Press, 2016.

Smith, Matthew J. "Tragedy 'Before' Pity and Fear." In *The Palgrave Handbook of Affect Studies and Textual Criticism,* edited by Donald R. Wehrs and Thomas Blake, 391–412. London: Palgrave Macmillan, 2017.

Smith, Rosalind, Michelle O'Callaghan, and Sarah C. E. Ross, "Complaint." In *A Companion to Renaissance Poetry,* edited by Catherine Bates, 339–52. Malden, MA: Wiley-Blackwell, 2018.

Spurgeon, Caroline. *Shakespeare's Imagery.* Cambridge: Cambridge University Press, 1935.

214 BIBLIOGRAPHY

Steggle, Matthew. *Laughing and Weeping in Early Modern Theatres*. Burlington, VT: Ashgate, 2007.

Stoll, Abraham. *Conscience in Early Modern English Literature*. Cambridge: Cambridge University Press, 2017.

Streete, Adrian. *Protestantism and Drama in Early Modern England*. Cambridge: Cambridge University Press, 2009.

Streeter, Ashley. "The Beleaguered Virtue: Robert Wilson's *The Three Ladies of London* and the Problem of Conscience." *Exemplaria* 24, no. 12 (2012): 78–94.

Strier, Richard. *The Unrepentant Renaissance: From Petrarch to Shakespeare to Milton*. Chicago, IL: University of Chicago Press, 2011.

Strohm, Paul. *Conscience: A Very Short Introduction*. Oxford: Oxford University Press, 2011.

Sullivan Jr., Garrett A. *Sleep, Romance, and Human Embodiment: Vitality from Spenser to Milton*. Cambridge: Cambridge University Press, 2012.

Swann, Elizabeth L. "Nosce Teipsum: The Senses of Self-Knowledge in Early Modern England." In *Literature, Belief and Knowledge in Early Modern England: Knowing Faith*, edited by Subha Mukherji and Tim Stuart-Buttle, 195–214. New York: Palgrave Macmillan, 2018.

Swärdh, Anna. "From Hell: *A Mirror for Magistrates* and the Late Elizabethan Female Complaint." In *Narrative Developments from Chaucer to Defoe*, edited by Gerd Bayer and Ebbe Klitgård, 97–115. New York: Routledge, 2011.

Syme, Holger Schott. *Theatre and Testimony in Shakespeare's England: A Culture of Mediation*. Cambridge: Cambridge University Press, 2012.

Tassi, Marguerite A. "Wounded Maternity, Sharp Revenge: Shakespeare's Representations of Queens in Light of the Hecuba Myth." *Explorations in Renaissance Culture* 37, no. 1 (2011): 83–99.

Thompson, Ayanna. "*Desdemona*: Toni Morrison's Response to *Othello*." In *A Feminist Companion to Shakespeare*, edited by Dympna Callaghan, 494–506. Malden, MA: Wiley-Blackwell, 2016.

Thompson, Ayanna. "Shakespeare and Race." Interview by Farah Karim-Cooper. *Such Stuff*. September 28, 2018. Podcast, 35:35. https://www.shakespearesglobe.com/discover/blogs-and-features/2018/09/28/such-stuff-s1-e4/ (last accessed on January 18, 2023).

Thorne, Alison. "'O, lawful let it be/ That I have room...to curse a while': Voicing the Nation's Conscience in Female Complaint in *Richard III*, *King John*, and *Henry VIII*." In *This England, That Shakespeare: New Angles on Englishness and the Bard*, edited by Willy Maley and Margaret Tudeau-Clayton, 105–24. Burlington, VT: Ashgate, 2010.

Tillyard, E. M. W. *Shakespeare's History Plays*. London: Chatto and Windus, 1944.

Tilmouth, Christopher. "Shakespeare's open consciences," *Renaissance Studies*, 23, no. 4 (2009): 501–15.

Turner, Henry S. *The English Renaissance Stage: Geometry, Poetics, and the Practical Spatial Arts*. Oxford: Oxford University Press, 2006.

Vaught, Jennifer C. *Masculinity and Emotion in Early Modern English Literature*. Burlington, VT: Ashgate, 2008.

Vaught, Jennifer C. "'Sad Stories of the Deaths of Kings': Lyric and Narrative Release from Confining Spaces in Shakespeare's *Richard II*." *Quidditas: Journal of the Rocky Mountain Medieval and Renaissance Association* 20 (1999): 173–92.

Vinter, Maggie. *Last Acts: The Art of Dying on the Early Modern Stage*. New York: Fordham University Press, 2019.

Visser, Arnoud S. Q. *Reading Augustine in the Reformation*. Oxford: Oxford University Press, 2011.

Walsh, Brian. *Shakespeare, the Queen's Men, and the Elizabethan Performance of History*. Cambridge: Cambridge University Press, 2009.

Walsham, Alexandra. *Providence in Early Modern England*. Oxford: Oxford University Press, 2001.

Warley, Christopher. "Specters of Horatio." *ELH* 75, no. 4 (2008): 1023–50.

Wells, Stanley. "The Lamentable Tale of 'Richard II.'" *Shakespeare Studies* (Tokyo) 17 (1978): 1–23.

Wells, Stanley. "Staging Shakespeare's Ghosts." In *The Arts of Performance in Elizabethan and Early Stuart Drama: Essays for G. K. Hunter*, edited by M. Biggs et al., 50–69. Edinburgh: Edinburgh University Press, 1991.

Wheeler, Richard P. "History, Character and Conscience in *Richard III.*" *Comparative Drama* 5, no. 4 (1971–2): 301–21.

Whigham, Frank. *Seizures of the Will in Early Modern English Drama*. Cambridge: Cambridge University Press, 1996.

Whipday, Emma. *Shakespeare's Domestic Tragedies: Violence in the Early Modern Home*. Cambridge: Cambridge University Press, 2019.

Whitney, Charles. "Ante-aesthetics: Towards a Theory of Early Modern Audience Response." In *Shakespeare and Modernity: Early Modern to Millennium*, edited by Hugh Grady, 40–60. London: Routledge, 2000.

Whittington, Leah. *Renaissance Suppliants: Poetry, Antiquity, Reconciliation*. Oxford: Oxford University Press, 2016.

Wilks, John S. *The Idea of Conscience in Renaissance Tragedy*. New York: Routledge, 1990.

Williams, Katherine Schaap. "Enabling Richard: The Rhetoric of Disability in *Richard III*," *Disability Studies Quarterly* 29, no. 4 (2009).

Wilson, Luke. *Theaters of Intention: Drama and the Law in Early Modern England*. Stanford, CA: Stanford University Press, 2000.

Wiseman, Susan, ed. *The Rhetoric of Complaint: Ovid's Heroides in the Renaissance and Restoration*. Special issue, *Renaissance Studies* 22, no. 3 (2008).

Witmore, Michael. *Shakespearean Metaphysics*. London: Continuum, 2008.

Wolfson, Susan, ed. *Reading for Form*. Special issue, *Modern Language Quarterly* 61, no. 1 (2000): 1–16.

Woodbridge, Linda. *English Revenge Drama: Money, Resistance, Equality*. Cambridge: Cambridge University Press, 2010.

Zamir, Tzachi. *Double Vision: Moral Philosophy and Shakespearean Drama*. Princeton, NJ: Princeton University Press, 2006.

Žižek, Slavoj. *Violence: Six Sideways Reflections*. New York: Picador, 2008.

Index

For the benefit of digital users, indexed terms that span two pages (e.g., 52–53) may, on occasion, appear on only one of those pages.

Adams, Henry Hitch 173–4, 173n.8
Adelman, Janet 51n.92, 90n.100
aesthetic theory, early modern 23–4, 137–8
  intersections with female complaint 3, 23–4, 136–9, 143, 145–52, 155–8, 167–9
Ahmed, Sara 19n.75, 39n.52, 171, 183n.26
Akhimie, Patricia 39n.52
Alfar, Cristina León 77–8
Ames, William, *Conscience, with the Power and Cases Thereof* 65, 82n.70
Anderson, Thomas P. 94n.1
Archer, Harriet 98n.10, 109n.48
Arden of Faversham 176–8, 192, 194–5, 197
Aristotle
  and eudaimonia 10–12
  Ethics 10n.33, 95–6
  Poetics 9n.27, 111–12, 143n.34
  Rhetoric 4n.7
  and natural philosophy 95n.4
  and political theory 58n.102
  and the tripartite soul 127–8
  and virtue ethics 15–19, 101–2, 133–4
Arthur, Jake 6–7
Augustine 33, 97–8, 101–2
  Confessions 99–101, 110–11, 119, 128–9, 167–9
  City of God 116–17
Austin, J. L. 14n.51

Bailey, Amanda 61
Baldwin, William 7–8, 72–3, 98n.10, 105
  see also Mirror for Magistrates
Baldo, Jonathan 125n.78
Barish, Jonas A. 136n.7
Barnfield, Richard, *The Complaint of Poetry* 4–6
Bates, Catherine 11–12, 135n.2
Beaumont, Francis, *The Maid's Tragedy* 145–8
Becon, Thomas
  The Governance of Vertue 102
  The Sicke Man's Salve 41–2
Belsey, Catherine 116n.64
Bengtsson, Frederick 173n.8
Benjamin, Walter 28n.11, 47–8

Benson, Sean 172n.3
Berlant, Lauren 168n.97
Bernard, Richard, *Christian See to Thy Conscience* 65n.13
Bevington, David 76n.55
Bloom, Gina 76n.56
Boethius, *De consolatione philosophiae* 4–6, 26, 40–1
Bolam, Robyn 162n.88
Bonetto, Sandra 89n.95
Bouwsma, William J. 102n.28
Braden, Gordon 8n.22
Braun, Harald E. 65n.9, 93n.107
Bristol, Michael D. 20n.79
Brooke, Tucker 98n.10
Brooks, Harold F. 74n.51
Brown, Georgia 153–4
Budra, Paul 162
Burton, Ben 19n.74
Bushnell, Rebecca 7n.20
Butler, Judith 21, 63–4
Butts, Thomas 13–14

Cadman, Daniel 7n.20, 38n.44
Calvin, John 97–8
  Genesis 33, 128–9
  Institutes 12n.42, 27–8, 32–3, 37, 40–2, 46–7, 83–4, 100–3, 107n.47, 109–11, 119, 121, 128, 131–2
  Job 27–8, 30–1, 38nn.45, 47, 44, 46
  Romans 100–2, 107
Calvinist theology
  importance in early modern England 21–2, 30–1, 33, 38–9, 102–3
  intersections with Stoic moral philosophy 30–1, 38–47
  see also Calvin, John; conscience; creatureliness; desire; grace; moral psychology; Original Sin; providence; suffering
Cary, Elizabeth, *The Tragedy of Mariam* 8–9
catharsis 9n.27, 143n.34
Cavarero, Adriana 63–4, 89n.96
Cavell, Stanley 14n.51, 61–2

218 INDEX

Chapman, Alison A. 150n.51
Charnes, Linda 74n.52, 91n.104
Charron, Pierre, *Of Wisdom* 39–41, 103,
 129, 169
Chaucer, Geoffrey 5n.9, 7–8, 26n.1
Churchyard, Thomas, *Shore's Wife* 152–7, 163
Clarke, Danielle 135nn.1–2
Cleaver, Robert, *A Godlie Forme of Householde
 Government* 174
Clemen, Wolfgang 8n.24, 44n.71
Clody, Michael C. 60n.106
Cochran, Elizabeth Agnew 30n.17
Cohen, Stephen 19n.74
Combe, Kirk 16n.61
Comensoli, Viviana 173n.8, 174n.12
complaining
 as address to power 14–15, 58–63, 68–78
 efficacy of 9–10, 19, 76n.56, 148
 as ethical thinking 10–12
 ethics of 12n.44, 22, 26–8, 30–1, 37–49, 53
 and fantasy 26–30, 34–7, 45–7, 54–7
 gendering of 31, 39–40, 44, 46–7
 and the human condition 4, 9–10, 29n.16,
  32–4
 as irrational response to suffering 29–31,
  34–5, 38–40, 44–5
 pleasure in 12n.44, 36–7
 racializing of 39–40
complaint
 against the times 4–6, 15–17
 amorous/ erotic 11–12, 190
 definition of 4–7, 4n.7
 and ethical discourse 3, 11–19, 21–5
 as form of ethical thought, *see* complaint,
  deathbed; complaint, existential; complaint,
  female; complaint, judicial; complaint,
  spectral
 and forensic rhetoric 14–15, 70, 75–9,
  97–8, 192
 genealogies of 5n.9
 in legal contexts 4n.8, 14–15, 70–5, 79
 as poetic form 4n.8, 12–13
 as speech act 14–15, 73–6
complaint, deathbed 3, 12–13, 24, 171–3,
 175–84, 189–97
 as confession of wrongdoing 12–13, 24,
  171–2, 175, 181–2, 189–90, 192–5
 definition of 12–13, 171–2, 175, 181–2,
  189–90
 in domestic tragedy 24, 173, 175–82, 187,
  189–90, 192, 194–7
 as affirmation of happiness script 24, 171–2,
  175–6, 179, 181–2, 189–90, 195–7
 in *Othello* 24, 172–3, 182–4, 189–97

 as expression of repentance 12–13, 24, 171–2,
  175–82, 189–90, 194–7
complaint, existential 3, 12–13, 22, 28–37, 41–8,
 50–1, 53–62, 171
 as expressive of creatureliness 3, 22, 28–37,
  41–8, 50–62
 definition of 12–13, 28–9, 171
 in ethical discourse 30–1, 37, 41–7, 50–3
 and fantasy 29–30, 34–7, 45–7, 53–8
 in *King Lear* 3, 22, 47–8, 50–1, 53–62
 as interpretation of suffering 28–37,
  45–7, 53–62
 as form of tragic-existential
  discourse 28–37, 51–3
complaint, female 2n.2, 3, 12–13, 23–4, 74n.51,
 76n.56, 135–6, 138–71
 as articulation of aesthetic theory 3, 23–4,
  136–9, 143, 145–52, 155–8, 167–9
 definition of 12–13, 135–6
 as creating lamentable aesthetic
  objects 146, 150–65
 and Ovidian complaint 135, 143–6
 in *Richard II* 3, 23–4, 138–42, 151–2, 157–70
 as model of sympathetic reception 12–13,
  23–4, 135–6, 138–54, 156–7, 167–9
 in tragic historical poetry 23–4, 138–9, 152–7
complaint, judicial 3, 12–13, 22, 63, 68–83,
 86–93, 156, 171
 in accounts of conscience 3, 22, 63–8,
  71–2, 79–93
 definition of 12–13, 63, 69–72
 as focalizing ethical responsibility 22, 63–5,
  68, 71–5, 82–93
 as demand for justice 12–13, 63, 68–82
 in *Richard III* 3, 22, 64–8, 73–83, 87–93
complaint, spectral 3, 12–13, 23, 94–8, 105–9,
 111–16, 120–3, 125–9, 133–4, 171
 definition of 12–13, 94
 as figure for enigmatic motive 23, 94–8,
  105–9, 111–16, 120–3, 125–9, 133–4, 171
 in *Hamlet* 23, 94–8, 111–16, 120–3, 125–9,
  133–4, 171
 in the *Mirror for Magistrates* 23, 97–8, 105,
  111–12
 in revenge tragedy 94, 113–16, 121
complaint-shaming, rhetoric of 26, 30–1,
 39–40, 45, 162
*Complaynt agaynst the wicked enemies
 of Christ, A* 4–6
confession 2n.3, 4–6, 12–13, *see also* complaint,
 deathbed
conscience 3, 21–2, 63–8, 71–5, 80–93
 in Calvinist theology 64–7, 83–5, 92–3
 as complaining 3, 22, 63–8, 71–3, 80–1, 83–6

as paradigmatic ethical demand 22, 64–6, 68,
    82–4, 91–3
ghosts as figures for 78, 80–1, *see also*
    Richard III
and judicial complaint 3, 22, 63, 68, 79–93
as internal voice 3, 65–8, 83–6
and the moral law 22, 64–5, 84–6, 90
and relationality 64–5, 68, 82–3, 86–93
in *Richard III* 3, 22, 63, 66–8, 73–5, 80–1,
    86–93
consolation 4–6, 30–1, 39–47
contemptus mundi theme 17, 32
Cormack, Bradin 71n.34
Cox, John D. 18–19, 20n.80, 92n.105
Crane, Mary Thomas 95n.4
Craik, Katharine A. 136n.6, 150n.49, 181–2
creatureliness 3, 22, 26–62
    and authority 21–2, 28n.11, 30–1
    in Calvinist theology 3, 22, 26–34, 37–48
    ethical scripts about 3, 21–2, 26–8,
        30–1, 37–48
    as expressed in existential complaint 3, 21–2,
        28–37, 41–8
    and intensity of feeling 32–4
    in *King Lear* 3, 22, 47–61
    and psychoanalysis 34n.36
Critchley, Simon 63n.1
Curran, Kevin 20n.81, 71, 86, 92–3, 92n.105
Cutrofello, Andrew 97n.7

Dailey, Alice 160–1
Daniel, Drew 119n.70
Daniel, Samuel
    The Civil Wars 15, 139–40, 159
    The Complaint of Rosamond 23–4,
        152–7, 163
desire
    in Calvinist theology 11–12, 100–2, 110–11
    in classical moral philosophy 10–12
    as animating complaint 4–7, 10–13, 171
    as shaped by complaint 3, 13, 19, 24–5
    as irrational 11–12, 106–7, 110–11,
        128–9, 134
    in psychoanalytic theory 11–12,
        104n.40, 106–7
DiGangi, Mario 66n.16, 78n.61
Dionne, Craig 62
Dolan, Frances E. 173–4
Dollimore, Jonathan 48n.83
Donne, John 26
Drayton, Michael
    Englands Heroicall Epistles 4–6, 153–4
    Matilda 23–4, 45–7, 152–7
    Peirs Gaveston 152–7, 163

Driver, Julia 168n.96
Dubrow, Heather 12n.45, 19n.74, 153n.56
Dunne, Derek 121

Edelman, Lee 111–12
Eisendrath, Rachel 137–8, 148
Elam, Keir 78n.65
Elton, William 47n.82
Engle, Lars 20n.80
Enterline, Lynn 4–6, 135nn.1–2, 143–4, 148
Erickson, Peter 172n.4
ethical discourse, early modern 18–19
    see also conscience; creatureliness; happiness
        scripts; moral psychology; reception

Felch, Susan M. 7n.18, 15–17
Ferguson, Margaret 136n.7
Finn, Kavita Mudan 153n.58
Fletcher, Giles, *The Rising to the Crowne of
    Richard the Third* 156–7
Fletcher, John, *The Maid's Tragedy* 145–8
Floyd-Wilson, Mary 140n.20
Foakes, R. A. 60n.105, 61n.107
Forker, Charles 140nn.17, 21, 141n.24,
    158n.79, 159n.81, 162n.88
formalism, historical 19n.74
formalism, new 13n.46
Fox, Cora 183n.26
Freud, Sigmund 11–12, 86, 90n.100,
    104n.40, 106–7
Freinkel, Lisa 33, 97n.8, 104n.40

Garrett, Aaron 18–19
Gascoigne, George
    "An absent dame thus complaineth," 11–12
    "The View of Worldly Vanities," 32
Geng, Penelope 59n.103, 62, 71n.34
Giancarlo, Matthew 71n.34
Gil, Daniel Juan 56–7
Gillies, John 109n.52
Gold, Moshe 20n.81
Golding, Arthur 27n.7, 30–1, 38n.45
Goodman, Godfrey, *The Fall of
    Man* 10–11, 33–4
Gouge, William, *Of Domesticall Duties* 174
grace 100–2, 107–9, 119, 121
Grady, Hugh 48n.83, 49n.88, 137–8, 147–8,
    150–1, 167
Gray, Patrick 20n.80, 21, 86, 92n.105,
    143n.34, 158n.78
Greenberg, Mitchell 24–5
Greenblatt, Stephen 48n.83, 116n.65
Greene, Robert, *Selimus* 34–6, 54
Grier, Miles 197n.47

220 INDEX

Griswold, Jeffrey B. 58n.102
Grossman, Marshall 136n.6
Guy, J. A. 70n.32

Hadfield, Andrew 109n.48
Hall, Edward, *The Union* 66n.18, 73–5, 85–9
Hall, Kim F. 172n.4, 184n.28
Hall, Joseph
  Characters of Vertues and Vices 30–1
  Meditations and Vowes 4, 38–9, 41
  Salomons Divine Arts 10n.33, 18n.71
  Two Guides to a Good Life 18–19, 39–41
  Virgidemiarum 7n.21
Hamlet 3–4, 23, 26, 33–4, 39n.51, 53n.94,
    87n.92, 94–100, 109–34, 142–3, 171
  scenes of animation in 96–9, 111–12, 115–19,
    123–9, 132–4
  treatment of Calvinist moral psychology 23,
    94, 97–102, 109–13, 115–17, 119–23,
    128–32
  enigmatic motive/ command motif 3, 23,
    94–9, 110–12, 115–29, 132–4
  inaction 23, 96–100, 117–21, 123–6
  insufficiency of reason and will in 96–102,
    109–23, 128–34
  revenge 94, 110–11, 113–17, 120–2
  spectral complaint in 3, 23, 94–8, 111–16,
    120–3, 125–9, 133–4, 171
Hamlin, Hannibal 50n.89
Hamlin, William 87n.91
Hammill, Graham 28n.11
happiness scripts 19, 24, 171–84
Harvey, Elizabeth D. 135n.2
Helgerson, Richard 153–4, 156–7
Hendricks, Margo 184n.28
Herbert, George, "Complaining," 29n.16
Herman, Peter C. 136n.7
Heywood, Jasper
  Thyestes 113–14
  Troas 7–8, 113, 115–16
Heywood, Thomas
  Apology for Actors 122n.76, 137
  Edward IV, Part 2 176–7, 181n.22
  A Woman Killed with Kindness 176–7, 179–81,
    194–5, 195n.42, 197
Higgins, John 98n.10, 105–6, 136–7
  see also Mirror for Magistrates
Hirschfeld, Heather 38n.46, 109n.52, 188–9
Holbrooke, William, *Loves Complaint* 15–17
Holderness, Graham 67n.21
Honig, Bonnie 77–8
Honigmann, E. A. J. 192n.38, 193n.40
Howard, Jean E. 76n.56, 161
Hoxby, Blair 7n.20, 9
Hughes, Daniel E. 67n.21

Hui, Andrew 130n.82
humoral theory 13–14, 36–7, 44
Hutson, Lorna 70n.32, 71n.34

Jackson, MacDonald P. 1n.1
James I, *The True Lawe of Free Monarchies*
    70n.33
James, Heather 150, 167–9
Job, Book of 4–6, 26, 41–2, 46, 53, 56–7
  see also Calvin, John
Johnson, Toria 58n.100
Joughin, John J. 60
Jowett, John 78–9

Kahn, Coppélia 90n.100
Kahn, Victoria 66n.16, 137–8
Kantorowicz, Ernst 28n.11, 158n.76
Karim-Cooper, Farah 196n.46
Kearney, James 58n.101
Kerrigan, John 2nn.2–3, 4–6, 71n.34, 98n.9,
    121n.73, 135n.2, 156n.74
Kiefer, Frederick 106n.45
Kietzman, Mary Jo 6n.13
King Lear 3, 22, 31, 44, 47–62, 171
  and creatureliness 3, 22, 47–61
  on the ethics of complaining 3, 22, 47–53,
    56–62
  existential complaint in 3, 22, 47–8, 50–1,
    53–62
  and feeling 48–53, 57–62
  immanence vs. transcendence 47–8, 50–1, 61
  and sovereign authority 50–1, 56–61
  and tragic-existential discourse 22, 49–54,
    59–61
Kingsmill, Thomas, *A Complaint against
    Securitie* 15–17
Kottman, Paul 20n.81, 138n.12
Kraye, Jill 10n.33, 30n.17
Kuchar, Gary 85n.82
Kuzner, James 20n.81, 21, 24–5, 92n.105,
    133–4
Kyd, Thomas
  The Spanish Tragedy 36, 115–16, 118n.69,
    121–2
  The Tragedy of Soliman and Perseda 36–7

La Primaudaye, Pierre de, *The French
    Academie* 4, 32, 97n.8, 103–5, 119–20
Lacan, Jacques 11–12, 104n.40
*Lamentable Complaint of the Commonaltie,
    The* 4–6, 71–2
Lamentable Tragedie of Locrine, The 9, 39–40
lamentation 6n.17, 17, 75–8
  see also complaint, female
Lamentation of Melpomene, The 17

Lane, John, "Tom Tel-Troth's Message, and His Pens Complaint," 4–6
Laplanche, Jean 38n.46
Lehtonen, Kelly 59n.103
Lemon, Rebecca 27n.7, 65n.8, 79
Levinas, Emmanuel 63–4
Levine, Caroline 13n.46
Levinson, Marjorie 13n.46
Levy, Eric P. 118n.68
Lewis, Rhodri 20n.80
Lichfield, William, *The Remors of Conscyence* 65–6
Lille, Alain de, *De planctu naturae* 5n.9
Lipsius, Justus, *Two Bookes of Constancie* 39–41, 65
Little, Jr., Arthur L. 184n.28, 185, 196–7
Lobis, Seth 140n.20
Lodge, Thomas, *Tragicall Complaint of Elstred* 152–7, 163
Loewenstein, David 24n.90, 47n.82
Long, Zackariah C. 67n.21
Lopez, Jeremy 158
Lorenz, Philip 28n.11
Lukacher, Ned 87–8
Lupton, Julia Reinhard 20n.81, 21, 26–8, 28n.11, 53
Lydgate, John 5n.9, 7–8

MacDonald, Joyce Green 184, 196–7
Macpherson, Sandra 13n.46
Magnusson, Lynne 73–6, 167–9
Mallette, Richard 132n.84
Manley, Lawrence 16n.58
Marcus, Leah S. 51n.91
Marlowe, Christopher
    Tamburlaine 7–8, 13–14, 34–5
    Edward II 39–40
Marshall, David 168n.96
Matz, Robert 136n.7
Maus, Katharine Eisaman 91n.102
McEleney, Corey 137, 148
McKeithan, D. M. 53n.93
McMillin, Scott 160n.82
Meek, Richard 140n.18, 151–2, 158–9
melancholy 12n.44, 47–8, 119n.70
Menon, Madhavi 111–12
Meyer, Liam J. 70n.32
Middleton, Thomas, *A Yorkshire Tragedy* 175–6
Milton, John
    Paradise Lost 26
    Samson Agonistes 9n.27
Mirror for Magistrates, The 4–8, 15–17, 23, 30–1, 72–3, 90, 97–8, 105–12, 133, 136–7, 139–40, 152–4, 162

Montaigne 20n.80, 44, 83n.72
moral philosophy 10n.33, 18–19, 21, 63–4, 101–5, 129–31
moral psychology 94, 185–8
    implications of Calvinist theology for 97–109;
        see also Hamlet
    intellectualist models of 97–8, 101–9, 114–15, 121, 127–30
    see also reason; will; desire
More, Thomas, *The History of King Richard III* 90
Mousley, Andy 49n.87
Mukherji, Subha 71, 76n.53
Mulcaster, Richard, *A Comforting Complaint* 4–6
Mullan, John 168n.96
Mullaney, Steven 24–5
Munday, Anthony, *Mirrour of Mutabilitie* 15–17
Muschet, George, *The Complaint of a Christian Soule* 102

Nandi, Miriam 147n.43
Nashe, Thomas, *Christs Teares Over Jerusalem* 15–17
Neill, Michael 185
Ngai, Sianne 97n.6, 136, 146
Norton, Thomas, *Gorboduc* 8–9
Nussbaum, Martha 40n.57
Nuttall, A. D. 20n.79

O'Callaghan, Michelle 5n.9, 6–7, 7n.18, 19n.77, 135n.1
Ojakangas, Mika 65n.7
Oldenberg, Scott 70n.32
Original Sin 11–12, 28, 32–3, 38n.46, 83n.75, 100–1, 103–4, 112–13, 128–9
Orlin, Lena Cowen 172n.3, 173–4, 177n.19, 181–2
Othello 3, 24, 172–3, 176–7, 179–80, 182–97
    fragmentation of deathbed complaint 24, 172–3, 189–97
    relation to domestic tragedy 24, 172–3, 176–7, 179–80, 182–5, 189–90, 194–7
    abdication of ethical authority 24, 172–3, 189–90, 195–7
    fantasy of "adulterous" interracial marriage 184–5
    treatment of racist happiness script 24, 172–3, 183–4, 188–90, 194–7
    sexual repentance motif 185–9, 194–7
Ovid
    Heroides 4–6, 135, 143–5, 152–3
    Ibis 78, 80–1
    Metamorphoses 143–4, 152–4

222 INDEX

Parr, Katherine, *The Lamentacion of a Sinner* 4–6
Parvini, Neema 18–19, 20n.80
passability 13–14, 21
passion 9, 13–14, 28, 36–7, 40–7, 88, 142–3, 148, 167–9
Paster, Gail Kern 14n.47, 54n.96
patience 39–42, 51–3, 60–1, 77–8
Patterson, Annabel 70n.32
Patterson, Lee 9n.31
Peacham, Henry, *The Garden of Eloquence* 4, 70
Perkins, William
  Discourse of Conscience, A 64–7, 83–6, 83n.75, 86n.88, 90, 92
  Salve for a sicke man, A 41
Perry, Curtis 8n.22, 44n.71, 48n.83
Peter, John 16n.61, 32n.24, 197–8
petitionary discourse 71–2, 71n.34
Pigman, G. W. 45n.75
Plutarch, *Morals* 19–20, 39–40
Pollard, Tanya 8n.22, 99n.11, 136nn.3, 6, 150n.49
Powel, Gabriel, *The Resolved Christian* 26–7
Prendergast, Maria Teresa Micaela 16n.58
providence 22, 27–8, 30n.17, 37–8, 46–7, 48n.83, 106, 131–2
Puttenham, George, *The Art of English Poesy* 17
Pye, Christopher 138n.12

Quinn, Kelly 153n.57
Quintilian, *Institutio oratoria* 70, 79, 139–40

Rackin, Phyllis 74n.51, 76n.56
Raman, Shankar 60n.106, 99n.12
Rasmussen, Mark David 19n.74
reason
  as infected by concupiscence 100–1
  as limited 37, 97–8, 101–3, 108–12, 129–30
  as sovereign 97–8, 103–9
  as tempering passion 39–47
reception, ethical paradigms of literary 3, 19–20, 23–4, 136–9
  see also reception, sympathetic
reception, sympathetic 23–4, 135–6, 140–52
  as integral to scenes of female complaint 12–13, 136, 141–8
  as virtuous 138–9, 141–50, 152–4, 156–7, 167–70
  as concern of *Richard II* 138–42, 151–2, 157–70
  as concern of tragic historical poetry 138–9, 152–7
Reiss, Timothy J. 7n.20, 13–14, 21
relationality 21–2, 63–5, 68, 86, 91–3

revenge, and complaint 4–6, 72–3, 75–6, 78–82, 94, 113–16, 121
Richard II 3, 23–4, 69–70, 73–5, 138–41, 151–2, 157–71
  appropriation of female complaint 138–42, 151–2, 157–70
  conversion of Richard into lamentable aesthetic object 3, 152, 157–67, 169–70
  self-reflexivity as ethical anxiety 23–4, 138–9, 158–9, 169–70
  and sympathetic reception 138–42, 151–2, 157–70
Richard III 3, 22, 63–8, 73–83, 85–93, 171
  and conscience 3, 22, 63, 66–8, 73–5, 80–1, 86–93
  and ethical responsibility 22, 63, 68, 82–3
  ghosts in 63, 66–8, 73–5, 78–82, 87–93
  relation to historiographical sources 66–7, 73–5, 85–6, 89–90
  judicial complaint in 3, 22, 64–8, 73–83, 87–93
  and relationality 64–5, 68, 82–3, 86–93
Robinson, Richard
  The Rewarde of Wickednesse 15–17
  The Vineyarde of Vertue 29
Robson, Mark 138n.12
Rosendale, Timothy 28n.10, 106n.45
Ross, Sarah C. E. 5n.9, 6–7, 7n.18, 19n.77, 135n.1, 142
"Ruful Complaynt of the Publyke Weale to Englande, A" 4–6
Ruti, Mari 93n.109
Ryrie, Alec 102n.32

Sabies, Frances, *Adam's Complaint* 32, 46–7
Sacks, Peter 72–3
Sackville, Thomas, *Gorboduc* 8–9
Salzman, Paul 12n.44
Sanchez, Melissa 11n.41, 97n.8, 100n.17, 110–11, 186n.33
Santner, Eric L. 34n.36
satire 16n.61, 197–8
Scase, Wendy 6–7, 15n.52, 71n.34
Scherer, Abigail 147n.43
Schliesser, Eric 136n.5
Schmitz, Götz 167–9
Schoenfeldt, Michael C. 30n.17, 150
Schwarz, Kathryn 97n.8, 103n.37
Schwyzer, Philip 94n.1
Scott, William, *The Model of Poesy* 4–6, 10–11
Scott-Bauman, Elizabeth 19n.74
Seneca 83n.72
  De Providentia 38–41, 44
  De Ira 114

Phaedra 115n.61
Thyestes 113–14
Troades 7–8, 113, 115–16
Shakespeare, William 3, 19–25
Antony and Cleopatra 158n.78
Coriolanus 69–70
Henry V 72
2 Henry VI 69–70, 84–5
3 Henry VI 78–9, 89–92, 162–3
Henry VIII 69–70, 91n.103
Lover's Complaint, A 1–3, 11n.41,
156n.74, 164–5
Macbeth 9–10, 84–5, 87n.92
Measure for Measure 68–9, 83
Merchant of Venice, The 15, 69–70, 84–5
Midsummer Night's Dream, A 69–70
Rape of Lucrece, The 14–15, 23–4, 136,
141–52, 147n.45, 155–7, 164–7, 169
Tempest, The 85–6
Titus Andronicus 44–5, 59n.104, 141–2
Troilus and Cressida 8–9
Twelfth Night 69–70
Two Gentlemen of Verona, The 143–5
Venus and Adonis 141–3
see also Hamlet; King Lear; Othello;
Richard II; Richard III
Shannon, Laurie 27n.5, 50n.90
Sherman, Donovan 160–1, 166n.91
Shortslef, Emily 7n.18
Shuger, Debora 18n.71
Sidney, Philip 4–6, 143n.34
The Countess of Pembroke's Arcadia 10–12,
28–30, 43, 53n.93
Astrophil and Stella 11–12
The Defence of Poesy 19, 121–2, 128–9, 167–9
Sinfield, Alan 132n.84
Skinner, Quentin 15n.52, 70n.30, 72n.40, 94n.2
Slights, Camille Wells 83, 84n.76
Smith, Hallett 153n.56
Smith, Ian 197n.48
Smith, Matthew J. 9n.27
Smith, Rosalind 5n.9, 6–7, 19n.77, 135n.1
Spenser, Edmund
Complaints 4–6
The Teares of the Muses 7–9
The Visions of Petrarch 17
Spurgeon, Caroline 49n.86
Standish, Arthur, *The Commons*
Complaint 15–17
Steggle, Matthew 151n.54
Stoicism 30–1, 38–47, 38n.44
intersections with Calvinist theology 30–1,
38–47
Stoll, Abraham 66

Streete, Adrian 21–2, 34n.37, 101n.25, 102–3, 109
Streeter, Ashley 85n.82
Strier, Richard 41n.64
Strohm, Paul 65n.7, 66n.16, 84n.77
subjectivity, *see* creatureliness; passability;
relationality
Sullivan, Jr., Garrett A. 88n.93
suffering
theological frameworks for interpreting
30–1, 37–47
virtuous responses to 37–47
supplication 14–15, 71–2
Swann, Elizabeth L. 102n.32
Swärdh, Anna 153n.56
Syme, Holger Schott 71nn.34, 38
sympathy 136, 139–41, 150, 167–9
as aesthetic emotion 136, 138–9, 146–51,
153–7, 163
see also reception, sympathetic

Tassi, Marguerite A. 76n.55
Thompson, Ayanna 172–3, 194n.41, 195–7
Thorne, Alison 15–17, 77–8
Tillyard, E. M. W. 73n.48
Tilmouth, Christopher 83n.72
tragedy
affinity with complaint 7–10, 167–9
and cause 111–12
and pathos 9, 153–4
tragedy, de casibus 7–8, 94, 97–8, 152–3, 162
see also Mirror for Magistrates
tragedy, domestic 24, 171–85, 189–90, 192, 194–7
function of deathbed complaint in 24, 171–3,
175–7, 179, 181–2, 189–90, 197
and domestic ideology 24, 171–5, 181–2
relation of *Othello* to 24, 172–3, 176–7,
179–80, 182–5, 189–90, 194–7
tragedy, Greek 5n.9, 7–8, 143–4
tragedy, revenge 110–11, 113, 115–16, 121–2
function of spectral complaint in 94,
113–16, 121
tragedy, Senecan 7–8, 44n.71, 48n.83, 97–8,
110–11, 113–16, 143–4
tragic-existential discourse 9–11, 22
see also complaint, existential
tragic historical poetry 152–7
function of female complaint in 23–4, 138–9,
152–7
function of spectral complaint in 94,
105–6, 111–12
True Tragedy of Richard the Third, The 67–8
True Tryall and Examination of a Mans owne
Selfe, The 82–3
Turner, Henry S. 49n.88

224 INDEX

Vallence, Edward 65n.9, 93n.107
Vaught, Jennifer C. 160n.82
Vinter, Maggie 40n.59, 160–1
Virgil, *Aeneid* 195
Visser, Arnoud S. Q. 101n.20

Walsh, Brian 67nn.23, 24, 73–5, 78
Walsham, Alexandra 28n.10
Warning for Fair Women, A 9, 115–16, 122n.76,
  167–9, 173–4, 176–9, 192, 194–5, 197
Ward, Samuel, *Balm from Gilead to Recover
  Conscience* 83–5
Warley, Christopher 130n.82
Webbe, William, *A Discourse of English Poetrie*
  7–8, 10–11
Webster, John, *The Duchess of Malfi* 42–4
Wells, Stanley 67n.23, 151n.53
Whately, William, *A Bridebush* 174–5, 188–9
Wheeler, Richard P. 67n.21
Whetstone, George, "Cressid's Complaint," 2n.2
Whigham, Frank 97n.8
Whipday, Emma 172n.3, 173n.8
Whitney, Charles 136n.6
Whittington, Leah 71–2
Wilks, John S. 67n.21

will
  as bondaged or free 101n.21, 107–9
  as infected by concupiscence 23, 100–4,
    107–9, 128–9
  as divided 99–100, 119
  as following reason 23, 97–8
  volitional excess 96–7, 99–101, 108, 110–13,
    115–17, 119–21, 128–9, 133–4
  voluntas 114
Williams, Katherine Schaap 90n.101
Wilson, Luke 71n.34, 102–3, 109–11
Wilson, Thomas, *Arte of Rhetorique* 70, 141
Wiseman, Susan 135n.1
Witmore, Michael 20n.81, 24n.90
Wolfson, Susan 13n.46
Woodbridge, Linda 76n.54
Wroth, Mary, *The Countess of Montgomery's
  Urania* 135
Woolton, John, *Of the Conscience* 65–7,
  81n.68, 89–90
Wilcox, Helen 29n.16
Wright, Thomas, *The Passions of the Minde* 88, 103

Zamir, Tzachi 20n.79
Žižek, Slavoj 109n.51